The E Coast Path

Book 1: The South Coast

by Christopher Goddard

GRITSTONE
PUBLISHING

The South Coast Overview

Start: Woolwich
Finish: Exmouth
Total Distance: 1136.9km (706 miles)
Total Ascent: 11,240m (36,880ft)
Days: 54

Map Key *(for route maps throughout book)*

- – – – Official main route
- ▬○▬ Official alternative route
- – – – Unofficial alternative route (unsigned)
- •••••• Other path or ferry route
- ▬▬▬ Road
- ◾• Buildings
- P Car park
- T Train station
- B Bus stop
- WC Public toilet

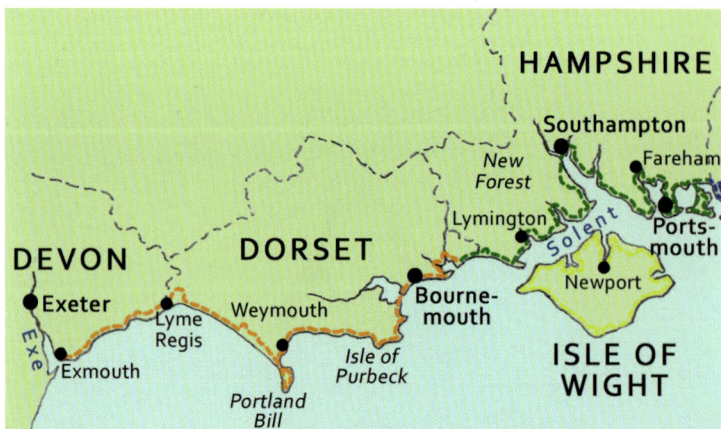

CONTENTS

INTRODUCTION – The English Coast

Oh, I do like to be beside the seaside,
Oh, I do like to be beside the sea,
Oh, I do like to stroll along the prom, prom, prom,
Where the brass bands play tiddley-om-pom-pom,
So, just let me be beside the seaside,
I'll be beside myself with glee.

John H. Glover-Kind, *I Do Like to be Beside the Seaside*

For someone born in the heart of England, in Sheffield, and never having lived closer than 50 miles from the sea, the seaside was always a treat, associated with holidays and day trips. So what if dull grey days picking sand out of your candy floss, tearing clothes on old funfair rides and eating in drab modernist cafes never really lived up to the image of it – it was still the seaside. Even now I get a leap of excitement when I first glimpse the sea at the end of a long drive, then love to stand on the front and gulp in the salty sea air, before pulling off my shoes and socks to dip my feet in the water. However cold and wet the day, it brings back a childish thrill that I doubt leaves any of us.

There is a magic to the rhythmic swoosh of waves on the shore, the crinkle of shells underfoot, flocks of birds wheeling overhead in formation, and the sense that the evanescent land between the tide lines is constantly being remade. Even the most elaborate sand castles stand only until the next tide and each step feels like it can never be repeated. Footsteps form in the sand only to be swallowed up as the waves rush in.

This trick can be hard to pull off at times though. It's easy to regard the English coast as being ruined and mourn the loss of its innocence. As Edmund Gosse bemoans in Father and Son, 'No one will see again on the shore of England what I saw in my early childhood, the submarine vision of dark rocks, speckled and starred with an infinite variety of colour, and streamed over by silken flags of royal crimson and purple.' The seaside somehow

manages to appear simultaneously over-developed and under-nourished. Every year over 150 million visits are made to the English coast, pumping £13.7 billion into the local economy and, in summer, the roads anywhere within a couple of miles of the sea are snarled up and every inch of the seafront lined with bright tat, car parks and caravan sites. Yet some of the country's poorest communities are to be found in faded ports and resorts, whose connection with the sea itself appears to have been lost. The fishing industry is massively diminished and our trade is via container ships the size of islands, reducing our shore from a working landscape, busy with boats of all sizes and a bustle of activity, to a seasonal tourist economy.

England is a maritime nation that was for so long defined by the sea that surrounds it on most sides. The sea was our route of trade, exploration and empire-building, a place of boundless possibility. Yet it has also represented great danger, most invasions having reached England by sea and a series of Great Storms and tsunamis having laid waste to its shores. For centuries we were governed by the rhythm of the tide and the pull of the moon – the fishing industry and the movement of goods were limited by the slow draw of the ocean. There are few better ways to reconnect with these aspects of the past than walking around England's coastline.

To walk the England Coast Path is to experience the edge of the land differently and to realise that we do, after all, like to be beside the seaside. To walk some of the more remote, wild and windswept sections of the coastline, and round a headland to be dazzled by the bright lights of the promenade is to be given a true perspective on the contrasts of our frontier. If you drive to the coast you might come to think of the coast as monotonous and over-developed, but to walk into Brighton, Skegness, Weston-super-Mare, Southend or Bournemouth after a long hike, is to be granted a real sense of how special these places are.

In Jonathan Raban's wonderful description of his journey round Britain by boat, the land is reduced to 'a dark smear between the sea and the sky like the track of a grubby finger across a windowpane'. But from the land it is the sea that is often reduced to a benign body, just a line on the horizon. So it is edifying, when the wind is up and the water is frothing with white horses crashing violently on the rocks, to remember that the sea is ultimately in charge here. Our fragile island is constantly reshaped by it, eaten away along the crumbling clays of the east coast, and built up in places like the steadily growing heaps of shingle and sand at Dungeness, Orford Ness and Spurn Point. But these can just as easily be swept away again by the vagaries of the currents – a previous incarnation of Spurn Point with its medieval port of Ravenser Odd now lies beneath the waves two miles offshore, along with dozens of settlements all round the English coast. Sea levels, such an important concern for our immediate future, have changed throughout history. Once connected to the continent by Doggerland, Britain is full of reminders of former sea levels with raised beaches being found several metres up the existing cliffs. Even the chalk cliffs, that defiant face that England shows the rest of Europe, are fragile and vulnerable to the corrosive power of the sea. We might think of England as a changeless entity, but on the coast we are forced to accept that it is changing rapidly with every wave, every tide, every storm.

The South Coast

The south coast of England technically runs all the way from the North or South Foreland in Kent to Land's End in Cornwall, though the term is most often used to refer to the coast through the counties of Kent, Sussex, Hampshire and parts of Dorset. This distinguishes it from the

Beachy Head Lighthouse

well-known south west coast and focuses on the parts of the south coast that lie within relatively easy access of London. It is this definition I have stuck closely to with this book, the first of four that trace the England Coast Path around its circuit of England. I have also included the Thames estuary shoreline on the north side of Kent and the first part of the South West Coast Path through Dorset and east Devon. This gives a satisfying journey from one great river estuary in the Thames to another in the Exe, covering over 700 miles between Woolwich to Exmouth.

Though often overlooked in favour of the spectacular coasts of Cornwall and

The Isle of Wight coast near Ventnor

Devon, the south coast is arguably the most varied coastline in England. It has towering cliffs, mostly composed of chalk, and some of the country's most iconic coastal sites – the White Cliffs of Dover, Beachy Head and the Seven Sisters, the Needles, Great Harry Rocks, Lulworth Cove and Durdle Door, Portland Bill and Golden Cap. It has open marshes along the Thames estuary and around the Hampshire harbours, where wading birds feed on the mudflats and oysters are harvested. It has miles of the finest beaches stretching along much of the Sussex coast, round Christchurch and Poole Bays and across much of west Dorset. It has many of the most famous seaside resorts in the country; Margate, Eastbourne, Brighton, Bognor Regis, Bournemouth, Weymouth, Swanage and Lyme Regis to name just a few. In between there are historic settlements like Faversham, Sandwich, Rye, Beaulieu, Christchurch and Abbotsbury and some of the most important ports in England at Portsmouth, Southampton, Dover, Poole, Ramsgate and Chatham. Though it contains some of the most built-up parts of the English coast, there is plenty of variety in the walking as the coast path dips in and out of all these very different landscapes.

As a northerner I'm always surprised by how much the south of the

Whitstable oysters

country looks to France and greater Europe, in both positive and negative ways. The English Channel acts both as a border between Britain and the continent, and a link between the maritime ports on both sides. France is clearly visible across the water from Kent and, for centuries, when trade was easier by boat than land, much of the south coast was more closely linked with France than it was with places far closer inland. Until the arrival of the railways in the mid 19th century, trade with London was undertaken by sea rather than land, and it was far easier to bring hops, cereals and fruit from Kent along its rivers to the Thames estuary than transport them across the Downs. The Cinque Ports between Sandwich and Hastings were established in the 12th century and controlled the maritime trade in this part of the English channel until the 15th century, often aggressively so (as a 1321 attack on ships in Southampton would attest). More recently, ferry ports like Dover, Folkestone, Portsmouth and Southampton became our primary link with the Continent and the Channel Tunnel linked us even more closely geographically.

Though the south west is most closely associated with smuggling in our national imagination because of Devon and Cornwall's romantic coves and stories like *Poldark* and *Jamaica Inn*, the vast majority of this 'free trade' actually took place on the south coast, particularly on the remote shingle beaches of Sussex and Kent. It was possible to row relatively small boats to France in two hours and return with a valuable hoard of tobacco, tea, wine or spirits, with a network ready to distribute the contraband across the country. At its peak in the 18th and early 19th centuries, before many import duties were removed, it is estimated that two thirds of the tea drunk in England had arrived via this route.

From the late 18th century, bathing in saltwater and drinking it became fashionable – a pint of seawater every morning was said to help the bowels. Resorts began to spring up along the south coast, particularly after King George III began visiting Weymouth in the 1790s. The world's first bathing machine (a shed that could be wheeled into the water to preserve the bather's modesty) was developed in Margate, where the Royal Sea-Bathing Infirmary was founded in 1791, the first of its kind. Focusing on the health benefits of the immersion cure, this wasn't bathing as leisure, but it began the process of transforming much of the south coast into that we are familiar with today, what travel writer Paul Theroux has called 'the holiday coast'.

The England Coast Path

> I had an impression that there was a continuous footpath that went round the whole coastline of Great Britain… Usually it was a muddy twelve-inch path, with a brisk figure approaching in plus-fours and thick-soled shoes and a crackling plastic mackintosh, and carrying a bag of sandwiches and an Ordnance Survey map. I imagined this person to be just another feature of the British coast, like old gun emplacements, and the iron piers, and the wooden groynes, and the continuous and circling footpath.
>
> Paul Theroux, *The Kingdom by the Sea*

Despite Theroux's impression, there has never until now been a continuous path around the coast of England. John Merrill famously walked nearly 7,000 miles around the whole coast of Britain in just 10 months in 1978, the first person known to do so, but this was his own bespoke route that in places required straying inland and in others involved trespassing. Others have followed parts of his journey over the years and several long distance routes have been promoted along the English coast, most notably the South West Coast Path. However, it was far from a complete circuit, with the more difficult parts around estuaries and through private estates avoided by these routes, making it hard to complete a meaningful circumnavigation without Merrill's meticulous planning and sheer determination.

The England Coast Path began with the Marine and Coastal Act 2009, which created a statutory duty for Natural England to establish a long distance trail around the whole coast of England and designate a coastal margin for open access to all beaches, cliffs and shoreline. These two parts have been worked on in tandem, meaning it is a far more complicated proposition than the Wales Coast Path, the 870-mile route around Wales that opened in 2012.

One of the most powerful elements of the new legislation is the idea of 'roll-back', with the new coast path automatically moving inland as cliffs eroded or collapsed without the need for any further negotiations with landowners – this is particularly important in parts of the east coast where the land is disappearing at rates of up to 2m per year. At estuaries, discretion can be used to extend the trail along (and potentially beyond) any tidal waters as far as the first bridge or crossing with pedestrian access. As such, it represents a great opportunity to secure coastal access in areas where there previously was none, linking existing coastal trails and providing recreation benefits for residents, businesses and visitors alike.

The coast has been broken down into 67 sections, with statutory reports being created for each, recommending where the route should go and identifying a suitable coastal margin in each area. After a period of consultation, during which objections could be lodged, these reports were to be presented to the Secretary of State for Environment, Food and Rural Affairs for approval or amendment. Only then could work begin on the path itself, with each section declared open once signs, gates, bridges and other furniture had been installed by the relevant local authority.

The coastal margin is a single continuous corridor of all the land to the seaward side of the new trail and occasionally further areas of beach, dune or foreshore on the landward side. Any buildings and their immediate curtilage or gardens are automatically excluded, as well as Military Lands, railways, quarries, schools, racecourses, aerodromes, golf courses, burial grounds, caravan parks and any fields that have been cropped in the previous 12 months. Other areas may also be excluded, including those with statutory environmental designations like Marine Conservation Zones and Sites of Special Scientific Interest. These cover most of the estuaries and marshes of the country and, together with the above, exclude a lot of land, but what these new rights do ensure is still important. Any beach or stretch of non-designated foreshore can now be freely accessed by anyone on foot or by wheelchair for walking, climbing or picnicking, though these rights do not extend to camping, cycling or horse riding.

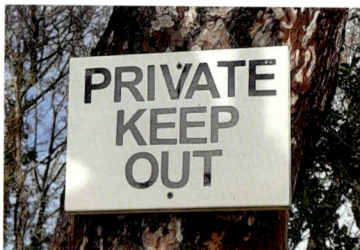

Initially it was estimated that the England Coast Path would take just a few years to establish, but cuts to Natural England's budget and a reluctance by landowners to acquiesce to this new legislation hindered its progress. In 2014 the Coalition Government, in one of the Liberal Democrats' few lasting legacies from their brief stint in power, pledged to allocate extra funding to deliver the completed route by 2020. This allayed fears that the path would become a victim of political vagaries and this great opportunity to change the face of the English coast would be lost, but of course it was never going to be as simple as the politicians thought.

By the end of 2020, just 387 miles of the England Coast Path was officially open with the new coastal access rights in place, approximately 14% of the whole route. For those of us working on books on this route and groups like the Ramblers and Long Distance Walkers

Association, it was quite dispiriting. The first short section had opened in June 2012 between Weymouth and Lulworth Cove and I'd walked my first parts of the route in Durham and Cumbria soon after they opened in April 2014, but since then it has felt at times that things have progressed at a snail's pace. Most of the work though was going on behind the scenes at Natural England, negotiating a route that satisfied both environmental bodies and local landowners. Continued budgetary restraints and a global pandemic haven't helped, and we have had to keep the faith that the small team at Natural England could still deliver this huge national project.

So here we are in 2023 (which is being celebrated as the 'Year of the Coast') and the England Coast Path is still not yet complete, but there is enough of it ready in parts of the country for me to launch the first book in this series. There are still gaps that will hopefully soon be filled, but in these cases I have suggested the best route currently available at time of publication. If you find newly opened sections with clear signage, you should follow these, but in their absence I have provided the best available route I can. There are sections that are not yet signed as the England Coast Path and more care will be needed to stay on the route here, but hopefully my route descriptions are detailed enough to follow and, if in doubt, always keep the sea on your left!

Signage of the England Coast Path varies greatly in terms of style and reliability. All signs have been installed by local authorities, with 90 different governmental bodies signing different sections of the route, so naturally there will be some inconsistency. Some of this was done in 2012 and some more than 10 years later, with the result that the newer sections will be less worn but hopefully better signed. There are also parts of the route that continue to be signed as parts of the long distance path of which they were originally part (e.g. the South West Coast Path, the Cleveland Way or the Norfolk Coast Path). Here are some examples of the variety of signage encountered on the south coast part of the England Coast Path.

Walking the England Coast Path

The England Coast Path is by its nature a circuit of the whole country (bar the land borders with Wales and Scotland) and can in theory be started anywhere along the route. According to Natural England, the route begins at Aust by the Severn Bridge and continues anti-clockwise to the Welsh border on the Dee estuary between Neston and Shotton. The route though can be undertaken in either direction, and I wanted the first two books to cover the south and south west coasts (where the path was likely to be ready to access sooner). I also liked the idea of starting in London on the route's only dead-end section, which runs along the south bank of the Thames out of London. So my description goes clockwise and starts at Woolwich, allowing the route to be broken into four roughly even sections, divided by significant river estuaries; the Thames, the Exe, the Severn and the Humber. This means the existing South West Coast Path is broken up between two books and the two sides of northern England are combined into a single volume, but it is the neatest way to break this substantial and unwieldy route into four manageable volumes.

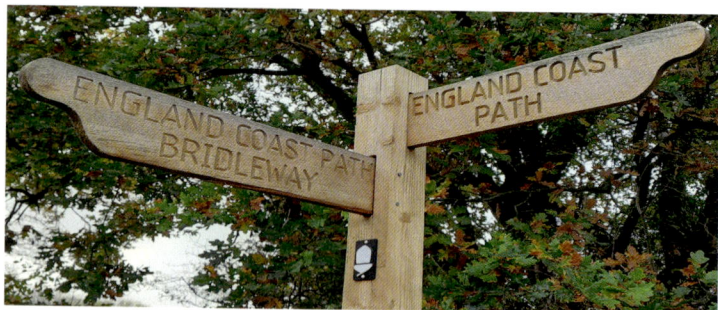

I have begun my series with the south coast, embarking on this venture in Woolwich, where the true coast feels a long way off. The route works its way along the south bank of the River Thames, before the estuary starts to open out. Beyond the Medway Delta and Isle of Sheppey, the coast path finally reaches the North Sea at the north east corner of Kent. Thereafter, the English Channel becomes the walker's companion for the rest of this book, as the route continues round the chalk cliffs of Kent and East Sussex and across the endless shingle beaches of Dungeness and West Sussex.

Beyond the myriad harbours of east Hampshire, the Solent creates its own little world, with the marshes and forest of west Hampshire sheltered by the Isle of Wight. A distillation of the whole south coast, the 86-mile circuit of the island is a rewarding additional loop reached by ferries from either Portsmouth or Southampton. The beaches of Christchurch and Poole Bays soon give way to the dramatic chalk and limestone of the Isles of Purbeck and Portland. Dorset soon slides imperceptibly into Devon, while the geologically dramatic Jurassic coast continues all the way to Exmouth, an appropriate place to break before the drama of the south west coast, which will be continued in Book 2.

The England Coast Path along the south coast incorporates parts of several existing trails – Saxon Shore Way, Sussex Border Path, Solent Way, Isle of Wight Coastal Path and the South West Coast Path – and yet there are variations from these routes in many places, as well as several new sections that have been created to improve coastal access.

There is little doubt that the most satisfactory way to walk a long distance path is to start at one end and walk continuously along it to its end, whether carrying a large rucksack full of camping gear, hopping between B&Bs and guest houses, or having your gear ferried along by a luggage transfer operator. However, the England Coast Path is hard to do all in one go – there is the sheer length of it (2,795 miles), the gaps along the Welsh and Scottish borders, and the fact that it has no true start and end. As there is no existing route along the Scottish border or coastline, the purist could start at the Scottish border near Berwick and finish at Gretna, adding the Wales Coast Path (or Offa's Dyke Path for a more direct route) from the Severn Bridge to Shotton to provide a complete linear route of nearly 3,800 miles.

For most people though, this will not be possible and the route will need to be broken into manageable sections and undertaken in what holiday windows are available. I did it all out of my camper van, generally using public transport to get me back to my starting point, though the way the route opened meant I did not complete the sections in order. I would often park in the middle of the day's route, whether for cheaper parking, quieter places to camp or to fit in with infrequent rural bus services. This meant that, though I have walked every step of the coast path, I didn't always get the sense of new parts of the coast unfolding in front of me. But each walker will doubtless find their own way that works for them.

I have tried to encompass all eventualities in this book, breaking the route into good walking days of between 11 and 16 miles where possible. Sometimes a shorter day forms a natural break, but sometimes there is nothing for it but to extend the day, though I have tried to keep all the days below 20 miles.

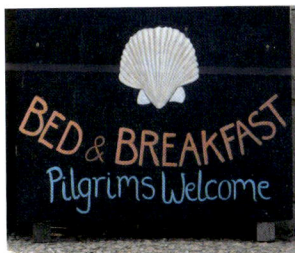

The terrain will affect this too, as 15 miles along the Cornish coast is not the same as 15 miles around the Essex marshes or the promenades of Sussex, though I would argue that the mental tiredness of some of these unchanging landscapes can be as taxing as climbing the equivalent of Ben Nevis in a day's walking. I appreciate that everyone has their different idea of a good day's walking but, while some will only want to cover 10 miles a day and others will be aiming for 20, I hope I have settled on a happy medium. Ideally you'll make good progress on the coast path, but have time to enjoy the walk, perhaps have a swim or explore somewhere off the route.

Information is provided for parking at either end of each day's walk, and public transport to take you back to the start. In nearly all cases there is some sort of public transport, although some days require more careful planning than others and occasionally you may need to resort to using a local taxi or even leaving a car at either end. If using public transport, Sundays present a problem in many areas, with most rural buses having no service, so careful planning is needed to avoid compulsory rest days every Sunday.

There is also information on accommodation, though details are provided only where this is limited, as larger towns and busier places have too many options to list. I have not tried the accommodation, so they are not recommendations, just a list of all the information I have been able to gather and check. In some cases the only options available are those found on Airbnb, which dominates this sector but can provide useful options. Where possible I've listed alternatives. Similarly the lunchtime refreshment options I have listed do not come from personal recommendation, but simply provide useful information it may be

Portland Bill

helpful to know before you set off the day, particularly on the more remote sections of the coastline.

For the backpacker or budget traveller, I have also listed bunkhouses, youth hostels and campsites where they coincide with the days I have created. While hotels, B&Bs and public transport tend to be found in and around larger towns, these places are often located on more remote sections of the route. If you're doing the route this way, you'll probably find yourself ignoring the way I've divided the route and working out ways to hop from campsite to campsite. Though this is easily possible in the more touristy seaside areas, there are plenty of more remote or very urban sections of the route where there is little or nothing to be found. There is also a pattern of smaller campsites disappearing, leaving the only options as vast caravan parks, which even where they do take tents are expensive and unsatisfying. Walking long distance paths with a backpack and a tent is certainly not as easy as it used to be.

I have often been asked about wild camping in England and Wales, which is strictly illegal without the landowner's permission. However, as Raynor Winn's journey along the South West Coast Path in *The Salt Path* attests, it is perfectly possible to camp on the more remote parts of the English coast. That said, the coast is so developed in places, particularly in the south east of England, that I imagine it would often be difficult to find somewhere suitable. As a general rule, if you can't find a landowner or farmer to ask permission from, pitch up late and unobtrusively and strike camp early, leaving no trace – it's hard to imagine you'd come to much bother this way, even on our crowded isle.

The route descriptions are designed both to aid navigation and as a companion to the walk, dropping in snippets of historical, geological or biological information. I have eschewed Ordnance Survey maps for my own hand-drawn overviews of each day. Though these won't tell you whether to turn left or right at a particular junction, they should be detailed enough to work out the shape of the day without needing to invest in all of the OS maps needed to cover the whole coastline (which would potentially mean carrying 45 Landranger or 74 Explorer maps).

A well waymarked National Trail following the coastline is on the whole not the hardest route to follow. 'Keep the sea on your left' is a safe direction for most of the way and you should be able to keep the book in your pocket for long sections. However, there are always a few places where the route is not obvious. Urban areas are particularly difficult to waymark (signs have a habit of disappearing or getting turned to point in the wrong direction) and you often find yourself abandoned just when you most need help, with the sea invisible behind an industrial estate or dockyard. Sand dunes and forests can be equally disorientating, presenting mazes of paths that all look the same. So I do hope that the combination of map and text in this book provides enough information to avoid striking off in the wrong direction and having to backtrack.

The Ordnance Survey app is a good backup if you don't mind reading maps off your phone and I find it useful in areas for which I don't have the paper map. Do, however, make sure you have downloaded the map squares covered by the route before setting off as phone reception remains unpredictable on some of the more remote parts of the coast. What my maps hopefully do is to show the location of points of interest, particularly those just off the route, and clearly display different route options. The main route is shown in red and any official alternatives (usually relating to high tides or seasonal ferries) in green, and I have added informal alternatives in orange. These are optional routes along beaches or other sections that the formal route has eschewed for safety or other reasons, although they often provide a

Durdle Door

more interesting walk than the main route. They may also plug occasional gaps in the route, where no safe route has been established yet – on the south coast, these gaps exist around Rye, the Osborne House estate on the Isle of Wight, and Lulworth Ranges in Dorset. All of these informal alternative routes are publicly accessible and, if you use basic common sense with respect to tides, roads or cliff edges, you shouldn't come to grief.

Of course there will be temporary and permanent diversions – indeed there already are in places – that will be necessary due to cliff collapses or landslips. The best place to check for diversions is on the official England Coast Path website at: *www.nationaltrail.co.uk/en_GB/trails/england-coast-path* as they can potentially have a significant effect on the length of a day's walking. Existing closures near Watchet in Somerset and Duporth in Cornwall, for example, add 1-2 miles of walking to already long days. As a general rule, you are best following any local guidance and signed diversions that are in place.

It should be stressed again that, at the time of publication, the whole of the England Coast Path is not officially open. New sections are being opened all the time as work is completed, but until these are all open it is likely you'll encounter parts of the route that are not yet fully signed. I have started with the south coast as there is existing public access on most sections of the route here and, though they may be signed as other long distance routes or in some cases not at all, you shouldn't have a problem walking at least one of the route options I have outlined. The only real exception to this is the Isle of Sheppey, where negotiations are still ongoing about some parts of the route and others have no existing public access or obvious alternatives. I would advise leaving this short two-day circuit, which is separate from the mainland route anyway, until the route here has officially opened. Otherwise, you just need to be aware that more care will need to be taken with navigation where the route has yet to be officially opened.

Lastly, the 'Song for the Day' is a bit of fun that you may use as another nugget of information or as a soundtrack to your walk. Each song relates in some way to the day's walk; some are very obviously about a place passed en route; some are by local bands or artists; some reveal an interesting local story; while others are more loosely connected to the area by a key word or are about a broader aspect of the area. I have put together individual playlists for each chapter on my YouTube channel at: **www.youtube.com/@englandcoastpath**

Most of all though, I do hope you enjoy exploring this fantastic new National Trail as much as I have!

For further books in this series, more information and a feedback/query form, please visit my website at **www.englandcoastpath.com**

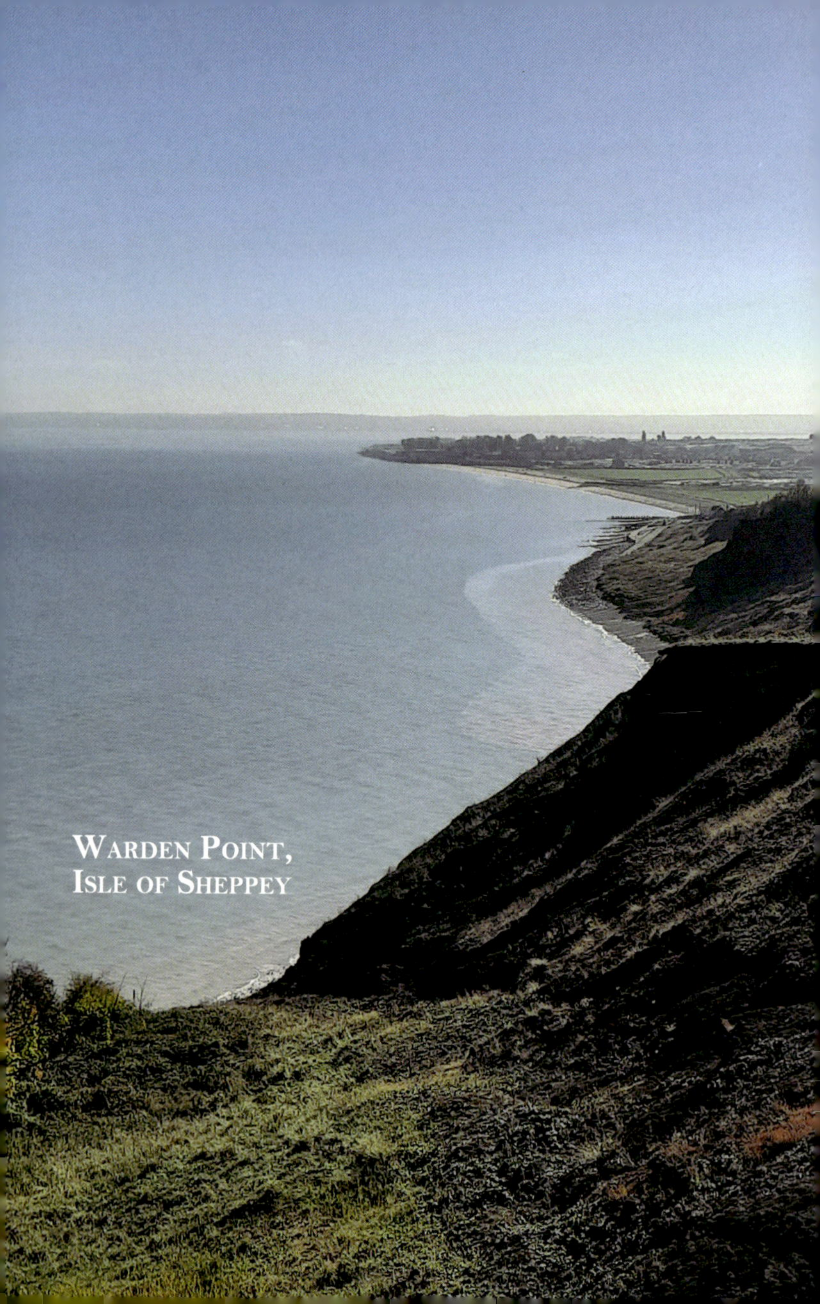
WARDEN POINT,
ISLE OF SHEPPEY

Part 1:
The North Kent Coast

The North Kent Coast

Start: Woolwich
Finish: Margate
Total Distance: 261.0km (162 miles)
Total Ascent: 790m (2,590ft)
Days: 11

> ...the dark flat wilderness beyond the churchyard, intersected with dykes and mounds and gates, with scattered cattle feeding on it, was the marshes; and the low leaden line beyond, was the river; and the distant savage lair from which the wind was rushing, was the sea...
>
> Charles Dickens, *Great Expectations*

The north Kent coast stretches along the River Thames from the outskirts of London to the North Foreland headland just beyond Margate. A landscape of muddy estuary shores, it has more in common with the rest of the east coast than the long beaches of the south coast. Only east of the Medway are there any true beaches, with Margate's the first sandy expanse encountered. Soft and crumbling cliff

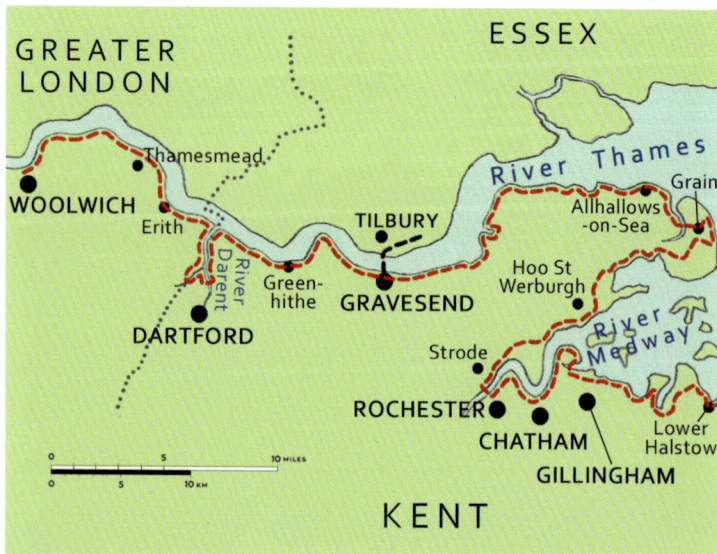

faces are found on the Isle of Sheppey and between Herne Bay and Reculver, with the walls of chalk that will become a defining characteristic of the south coast first rearing up on the Isle of Thanet.

The Thames is a very shallow estuary, strewn with sandbanks that are treacherous for shipping, and when the tide goes right out it can look like the mud continues all the way from the Isle of Grain to Canvey Island in Essex. There are myriad channels marked by lines of buoys and it resembles more a vast Norfolk Broad than the open sea, as does the River Medway's broad delta. Further out there are huge wind farms and the Maunsell Towers, abandoned World War II sea forts that look like old camera tripods or something out of *Star Wars*, betraying that this is not quite the real open sea.

The low-lying marshes of north Kent are brooding places and were a lawless hinterland, once home to gypsies, livestock and escaped convicts like Dickens' Magwitch. They have been tamed somewhat by the creation of the Thames' modern river banks, reclaiming marshland to build new settlements like Thamesmead and Ebbsfleet, as London continues to sprawl outwards. The Thames' vast delta, for all the efforts to corral it by land reclamation, often gives the impression of being easily taken back by the sea, as it was in the devastating North Sea flood of 1953.

The name Kent (like Canterbury) derives from Cantium, the Roman name for large parts of the south east of England that were once

The Red Towers Maunsell sea forts

occupied by the Cantiaci, a Celtic tribe described by Julius Caesar as the most civilised in Britain. Kent was the only county in England to have two ancient cathedrals, at Canterbury and Rochester, and claims to be the only place not conquered by the Normans, with whom the Men of Kent made a deal to keep some of their hereditary customs *(see p47)*. This is why the white horse symbol of Kent is known as Invicta, meaning 'unconquered'.

Historically, north Kent was closely linked with London, with shallow sailing boats called hoys loading oats, barley, fruit and hops from the muddy quays and creeks of Kent to ship to the capital. Oysters were (and indeed still are) farmed on the tidal flats, particularly around Whitstable and Faversham, and traded to fish markets in London and Holland. Kent's historical reputation as the 'Garden of England' had more to do with its maritime transport links with London than particularly superior soil.

Kent was also at the heart of the naval industry, with warships built and repaired at dockyards along the Thames and Medway, at Deptford, Woolwich, Chatham and Sheerness. Deptford and Woolwich were first established by Henry VIII, while Chatham grew to be the largest, surviving a century longer before its eventual closure in 1984.

As the fishing industry gradually gave way to tourism from the late 18th century, fishing villages remodelled themselves as seaside resorts. Early resorts included Erith, Greenhithe and Gravesend, within easy access of London via packets and steamers, but as transport improved so the resorts of Whitstable, Herne Bay, Margate, Broadstairs and Ramsgate expanded, particularly after the arrival of the railways in the 1840s.

Wedged between the Thames estuary and the continent, Kent is surrounded by water on more sides than any other county apart from Cornwall. Modern Kent now begins at Dartford, meaning that part of this section runs through Greater London, but Kent once continued all the way into London to meet Surrey just beyond Deptford.

Parts of the England Coast Path through north Kent are entirely new, particularly around the Isles of Grain and Sheppey, while large sections follow the existing Saxon Shore Way between Gravesend and Margate. The first part of the route is very urban, following the river's great curves from Woolwich to Gravesend, beyond which the city is left behind. As the estuary widens, great forts – Tudor, Napoleonic and 20th century – dot the shoreline. The Hoo Peninsula, Isle of Grain and Isle of Sheppey surround the mouth of the River Medway, whose intricate shoreline surrounds the trio of historic Medway towns; Rochester, Chatham and Gillingham.

The Isle of Sheppey, a 30-mile circuit off the mainland route, is a fascinating place, with crumbling clay cliffs and great marshes, though this is one of the few sections that is hard to complete until the new coast path is fully open. The marshes of the Swale lead on past the attractive towns of Sittingbourne and Faversham to what finally feels like the open sea at the resorts of Whitstable, Herne Bay and Margate. Though facing north, the latter is the first time you encounter the beaches, amusement parks, donkey rides and candy floss that characterise much of the south coast. It is a gentle start to the England Coast Path, a flat but interesting route with largely very good public transport links.

Reculver Towers and Bishopstone Cliff

Useful Information

Tourist Information – *www.visitsoutheastengland.com*
Southeastern Rail – 0345 322 7021 *(www.southeasternrailway.co.uk)*
Stagecoach South East – 0345 2418000 *(www.stagecoachbus.com)*
Arriva Kent & Surrey – 0344 8004411 *(www.arrivabus.co.uk)*
Chalkwell Garage & Coach Hire – 01795 423982 *(www.chalkwell.co.uk)*
Kent Travel – *www.kent.gov.uk/roads-and-travel/travelling-around-kent*
Train Times – *traintimes.org.uk*
Bus Times – *bustimes.org*
Traveline – *www.traveline.info*

COUNTY ANTHEM

The Albion Dance Band – *Hopping Down In Kent*

This traditional folk song recounts the experiences of one of the hop-pickers who used to head down from London to Kent in September every year. Around the turn of the century as many as 80,000 East Enders made the annual pilgrimage with their families for what was essentially a working holiday, though this song makes clear they went back with little in their pocket. This tradition continued until the 1960s, when pickers began to be replaced by more efficient machines. This version was recorded in 1977 and released on *The Prospect Before Us* album by an iteration of the Albion Band that focused on traditional English dance songs.

Herne Bay Pier

Section 1.1 – Woolwich to Dartford

Distance: 20.6km (13 miles)

Height Gained: 60m

Parking: Pay car parks in both Woolwich and Dartford. Free parking along the route at Erith.

Public Transport: There are regular trains from Dartford (whose station is 1 mile from the route along Darent Creek) to Woolwich 7 days a week.

Refreshments: Various cafes and pubs in Erith, roughly halfway through the day's walk.

Accommodation: As well as rooms at the Royal Victoria & Bull Hotel (01322 224415) and the Fulwich (01322 223683), there are various options on Airbnb, but there are no campsites this close to London.

Overview: The only section of the England Coast Path in London, this is inevitably a very urban day following a tarmac cycleway for most of its course. As it doesn't link with the route on the other side of the Thames Estuary, which ends at Tilbury, it's likely to be an optional extra that some walkers will choose to forego. However, it feels like a good way to start the coast path, leaving London behind for the open vistas of the English coast. The route follows the Thames Path Extension as far as Crayford Ness, then opens out on Erith Saltings and along Dartford Creek, with some fascinating industrial sites along the great river.

Route Description

The England Coast Path starts on the south side of the Thames Estuary at **Woolwich Foot Tunnel**, which opened in 1912 and runs ¼ mile under the river to North Woolwich. You follow the route of the Thames Path Extension, which runs along the river bank beside the Q14 cycleway all the way to Crayford Ness, and is not signed as the England Coast Path until this point. If you're really keen, you could actually start the route right in the middle of London, adding another 11 miles along the Thames Path from London Bridge via Rotherhithe, Deptford and Greenwich, before passing the Thames Barrier to reach Woolwich.

The riverside promenade soon opens out by the start of the **Royal Arsenal**, which once stretched for over 3 miles along the river to Cross Ness. Continue alongside the river bank out of Woolwich, crossing the **Ordnance Canal** to pass the new estates of Thamesmead West. The

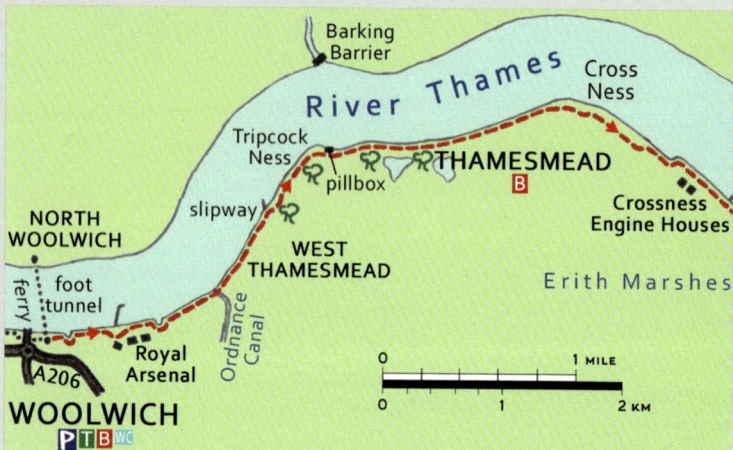

path is greener round **Tripcock Ness**, which is marked by a red navigation light. The opposite side of the river is dominated by Barking Barrier, a tidal flood barrier at the end of Barking Creek. The broad promenade continues past **Thamesmead**, a settlement created in the 1960s on the site of the former arsenal and greatly expanded in recent years. It is marked by a series of striking man-made hills, constructed from waste material created in the landscaping of the site.

Beyond the next navigation light at **Cross Ness**, the path crosses

Woolwich Arsenal

Woolwich's Royal Arsenal was once the world's largest munitions site, supplying the Royal Navy from the early 18th century until the ordnance factory closed in 1967 and employing 80,000 people at its peak. Among the twenty remaining buildings are the grand stores, a rifle shell factory, a carriageworks and some of the barracks. In 1886 workers from the

armament factory formed a football team then called Dial Square (after the sundial above the factory entrance) – they would become Arsenal FC and eventually move across the river to Highbury in 1913.

Erith Marshes, a landscape that has been dominated by its sewage works since 1865, when Joseph Bazalguette built the huge **Crossness Engine Houses** to pump London's untreated sewage into the Thames at high tide to be washed out to sea. After treatment works were developed, the sludge that had settled from the sewage was still taken out into the estuary to be dumped, though it is now used to create electricity at the modern generator building immediately beyond. The remarkably ornate cast iron and brass interiors of the pumping station, modelled on Norman cathedrals, have been preserved as an industrial

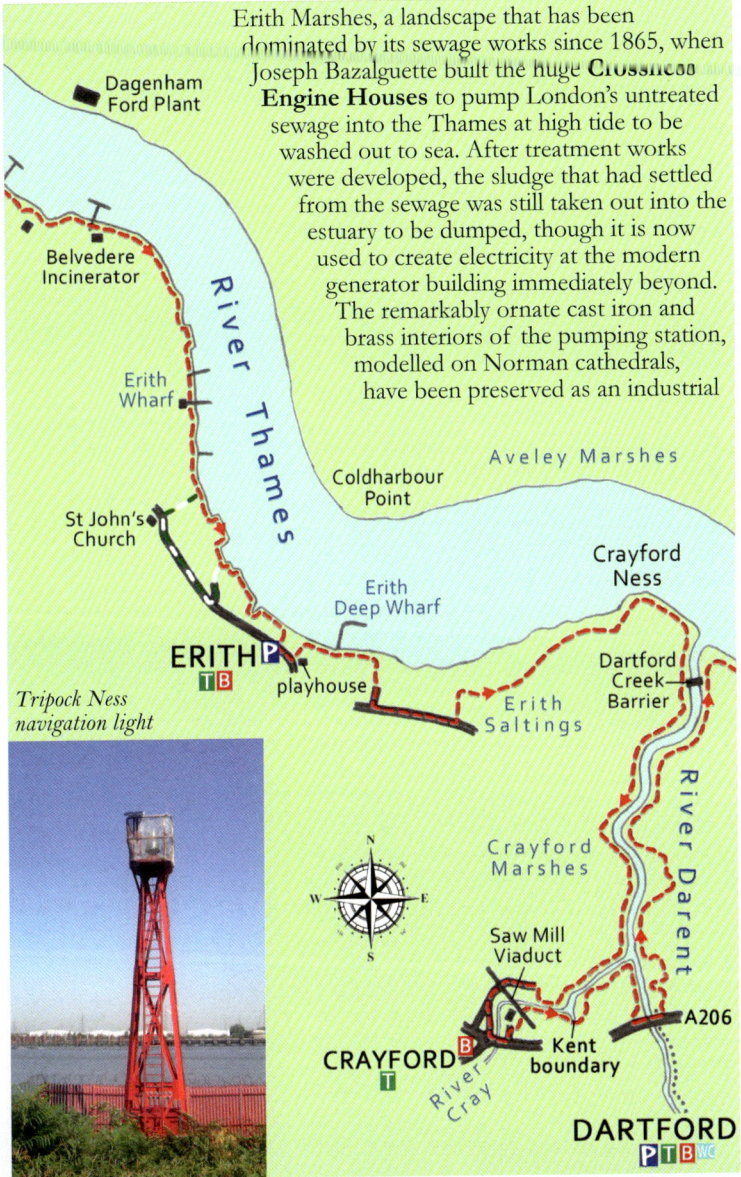

Dagenham
Ford Plant

Belvedere
Incinerator

River Thames

Erith
Wharf

Coldharbour
Point

Aveley Marshes

St John's
Church

Erith
Deep Wharf

Crayford
Ness

ERITH P
T B
playhouse

Dartford
Creek
Barrier

*Tripock Ness
navigation light*

Erith
Saltings

River Darent

Crayford
Marshes

Saw Mill
Viaduct

A206

CRAYFORD B
T
River Cray

Kent
boundary

DARTFORD
P T B WC

museum. On the opposite side of the river lies Ford's enormous plant at Dagenham, which has produced over ten million cars since 1931, though there are now plans to build 3,500 new homes on the site.

The cycleway stays along the shore past the **Belvedere Incinerator** (a generator burning rubbish on the site of Belvedere Power Station) and beneath several piers at Erith Wharf to reach the edge of Erith. Where the cycleway (and alternative route) turns right to join the road briefly, a path continues straight ahead, following the lower walkway around the wharfs. Rejoining the cycleway, keep left on the lower walkway to reach Riverside Gardens, before being forced up to join **Erith** High Street. Follow it left, then turn left just before Erith Playhouse and head down steps to the river bank again. You soon reach **Erith Deep Wharf**, London's longest pier and a fine detour out over the river. The first pier was built at Erith (pronounced 'ear-ith' and meaning 'old harbour') in the 1840s, when it brought day-trippers to the town's pleasure gardens. Its short-lived popularity ended with the development of the sewage works at Crossness, the tide failing to take its effluent as efficiently out to sea as was originally envisaged.

The Gypsies of Belvedere Marshes

Romany travellers gathered on the low-lying and poorly-drained land of Belvedere Marshes from the late 19th century, spending the winter here after travelling around Kent the rest of the year, picking hops, apples, potatoes and fruit. By the 1940s it had developed into the largest gypsy camp in England, with up to 1,700 people staying during the winter and hundreds of ramshackle huts erected. However, the 1953 flood that so devastated the south east of England also washed away the camp, claiming 300 lives there, and local council pressure ensured the gypsies were moved to designated sites by the 1960s.

Follow the riverside walkway until you have to head right to join the road. At the end, go left on Manor Road for nearly ½ mile, eventually turning left towards **Erith Yacht Club**. Here the tarmac finally ends and a track leads out onto the blissfully open ground of **Erith Saltings**, one of the last remnants of the Thameside saltmarsh that once extended from Erith to Stone. You pass several concrete World War II battery buildings on the way out to the mast on **Crayford Ness**. Here the Thames Path extension abruptly stops, but the England Coast Path continues along the embankment to the **Dartford Creek tidal barrier** – the 160-tonne gates are closed only when flooding is likely. Sadly there is no way across the creek on foot until you reach the A206 and it is nearly 5 miles round to the opposite bank.

Keep left to follow the River Darent to its junction with the River

Cray, which the path then follows towards **Crayford**. Join a road to head under Saw Mill Viaduct, then keep left to join the main road briefly. Turn left immediately, then bear right onto a path along the other side of the creek back under the viaduct. Here you leave Greater London and enter Kent and, after tracing the creek back to the **River Darent**, you soon reach the A206 heading left over the water. The route continues left back out onto the marshes, but turning right alongside the creek leads into **Dartford** past the industrial estates – it is about 1 mile to the railway station. Dartford is a shortening of Darentford and was established by the Romans on the line of Watling Street between London and Canterbury, later becoming an important stopping point for pilgrims on the way to Canterbury Cathedral.

SONG OF THE DAY

Callender's Cable Works Band – *A Sailor's Life*

This song was recorded for the BBC in 1928 by an amateur brass band made up of workers at Callender Cable & Construction Co. (based at Erith Works). A traditional folk song about a woman searching for her lover only to discover that he has drowned, it would later be picked up by Sandy Denny, who recorded a more famous version with Fairport Convention.

Horses on Crayford Marshes

Section 1.2 – Dartford to Gravesend

Distance: 18.7km (11½ miles)

Height Gained: 80m

Parking: Pay car parks in Dartford and Gravesend.

Public Transport: Regular trains from Gravesend to Dartford (the station is 1 mile from the route along Darent Creek) 7 days a week.

Refreshments: At the midpoint of the day's walk, Greenhithe has a small selection of places, including the Pier Hotel, Café de Dawn and various fast food outlets.

Accommodation: There are no campsites near Gravesend, but the town has plenty of hotels and B&Bs, including the Clarendon Royal Hotel (01474 362221) right on the route.

Overview: Another optional extra day for completists, linking London with the main circuit at the Tilbury to Gravesend ferry crossing. This section blends former saltmarshes with heavy industry and, though the latter part of the walk is unremittingly industrial, it is a great contrast to the open marshes that lie ahead and has plenty of fascinating sights, including passing far beneath the M25 at the Dartford Crossing.

Route Description

Rejoin the route at the A206, turning left onto a path along the meandering embankment on the east side of **Dartford Creek**. The circuitous route passes several ruined ammunition stores for the anti-aircraft guns that were sited on **Dartford Marshes** during World War II to protect London. Beyond is the former site of a World War I airfield and isolation hospital at Joyce Green, though much of this history is now being erased by aggregate quarrying. The marshes are still home to many beautiful grazing horses, which belong to local Romany families who were granted land here by Henry VIII to breed horses for him.

Beyond the tidal barrier, the path rejoins the bank of the River Thames as it is drawn towards the giant **Queen Elizabeth II Bridge**, carrying the southbound M25 across the estuary. Pass the site of the **Littlebrook Power Stations**, the last of which was pulled

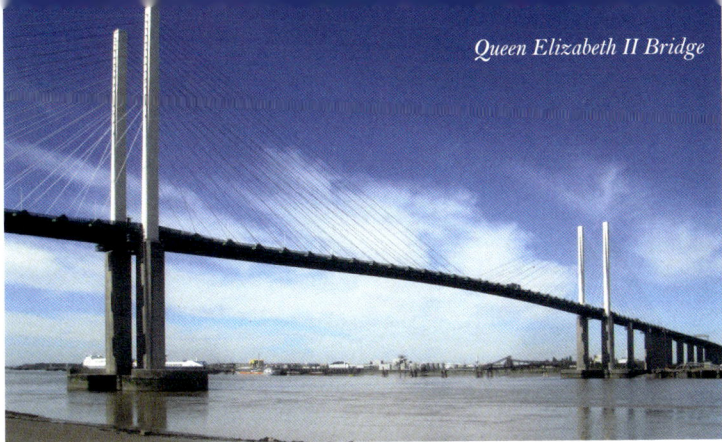

Queen Elizabeth II Bridge

Queen Elizabeth II Bridge

The bridge opened in 1991, just five years after the M25 was completed, as the two Dartford Tunnels that had been dug beneath the river were insufficient for the new road's traffic. The name was a compromise after residents on either side of the estuary rejected the originally proposed names of either Dartford Bridge or Tilbury Bridge.

down in 2019, before ducking beneath the bridge's feet. The gravel path continues until it is forced right to the road by the heaps of sand and gravel at **Greenhithe Wharf**. Keep left on the road and turn almost immediately left on a grassy path before the supermarket. Reaching the riverside flats, turn left up some steps to return to the river bank until forced to rejoin the road by the John Franklin pub in the small town of **Greenhithe**. A landing place since Roman times (*hythe* meaning a wharf), this was once a popular Victorian resort with a pier and a stream of pleasure steamers arriving from London.

Follow the road left, then go left into Frobisher Way and turn next right as the route skirts around the modern wharfside flats. A narrow pathway at the end emerges by the **Pier Hotel**. Turn left into the riverfront green of **Ingress Park**, named after the nearby Ingress Abbey (said to have been built with stone from the old London Bridge). Make sure you follow the lower walkway along the river bank to emerge on **Swanscombe Marshes** at the end of the houses. It is an area touted for development as the London Resort, a theme park based on British and Hollywood film and television.

At the end of the embankment head straight on, then follow a vehicle track left towards the old jetty at **Bell Wharf**, before turning right towards the massive pylon that dominates this landscape. Pass underneath the feet of this impressive structure that carries cables

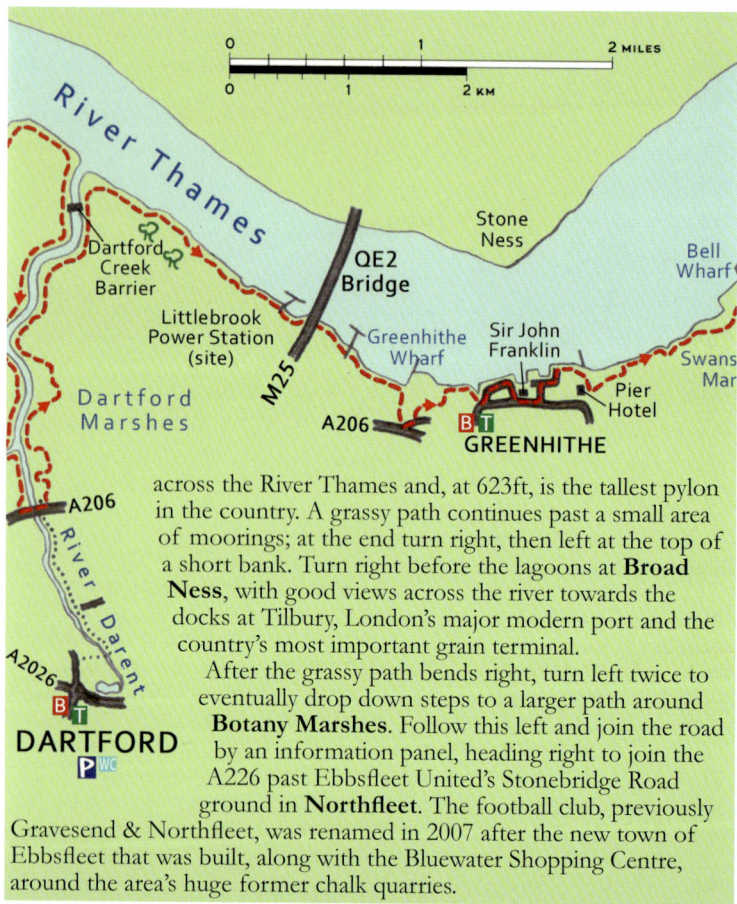

Map labels:

River Thames

0 ... 1 ... 2 MILES
0 ... 1 ... 2 KM

Dartford Creek Barrier

QE2 Bridge

Stone Ness

Bell Wharf

Littlebrook Power Station (site)

Greenhithe Wharf

Sir John Franklin

Swans Mar

M25

Dartford Marshes

A206

Pier Hotel

B T GREENHITHE

A206

River Darent

A2026

B T DARTFORD

P WC

across the River Thames and, at 623ft, is the tallest pylon in the country. A grassy path continues past a small area of moorings; at the end turn right, then left at the top of a short bank. Turn right before the lagoons at **Broad Ness**, with good views across the river towards the docks at Tilbury, London's major modern port and the country's most important grain terminal.

After the grassy path bends right, turn left twice to eventually drop down steps to a larger path around **Botany Marshes**. Follow this left and join the road by an information panel, heading right to join the A226 past Ebbsfleet United's Stonebridge Road ground in **Northfleet**. The football club, previously Gravesend & Northfleet, was renamed in 2007 after the new town of Ebbsfleet that was built, along with the Bluewater Shopping Centre, around the area's huge former chalk quarries.

Grays from Broad Ness

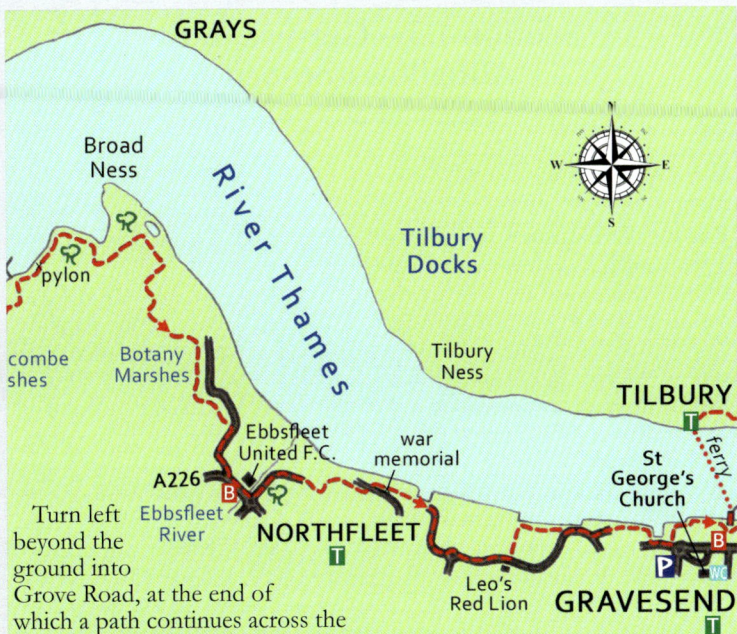

GRAYS

Broad Ness

River Thames

Tilbury Docks

pylon

combe shes

Botany Marshes

Tilbury Ness

TILBURY

Ebbsleet United F.C.

war memorial

ferry

St George's Church

A226

Ebbsfleet River

NORTHFLEET

Leo's Red Lion

GRAVESEND

Turn left beyond the ground into Grove Road, at the end of which a path continues across the industrial wasteland beyond. Turn left back towards the estuary and follow the well signed path through the Bevans Cement Works, where you pass a **war memorial** for its workers in the form of a statue of Britannia. At the far end of the works, push through a heavy metal gate and join a road leading right through the industrial estate. Opposite **Leo's Red Lion** (a famous live music venue), turn left and follow the estuary shore briefly before rejoining the road. Keep left and soon pick up another walkway leading along the river past Baltic Wharf. At its end, follow the road left to a roundabout near the centre of **Gravesend**. The route turns left to rejoin the riverside walkway via a series of steps and soon reaches **Gravesend Town Pier**, where the ferry from Tilbury and the east coast continuation of the coast path arrive.

SONG OF THE DAY

Rolling Stones – *Waiting on a Friend*

Both Mick Jagger and Keith Richards grew up in Dartford, going to the same primary school, but they met as adults for the first time on October 17 1961 on platform 2 at Dartford station. A blue plaque marks the place where they bonded over blues records, and this single, originally recorded in 1972 but only released on 1981's *Tattoo You*, can be seen as remembering this meeting.

Section 1.3 – Gravesend to Allhallows-on-Sea

Distance: 28.5km (17½ miles)

Height Gained: 30m

Parking: Free car park in Allhallows-on-Sea and pay car parks in Gravesend.

Public Transport: Bus 191 (Arriva Kent & Surrey, towards Chatham) runs every two hours from Allhallows-on-Sea to both Rochester and Chatham railway stations, from which regular trains run to Gravesend. Both services run 7 days a week.

Refreshments: Nothing is passed on the route between Gravesend and Allhallows-on-Sea, with the Six Bells in Cliffe, 1½ miles off the route, being the closest.

Accommodation: The only accommodation in Allhallows-on-Sea is on Airbnb, mainly chalets in the holiday park. Camping is available a mile inland at Allhallows Place Touring Park (07387 678302).

Overview: A long day across the remote marshes of the Hoo Peninsula as the Thames Estuary finally opens out and leaves the city behind. After escaping the industrial outskirts of Gravesend, there is little other than birds and grazing horses for company. The quiet marshes are littered with the eerie shells of abandoned forts, camps and stores that once lined the Thames shore.

Gravesend

Gravesend was an important outer port for London, with strong links to the New World. Despite widely held myths about bodies washing up here or being buried away from London during the Bubonic Plague in the 1660s, its name does not relate to graves, but instead possibly a grove or a Dutch word *graaf* for a count. Gravesend's most prominent landmark is St George's Church, an 18th-century Georgian edifice with a striking white spire. It stands on the site of the old churc, alongside which the Native American princess Pocahontas was buried in 1617.

Route Description

From the ferry terminal at **Gravesend Town Pier** (the oldest remaining cast iron pier in the world), the route follows the walkway through St Andrews Gardens past the striking red lightship, the last of its kind to be built, in 1963. At its end, join the road to pass the footings of a 16th-century blockhouse and the Royal Terrace Pier. Turn left at the next junction, then left on Commercial Place to skirt around **New Tavern Fort** and join Gordon Promenade. The fort was built to defend London during the Napoleonic War in the 1780s and is open to look round at weekends.

Continue past the canal basin and follow the rough cobbles between old warehouses. At the end, a narrow fenced pathway cuts through to Wharf Road. Turn left at the crossroads to reach **Denton Wharf**, where a path leads right along the river bank past the **Ship & Lobster**. Climb some concrete steps to leave the walkway and join a grassy path across the open marshes. Stay along the shore past the rifle range to reach the ruins of **Shornemead Fort**, one of several artillery forts constructed in the 1860s to protect London from attack by sea as part of the Palmerston defences.

Lightship, Gravesend

Follow the lower path close to the bank around Shorne Marsh and Higham Bight. The modern channel marker replaced the nearby **Shornemead Lighthouse**, of which only the base remains – you passed its red tower earlier, among the warehouses at Denton Wharf. Nearing the first lagoons of Cliffe Pools, turn left on a narrow causeway out towards Cliffe Fort. Higham Bight's muddy shore is littered with the wreckage of **Alpha Wharf**, the ruins of **Nore Fort** (which stood in the estuary off Sheerness during World War II) and the hulls of several ships that were abandoned here, including the *Hans Egede*, a Norwegian boat that began to sink in the Thames in the 1950s.

The path skirts left around **Cliffe Fort**, steps leading you down across the former launching bay of the 19th-century Brennan torpedo. Beyond the gravel works that overshadow the fort, the path bends right around **Cliffe Creek**. Keep left at its end and join the broad vehicle track running parallel to the sea wall all the way round Cliffe Marshes.

Half a mile beyond the boundary obelisk on **Lower Hope Point**, bear left to join a path along the sea wall. Views now open out across the estuary to London Gateway Port and towards the edge of the hills inland. The buildings arranged across the marshes were part of **Cliffe Explosives Works**, a 114-hectare gunpowder and chemical explosives factory from 1892 and 1921, and most famous as Curtis's & Harvey Ltd.

This remote section of the coast path continues for a couple of miles to **Salt Fleet Flats**, where the route turns right around a newly breached area of mudflats. This nature reserve was created as compensation for an area of saltmarsh lost in the creation of the deep sea container terminal across the river at London Gateway. Follow the track round the new reserve, then rejoin the old sea wall to skirt around **Egypt Bay**, thought to have gained its name after a Phoenician coin was found nearby.

Beyond the remains of a World War II camp, continue round **St Mary's Bay** and the surprising sandy beach beyond West Point. The buildings here were magazines for storing and packing explosives around the turn of the 20th century. Follow the sea wall until **Coombe Point Beach**, then turn left, not along a reedy path across the marshes, but on a new path along the edge of the field beyond. Cut left then right to cross a stile and follow the edge of the fields, staying on the dry side of **Dagnam Saltings** between a series of World War II pillboxes. Reaching the golf course of **Allhallows Leisure Holiday Park**, keep left over the bridge and along the marsh edge to join a walkway

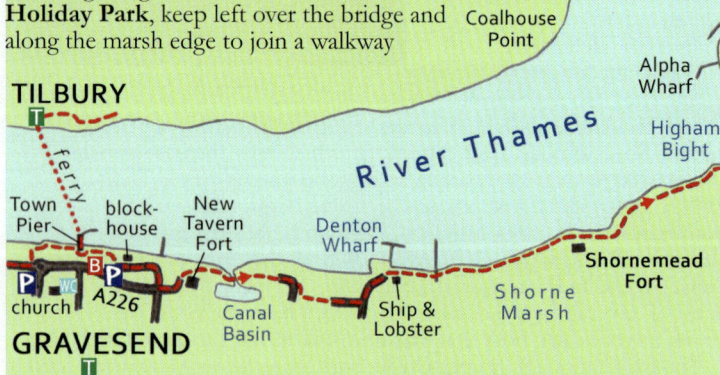

Coalhouse Point

Alpha Wharf

TILBURY

River Thames

Higham Bight

Town Pier

block-house

New Tavern Fort

Denton Wharf

church   A226

Canal Basin

Ship & Lobster

Shorne Marsh

Shornemead Fort

GRAVESEND

behind the beach. This soon opens out on the grassy shore of the holiday park, home to a funfair through most of the summer.

To reach the village of **Allhallows-on-Sea** you can turn right at the end of the holiday park and follow a public footpath up through the chalets to the main entrance, or turn right after another ½ mile to head back to the car park and **British Pilot** pub at the end of the road. The

Map labels:

Canvey Island

London Gateway Port

River Thames

Lower Hope Point

obelisk

Cliffe Explosives Works

Cliffe Fleet

Salt Fleet Flats

Egypt Bay

Halstow Marshes

Cliffe Marshes

Hoo Peninsula

Cliffe Creek

Cliffe Fort

CLIFFE

Cliffe Pools

Boundary obelisk, Lower Hope Point

Full Metal Jacket

The expanse of Cliffe Marshes was used as a location in Stanley Kubrick's 1987 film *Full Metal Jacket*, which was entirely filmed in England as Kubrick was famously afraid to fly, despite owning a pilot's licence. He recreated the Vietnam countryside of the second half of the film on the Thames marshes and the Norfolk Broads, importing hundreds of palm trees and tropical plants. He also used Beckton Gas Works and the Isle of Dogs in East London for scenes of urban warfare, even having some buildings selectively demolished.

The wreck of the Hans Egede at Higham Bight

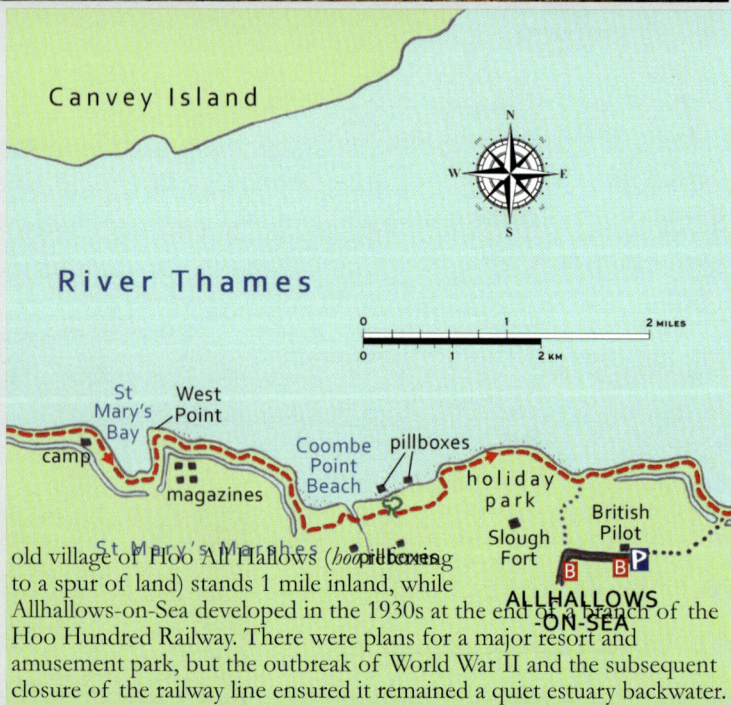

Canvey Island

River Thames

St Mary's Bay

West Point

camp

magazines

St Mary's Marshes

Coombe Point Beach

pillboxes

holiday park

Slough Fort

British Pilot

pillboxes

ALLHALLOWS-ON-SEA

old village of Hoo All Hallows (*hoo* referring
to a spur of land) stands 1 mile inland, while
Allhallows-on-Sea developed in the 1930s at the end of a branch of the
Hoo Hundred Railway. There were plans for a major resort and
amusement park, but the outbreak of World War II and the subsequent
closure of the railway line ensured it remained a quiet estuary backwater.

> **Great Expectations**
>
> 'Ours was the marsh country, down by the river, within, as the river wound, twenty miles of the sea', begins Charles Dickens' *Great Expectations*. The bleak landscape of the Hoo Peninsula is the setting for Pip's childhood, with the opening scene where Pip meets the convict Magwitch thought to be set in St Mary's Church near Lower Higham. Dickens had lived in Chatham between 4 and 11 and would return to Lower Higham when he could afford to in 1856 – it was here that he wrote *Great Expectations* and where he would die 14 years later.

SONG OF THE DAY — **Neil Young** – *Pocahontas*

Pocahontas, a Native American princess of the Powhatan people, was captured and brought to London by her husband John Rolfe under her assumed name Rebecca and was the first Native American to visit Europe. In 1617, at the age of 21, just after setting sail to return to her homeland she died of unknown causes and the ship stopped to allow her to be buried in Gravesend. Her tragic story is recounted in this acoustic ballad by Neil Young that was first released on his 1979 album *Rust Never Sleeps*.

Section 1.4 – Allhallows-on-Sea to Hoo St Werburgh

Distance: 24.8km (15½ miles)

Height Gained: 60m

Parking: Free car parks in Allhallows-on-Sea, Grain and Hoo St Werburgh.

Public Transport: Bus 191 (Arriva Kent & Surrey, towards Grain) runs from Hoo St Werburgh to Allhallows-on-Sea every two hours 7 days a week.

Refreshments: The Hogarth Inn in Grain and Arnie's Cafe at Kingsnorth Industrial Estate are passed on the route, while Rose's Tea Room in Lower Stoke is ½ mile off it near Stoke Medway Airfield.

Accommodation: There is no accommodation in or particularly close to Hoo St Werburgh, the closest being the Tudor Rose Inn (01634 714175), 2½ miles further along the route in Upper Upnor. Otherwise you can catch Bus 191 (Arriva Kent & Surrey, towards Chatham) that runs every 20 minutes into Strood or Rochester. The closest campsite is back in Allhallows at Allhallows Place Touring Park (07387 678302), though the buses to here only run every 2 hours.

Overview: Though dominated by the Isle of Grain's power stations, container port and gas terminals, this is a pleasantly varied day. Starting along the Thames estuary and ending along the Medway shore, the route has plenty of interest along the Grain waterfront, the marshes of Stoke Saltings and an inland section past Stoke. Only the 2-mile road section out of Grain really drags.

Route Description

Rejoin the sea wall at **Allhallows-on-Sea**, either through the holiday park or via the path from the end of the road by the British Pilot. The embankment soon bears right by the mouth of Yantlet Creek, across which you can see the **London Stone** obelisk beyond a collapsed navigation beacon. Joining the bank of **Yantlet Creek**, the route passes a memorial to Geoffrey John Hammond and a monument commemorating the creation of the Thames flood defences in the 1970s.

Continue around Allhallows Marshes, on which there are the remains of a World War II decoy designed to draw bombers away from the nearby oil installations, then turn left to cross the creek onto the **Isle of Grain**. Soon bear right off the track to a gate and follow a path along the edge of a field, emerging alongside the access road to **Yantlet Range**, which was established in 1920 as part of the experimental firing ranges at Shoeburyness – long range guns fired shells across the Thames to be recovered from the sands off the Essex coast.

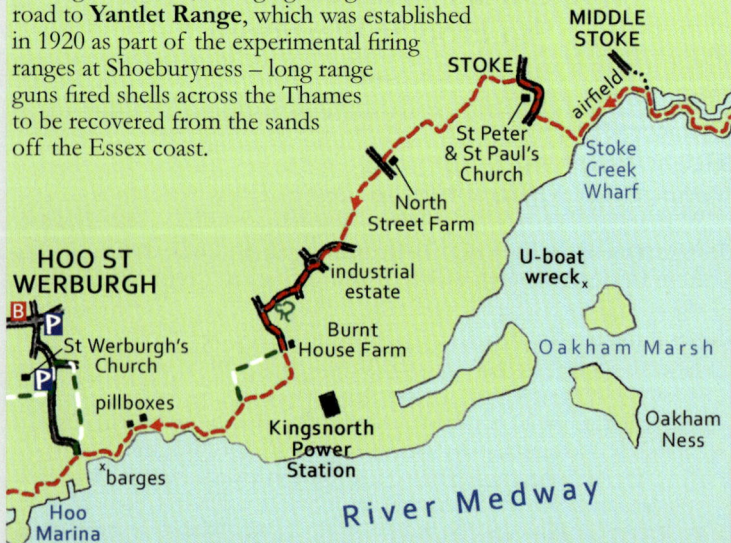

MIDDLE STOKE

STOKE

airfield

St Peter & St Paul's Church

Stoke Creek Wharf

North Street Farm

U-boat wreck ×

HOO ST WERBURGH

industrial estate

Burnt House Farm

Oakham Marsh

B

P

St Werburgh's Church

P

pillboxes

Kingsnorth Power Station

Oakham Ness

× barges

Hoo Marina

River Medway

Follow the embankment inland alongside the road until some steps lead down to join it all the way into **Grain**. Turn left at the end of West Lane and left again on High Street, passing the Hogarth Inn and **St James' Church** to reach the seafront at the end of the road. Entering Grain Coastal Park, continue down to the small beach, with great views across the mouth of the Thames estuary, and follow a walkway right along the sea wall. Bending round towards the mouth of the **River**

The Yantlet Line

The Yantlet Line represents the end of the Port of London Authority's jurisdiction and is marked by the London Stone near the mouth of Yantlet Creek and the Crow Stone at Chalkwell, near Southend. Richard I first bought these rights to fish and raise tolls along the Thames and part of the Medway in the 12th century, and one of the older London Stones in Lower Upnor is marked '1204'. In 1857 the Thames Conservancy Act transferred these rights to the Crown and the two modern obelisks were erected on the tidal estuary shore as memorials to the former extent of London's reach.

The London Stone

Medway, pass a couple of concrete shelters and the overgrown site of Grain Fort to reach a narrow causeway leading across the mud to **Grain Tower** – this striking fort was built in 1855 to defend the approach to Sheerness Dockyard and can be approached with care at low tide.

Join a path along the top of the sea wall soon after the causeway, then turn right down some steps and follow a path across the marsh past the remains of **Grain Battery** (later known as Dummy Battery because it suffered from subsidence) to reach Port Victoria Road. Follow it briefly right, then turn left on a tarmac pathway through the dense scrub to join the access road to **Grain Power Station**. This gas-powered turbine replaced the old oil-powered power station that was demolished in 2015-16, including its iconic 244m-tall chimney (the highest structure in the country ever to be pulled down).

At the end of the access road, turn left along the B2001 and follow it for nearly 2 miles between the liquefied natural gas (LNG) facility

St James' Church, Grain

whose storage containers dominate the island's skyline, Medway Power Station, and the **London Thamesport** deep water container terminal, built on the site of the former Kent Oil Refinery. After crossing the access road to **Grain LNG** and the railway at Grain Crossing, cross the road and join a gravel path along its left side. This soon leads onto the sea wall and heads left out across **Stoke**

Marshes to the shore of Colemouth Creek, before doubling back towards the road.

Stay on the embankment past the flyover that leads onto the Isle of Grain, this side of the island now less clearly defined following land reclamation of the former marshes. Hug the intricate shore of Stoke Saltings, in whose thick mud lie several former wharfs and abandoned boats, including the country's last **U-boat wreck**, the only one remaining after nearly 100 were scrapped on the River Medway following World War I.

Keep left past **Stoke Medway Airfield** to reach the boatyard at Stoke Creek, where you turn right to cross the railway and follow Creek Lane up to the road. Follow this right into the village of **Stoke**, passing St Peter and St Paul's Church, then bear left on Vicarage Lane. Fork right twice to enter the fields, then turn left on a path that soon becomes a vehicle track. Keep straight on to the buildings at Tudor Farm, turning right then left here to follow a broad track across a shallow valley to **North Street Farm**. Head straight across the road and cross the railway in the far corner of the field, then follow a path to the road by Kingsnorth Industrial Estate. Turn right along the road and head straight across the roundabout, then keep straight on past the entrance to the decommissioned coal- and oil-fired **Kingsnorth Power Station**.

Turn left at the end of Eschol Road to a point where the route divides by **Burnt House Farm**. The main route continues straight on to the edge of the marshes, where it turns right and hugs the hedgeline past a couple of pylons. Cross the scrub to a gate, *where an alternative route arrives, having followed a well defined track across the fields in case the marshes are flooded at spring high tides*. The unified route now follows the field edge round to a gate, then bears left up onto the low sea wall and follows it

The causeway leading out to Grain Tower

The Isle of Grain

Grain derives its name from the Old English *greon*, meaning gravel, and was historically part of the manor of Gillingham, despite being on the opposite side of the Medway estuary. The island was then separated from the Hoo Peninsula by Yantlet Creek (also known as the Stray), which was the main route of ships from the Medway towns to London. Even after the first road causeway was created in the 18th century, the Mayor of London ordered it be severed in 1823 to allow boats to be able to pass. The road was re-established by 1835 and the Thames and Medway Canal was built soon after to link Strood and Gravesend.

along the Medway shore to rejoin the route of the Saxon Shore Way. Continue past the remains of Abbot's Court Wharf, a pair of pillboxes behind the sea wall, and the graveyard of a number of Thames sailing barges used to transport cement along the river.

Reaching the edge of **Hoo Marina**, the main route continues straight on, but to reach Hoo St Werburgh you are best following the alternative route along the lane right, then bearing right on a path across the field towards the village. Turn left on the road at the end and, where the route continues left to pass **St Werburgh's Church**, head right to reach the bus stop in the centre of the village. **Hoo St Werburgh** (generally known simply as Hoo) is an ancient settlement, its 12th-century church dedicated to a 7th-century Anglo-Saxon princess who is also the patron saint of Chester.

SONG OF THE DAY

The Dubliners – *McAlpine's Fusiliers*

A song about the brutal labour undertaken by Irish navvies who came to Britain for work in the 20th century, this was arranged by Dominic Behan in the 1960s and features many lines from traditional Irish verse. McAlpine is a reference to the construction company who were a major employer of the navvies, including for the power station built on the Isle of Grain in the 1950s, and it features the lyrics 'I stripped to the skin with Darky Flynn, Way down upon the Isle of Grain'.

Houseboats at Port Werburgh

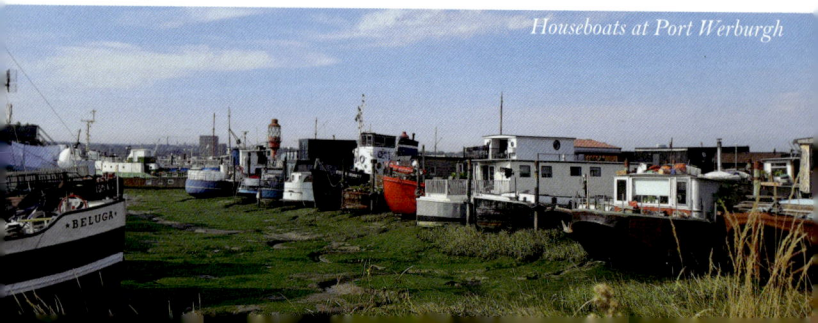

Section 1.5 – Hoo St Werburgh to Gillingham

Distance: 18.4km (11½ miles)

Height Gained: 80m (or 130m via alternative route)

Parking: Pay car parks in Rochester, Chatham and Gillingham. Free car parks in Hoo St Werburgh and Lower Upnor.

Public Transport: Bus 1 (Arriva, towards Chatham) runs every 30 minutes from the A289 through Gillingham to Chatham bus station, from which Bus 191 (Arriva, towards Hoo/Grain) runs every 20 minutes to Hoo St Werburgh. Less frequent service on Sundays.

Refreshments: The Boat House in Strood or various options on or close to the route through Rochester and Chatham.

Accommodation: The Premier Inn Chatham/Gillingham (0333 3219353) is close to where the route emerges on the A289 through Gillingham, while the Ship & Trades (01634 895200) is passed closer to St Mary's Island. The nearest campsites are at Overshore Caravan Park (01634 374880) near Otterham Quay, right by the route some 4½ miles beyond Gillingham, and just beyond at Five Acres (07377 625979) in Upchurch.

Overview: A largely urban but nonetheless fascinating day's walk around the River Medway as it winds inland through its historic towns and dockyards. Beyond the estuary shore at Hoo Marina and beautiful Upnor, the walking is all on hard surfaces as the route links the Medway Towns of Strood, Rochester, Chatham and Gillingham. Rochester and Chatham are particularly appealing, the latter's famous docks surrounded by historic fortifications and new riverside developments at Rochester, St Mary's Island and Gillingham's Pier Quays.

Route Description

Pick up the main route again at **Hoo Marina**, where a path cuts through the boatyards and industrial units to emerge by the entrance to Port Werburgh. The route continues along the fence beyond, keeping left to briefly join Marine Drive, then bearing left on a path through the boats of Hoo Ness Yacht Club. Continue past the houseboats beyond, before joining the tidal and often slippery estuary shore for the next ½ mile. There is no escape into the woods behind, but the most precarious section is passing the redbrick wall of

Cockham Wood Fort, built in 1669 to defend Chatham Docks and abandoned by the early 19th century. Continue past Wilsonian Sailing Club and Upnor Boat Yard, before joining a walkway by Medway Yacht

Club. Follow the access road into **Lower Upnor**, where the routes converge by an obelisk that is one of a pair of London Stones, marking the extent of London fishermen's rights. Another stone just beyond commemorates the Navy training ship *Arethusa*, which was built in 1849 and served in Crimea as the last British ship to go into battle under sail before being used to train cadets on the Medway.

ALTERNATIVE ROUTE: *As well as avoiding the tidal shore, this is a particularly useful route as it passes so close to the centre of Hoo St Werburgh. After following the road past the small car park near ST WERBURGH'S CHURCH, the alternative route turns right beyond the last house in the village. Follow the lane past Cockham Cottage and Cockham Farm, bearing left by the latter to follow a vehicle track between the fields. At its end by Tamarisk, a fenced path continues straight on between the houses of CHATTENDEN. Turn left on the second road and, at its end, head straight into Cockham Wood. Two paths bear round to the right and converge to bend left and head down the hill to rejoin the main route in Lower Upnor.*

Stay along the waterfront to join the road in front of the Pier pub and continue past the **Ordnance Yard**, before turning left up some steps. Follow the wall of the yard, built in the 19th century to store gunpowder and artillery shells for Upnor Castle, and join Upchat Road. Keep left before the Kings Arms, following the cobbled High Street down through picturesque **Upper Upnor**. At the end, **Upnor Castle** can be visited to the left, while the route continues down to the soggy tidal shore. *An alternative route follows the next road back up through the village if the*

Upnor Castle and the River Medway

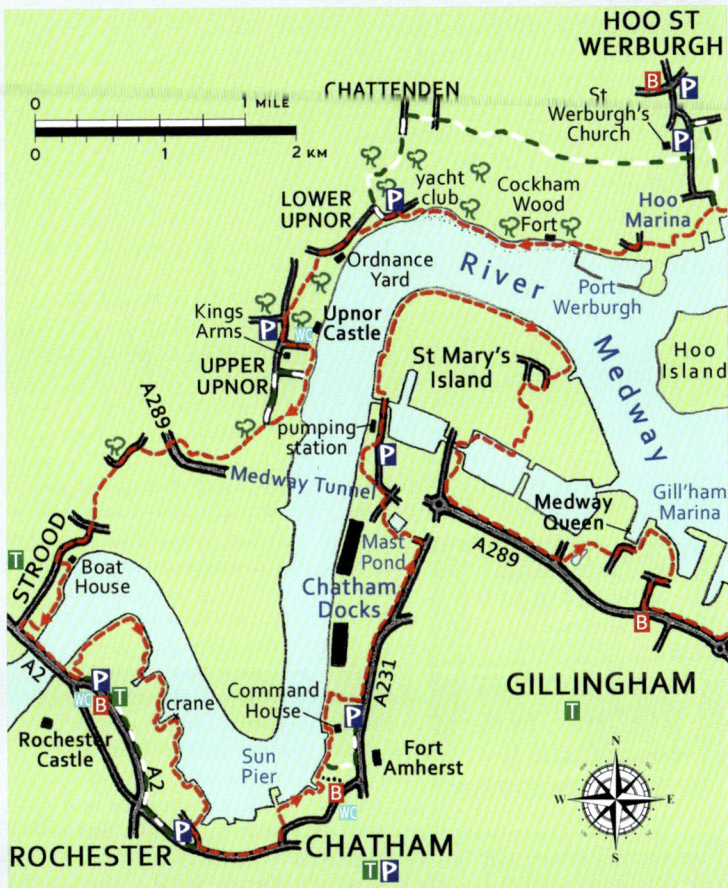

HOO ST WERBURGH

CHATTENDEN

St Werburgh's Church

yacht club

Cockham Wood Fort

Hoo Marina

LOWER UPNOR

Ordnance Yard

River Medway

Port Werburgh

Hoo Island

Kings Arms

Upnor Castle

St Mary's Island

UPPER UPNOR

A289

pumping station

Medway Tunnel

Medway Queen

Gill'ham Marina

STROOD

Boat House

Mast Pond

Chatham Docks

A289

A2

crane

Command House

A231

GILLINGHAM

Rochester Castle

Sun Pier

Fort Amherst

A2

ROCHESTER

CHATHAM

0   1 MILE
0   1   2 KM

N
W   E
S

Kentish Man or Man of Kent

The River Medway roughly cleaves Kent in two and famously divides its people between the Kentish Men and Maids to its west, and the Men or Maids of Kent to the east. This divide is thought to have arisen because Saxons settled west of the river and Jutes to the east. However, another story suggests that William the Conqueror passed easily through West Kent but was prevented from travelling through East Kent until he promised to protect the area's gavelkind inheritance law, by which the land was equally divided between male heirs. The Men of Kent proudly clung to their archaic system until it was abolished in 1925.

marsh is impassable at high tide. Upnor developed around the Elizabethan castle that was built to defend Chatham's royal dockyards and remained in use as a gunpowder store until 1945.

The two routes converge by the entrance to the MOD's **Upper Upnor Depot**, the onward path hugging the perimeter fence before bending round to reach the A289. Over the pedestrian crossing, follow a path heading up some steps into the scrub, then join the road at the top. Keep left on a cycleway along the high ground above the Medway City Industrial Estate that covers this spur of the River Medway, then bend left to drop back down to the road. Go straight on into Riverside, following it round past the line of the **Thames and Medway Canal**, which provided a shorter goods route to London, cutting through the 2-mile Higham and Strood Tunnel that it shared with the railway to reach the Thames at Gravesend.

A path leads left just beyond the Boat House, following the river bank through **Strood** (its name, like Stroud, derived from an Old English word *stod* for a marshy area overgrown with scrub) until you are forced back to the road. Turn left under the railway, then left again to follow the A2 across the Medway at **Rochester Bridge**. The bridge was built in the 1850s, replacing a medieval bridge that had been blown up to allow larger boats to pass, and was widened in 1970. Over the bridge, Rochester's attractive High Street and well preserved 12th-century **castle** are reached to the right. **Rochester**'s layout mirrors the Roman town of Durobrivae, which was built on the site of an Iron Age settlement and alongside the first bridge over the Medway. Its cathedral, founded in 604, is the second oldest in the country after Canterbury, though the present building is Norman. The town features in several works by Charles Dickens, who lived in Chatham between the ages of 4 and 11, and returned to the area in his later years.

The route doubles back left to join a new walkway along the river bank. This will hug the shore past Cory's Creek, Blue Boar Creek and Furrell's Wharf, passing a refurbished crane that was used to unload aggregate for the local cement industry, and eventually emerging on Doust Way. *However, the flats of* **Rochester Riverside** *are still being built and there may be no way through the building site, so a temporary route stays on the A2 alongside the railway – you may prefer to follow Rochester High Street past the cathedral and Huguenot Museum. The temporary route turns left on the High Street where it crosses the A2, following it under the railway to rejoin the long-term route*

Chatham Dockyards from Mast Pond

just beyond. Both routes now follow the road as Rochester runs seamlessly into **Chatham**. Turn left on Medway Street, then left again towards **Sun Pier**; named after the Sun Hotel and built in 1886, paddle steamers moored here until 1963 and the pier had its own pavilion until it was destroyed by fire in 1972.

A walkway leads on along the river bank to **Riverside Gardens**, where you can see the impressive barrier ditch created in the 1750s to protect Chatham Dockyards from an attack by land. Known as the Chatham Lines, it was linked to **Fort Amherst** on the hill above and protected by cannons fired from the casemates (gun emplacements) that can be seen exposed at the foot of the ditch. Continue along the riverside walkway *(the alternative route along the road only need be used when part of this route is closed between 8pm-8am)* past the **Command House** and Gun Wharf, until you are forced up some steps to join the A231. Follow the main road past an entrance to Chatham's Historic Dockyard and stay along the dock wall past the roundabout. Finally turn left after ¾ mile, shortly before the next roundabout, to circle around the left side of Mast Pond in the lee of the vast covered slips at the far end of the dockyards. **Chatham Dockyards** were established in the mid 16th century and developed into the largest naval dockyard outside Portsmouth, building more than 500 Navy ships, including Nelson's Flagship *HMS Victory* in 1759, and later specialising in submarine construction. It closed in 1984 and its well preserved Georgian buildings are now a tourist attraction.

Crane, St Mary's Island

Follow the road right from **Mast Pond**, then turn left at the roundabout on Leviathan Way and soon bear left to rejoin the river bank above the line of the Medway Tunnel. Follow the walkway before rejoining Leviathan Way to pass the redbrick former pumping house for the dry dock. Cross the bridge onto **St Mary's Island**, then turn left to follow a walkway around St Mary's Wharf, past another blue dock crane. The docks here were constructed in the 1860s on an area of former saltmarsh to serve as an extension of Chatham Dockyards – the work was done by convicts from Chatham Prison, which had been built on St Mary's Island in 1856.

The path continues round the island's shore to **Finsborough Ness**, where it cuts through to the road. Follow this to its end, then join a path leading up onto the high ground of East Bund. This eventually drops down to one of the dock basins on the other side of the island, where you head through a gate and follow the wooden walkway along the edge of the dock. Turn left at the far end to cross a bridge off St Mary's Island, then leave the dock side and join a path alongside Maritime Way. Head straight on at the first roundabout, then turn left at the second to join the side of the busy A289 dual carriageway. Stay on this to the next junction, where you turn left at the far side of Gillingham Gate Road and follow a path between the Mast & Rigging and a small pond. Bear right across the front of the supermarket, then turn left on the road at its end to reach **Gillingham Pier**, where the *Medway Queen* is moored. This paddle steamer made seven trips to France during the evacuation of Dunkirk, rescuing over 7,000 men, and was recently restored to become the last of its kind still mobile in the country.

Follow a broad walkway out towards the river, then head up some steps and follow the riverfront round past **Gillingham Marina**. Turn right then left on the broad avenues between the new developments of Pier Quays to return to the A289. Buses leave from the other side of the road for Chatham, or you can head up one of the roads opposite to reach the railway station in the centre of Gillingham. **Gillingham**'s name is thought to relate to Gylling in Jutland, whose people settled in this part of Kent in the 5th century, but a long-held story suggests that a warlord led his warriors into battle while shouting and acquired the name Gyllingas from an Old English word *gyllan*, meaning 'shout'.

SONG OF THE DAY

Wild Billy Childish & His Famous Headcoats – *Chatham Town Welcomes Desperate Men*

Chatham-born Steven John Hamper has been at the heart of a vibrant Medway art and music scene since forming the punk band the Pop Rivets in the late 1970s. Under his alter ego Billy Childish, he has also performed with Three Milkshakes, the Chatham Singers, The Buff Medways, The Musicians of the British Empire and CTMF, and featured prominently on Tracey Emin's famous tent *Everyone I Have Ever Slept With 1963-1995*. This scuzzy Medway Delta blues song is taken from his 2000 album *I Am the Object of Your Desire* with Thee Headcoats.

Gillingham Marina

Section 1.6 – Gillingham to Swale

Distance: 25.0km (15½ miles)

Height Gained: 90m

Parking: Free parking at various places in Riverside Country Park, and very limited free parking at Swale railway station.

Public Transport: Trains run at least once an hour 7 days a week from Swale railway station to Sittingbourne, from where more regular trains run to Gillingham, whose station is ¾ mile from the route.

Refreshments: The Riverside Country Park Cafe is passed early on, with the only options thereafter being the Crown at Upchurch and the Three Tuns in Lower Halstow.

Accommodation: There is nothing close to Swale railway station as it is in the middle of nowhere, but there are regular trains in both directions to Sittingbourne, Queenborough or Sheerness. The Queen Phillippa (01795 228756) is opposite Queenborough station and the Royal Hotel (01795 662626) is alone in offering rooms near the centre of Sheerness, although Sittingbourne has plenty of options, including Travelodge Sittingbourne (0871 9846562) right next to the station. The closest campsites are back near Upchurch at Five Acres (07377 625979) and Overshore Caravan Park (01634 374880).

Overview: A fine walk along the intricate southern shore of the broadening Medway delta, particularly where the route hugs the estuary through Riverside Country Park, from Ham Green to Lower Halstow, and across Chetney Marshes. In between, there are some unpleasant road sections, particularly if new parts of the England Coast Path aren't yet in place, but the Saxon Shore Way often provides a good alternative with some pleasant walking just inland.

Route Description

Follow the A289 dual carriageway through **Gillingham** to the Strand roundabout, where you turn left on Strand Approach Road. Head straight on at the end on a path across the green, keeping the **Strand Leisure Pool** to the left to join the estuary shore beyond. The Strand was a bathing pool created on the mudflats by Thomas Cuckow in 1896, with further land reclaimed from the estuary to create the waterfront park that provided a focal point for Gillingham's seafront throughout the 20th century.

The promenade leads round past a line of derelict **Medway barges** and through the boatyards of Medway Cruising Club, before being

Map labels:

1 MILE
1 KM / 2 KM
0

Darnet Fort
Bishop Saltings
Hoo Island
Hoo Fort
River Medway
Nor Marsh
Gillingham Marina
The Strand
x barges
P WC
B
A289
GILLINGHAM
T
Cinque Port Marshes
Sharp's Green Bay
Horrid Hill
A289
P
former stables
Riverside
P WC
Bloors Wharf
Country Park
LOWER RAINHAM
B
P

forced right along Owens Way. Round
the corner, turn left on a path along the
corrugated fence to rejoin the shore around the mudflats of Cinque
Port Marshes. There are good views across the Medway towards **Hoo
Fort**, a 19th-century circular fortification on the tip of Hoo Island. It is
twinned with Fort Darnet, which stands on a smaller island in the
broadening estuary, and both were plagued with subsidence problems,
consequently never seeing any military action.

Follow the sea wall round to enter **Riverside Country Park** at
Copperhouse Lane, its name referring to a copperas works that once
extracted iron sulfate on one of the small islands on the marshes here.
The path hugs the shore past a disused riding school and the former
landfill site of Eastcourt Meadows. Keep left beyond the car park at
Sharp's Green to reach the causeway that leads out to the small cement
works that once stood on the island of **Horrid Hill**. The route
continues along the estuary shore to **Bloors Wharf**, a former scrapyard
for dismantling boats that projects out into the mudflats. Either follow
the path on through the trees, or the wharf itself, to rejoin the shore
beyond. Keep left past Motney Hill Car Park and follow a path parallel

to the road, before joining it to cut across the shoulder of **Motney Hill**, itself once an island in the estuary, and finally leave the country park.

Turn right before the wastewater treatment works and cut across to join the embankment alongside **Otterham Creek** on the far side of the headland. Follow this right to the head of the estuary, cutting through the trees to skirt around an industrial estate, before joining its approach road to reach Otterham Quay Lane. The new route of the England Coast Path will turn immediately left here through Beckenham & Otterham Residential Parks, then turn right at the end to skirt around the edge of the field beyond. You'll then turn right at the far end across a former tip, then head left around the edge of a series of fields on the fringe of **Horsham Marsh**, before cutting left to head up through the trees to rejoin the existing Saxon Shore Way.

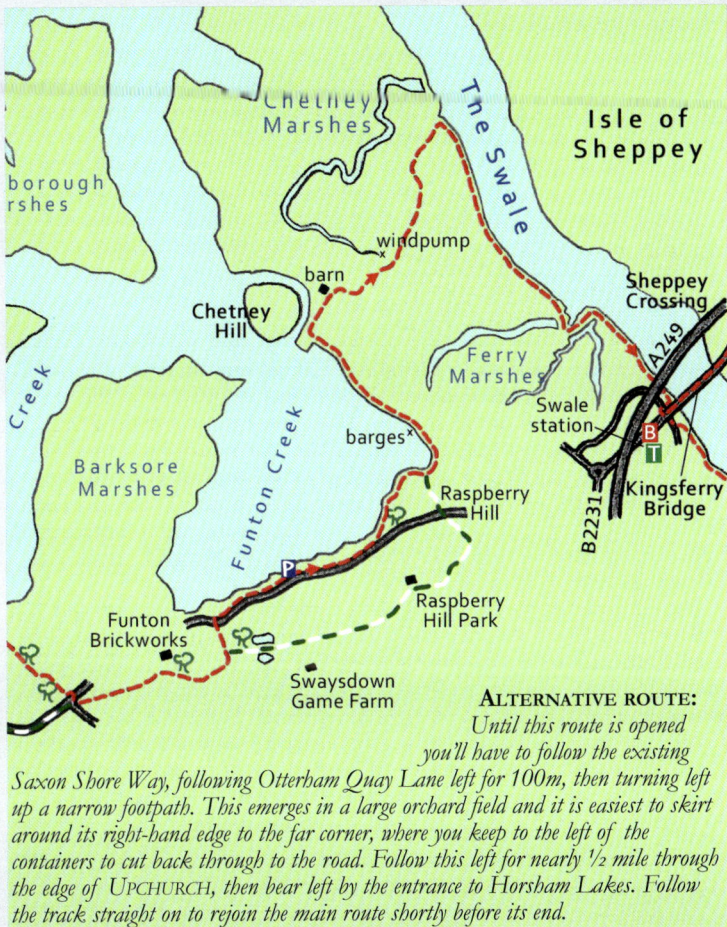

Isle of Sheppey

Chetney Marshes

The Swale

borough rshes

windpump
×

barn

Chetney Hill

Sheppey Crossing

A249

Ferry Marshes

Creek

Funton Creek

barges ×

Swale station

Barksore Marshes

Raspberry Hill

B

Kingsferry Bridge

B2231

P

Raspberry Hill Park

Funton Brickworks

Swaysdown Game Farm

ALTERNATIVE ROUTE:
*Until this route is opened
you'll have to follow the existing*
*Saxon Shore Way, following Otterham Quay Lane left for 100m, then turning left
up a narrow footpath. This emerges in a large orchard field and it is easiest to skirt
around its right-hand edge to the far corner, where you keep to the left of the
containers to cut back through to the road. Follow this left for nearly ½ mile through
the edge of* UPCHURCH, *then bear left by the entrance to Horsham Lakes. Follow
the track straight on to rejoin the main route shortly before its end.*

Medway marshes between Bloors Wharf and Motney Hill

Medway Prison Hulks

From the late 18th century, overflowing prisons led to England making use of condemned and captured boats beached in the estuaries of the south east to house convicts. The first prison hulks were on the Thames near Woolwich, but this system spread to the many hulks on the Medway estuary, which were often used to house French prisoners of war. Conditions were dire and up to a third of the prisoners died, so escape attempts were often made to nearby islands in the estuary – if captured it is said they were hanged on Horrid Hill, one possible origin of its curious name. The system ended in the 1850s, when most survivors were transferred to the newly built Chatham Prison and the boats were burned or towed away.

At the end of the track by **Horsham Lakes**, keep straight on along a path past the fishing lakes and cut through the hedge to cross the open field beyond. Go left on the road for 200m, then turn right on a path just beyond the access road to Upchurch Poultry Farm. This cuts through the paddocks past a World War II **anti-aircraft gunsite**, then heads straight on across the orchard beyond, following a vehicle track to Ham Green. Turn right on the road, then immediately left on Shoregate Lane, before turning right at its end by **Shoregate Wharf** to rejoin the estuary shore by Hamgreen Saltings.

The embankment leads right to pass through a small boatyard and follows the edge of the marsh round to **Twinney Wharf**. Head straight across the track to stay on the embankment past Twinney Saltings and keep left around the former brickfields to emerge at the picturesque wharf on **Halstow Creek**, where a fine Thames barge, the *Edith May*, is usually moored. **Lower Halstow** grew around Eastwoods Brickworks from the 1840s until their closure in 1966. Halstow means 'holy place' in Old English, and the village's church (dedicated to St Margaret of Antioch) is of Saxon origin, with a 13th-century tower.

Halstow Wharf & the Edith May

The new England Coast Path will stay on the shore past the church, following the embankment past **Lower Halstow Yacht Club**. Where it reaches the road, the new route will turn immediately left and follow the edge of the field, before turning right near the far end to follow a band of trees, first on the right then the left, past **Great Barksore Farm**.

Bar-tailed godwit on the Medway estuary

ALTERNATIVE ROUTE:
If this new route is not yet in place, you'll need to follow the Saxon Shore Way up the lane past the church. Head straight on at the end, following a path through the orchards to re-emerge on the road, following this for ¼ mile to the junction with Basser Hill, where the new route appears from the left.

From the junction with Basser Hill, follow a footpath across the wheatfields inland of the busy road, then bear right up the slope above the remains of **Funton Brickworks**, which produced the classic yellow London bricks until 2008. A clear line continues across the heart of a large wheatfield with good views over the marshes, before turning left down a rough track. The new route will continue down to the road and follow a new path along the edge of the marsh beside it for ¾ mile, before turning left along the shore where the road starts to climb up **Raspberry Hill**.

ALTERNATIVE ROUTE: *However, this road can be unpleasant to walk along, so you are best staying on the Saxon Shore Way until the new route is open, turning right off the track after just a few metres. A lovely path passes between a couple of ponds before crossing the open fields below Swaysdown Game Farm. Keep straight on, even where the line is ill defined, following a series of white posts across further wheatfields to reach a high fence around RASPBERRY HILL PARK. Join the broad track here and follow it to a signpost by a gate on the right; turn left here to cross the scrub and head straight over the road. Continue down off Raspberry Hill to rejoin the new route on the broad shore of Funton Creek.*

Follow the sea wall past a series of abandoned barges and out towards the main estuary. Turn right by the creek surrounding **Chetney Hill** and keep right of the barn to join a grassy embankment leading across **Chetney Marshes**, one of the earlier sea walls protecting this reclaimed land. Head straight across a vehicle track by a windpump to reach the far side of the peninsula by **the Swale**, the channel that separates the Isle of Sheppey from the mainland. Follow the sea wall right along its shore and keep left around Ferry Marshes to pass a couple of

Sheppey Crossing seen across Ferry Marshes

navigation markers as the channel narrows. Keep straight on beneath the **Sheppey Crossing** flyover carrying the A249 over the Swale, then turn right down some steps by the foot of the older **Kingsferry Bridge**. On the other side of the road, some rough steps head up the bank to the B2231, though you do have to clamber over the roadside barrier. The route continues left to the Isle of Sheppey, while Swale railway station is reached just a few yards to the right.

The Swale

The Swale's name means 'swirling water', a likely reference to the tidal flow through this narrow channel. It was originally a river valley, before the Isle of Sheppey was cut off from the mainland by rising sea levels around 6,500 BCE. Despite the existence of a short-lived medieval bridge near Harty called Tremseth Bridge, the island was reached only by ferries at Kingsferry, Elmley and Harty until a bridge was built at Kingsferry in 1860, a bascule bridge that carried only a railway to Sheerness. Road traffic could reach the island only after the present Kingsferry Bridge opened in 1960. Along with the railway it carries, this can be lifted to allow ships to pass, while the modern flyover was opened in 2006 to prevent the island being cut off when the bridge was damaged by boats.

SONG OF THE DAY

Wang Chung – *The Waves*

Wang Chung's frontman Jack Hues was born in Gillingham as Jeremy Allan Ryder, taking his pseudonym from a play on the French *j'accuse*. The new-wave band were formed in 1979 as Huang Chung, meaning 'yellow bell' in Mandarin Chinese, but the name was changed to Wang Chung by the time they released this song on their second album *Points on the Curve* in 1983. Hues sings, 'The moonlight falls upon the tears you weep, and you can hear the waves crash on the beach at night'.

Section 1.7 – Swale to Leysdown-on-Sea

Distance: 27.3km (17 miles)

Height Gained: 200m

Parking: Pay car parks in Sheerness. Free car parks in Queenborough, Warden and along the seafront between Sheerness and Minster Leas.

Public Transport: Bus 360 (Chalkwell, towards Sheerness) runs roughly hourly from Leysdown-on-Sea to Sheerness railway station, from where there are trains to Swale railway station at least once an hour. Both services run less frequently on Sundays.

Refreshments: Various options in Sheerness, the Little Oyster Tea Room above Minster Leas Beach, or the Coppice pub and Dickens Inn close to the route through Eastchurch Holiday Centre.

Accommodation: Leysdown and Warden are both full of holiday parks, so the only accommodation available are a handful of chalets and caravans on Airbnb. The closest rooms are at the Shurland Hotel (01795 881100) in Eastchurch, which is less than 1 mile off the route near Eastchurch Holiday Centre, but most easily reached by bus from Leysdown. Camping is available in Leysdown at Priory Hill Holiday Park (01795 510267), and in Warden at Warden Springs Holiday Park (01795 880888).

Overview: A long day necessitated by the distance round the Isle of Sheppey, which can just be squeezed into two days' walking. It is, however, a fine and varied walk that will, especially once the new sections have been opened, be a surprising highlight of the north Kent coast. The flat marshes and docks of west Sheppey house the fine promenades of Queenborough and Sheerness, before the clay cliffs of Minster and Warden rear up to provide great views across the mouth of the Thames estuary. However, this part of the island is dominated by holiday parks, so until the new route is established you are condemned to some unpleasant road walking in places and may prefer to get a bus from Minster to Warden Bay. Some try to follow the foot of the cliffs round this section at low tide, but even if you can time it right, the clay at the back of the beach can be so soft as to be impossible to walk on.

Route Description

Cross **Kingsferry Bridge** from Swale railway station to reach the Isle of Sheppey, doubling back left at the first opportunity to join the embankment around South Marshes. Follow the Swale shore past Queenborough Water Treatment Works and up some steps to join a vehicle track around Rushenden Marshes. After this bends right over a low brow, keep left to follow a track out round Ladies Hole Point, before returning past the pier at **Coal Washer Wharf**, built for a nearby coal-washing plant in 1908. The track continues around the Swale shore all the way to Alsager Avenue on the edge of Rushenden. At the end, turn left and follow the main road into Queenborough, crossing the creek just before reaching the site of **Queenborough Castle**. **Queenborough** was established by Edward III in the 1360s as a planned town around the newly constructed castle and became one of the most important ports in Kent, focused primarily on the wool trade. However, the castle was demolished following the Civil War and the port was soon superseded by Sheerness and the Medway towns until its recovery as an industrial port in the 19th century.

Turn left beyond the Queen Phillippa on the High Street, then fork left on South Street to pass the wharves on **Queenborough Creek**. Follow the road round to the right, then turn left on a narrow path beyond the Admiral's Arm to reach the attractive waterfront. Follow this right past the park and pier to follow a walkway alongside the Swale until you are forced inland near the junction with the Medway by the acres of imported cars at **Sheerness Docks**, which handle and store 400,000 imported vehicles from Europe each year. A concrete path skirts around the vast site and runs parallel to the A249, before dropping down some steps to join West Street heading left into **Blue Town**. Follow the dock wall past the former Royal Fountain Hotel and **Criterion Music Hall** (now a museum and cinema) through what was once a bustling dockside settlement. Blue Town developed around the first docks in the early 18th century, when a collection of wooden houses were painted blue using paint stolen from the naval stores.

Continue straight on to rejoin the A249 at a roundabout, crossing a

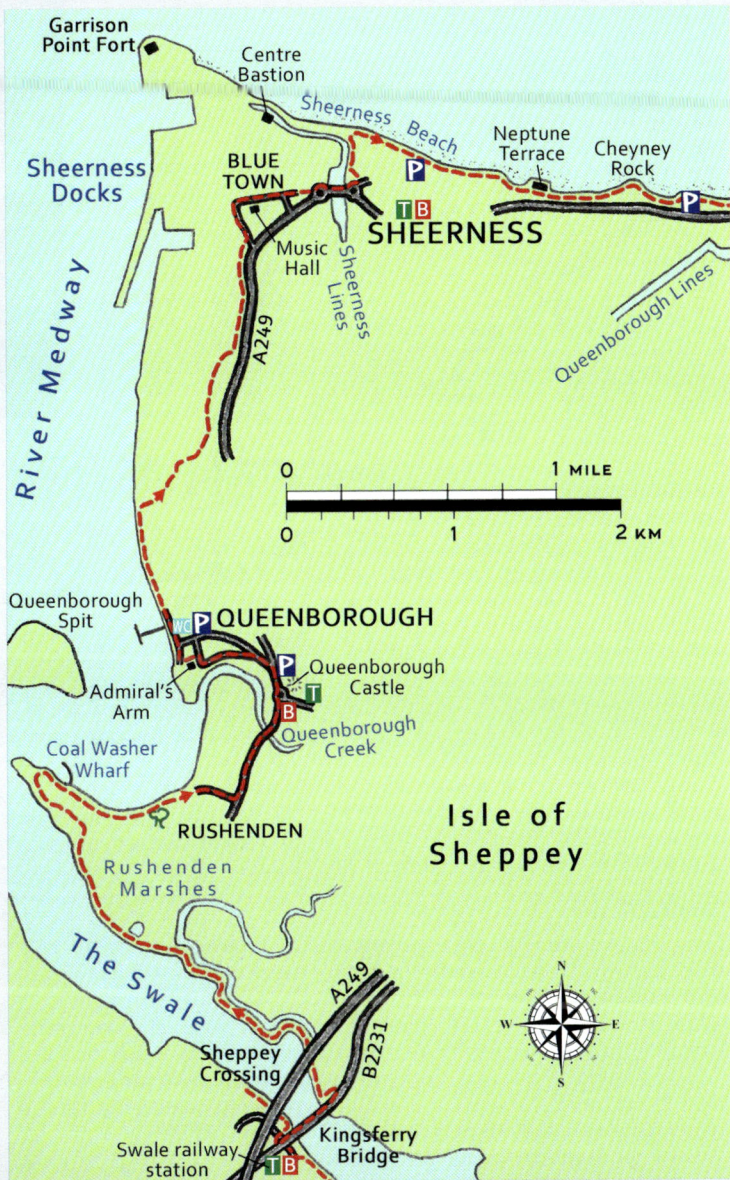

Garrison
Point Fort

Centre
Bastion

Sheerness Beach

Neptune
Terrace

Cheyney
Rock

Sheerness
Docks

BLUE
TOWN

P

T B

SHEERNESS

P

Music
Hall

Sheerness
Lines

Queenborough Lines

River Medway

A249

0   1 MILE

0   1   2 KM

Queenborough
Spit

WC P QUEENBOROUGH

P

T

Queenborough
Castle

Admiral's
Arm

B

Queenborough
Creek

Coal Washer
Wharf

Isle of
Sheppey

RUSHENDEN

Rushenden
Marshes

The Swale

A249

B2231

Sheppey
Crossing

N

W   E

S

Kingsferry
Bridge

Swale railway
station

T B

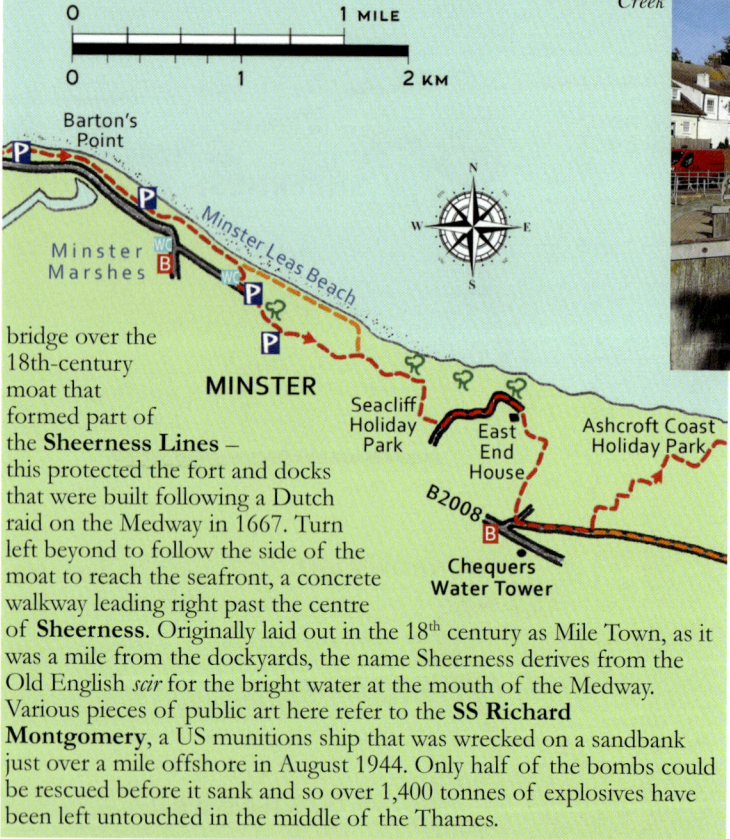

Queenborough Creek

Barton's Point

Minster Marshes

Minster Leas Beach

MINSTER

bridge over the 18th-century moat that formed part of the **Sheerness Lines** – this protected the fort and docks that were built following a Dutch raid on the Medway in 1667. Turn left beyond to follow the side of the moat to reach the seafront, a concrete walkway leading right past the centre

Seacliff Holiday Park

East End House

Ashcroft Coast Holiday Park

B2008

Chequers Water Tower

of **Sheerness**. Originally laid out in the 18th century as Mile Town, as it was a mile from the dockyards, the name Sheerness derives from the Old English *scir* for the bright water at the mouth of the Medway. Various pieces of public art here refer to the **SS Richard Montgomery**, a US munitions ship that was wrecked on a sandbank just over a mile offshore in August 1944. Only half of the bombs could be rescued before it sank and so over 1,400 tonnes of explosives have been left untouched in the middle of the Thames.

London Clay

The cliffs of north Sheppey are composed of London Clay, a soft yet stable blueish clay which underlies much of the south east and contains an abundance of plant fossils. Tropical seeds and fruits from various palms, as well as shark's teeth, molluscs and snake skeletons, have been found on the Sheppey foreshore from a warmer period during the early Eocene around 50 million years ago. The clay's distinctive properties allowed the tunnels of the London Underground to be dug, but also prevented skyscrapers from being built in the city until recent technological advances made this possible.

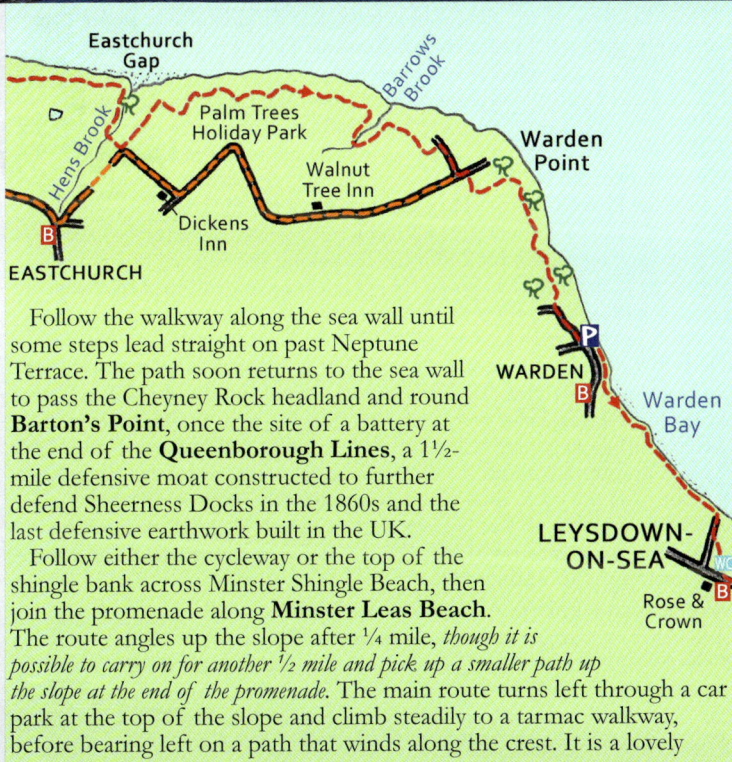

Follow the walkway along the sea wall until some steps lead straight on past Neptune Terrace. The path soon returns to the sea wall to pass the Cheyney Rock headland and round **Barton's Point**, once the site of a battery at the end of the **Queenborough Lines**, a 1½-mile defensive moat constructed to further defend Sheerness Docks in the 1860s and the last defensive earthwork built in the UK.

Follow either the cycleway or the top of the shingle bank across Minster Shingle Beach, then join the promenade along **Minster Leas Beach**. The route angles up the slope after ¼ mile, *though it is possible to carry on for another ½ mile and pick up a smaller path up the slope at the end of the promenade.* The main route turns left through a car park at the top of the slope and climb steadily to a tarmac walkway, before bearing left on a path that winds along the crest. It is a lovely

Minster Leas Beach and the cliffs of north Sheppey

route, with the soft clay cliffs of north Sheppey laid out ahead.

Hug the edge of the field to reach Seacliff Holiday Park, where you turn right on a track between the caravans. Turn left at the top and left again on the road, which soon becomes a rough track to pass **East End House** and a pair of wartime Nissen huts. After it becomes a grassy path, turn right alongside a small caravan park and join a gravel track to reach the road. Follow the road left up the hill near the **Chequers Water Tower** on top of the Mount, the highest point on Sheppey.

Beyond Plough Leisure Park and Golden Leas Holiday Park, the new England Coast Path will turn left on a track towards Punnetts Farm before turning right after 200m to wind along the edge of the fields. Reaching a tarmac track, you'll follow it left to the entrance of Ashcroft Coast Holiday Park, then skirt right around its perimeter to rejoin the crumbling clifftops. Head steadily down to **Eastchurch Gap** and follow Hen's Brook inland to a new access point into the holiday parks at the end of Fourth Avenue. Turn left beyond Brookside Leisure Park, following First Avenue to its end, then turning right on Third Avenue. After 100m, a new path will turn left beyond the entrance to Fine Acre Stables and briefly rejoin the clifftops to Palm Trees Holiday Park. Keep left through the park, then turn left to rejoin the clifftop along the edge of the fields beyond. Cross Barrows Brook and keep left around the field edge to emerge on Manor Way by **Warden radar mast**, following the track right up to the road.

ALTERNATIVE ROUTE: *Until the new coast path is officially open, much of this section is inaccessible, and the only alternative is to stay largely on the roads inland. Continue past the entrance to Punnetts Farm and drop down the hill for ¾ mile, before turning sharp left on the junction into First Avenue. Continue straight on as this briefly becomes a muddy path through the trees, then turn right at the junction of First and Fourth Avenues, following the latter over the brow through EASTCHURCH*

HOLIDAY CENTRE to emerge on Warden Road by the Dickens Inn. Follow this left for over a mile past the WALNUT TREE INN to rejoin the main route at the end of Manor Way. There is no verge on these road sections and, though the roads can be quiet out of season, they can be unpleasant to walk along in summer.

The routes converge to follow Warden Road briefly, before turning right by the entrance to Warden Springs Caravan Park. By a gate, head immediately left into the meadow, at the far end of which a path leads on to **Warden Point**, at the foot of whose crumbling cliffs lie the buildings from a World War II radar station, with two former parish churches lying further offshore. The new onward route will continue through the scrub beyond, but in the meantime you can cut through the adjacent caravan park to join the greensward along the top of the cliffs. A path continues through the trees beyond to reach the rough track of Cliff Drive, which leads down to the **Warden** seafront. Turn left and head down some steps to join a walkway along the sea wall that leads into a path around the beach of **Warden Bay**. Continue past the private Central Beach to join the promenade into Leysdown-on-Sea. Follow the road right up through the amusement arcades for which this small resort is famed, then bear left across the park to reach a bus stop on the main road. **Leysdown-on-Sea** developed around the short-lived Sheppey Light Railway, which ran from Queenborough to Leysdown until 1950.

Boris Island

It is off Leysdown-on-Sea that Boris Johnson proposed building a new airport for London during his time as Mayor of London. The proposal for a 6-runway London Britannia Airport on an artificial island nicknamed 'Boris Island' would have costed nearly £50 billion, but was rejected in 2014 in favour of upgrading Heathrow. Proposals for a Thames estuary airport to replace Heathrow or Gatwick have been put forward since the 1940s, with other sites considered including Cliffe and the Isle of Grain in north Kent and Foulness Island in Essex.

SONG OF THE DAY **Michael Crawford** – *The Music of the Night*

As a young boy, Crawford lived at Halfway on the Isle of Sheppey, before making his name as Frank Spencer in *Some Mothers Do 'Ave 'Em*. The 1975 Christmas special was filmed on the island, featuring Frank learning to drive and becoming stranded on Kingsferry Bridge before driving his car off Sheerness Pier into the sea. From 1986, he would become the original star of Andrew Lloyd Webber's *The Phantom of the Opera*. Though Crawford had performed on Broadway and the West End, he was considered an unlikely casting by many, yet went on to perform the part on stage over 1,300 times.

Section 1.8 – Leysdown-on-Sea to Swale

Distance: 26.7km (16½ miles)

Height Gained: 40m

Parking: Free car parking along the seafront between Leysdown and Shellness, and very limited free parking at Swale railway station.

Public Transport: Trains run at least once an hour from Swale railway station to Sheerness railway station, opposite which Bus 360 (Chalkwell, towards Leysdown) runs roughly hourly to Leysdown-on-Sea, with a less frequent service on Sundays.

Refreshments: The Ferry House Inn on the Isle of Harty is the only option passed on the route, though it is not always open at lunchtime during the week.

Accommodation: There is nothing close to Swale railway station, though glamping and lodge accommodation are available at Elmley Nature Reserve (01795 664896), 2 miles back along the route. There are also regular trains in both directions to Sittingbourne, Queenborough or Sheerness. The Queen Phillippa (01795 228756) is opposite Queenborough station and the Royal Hotel (01795 662626) is alone in offering rooms near the centre of Sheerness, but Sittingbourne has plenty of options, including Travelodge Sittingbourne (0871 9846562), right next to the station.

Overview: A flat and largely uneventful walk around the quiet marshes on the south side of the Isle of Sheppey. Apart from the low eminences of the Isle of Harty and Elmley Island, the route follows the 20th-century sea walls alongside the Swale, spending most of the day in the Swale and Elmley National Nature Reserves. However, the lack of public access on Harty Marshes means that until the new coast path is officially opened, there is no continuous legal route across the south side of the island and no obvious alternative inland.

Route Description

Follow the main road through **Leysdown-on-Sea** past Nutts Farm and Priory Hill Caravan Parks, then bear left across the car park to join the shore beyond the beach huts. Follow the seafront alongside the road, soon joining a sea wall past Neptune's Beach Cafe and the site of the **Short Brothers' aircraft factory**. Continue alongside the road past some beach houses on Shellness Beach and the Swale Naturist Beach. At the end of the road, turn right along the grass embankment – the hamlet of **Shellness** itself is private, occupying part

The Short Brothers

Shollness Beach was home to the world's first aircraft factory, which was opened by the Short Brothers in 1909 to mass manufacture their own aircraft design (the Shorts) and planes designed by the Wright Brothers. Eustace, Oswald and Horace Short had previously built balloons for the Indian Army and would soon move their operations to Eastchurch and later Rochester, becoming world leaders in seaplane manufacture. Yet it was here that the first mile-long flight in the UK took place on 2nd May 1909, when John Moore-Brabazon flew their Shorts No. 2 and claimed a £1,000 prize that the *Daily Mail* had offered for this achievement.

of the Shell Ness spit that is composed of millions of cockle and oyster shells from the extensive beds near Whitstable and is an important habitat for nesting birds.

Follow the sea wall through the **Swale National Nature Reserve** at the eastern entrance to the Swale, crossing some of the extensive reclaimed marshland that covers the southern side of the Isle of Sheppey. Beyond the Seawall Hide, a series of mounds to the right are thought to be composed of the waste products from **medieval saltworkings**. Although the Romans began the reclamation of the Kent marshes, large areas like this remained saltmarsh until modern sea walls were built following the devastating flood of 1953 and were an important source of salt for centuries.

At the end of the sea wall, bear left to a gate where a marker commemorates the first pig to fly, after John Moore-Brabazon took a piglet he dubbed Icarus II with him on his landmark flight in 1909. Follow the track inland, then turn left at the end to join the road by the **Church of St Thomas the Apostle** in Harty; built in the 11th century, it still possesses its original door, as well as a 14th-century carved wooden chest. Beyond the farm buildings, bear

Church of St Thomas the Apostle, Harty

diagonally left across the field and continue through the crops in the next field (no matter how unpromising it may look at first). The path continues through the hedge and across the scrub beyond to reach the road by the **Ferry House Inn**, following it left down to its end on the foreshore. It was from here that the Harty Ferry ran across the Swale to Oare Marshes until the 1940s. A historic rowing boat service, it was operated by the publican at the Ferry House, who also provided sustenance for passing travellers.

A new path beyond will skirt along the edge of the marsh, following the edge of the dry ground around the edge of what was once the **Isle of Harty**, a separate island cut off by tidal marshes from the rest of Sheppey. *In the meantime, at most states of the tide you can skirt around the edge*

of the rushes and pick up this line to reach the resumption of the sea wall, though there is no public right of access in place yet and a locked gate bars the route by Capel Fleet at present. Once open, the route will follow the sea wall for over a mile across Harty Marshes to reach a track near **Mocketts Pumping Station**, following it inland towards the grain silos of Little Bells Farm. Turning left here you rejoin an existing public footpath to cross Bells Creek and follow the track across the marsh for another mile, before climbing up onto the embankment across Windmill Creek. Here you enter **Elmley National Reserve**, the only one of its kind run by a farming family. Stretching for 3,200 acres across the south of the island most of the way to Kingsferry Bridge, it has the country's largest lowland population of breeding waders.

Leysdown Beach

B2231

LEYSDOWN
-ON-SEA

café

Short Brothers
memorial

Shellness Beach

Sheppey

The Swale National
Nature Reserve

SHELLNESS

pillbox

Seawall
Hide

Isle of Harty

Shell
Ness

HARTY

medieval
saltings

Ferry
House
Inn

St Thomas'
Church

0   1   2 MILES

0   1   2 KM

    The England Coast Path will follow a new route left
along the sea wall to round the hide on **Spitend Point** and
follow the bank of the Swale around Spitend Marshes. *However, in the
meantime, a public footpath follows the vehicle track across the marshes, passing right
by* COD'S HOUSE *(all that remains of the hamlet of Spitend) before crossing
Elmley Fleet and passing South Fleet Hide.* The routes converge at the sea
wall by **Wellmarsh Creek**, both following the vehicle track across the
marshes beyond and staying on the landward side of the sea wall at

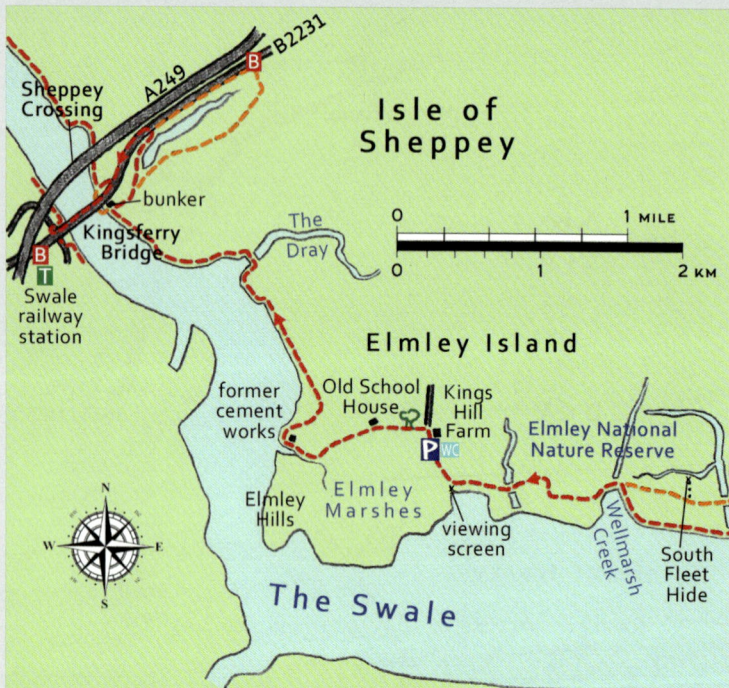

Isle of Sheppey

B2231

A249

Sheppey Crossing

B

bunker

Kingsferry Bridge

B

Swale railway station

The Dray

0   1 MILE

0   1   2 KM

Elmley Island

former cement works

Old School House

Kings Hill Farm

P   WC

Elmley National Nature Reserve

Elmley Hills

Elmley Marshes

viewing screen

Wellmarsh Creek

South Fleet Hide

N   W   E   S

The Swale

Sharfleet Creek. Follow the track up to the main car park at **Kings Hill Farm**, so named as James II was held here after being captured by local fishermen while trying to flee the Protestant country disguised as a Jesuit priest. It forms part of **Elmley Island**, first recorded as the Isle of Elms in 1250, when it was still surrounded by tidal saltmarsh.

Follow the track past the farm buildings, then turn left on another to pass the ruins of the **Old School House**, which stood beside St James' Church and was said to be the smallest school in England in 1919, when it had only five pupils. Drop back down to the marshes and turn right before a gate onto a grassy path alongside the drain. Keep straight on through the rubble remains of the **Turkey Cement Works**, which include its wharf, workmen's cottages and a Shepherd Neame pub called the Globe, all having been abandoned after the works closed in 1900.

Reaching the Swale at an old slipway, turn right along the embankment and follow it across **Elmley Marshes**, crossing the Dray to finally leave the nature reserve. Soon reaching the small boatyard and World War II bunker by **Kingsferry Bridge**, you find yourself on the wrong side of

> ### The Gypsy Tart
> The gypsy tart is a very sweet tart made from evaporated milk, muscovado sugar and pastry, and was at one time a staple of school dinners in the region. It is said to have originated on the Isle of Sheppey after an elderly local woman created it using the only ingredients she had available. She had seen some of the Romani children, who commonly travelled around north Kent, playing nearby and, thinking they looked undernourished, created the gypsy tart.

the railway, so the new coast path will follow the track right for 200m, before bearing left alongside the railway to join the B2231, which leads back over the Swale to the railway station and bus stop the other side.

ALTERNATIVE ROUTES: *However, if this section of path is not yet in place, it is a mile along the track to the road, where there is a bus stop, or a mile walk back along the road to the bridge. The other alternative is to take your boots and socks off and follow the old ferry slipway down to the river, then duck under the bridge to join the road the far side – note that the surface here is muddy and only safely accessible for around 3 hours either side of low tide.*

SONG OF THE DAY

Touriste – *Battle On*
A melodic indie anthem that was released as a debut single in 2006 by the Sheppey-based quartet, formed by brothers Sammie and Kris Harris. The island is not particularly renowned for its music scene, the band quipping 'In Sheppey you either play football or eat a kebab', and Touriste's rise was cut short by frontman Sammie being badly injured in a car accident.

Shellness Beach, looking across Whitstable Bay

Section 1.9 – Swale to Faversham

Distance: 29.0km (18 miles)

Height Gained: 30m

Parking: Free parking along the route at Oare Marshes Nature Reserve and by the Albion Tavern on Faversham Creek, with pay car parks in Faversham.

Public Transport: Trains run regularly from Faversham to Sittingbourne, where you change for the Sheerness train, which stops at Swale railway station at least once an hour 7 days a week.

Refreshments: Food is available at the Ship Inn in Conyer and the Cafe by the Creek in Oare.

Accommodation: Rooms can be found in Faversham at Creekside B&B (07990 586884), The Quay (01795 530388), the Sun Inn (01795 535098), the Railway Hotel (01795 533173). The closest campsites are Woodhill Campsite (07762 527331) and Painters Farm (paintersfarm.co.uk), both in Bayfield, 2 miles outside Faversham.

Overview: Another long flat day around the quiet marshes and nature reserves of the Swale, this time on the south side of the channel. The route bypasses Sittingbourne but makes lengthy diversions around Milton, Conyer and Oare Creeks before reaching the beautiful historic town of Faversham.

Route Description

From Swale railway station, drop back down the rough steps to the lower road just before **Kingsferry Bridge** and head right beneath the B2231. Bear left onto a path just beyond to join the embankment along the shore of the Swale for 500m, then turn right down some steps and follow a path back to the road. Turn left then immediately right on a broad track around the industrial units at **Ridham Dock**, which was built in the 1910s to support the local paper-making industry.

Reaching the road at the other side of the dock, head straight on along a path that leads back out to the sea wall. Follow this right alongside the Swale to join a vehicle track in the lee of the giant K3 plant, which generates energy using waste products from the adjacent paper mill. Continue beneath Grovehurst Jetty and past some old grindstones from **Kemsley Paper Mill**, which was the largest paper mill in Europe when it opened in 1924 and is now Britain's largest producer of recycled paper. The path rounds the corner into Milton Creek,

The Paper Industry

Paper-making was recorded in Sittingbourne from the early 18th century, but developed greatly after publisher Edward Lloyd bought Sittingbourne Mill in 1863. Instead of cotton rag, which was becoming increasingly expensive, he used local straw as well as esparto grass imported from Spain and Algeria to produce the paper he supplied to his London printworks for newspapers including the *Daily Chronicle*. His son Frank built a horse-drawn tramway (which would become the Sittingbourne & Kemsley Light Railway) to a new dock at Ridham, allowing the mill to become the largest producer of newsprint in the world. In the 1920s he built a new paper mill at Kemsley and created a model village for the workers – this mill remains open, though Sittingbourne Mill was closed in 2006.

passing the paper mill by Kemsley Down Station, which stands at the end of the **Sittingbourne & Kemsley Light Railway**, created in 1904 for the paper industry and reopened in 2012 as a tourist attraction.

Keep left alongside **Milton Creek** until you pass under the B2005 by Churchfield Wharf, then turn right to join the road across the bridge. Shortly before the next roundabout, double back right on a path that leads down to the opposite shore of Milton Creek. Head right beneath the road and follow the shore past Marshalls works, before it opens out by the pools of **Little Murston Nature Reserve**. Keep left around the former oyster pond, rejoining the Swale shore to reach the raised causeway of Foley Spit that marked the historic route of the **Elmley Ferry**. The two wrecks alongside it are thought to have been American-built World War II minesweepers.

Follow the sea wall alongside the broadest part of the Swale, passing Blackett's Outfall before bending right at the mouth of **Conyer Creek**. Stay on the sea wall as it winds around the creek shore to reach Swale

Conyer

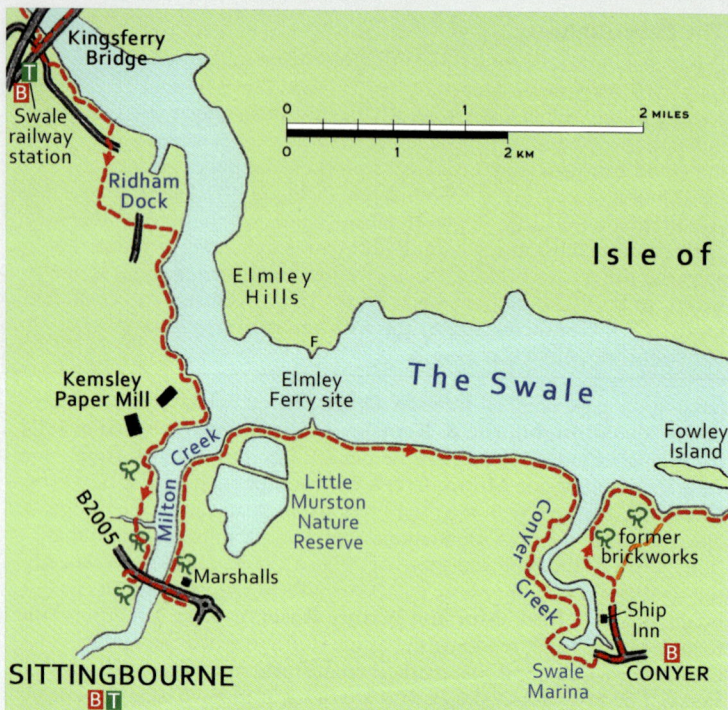

Kingsferry
Bridge

Swale
railway
station

Ridham
Dock

Elmley
Hills

Isle of

The Swale

Kemsley
Paper Mill

Elmley
Ferry site

F

Fowley
Island

B2005

Milton Creek

Little
Murston
Nature
Reserve

Conyer Creek

former
brickworks

Marshalls

Ship
Inn

SITTINGBOURNE

Swale
Marina

CONYER

Marina, where a path continues around the perimeter fence. Join the
road into **Conyer** and keep left to pass the Ship Inn, then head straight
on along a path around North Quay. The old Saxon Shore Way bears
right soon after, but (whatever the signs might appear to say) the new
England Coast Path continues left on the tarmac path. Passing the site

Gunpowder & Guncotton

Faversham was the site of the UK's first gunpowder works in the 16th
century, and the industry continued to thrive around the town until the
early 20th century. Guncotton (or nitrocellulose) was developed as a
more powerful explosive in the 1840s in Switzerland, and John Hall &
Son obtained the first patent to manufacture it in Faversham. In 1873 a
large new factory was constructed at Uplees by the Cotton Powder
Company and became a vital source of explosives during World War I.
On 2nd April 1916, a fire broke out and 200 tons of TNT exploded,
killing 115 people, though the bulk of the site's explosives remarkably
survived intact.

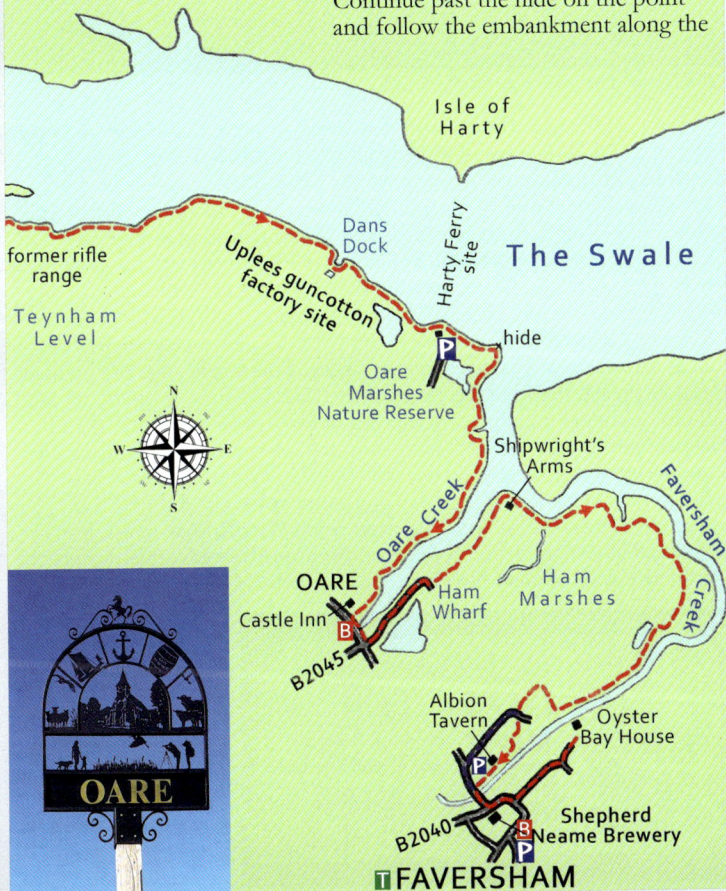

of a former brickworks, bear left onto a path that rejoins the shore of Conyer Creek to return to the Swale by the low outline of **Fowley Island**. Follow the sea wall for a lonely couple of miles past the disused rifle range on Teynham Level and the remains of a large **guncotton factory** near Uplees as the distinctive hump of the Isle of Harty rears up across the channel. Keep left by **Dans Dock** and the former jetty that served the gunpowder works to enter the local nature at **Oare Marshes**. By the car park and information centre, pass the slipway for the Harty Ferry, which ran across the Swale until the 1940s. Continue past the hide on the point and follow the embankment along the

Sheppey

Isle of Harty

former rifle range

Teynham Level

Dans Dock

Uplees guncotton factory site

Harty Ferry site

The Swale

hide

Oare Marshes Nature Reserve

Shipwright's Arms

Faversham Creek

Oare Creek

OARE

Castle Inn

Ham Wharf

Ham Marshes

B2045

Albion Tavern

Oyster Bay House

OARE

B2040

Shepherd Neame Brewery

FAVERSHAM

The Isle of Harty seen across the Swale

shore of Faversham Creek and Oare Creek towards the village of **Oare**, arranged along the edge of the higher ground above the marshes. Reaching the road, turn left to cross the creek, then keep left beyond the cafe and sailing club to follow a road along the other side of the creek. After it bends right, bear left on a path past the moorings at Ham Wharf. Turn right beyond the buildings of **Hollowshore** to follow the shore of Faversham Creek, passing the Shipwright's Arms before following the sea wall around **Ham Marshes**.

The creek bends round towards the wharves of Faversham, before being forced right by a new housing estate. Follow the edge of the field round to reach the road, bearing left then immediately right into a path alongside the former line of the creek before it was straightened and deepened in the 1840s. This path soon rejoins the creekside, though it can be flooded at high tide, so it may be necessary on occasion to retrace your steps and follow the alternative route around the road.

Continue past the Albion Tavern to reach New Bridge, which leads left into Faversham by the **Shepherd Neame Brewery**, from where the distinctive waft of malt fills the town's air. It is Britain's oldest brewery,

with origins in the 16th century, and there is a visitor centre round the corner. The route continues left, but turn right then left up Partridge Lane to reach the picturesque town centre, arranged around a 16th-

St Crispin

A 16th-century legend links St Crispin, the patron saint of shoemakers, with the town of Faversham. After their father's murder, he and his brother Crispianus fled Canterbury to avoid suffering the same fate for their faith. Passing a cobbler's workshop in Faversham, they took on an apprenticeship and eventually had their own shop in the town. The shoe shop and adjacent St Crispin's Well became a place of pilgrimage for those on the road to Canterbury. It now stands beneath the site of the Swan Inn, and there is an altar dedicated to St Crispin in the parish church.

century timber **Guildhall**, and the railway station beyond. **Faversham**, its name translating as 'metal-worker's village', is an ancient settlement around the wharf on Faversham Creek that came to prominence during the reign of King Stephen, when it briefly served as England's capital.

———— •◆• ————

SONG OF THE DAY

State of Undress – *The Faversham Girl*

This countrified song from the Dorset folk rockers' 2017 album *The Dance of Life* is about a particularly captivating but ultimately elusive girl from one of the band's previous gigs at the Anchor Inn in Faversham.

Oyster Bay House, Faversham

Section 1.10 – Faversham to Herne Bay

Distance: 22.5km (14 miles)

Height Gained: 20m

Parking: Pay car parks in Faversham and Herne Bay. Free parking for rail users at Herne Bay station, and free car parks along the route west of Seasalter and by the Albion Tavern by Faversham Creek.

Public Transport: Regular trains from Herne Bay to Faversham 7 days a week.

Refreshments: The Sportsman offers fine dining at Seasalter and the Forget Me Not Cafe & Tea Room just beyond more humble fare. However, Whitstable's famous oysters are the most obvious draw here, available at many seafront kiosks and cafes in the town.

Accommodation: There are various guest houses and B&Bs in Herne Bay, with camping available at Hampton Bay Park (07925 115741), just over 1 mile before Herne Bay.

Overview: A fine day contrasting the open marshes of South Swale Nature Reserve with the long shingle beaches and promenades of Seasalter, Whitstable and Herne Bay. There are some fine buildings in Faversham, Whitstable and Herne Bay, and it is an area rich in maritime history.

Route Description

Pick up the coast path in **Faversham** by the Shepherd Neame Brewery, keeping left along Belvedere Road, before turning left to follow a walkway alongside the creek. After being forced back to the road, a footpath cuts through to the end of Abbey Road, a short distance along which once stood **Faversham Abbey**. Keep left round **Standard Quay**, then follow a footpath to the right of **Oyster Bay House**, a 19th-century hop warehouse later used for storing fertiliser. Keep left through the maze of boats and warehouses of Iron Quay Boat Yard to reach a footbridge leading out onto the marshes.

Faversham Abbey

Founded in 1148 by King Stephen, the Cluniac monastery at Faversham Abbey would also be his burial site. When it was pulled down during the Dissolution, its stone was used to reinforce Calais against the French. Stephen's bones are said to have been thrown in Faversham Creek, then subsequently rescued and placed in an unmarked tomb in St Mary of Charity Church in Faversham.

Faversham Creek

The coast path follows **Faversham Creek**, keeping left to join the end of the road to **Nagden**, thought to have been the site of a Roman lighthouse (all evidence of which was sadly razed in the 20th century). Follow the track past the houses, then turn left along the edge of the field to rejoin the creek. It is a broad loop around the marshes at the mouth of the creek before joining the sea wall along the south side of the Swale. **South Swale Nature Reserve** extends along this shore, with a bird sanctuary at the shingle bar of **Castle Coote**. It is a breeding ground for the rare little tern, as well as a place sailors traditionally used to clean off the bottom of their boats at low tide. Despite strong local opposition, the whole of the marsh area inland between Nagden and Seasalter is destined to become Cleve Hill Solar Park, the UK's largest solar power station, with 880,000 individual solar panels.

Stay along the embankment, even where a path branches off to the left along the back of the shingle beach, and pass above the **Sportsman**. Rejoin the sea wall and shingle shore past Seasalter Sailing Club, before dropping down to the road by **Seasalter Pumping Station**. After a few yards, turn right to join a grassy path along the edge of Graveney Marshes parallel to the road. Rejoining the road, head straight across into a path behind the sea wall and along the back of **Seasalter**'s beach. You soon cross the shingle, hurdling the low wooden groynes, before rejoining the walkway at West Beach. Turn left at the far end of the beach huts, following the shingle round to a walkway that

Whitstable Oysters

Whitstable has been renowned for its native oysters since Roman times, when they were harvested to be sent back to Rome. The town developed around the profitable oyster trade, which peaked in the late 19th century. Whitstable Oyster Fishery Company remains the largest oyster farm in the country and there are still oyster sellers on every

corner. A heap of discarded shells forms part of the beach near the Royal Native Oyster Stores, though many of these are now non-native Pacific rock oysters carefully cultivated in the massive trestles standing just off the shore here.

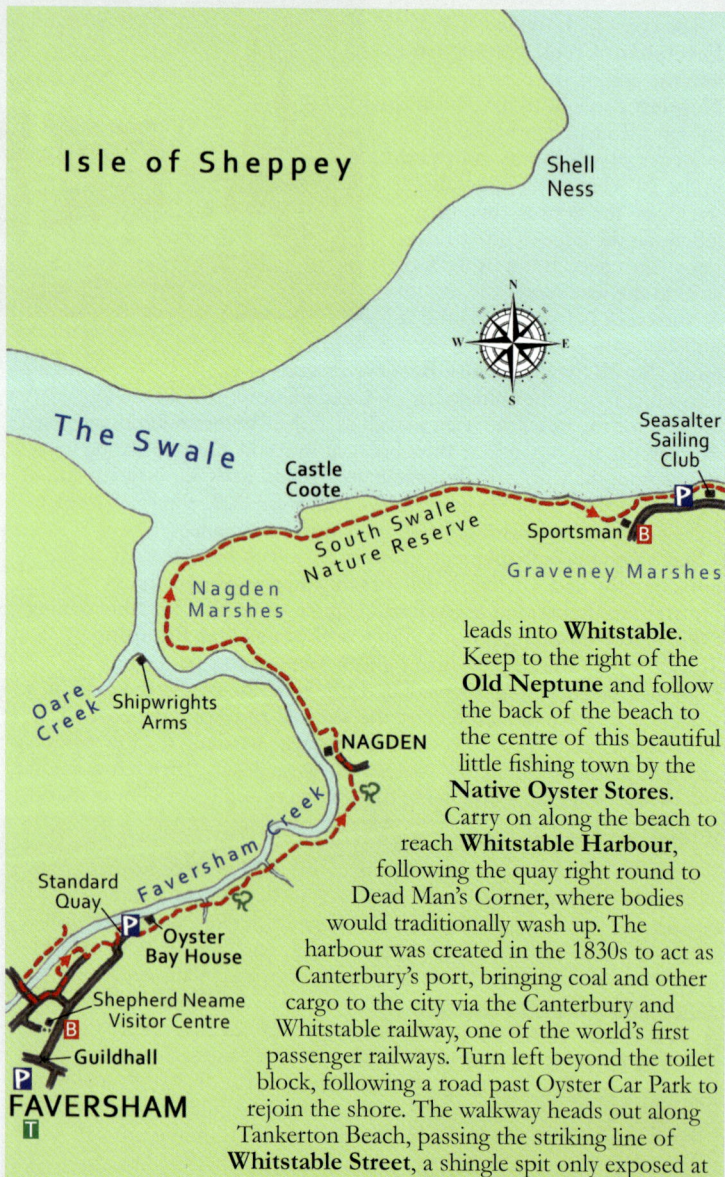

Isle of Sheppey

Shell Ness

The Swale

Seasalter Sailing Club

Castle Coote

South Swale Nature Reserve

Sportsman **B**

Graveney Marshes

Nagden Marshes

Oare Creek

Shipwrights Arms

NAGDEN

Faversham Creek

Standard Quay

Oyster Bay House

Shepherd Neame Visitor Centre

B

Guildhall

FAVERSHAM

leads into **Whitstable**. Keep to the right of the **Old Neptune** and follow the back of the beach to the centre of this beautiful little fishing town by the **Native Oyster Stores**. Carry on along the beach to reach **Whitstable Harbour**, following the quay right round to Dead Man's Corner, where bodies would traditionally wash up. The harbour was created in the 1830s to act as Canterbury's port, bringing coal and other cargo to the city via the Canterbury and Whitstable railway, one of the world's first passenger railways. Turn left beyond the toilet block, following a road past Oyster Car Park to rejoin the shore. The walkway heads out along Tankerton Beach, passing the striking line of **Whitstable Street**, a shingle spit only exposed at

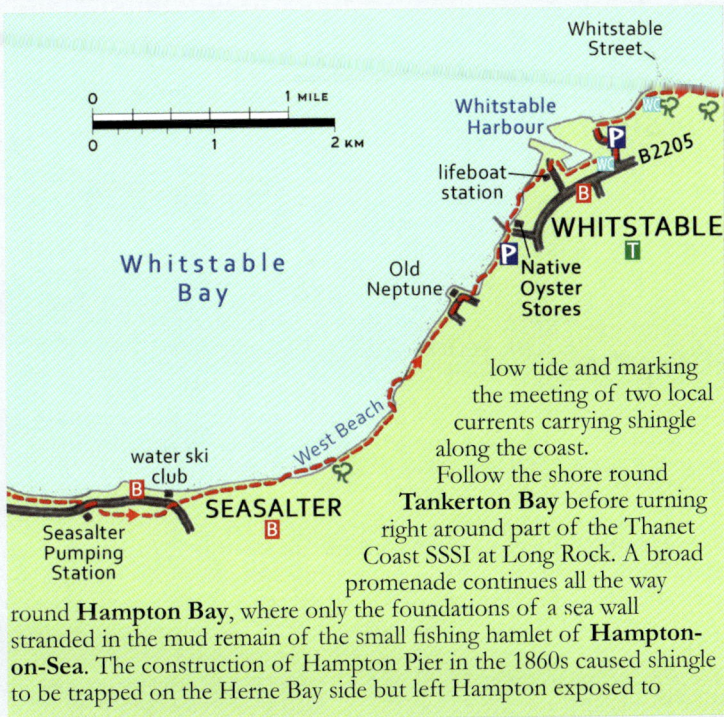

The map shows:

Whitstable Street

Whitstable Harbour

Whitstable Bay

lifeboat station

WHITSTABLE
B2205

Old Neptune

Native Oyster Stores

West Beach

water ski club

SEASALTER

Seasalter Pumping Station

0 ____ 1 MILE
0 ____ 1 ____ 2 KM

low tide and marking the meeting of two local currents carrying shingle along the coast.
Follow the shore round **Tankerton Bay** before turning right around part of the Thanet Coast SSSI at Long Rock. A broad promenade continues all the way round **Hampton Bay**, where only the foundations of a sea wall stranded in the mud remain of the small fishing hamlet of **Hampton-on-Sea**. The construction of Hampton Pier in the 1860s caused shingle to be trapped on the Herne Bay side but left Hampton exposed to

Beach huts at Whitstable

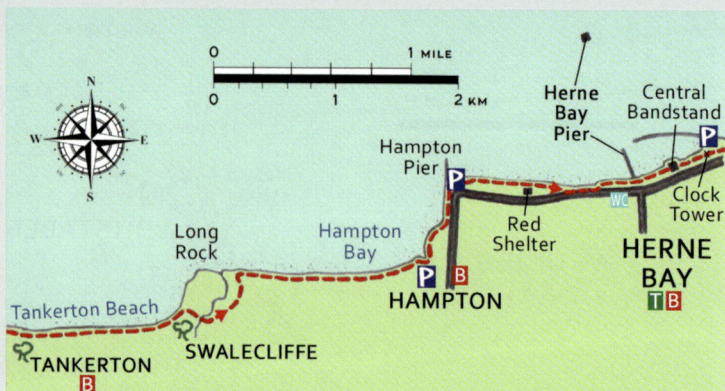

erosion and storms. During the 20th century, its houses were gradually abandoned until only a few traces are discernible in the bay. A tramway from the pier led to the mainline into London, as the Hampton and Reculver Oyster Fishery Company sought in vain to rival the success of its Whitstable counterparts.

At **Hampton Pier** turn right along the Spa Esplanade, passing the **Red Shelter** before having to join the road. The promenade resumes to reach the beautiful **Herne Bay Pier**, opposite which you can turn right along Station Road to reach the railway station. The original pier was the second longest in the country, but much of it was destroyed in a storm in 1978, leaving its far end still adrift over ½ mile offshore. The longer Neptune's Arm breakwater was constructed in the 1990s to protect the town from coastal erosion. Further out in the Thames Estuary stand the Kentish Flats Wind Farm and the Maunsell sea forts that were constructed during World War II to prevent air raids on London.

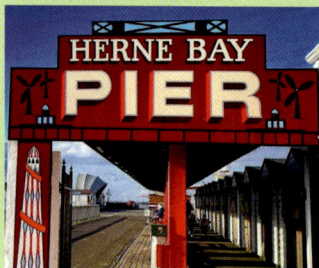

Amy Johnson

Amy Johnson, the famed aviator who had become the first woman to fly solo from the UK to Australia in 1931, died off the coast of Herne Bay on 5th January 1941. She had been delivering an RAF plane from Blackpool to Oxford when she was sighted parachuting into the sea as her plane came down. The captain of HMS Haslemere died trying to rescue her, but her body and most of her plane were never recovered. A bronze statue of Johnson adorns the promenade at Herne Bay.

The town centre is a short distance further along the seafront, near the art deco **Central Bandstand** and striking **Clock Tower**. Built of Portland stone, this structure was gifted to the town by Ann Thwaytes in 1837 and later memorialised those who had served in the Boer War. **Herne Bay** only developed as a seaside resort when direct steamers began arriving from London in the 1830s, at which point early investors had wanted to change its name to St Augustine's.

SONG OF THE DAY

Oysterband – *Over the Water*

Formed in Canterbury in 1976, the Oysterband began as a folk dance band known as the Oyster Ceilidh Band because of their close links with Whitstable. This love song from 2007's *Meet You There* is about the sea and the escape it offers.

Section 1.11 – Herne Bay to Margate

Distance: 19.5km (12 miles)

Height Gained: 100m

Parking: Various pay car parks in Herne Bay, Margate, Reculver and Birchington, with a free car park at Herne Bay station for rail users.

Public Transport: Regular trains run from Margate to Herne Bay 7 days a week.

Refreshments: Various cafes and pubs in Birchington and Westgate-on-Sea, including Minnis Bay Bar & Brasserie and West Bay Cafe close to the shore.

Accommodation: There are many accommodation options in Margate, including the Alpha Hostel (01843 221616) at Westbrook Bay, and a Visitor Information Centre (01843 577577). Unfortunately there are no campsites close to the town or this section of the route.

Overview: Although most of the walking is on a hard cycleway, this is a lovely day with varied scenery provided by Reculver's sandstone cliffs, Thanet's chalk formations and the broad marshes in between.

Route Description

Rejoin the promenade by the Clock Tower to head out of **Herne Bay** past the **King's Hall**. An Edwardian concert hall originally known simply as the Pavilion, it is built into the Downs, a spur of

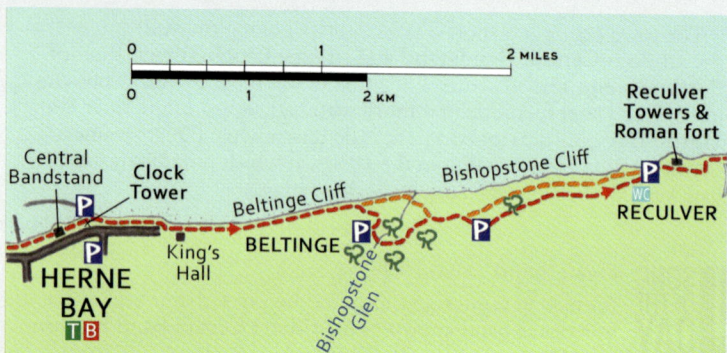

Reculver Towers Roman fort

Bishopstone Cliff

RECULVER

WC

Beltinge Cliff

BELTINGE

Bishopstone Glen

Central Bandstand

Clock Tower

King's Hall

HERNE BAY
T B

0   1   2 MILES
0   1   2 KM

clay and sandstone that ends at Reculver. Follow the promenade along the foot of Beltinge Cliff to a broad track leading up the slope to a car park by **Bishopstone Glen**. Keep left through the woods that were once known as the Fairy Glen and join an unsigned alternative path up from further along the beach (*reached via steps up the first, rather unstable, cliffs on the Kent coast*).

At the car park for Reculver Country Park, turn left either on the main track or a grassy path along the edge of the crumbling **Bishopstone Cliff**. It is a lovely walk through the rolling meadows to **Reculver**, which is dominated by **Reculver Towers**, the remains of a Saxon monastery's church. St Mary's Church was pulled down in 1805 due to erosion of the cliffs below, but the towers were kept as a navigational landmark. The monastery stood within the former site of the substantial **Roman fort** of Regulbium, with little but its outlines now imprinted on the grass.

Reculver Towers

Follow the path past Reculver Towers and through the fort's site, then turn left to join the broad cycleway that crosses **Chislet** and **Wade Marshes**. This was once part of the Wantsum Channel, which separated the Isle of Thanet from the rest of Kent, and the former tidal shore is marked by

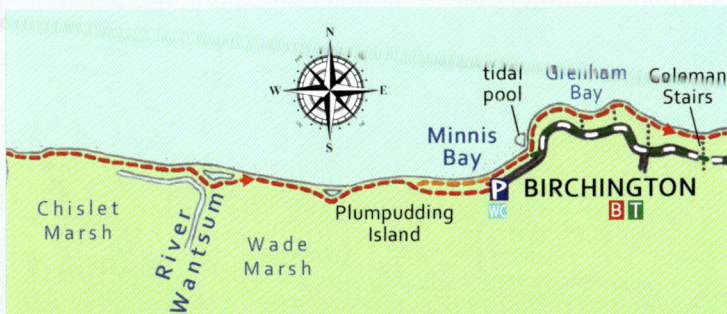

the mounds of medieval saltworkings. Divert around a couple of lagoons and pass **Plumpudding Island** to reach the broad beach at **Minnis Bay**, where the route bears right up the gentle slope that marks the start of the Isle of Thanet, though it is possible to continue across the beach itself.

The Isle of Thanet

The Isle of Thanet is a chalk outlier, on which Margate, Broadstairs and Ramsgate stand. Once separated from the mainland by a 2-mile wide channel, Thanet was an important prehistoric settlement site, with more Bronze Age burial mounds than anywhere else in Britain. Though folk tales link it to the Greek Thanatos (or 'Island of the Dead'), its name is more likely Celtic, referring to the holm oak or an ancient beacon fire. The Wantsum Channel steadily became silted up by deposits from the River Stour until it was a narrow channel that by 1485 could be crossed by the first bridge to Thanet.

At the car park rejoin the lower promenade and follow it past the tidal pool and round the foot of Kent's first chalk cliffs. *In storms or particularly high tides, it may be necessary to follow the alternative route along the road through Birchington above, but if in doubt there are plenty of escape routes up to the road.* Follow the shore round **Grenham Bay**, **Beresford Gap** and **Epple Bay**, passing several blocked-up tunnels, some of which were used by smugglers to bring contraband to houses some distance inland.

At Epple Bay, turn right either up the cycleway or the steps at the far end and join the road from Birchington to Westgate-on-Sea. Turn left down the first steps to **Westgate Bay** and skirt around the beach to follow the promenade round Ledge Point to **St Mildred's Bay**. Stay on the promenade along Westbrook Undercliffe, round **Westbrook Bay** and the last headland before the great expanse of **Margate Main Sands**. The tidal pool in the midst of it was one of two created by the

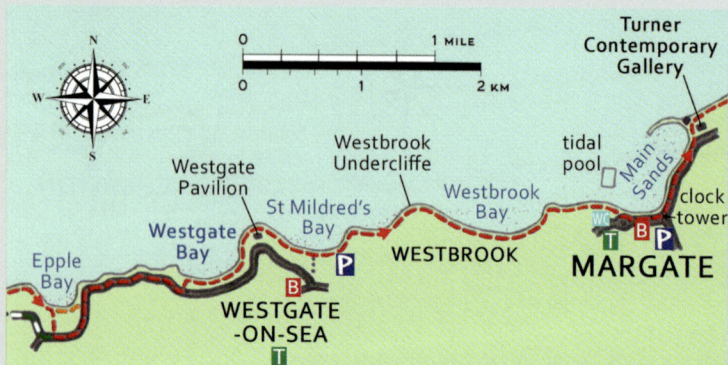

town in 1937; appropriate, since the town's name is a corruption of Meregate, meaning 'a pool reached through a gap in the cliffs'. Though the famous donkey rides, a fixture since 1790, were retired in 2008, there is a timeless quality to Margate's sandy beach.

Margate railway station is just 200m from the near end of the beach, but the town centre is reached by continuing round the promenade past the Dreamland Amusement Park and **Jubilee Clock Tower**. By the Harbour Arm at the far end of the beach is the visitor centre, housed in a replica of the original Droit House customs office that was destroyed in World War II, and the **Turner Contemporary Gallery**. J.M.W. Turner's love of Margate was inspired by skies he called 'the loveliest in

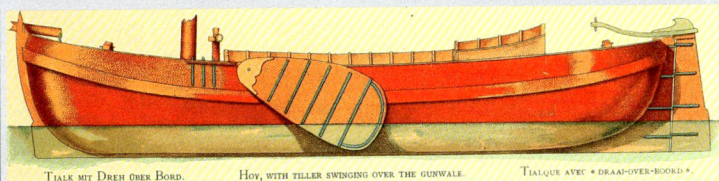

all Europe' and the gallery provides a similar view as from the lodging house he lived at between 1827 and 1847.

SONG OF THE DAY

Chas & Dave – *Margate*

This 1982 song was originally written for a Courage Best Bitter advert, but was later released as a single. However irritating they may have been, the Cockney duo's style was perfect for songs like this about the English seaside and everything that comes with it. Bright, cheesy and cheerful, they sing 'You can keep the Costa Brava and all that palaver, going no farther, me I'd rather have me a day down Margate with all me family.'

Margate's Harbour Arm and seafront at high tide

NORTH FORELAND

Part 2:

The South Kent Coast

The South Kent Coast

Start: Margate
Finish: Rye
Total Distance: 123.7km (77 miles)
Total Ascent: 1,210m (3,970ft)
Days: 6

The crows and choughs that wing the midway air
Show scarce so gross as beetles: half way down
Hangs one that gathers samphire, dreadful trade!
Methinks he seems no bigger than his head:
The fishermen that walk upon the beach
Appear like mice; and yond tall anchoring bark
Diminish'd to her cock; her cock a buoy
Almost too small for sight: the murmering surge,
That on the unnumber'd idle pebbles chafes,
Cannot be heard so high. I'll look no more;
Lest my brain turn, and the deficient sight
Topple down headlong.

William Shakespeare, *King Lear*

The south Kent coast is the county's more dramatic face to the outside world, presenting France and the continent with a severe line of chalk walls. The White Cliffs of Dover are, along with Beachy Head and the Seven Sisters, the most famous and recognisable images of England's south coast, and provide the backdrop to the above passage in *King Lear*, as well as Vera Lynn's iconic song. In fact the chalk, exposed where the North Downs meet the Strait of Dover, extends most of the way from Margate to Folkestone and covers half of this chapter. Elsewhere there are, around Deal and the vast promontory of Dungeness, the flint shingle beaches that characterise much of the rest of the south coast.

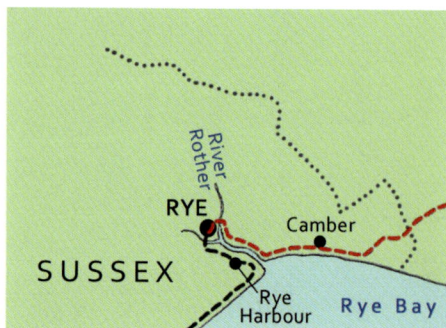

Picnic in St Margaret's at Cliffe

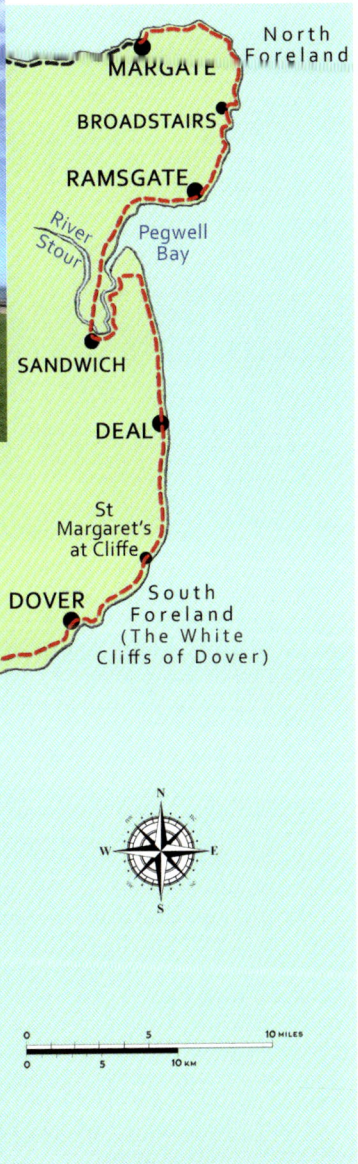

North
Foreland

MARGATE

BROADSTAIRS

RAMSGATE

River
Stour

Pegwell
Bay

SANDWICH

DEAL

KENT

St
Margaret's
at Cliffe

DOVER

South
Foreland
(The White
Cliffs of Dover)

FOLKESTONE

HYTHE

DYMCHURCH

St Mary's
Bay

Romney
Bay

Romney
Marsh

Greatstone-
on-Sea

Lydd

Lydd-
on-Sea

Dungeness

N

W   E

S

0   5   10 MILES

0   5   10 KM

Louisa Bay, near Broadstairs

The North Downs stretch inland across the heart of the county, leaving the far south of Kent to the flat marshes of Romney, Denge and Walland Marshes, a landscape of drainage ditches and sheep. At the southern tip of Kent, Dungeness is the closest thing we have to a desert in the UK, a status that had to be officially debunked by the Met Office in 2015. As a result, there is a great variety of landscape, although there is a marked contrast between flat days on long beaches and hilly days over chalk escarpments.

South Kent has been the obvious gateway to Britain for many of its invaders. Julius Caesar landed twice near Deal, years before Claudius' conquest of Britain; the first Saxon invasion came ashore at Pegwell Bay, the first bombs dropped on Britain landed near Dover Castle in 1914; and Hitler's unrealised plans to conquer Britain were to begin with an assault on Kent. From the 11th to 15th centuries, Sandwich, Dover, Hythe, Romney and Hastings comprised the Cinque Ports, which provided a royal fleet to defend the channel and received trading benefits in return. Later they would be joined by Rye and Winchelsea, as well as several subordinate ports around the south east coast.

The Camber around Rye Bay was once a populous area whose medieval ports were at the forefront of trade with Europe but as the coast shifted and all the harbours silted up, it became renowned for lawlessness. Smuggling began as a rebellion against 17th century taxes on the export of wool, and grew to encompass all manner of contraband on the area's remote shores. At the same time, ports further east grew in importance; the royal harbour of Ramsgate, at its peak in the 18[iii] century, was closely linked to the Baltic, and by the 19th century, Dover had grown to become the busiest ferry and cruise terminal in the world and one of the UK's most heavily defended ports.

Most of the coast path through south Kent follows the existing route of the Saxon Shore Way and was one of the first sections of the England Coast Path to open. From Margate the coast path continues its journey round the chalk outlier of the Isle of Thanet, rounding the North Foreland to leave the low-lying Thames estuary for the ramparts of the Strait of Dover. After working its way round the Stour estuary via Sandwich and crossing the shingle links around Deal, the chalk cliffs carry you dramatically past St Margaret's Bay and Dover to reach Folkestone. These great channel ports, just over 20 miles from France, remain more closely linked to the continent than anywhere else in Britain, Dover via its port and Folkestone as the terminal for the Channel Tunnel.

It is a long promenade around Romney Bay out to the unique shingle expanse of Dungeness and its nuclear reactors. Finally the route skirts around the army camp at Lydd to cross Camber Sands and reach the hilltop honeypot of Rye, just over the border into Sussex. Away from Dover and its cliffs, the coast path is quiet and there are some lovely sections of walking with good public transport links.

Useful Information

Tourist Information – www.visitsoutheastengland.com

Southern Rail – 0345 127 2920 (www.southernrailway.com)

Stagecoach South East – 0345 2418000 (www.stagecoachbus.com)

Kent Travel – www.kent.gov.uk/roads-and-travel/travelling-around-kent

Train Times – traintimes.org.uk

Bus Times – bustimes.org

Traveline – www.traveline.info

COUNTY ANTHEM

Vera Lynn – *The White Cliffs of Dover*

This famous wartime song that Lynn frequently sang for the British troops was actually written by an American songwriter, Nat Burton, and arranged by the American composer Walter Kent. Burton was unaware bluebirds were only found in North America and ironically have never been seen over the White Cliffs of Dover, but their presence signified happiness.

Section 2.1 – Margate to Sandwich

Distance: 24.8km (15½ miles)
Height Gained: 220m
Parking: Pay and display car parks in Margate and Sandwich. Free parking along the route at Pegwell Bay.
Public Transport: Hourly trains from Sandwich to Margate 7 days a week, most involving a change in Ramsgate.
Refreshments: Various cafes and pubs in Broadstairs and Ramsgate, with cafes passed in between at Louisa Bay Cafe, Sam's Bar at Dumpton Bay and Alison's Sea View Cafe in King George VI Memorial Park.
Accommodation: There are several accommodation options in Sandwich, with camping available just ½ mile from the route at Sandwich Leisure Park (01304 612681). The Tourist Information Centre (01304 613565) is at the Guildhall.
Overview: A long and varied day around the busy Isle of Thanet, with only the last few miles along the road into Sandwich lacking interest. The dramatic chalk cliffs of North Foreland shelter the popular resorts of Margate, Broadstairs and Ramsgate, before the quieter marshes of Pegwell Bay lead along the River Stour into Sandwich.

Route Description

Pass left of the Turner Contemporary Gallery to join the seafront promenade out of **Margate**, before the main route follows the cycleway up to the road by the former 1920s lido. This soon bears left past the car park and along Queen's Promenade above **Walpole Bay**, where the larger of Margate's two tidal pools was constructed on the rocky shore. Continue along the chalk clifftops around **Palm Bay** to reach **Foreness Point**, a prominent headland marked only by Margate Wastewater Pumping Station. *The unsigned alternative is to continue along the lower promenade beneath the cliffs. You have to cross the sand briefly at PALM BAY, but it is a more interesting route, and heading up the steps at Foreness Point brings you back to the main route.* This headland marks the end of the murky Thames estuary and the start of the noticeably greener waters of the Strait of Dover which, even when France is visible across the water, feels far more like the wild open sea than anything passed on the route thus far.

Follow the clifftop promenade round to **Botany Bay**, whose exquisite chalk stacks are the most striking feature on Thanet's coastline. Stay

Turner
Gallery
Walpole
Bay
Palm
Bay
Foreness
Point
Main Sands
WC
P
P
lido
tidal
pool
Botany
Bay
A28
T
B
MARGATE
WC
Neptune's
Tower
P
Kingsgate
Bay
Kingsgate
Castle
P
Joss Bay
North Foreland
Lighthouse
North
Foreland
Isle of
Thanet
B2052
Stone
Bay
BROADSTAIRS
T
B
P
WC
Viking Bay
bandstand
Louisa Bay
Dumpton
Bay
King George VI
Memorial Park
WC
East Cliff
Ramsgate
Tunnels
P
RAMSGATE
T
B
WC
Royal
Victoria
Pavilion
PEGWELL
Clock
House
Viking
longship
West Cliff
Pegwell
Bay
N
W
E
S
0
1
2 MILES
0
1
2 KM

The chalk stacks of Botany Bay

above the bay to pass round **Neptune's Tower**, a Henrican folly built in the 1760s by Lord Holland, possibly on the site of an ancient castle erected by the 5th-century warlord King Vortigern. Join the road to pass the Lord Digby pub and follow it above Kingsgate Bay and **Kingsgate Castle**, built as an extravagant stable block for Lord Holland's nearby Holland House. Where the pavement runs out, join the cycleway to the right of the road all the

way down to Joss Gap. Riddled with caves, **Joss Bay** was a notorious haunt for smugglers and is now regarded as Kent's finest surfing beach.

At the far end of the car park, a path leads along the top of the cliffs of **North Foreland**, with an octagonal lighthouse on the hill above that dates from 1691. Follow a path parallel to Cliff Promenade, then join the road by the top of some steps down to a private beach – now concrete but once wooden, these cut through a series of chalk tunnels and inspired the 39 Steps in John Buchan's spy novel when he stayed here in 1914.

Follow the road round to meet the main road and keep left on the B2052, then turn left on a footpath that cuts down through the cliffs to **Stone Bay**. The promenade leads along the foot of East Cliff to the car park at Broadstairs Harbour. **Broadstairs** is a popular resort known as 'the jewel in Thanet's crown', although it originally developed around the medieval Shrine of Our Lady Star of the Sea and its name came from the steps that reached it from the bay below. St Mary's Chapel on the B2052 now occupies the site of the shrine, and is not far from the Dickens House Museum, Charles Dickens having spent many summers near the harbour and writing *David Copperfield* while staying here.

Follow the road briefly, then join a path around the back of **Viking Bay**'s busy and colourful beach. At the far end, join the broad promenade beneath the cliffs round the headland to **Louisa Bay**. Continue around Dumpton Point to **Dumpton Bay**, where the promenade runs out. Though it is possible at most states of the tide to follow the sand round the bottom of the cliffs to Ramsgate, the main route heads up the slope and joins the broad grassy clifftop promenade.

Ramsgate Harbour and Clock House looking like a Tintoretto painting

> **Ramsgate**
>
> Ramsgate was once the region's most important port for trade with the Baltic, specialising in importing hemp and timber for the naval dockyards at Chatham, Woolwich and Deptford. Its vast harbour was constructed in the 18ᵗʰ century after the Navy suffered great losses during the Great Storm of 1703. George IV bestowed upon it the unique title of a Royal Harbour in 1821 and a granite obelisk (known locally as 'the Royal toothpick') was erected in his name near the quayside Clock House, which is now home to a maritime museum.

Keep left through **King George VI Memorial Park** and, reaching another road, turn left along the promenade to some steps leading down to the foot of the cliffs. The lower promenade leads into Ramsgate past the museum at **Ramsgate Tunnels**, where an underground city was built during World War II to shelter up to 60,000 people. As well as providing air raid cover, hundreds of families lived in the tunnels for months after their houses were destroyed.

At the Royal Victoria Pavilion (now the largest Wetherspoons in the country), bear right around **Ramsgate**'s harbour-front and fork right at the roundabout to angle steadily up the slope. Keep left along the broad clifftop promenade past the Royal Crescent and Royal Esplanade Gardens. At the far end, turn right up the wall to reach Pegwell Road. Follow this left to the Pegwell Bay Hotel, turning left beyond on a track

Viking longship Hugin

out past the last cliffs of the Isle of Thanet. A fine path winds down to **Pegwell Bay**, emerging through the grassy car park to join the road at Cliffs End near the Hugin, a replica of a Viking longship. Commemorating the first Saxon invasion of Kent, which landed here in 449, the replica ship was remarkably sailed across the North Sea by a group of Danes in 1949. The bay was also the site of St Augustine's arrival in the 6ᵗʰ century – a missionary sent from Rome, he became the first Archbishop of Canterbury.

Follow the road briefly, then bear left around the edge of the marshes of Pegwell Bay Nature Reserve. Keep left throughout, passing the bird hide, then turn left to meander through the dune pastures of **Stonelees**. The path soon emerges back on the main road opposite Ebbsfleet Road. Though it is hoped that a permanent route will be created along the River Stour, for now the busy A256 has to be followed for longer

The cliffs of Pegwell Bay

than one would like. Keep left at four roundabouts to follow Ramsgate Road into Sandwich via the vast complex at Discovery Park. It is a long 2½ miles at the end of the day before crossing the old toll bridge into the town. The entrance to **Sandwich** is marked by the arch of the 14th-century **Barbican** and the station is reached ½ mile straight on up the attractive High Street.

The Origin of the Sandwich

The name Sandwich means 'village on the sands', but it is now most associated with the lunchtime snack. This was first created in the 18th century for the 4th Earl of Sandwich, John Montagu, who is said to have been unwilling to take time away from the gambling table for meals. He had the top layer of bread added to the traditional open sandwich to avoid getting grease on the cards. However, as First Lord of the Admiralty, it is now thought that it was more likely to have been his work that kept him from the dinner table.

SONG OF THE DAY

Half Man Half Biscuit – *She's in Broadstairs*

The irreverent Half Man Half Biscuit do a neat line in songs about unprepossessing British places and this example is taken from their 2002 album *Cammell Laird Social Club* (named after a working men's club in the band's home town of Birkenhead). The title is a spoof of the Bauhaus song *She's in Parties* and features the lines 'I'm on another planet, she's on the Isle of Thanet, I wake up on a trolley, and realise the folly.'

Section 2.2 – Sandwich to Deal

Distance: 16.6km (10½ miles)

Height Gained: 20m

Parking: Pay and display car parks in Sandwich and Deal, with free parking further north along the seafront in Deal and at Sandwich Bay.

Public Transport: Trains run regularly from Deal to Sandwich 7 days a week, as well as hourly Buses 80/81 (Stagecoach South East, towards Sandwich).

Refreshments: There is nothing between Sandwich and Deal, but the day should be short enough for you to sustain yourself.

Accommodation: Deal has a broad range of accommodation options and a Visitor Information Centre (01304 369576) at the Town Hall. There is camping 3 miles beyond Deal at Kingsdown Camping (01304 373713).

Overview: A short, flat straightforward day on the marshes of the River Stour and the dunes of Sandwich Bay. Those who are keen may wish to merge this with Section 2.3, particularly if you are short-cutting across the Shell Ness headland on one of the older long distance routes. Otherwise there is plenty of time for birdwatching, discovering rare orchids or moths, or dipping in the sea.

Route Description

From the toll bridge, follow the River Stour out of **Sandwich** past the quay and the remains of the 15th-century town wall. Keep left, crossing a cut (the wonderfully named Vigo Sprong) and following a path along the main river past **Sandwich Marina**. Reaching a road beyond North Stream, turn left on a brand new path, leaving the Stour Valley Way (a potential shortcut across the headland if you are trying to combine this and the following section in one day). Keep left along the embankment beside the River Stour until **Bloody Point**, where you join

---

The Port of Sandwich

A medieval harbour on the Wantsum Channel, Sandwich was once considered England's primary port and was one of the famous Cinque Ports. A Royal confederation of the ports of Sandwich, Dover, Hythe, Romney and Hastings, this was established before the Norman Conquest and remains in ceremonial use. Sandwich declined in importance after the Great Storm of 1283 as the River Stour steadily silted up to leave the picturesque haven it is today.

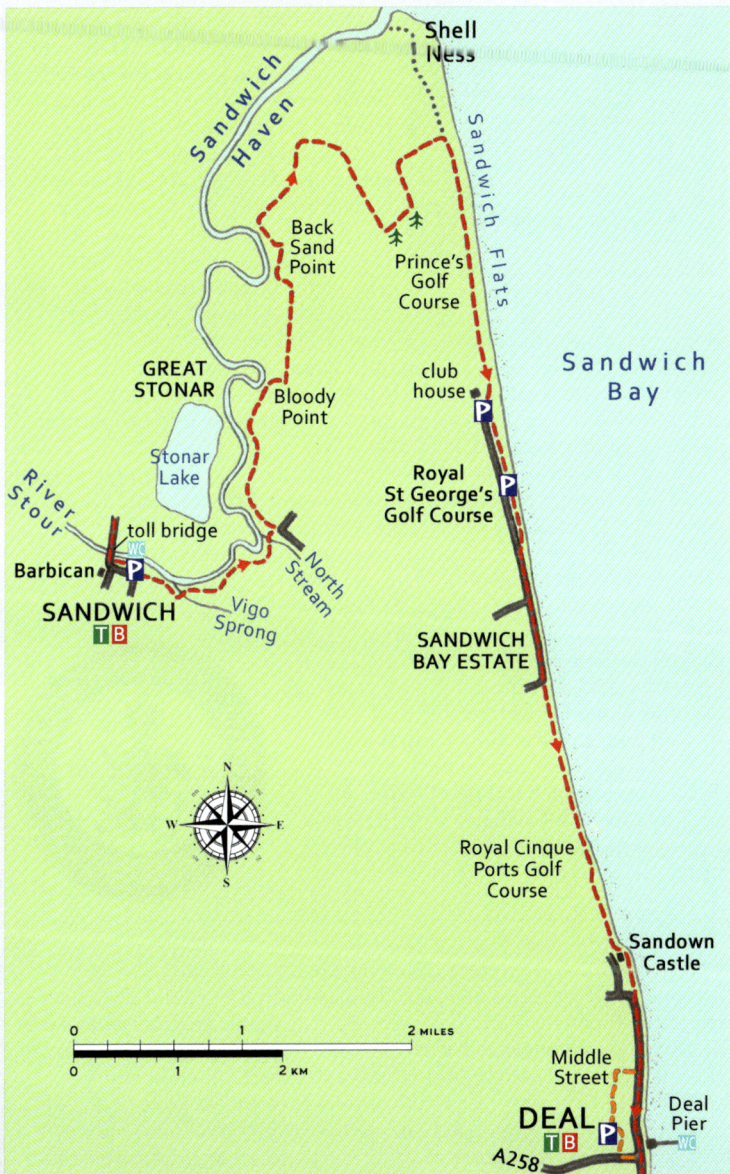

Shell
Ness

Sandwich Haven

Sandwich Flats

Back
Sand
Point

Prince's
Golf
Course

GREAT
STONAR

club
house

Sandwich
Bay

Bloody
Point

Stonar
Lake

Royal
St George's
Golf Course

River
Stour

toll bridge
WC
P

Barbican

North
Stream

SANDWICH

Vigo
Sprong

SANDWICH
BAY ESTATE

N
W   E
S

Royal Cinque
Ports Golf
Course

Sandown
Castle

0   1   2 MILES
0   1   2 KM

Middle
Street

Deal
Pier
WC

DEAL

A258

A Sandwich tern

a vehicle track heading right then left.

Rejoin the embankment at the end as it rounds **Back Sand Point**, then bends repeatedly right until you are heading back down the peninsula. Turn left along the edge of a small copse then keep left around the golf course, following the fence until it reaches the shoreline of Sandwich Bay about a mile south of **Shell Ness**. The whole of this area has been created since the 18th century by longshore drift, with pebbles and sand from Kingsdown and Deal moving inexorably north. It is an open landscape that is popular with birdwatchers and visited by oystercatchers and redshank. Though its little tern colony has disappeared, both the Sandwich tern and Kentish plover were first recorded at Sandwich Bay.

Though it is possible to follow the beach, the route turns right along a sandy line through the marram grass alongside **Prince's Golf Club** (ignore the intimidating signs). Follow one of the paths between the fence and the beach to reach the large car park at the end of Princes Drive and continue along the shore towards the grandiose mansions of the Sandwich Bay Estate. **Royal St George's Golf Club**, founded in 1887 and a regular host of the Open Championship, stands alongside.

Join the road past the estate and, at its end, continue along the firm pebbly track past the **Royal Cinque Ports Golf Course**. The edge of Deal is reached by the barely discernible site of **Sandown Castle**, an artillery fort built by Henry VIII to protect against invasion by the French. The three castles of Sandown, Deal and Walmer were

---

The Goodwin Sands

The Romans called it Infera Insula (meaning 'low island') and the island is thought to have been known as Lomea in the 11th century when it was owned by Godwin, the Earl of Wessex. Any usable land, however, was destroyed by storms in either 1014 or 1099, leaving only a great bank of shifting sand that stretches for 10 miles off the Kent coast and was exposed in places only briefly at low tide. Now protected by a ring of lightships, the Goodwin Sands are notorious for wrecks, having claimed over 2,000 ships, and buried treasure is still occasionally unearthed there.

linked by earthworks and known as the Castles of the Downs, referring not to the chalk hills but the natural harbour sheltered by the Goodwin Sands 6 miles off the coast of this part of Kent.

Join the promenade by **Deal**'s beautiful pebble beach and follow it all the way to the less charming pier, built in 1957. Immediately beyond, Broad Street leads ½ mile inland to the station. Probably the finest part of Deal, though, is its warren of narrow streets to the north of the town centre and an alternative route into town is to cut through to **Middle Street** running parallel to the promenade from halfway along the front. Despite not possessing a harbour, Deal was a busy naval port in the 18th century, as ships sheltered offshore in the lee of the Goodwin Sands. The town also had a lawless reputation, associated with smuggling and centred on the den of Middle Street, with tobacco, tea and spirits brought in and concealed in places where they are still being discovered today.

SONG OF THE DAY

Tori Amos – *That's What I Like Mick (The Sandwich Song)*
Amos is no stranger to unlikely covers – see her 2001 *Strange Little Girls* album – and this take on Chas & Dave's 1982 song about working-class mores was released as a B-side to the 1996 single *Caught a Lite Sneeze*.

Deal seafront

Section 2.3 – Deal to Dover

Distance: 15.6km (10 miles)

Height Gained: 390m

Difficulty: Moderate

Parking: Pay car parks in Deal and Dover. Free parking along the
seafront at Walmer and Kingsdown, and by the Dover Patrol
Memorial.

Public Transport: Hourly trains from Dover Priory station to Deal, as
well as regular Buses 80/81 (Stagecoach South East, towards
Sandwich) from Dover bus station, both 7 days a week.

Refreshments: Snack bar and pub by the beach at St Margaret's Bay, or
the Pines Garden Tea Room on the route just beyond.

Accommodation: There are various accommodation options in Dover,
including Dover Adventure Backpackers (07776 127592). The Visitor
Information Centre (01304 201066) is close to the route at Dover
Museum. The closest campsites are clustered at Capel-le-Ferne,
another 5-6 miles along the route to Folkestone; Little Satmar Holiday
Park (01303 251188), Little Switzerland Caravan Park (01303 252168)
and Folkestone Camping and Caravanning Club Site (01303 255093).

Overview: The famous White Cliffs of Dover dominate this short but
dramatic day, the chalk of the South Foreland rising precipitously
from the sea between Kingsdown and Dover. It is justly popular,
almost uncomfortably so on a sunny day, but it is a fantastic walk
around the part of England closest to the continent.

Route Description

From **Deal Pier**, follow the promenade past the rather stout edifice
of **Deal Castle**, a well preserved 16th-century artillery fort
surrounded by a moat. The tarmac pathway along **Walmer**'s green
seafront is accompanied by lines of boats on the shingle shore, and
leads pleasantly all the way to Kingsdown. It was on this beach that
Julius Caesar landed in 55 BCE and again the following year in the first
couple of failed invasions of Britain by the Romans.

At **Kingsdown** join the end of Wellington Parade and continue along
the shore to the Zetland Arms. Cross the pebbly beach of **Oldstairs
Bay** towards the white cliffs of the South Foreland. Join the road
briefly, then at the bend head up the steps to the clifftop and a lovely
walk across Kingsdown Leas. There are glimpses of the precipitous
chalk faces as the path climbs steadily towards the prominent **war**

memorial on Leathercote Point. It honours the men of the Dover Patrol, a fleet of naval ships, submarines and trawlers responsible for transporting troops across the Channel during World War I.

The route forks left shortly before the memorial and cafe but it is possible to continue to the memorial, then cross the road from it and descend to rejoin the coast path as it drops down towards **St Margaret's Bay**. Keep left in the trees to descend the cliff via steep steps to the stunning bay, the only place it is possible to look up at the chalk cliffs of the South Foreland. St Margaret's Bay, from where the first cross channel telephone cable was laid, is part of the larger village of **St Margaret's at Cliffe**, known for its famous residents, including Noel Coward, Ian Fleming and Peter Ustinov.

Follow the road up from the bay and bear left on the bend, before forking left along Beach Road past **St Margaret's Museum** and the Pines Garden. Continue along the rough track, soon doubling back to the left, where a gate leads left onto Lighthouse Down. All paths lead back up to the track, which climbs steadily towards **South**

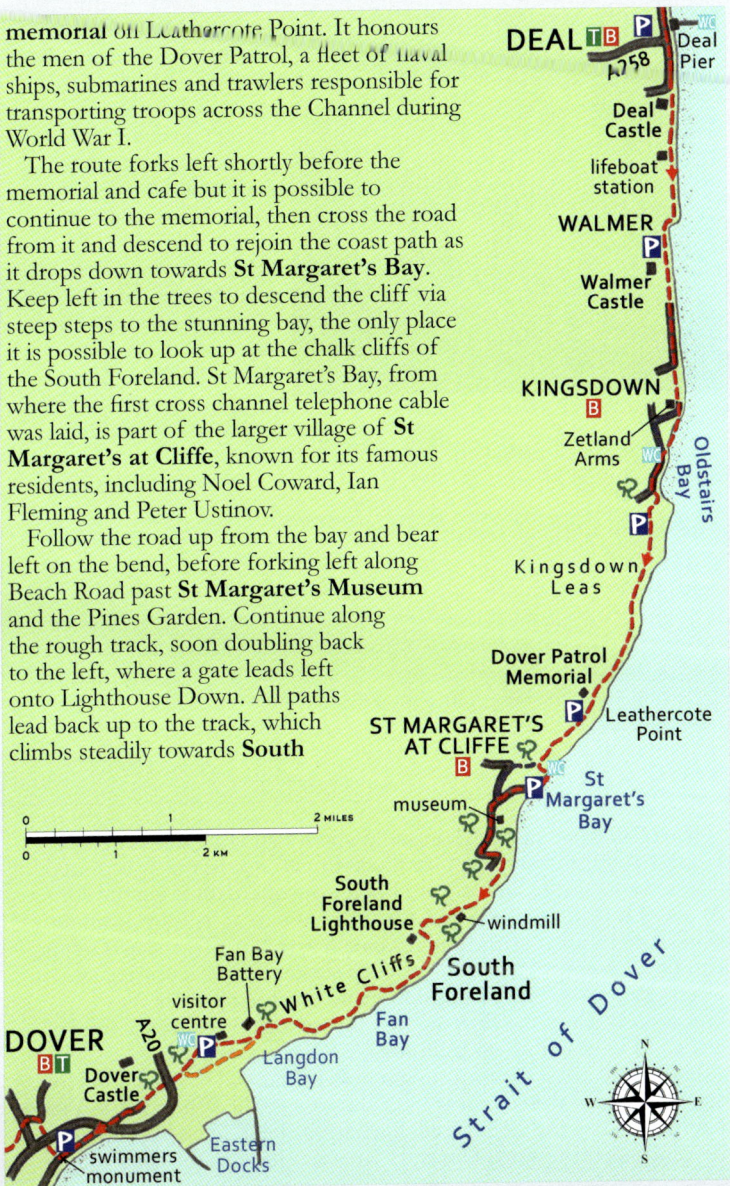

DEAL

Deal Pier

Deal Castle

lifeboat station

WALMER

Walmer Castle

KINGSDOWN

Zetland Arms

Oldstairs Bay

Kingsdown Leas

Dover Patrol Memorial

Leathercote Point

ST MARGARET'S AT CLIFFE

museum

St Margaret's Bay

South Foreland Lighthouse

windmill

South Foreland

Fan Bay Battery

White Cliffs

visitor centre

Fan Bay

DOVER

Dover Castle

Langdon Bay

Strait of Dover

swimmers monument

Eastern Docks

South Foreland Lighthouse

Foreland Lighthouse.
The lighthouse was built in 1843 to guide ships past the Goodwin Sands, though their shifting nature means it has since been decommissioned and given to the National Trust. Keep left of the lighthouse, following a path down to probably the busiest section of cliffs in the country, the iconic **White Cliffs of Dover**. Despite the hordes, it is a lovely walk along the dizzying chalk cliffs that are up to 350ft high – here the North Downs meet the sea and France is often clearly visible across the Channel.

The White Cliffs of Dover

The chalk from which the White Cliffs of Dover are formed was laid down at the bottom of an ocean between 66 and 100 million years ago. It is composed of millions of coccoliths, fragments of algal skeletons, compressed by the weight of subsequent deposits. The cliffs formed when glacial floods breached the ridge of chalk that linked Britain to the continent over 180,000 years ago, with the land bridge itself severed by rising sea levels just 10,000 years ago. It is thought the sight of these brilliant cliffs from across the sea gave Britain its ancient name of Albion.

The main route stays high inland of both Fan Hole and Langdon Hole, though some of the most dramatic cliff scenery is to be found where the land rises and falls, and well worn alternatives cut the corner. At **Fan Hole**, there is a World War I sound mirror halfway down the slope built to warn of the approach of enemy aircraft; it is part of the Fan Bay Battery complex, whose deep shelter has been opened as a tourist attraction. From **Langdon Hole** a disued path zigzags precariously down the cliff, only for the last section to have collapsed just short of the steps up from remote Langdon Bay.

The signed coast path forks right near the far end of Langdon Hole and climbs past the coastguard lookout to pass the **White Cliffs Visitor Centre**. Follow the access road down to the bend, then bear left to descend steeply towards Dover. If you stay closer to the cliffs with their

bird's eye view of the vast **Eastern Docks**, be aware that you must fork
right up the cliffs to rejoin the coast path – the lower path looks
promising but abandons you in dense scrub.

The path passes under the A2 before emerging on the edge of **Dover**.
At the end of East Cliff, bear left across the dual carriageway and join
the promenade around the surprising sandy beach found between the
town's busy docks. Turn right at the **Channel Swimmers Monument**,
then head straight on into the town centre via the underpass. The route
continues left before **Dover Museum**, although the station can be
reached in ½ mile by continuing straight on through the town centre.

The original settlement of Dover was a port on the River Dour, but
the silting of the river mouth led to the development of the artificial
docks that are now its primary feature. Dover has always been a
strategically important site because of its proximity to the continent.
The Romans established the town of Dubris here and built the first

The Dover Patrol Memorial above the cliffs of Kingsdown Leas

breakwaters, it was one of the primary Cinque Ports and would be the focal point of attempts to invade by Julius Caesar, William the Conqueror, Napoleon and Hitler. **Dover Castle**, first built by William the Conqueror and rebuilt by Henry II from Caen stone, is the largest in England and was long known as 'the key to England'.

Dover Castle

SONG OF THE DAY

Blur – *Clover Over Dover*
This melodic little song is one of the lesser known tracks on 1994's seminal album *Parklife*. The catchy tune is out of kilter with the suicidal theme – 'I'm on the white cliffs of Dover, thinking it over and over' – and is a play on the Sassy Lassies' racy 1944 song *Roll Me Over in the Clover*.

Section 2.4 – Dover to Hythe

Distance: 21.3km (13½ miles)

Height Gained: 550m

Parking: Pay car parks in Dover and Hythe. Free parking along the seafront in Hythe and at several car parks on Western Heights, along the route just out of Dover.

Public Transport: The Wave (Bus 102, Stagecoach South East, towards Dover) runs regularly from Hythe to Dover 7 days a week.

Refreshments: Various cafes, pubs and snack outlets are passed at Folkestone Harbour.

Accommodation: There is plenty of accommodation available in Hythe, with campsites towards Dymchurch at Fallow Fields Camping (0208 1468211) and Daleacres Club Campsite (01303 267679).

Overview: A beautifully varied route over the high chalk cliffs to Folkestone, then along the long beachfront promenade to Hythe. The first half is very up and down as it climbs over Dover's many hills and along a far quieter continuation of the White Cliffs of Dover past Samphire Hoe and East Wear Bay. The afternoon becomes a straightforward stroll along the promenade around the first part of Romney Bay's long arc.

Route Description

Rejoining the route in **Dover** on Queen Street, cross the A256 and turn left briefly, before heading right steeply up the hill. By the car park turn left up a long flight of steps, then turn right at the top to reach the impressive early 19th-century fortification of the **Drop Redoubt** on top of the Western Heights. There are great views across Dover; with Dover Castle perched on the hill opposite, you get a good impression of the garrison town that it became when invasion was thought imminent during the Napoleonic Wars. There were Roman lighthouses on both hilltops; that within the Drop Redoubt being known locally as the Devil's Drop of Mortar and likely to have given the fort its name.

Continue right around the fortifications until a path bears off right and drops down to the road. Follow this left and turn left at the next junction, bearing immediately right through a gate and descending a long flight of steps. At the bottom you can continue to the **Grand Shaft** (a triple helix staircase that once linked the garrison to the town below), though the route turns right and climbs again to pass the brick walls of **St Martin's Battery**.

At the car park, turn right then immediately left on Citadel Road. Fork left by the site of a 12th-century **Knights Templar Church**, then left again to follow a grassy path steadily down to **Aycliff**. Cut left to the road and follow King Lear's Way to the old main road, following it right to an underpass beneath the A20. The path climbs above **Shakespeare Cliff**, with the signed route now staying safely on the right side of the fence. Those with a head for heights can follow the old path closer to the crest, a fine serrated ridge of chalk edges said to have inspired

The observation tower at Samphire Hoe

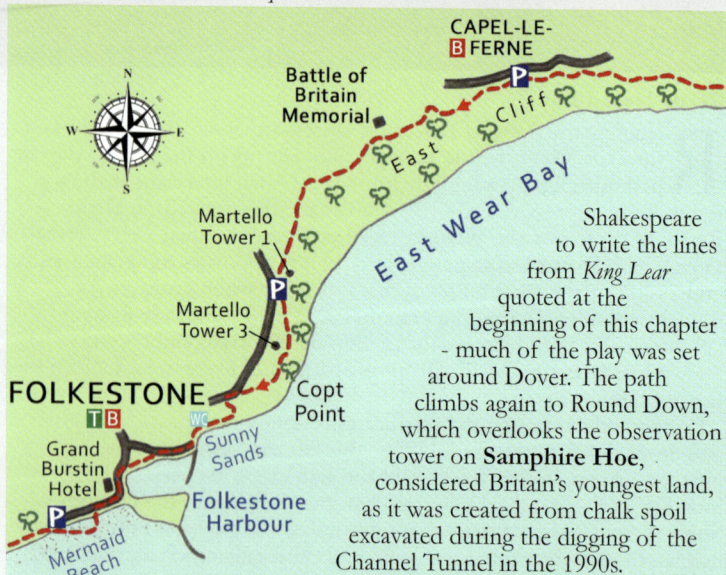

Shakespeare to write the lines from *King Lear* quoted at the beginning of this chapter – much of the play was set around Dover. The path climbs again to Round Down, which overlooks the observation tower on **Samphire Hoe**, considered Britain's youngest land, as it was created from chalk spoil excavated during the digging of the Channel Tunnel in the 1990s.

The coast path continues along the crest of the ridge above Samphire Hoe, passing a series of World War II defences that were part of **Lydden Spout Battery**. The roar of the A20 finally starts to abate as you near **Abbot's Cliff Sound Mirror**, an early warning system used in World War II to amplify the sound of approaching enemy planes. Soon after, fork left past the next lookout and follow a dizzying path overlooking Folkestone's **East Cliff** and the Warren below. The path skirts along the top of the cliff throughout, ducking in and out of the trees alongside the road on the edge of **Capel-le-Ferne**.

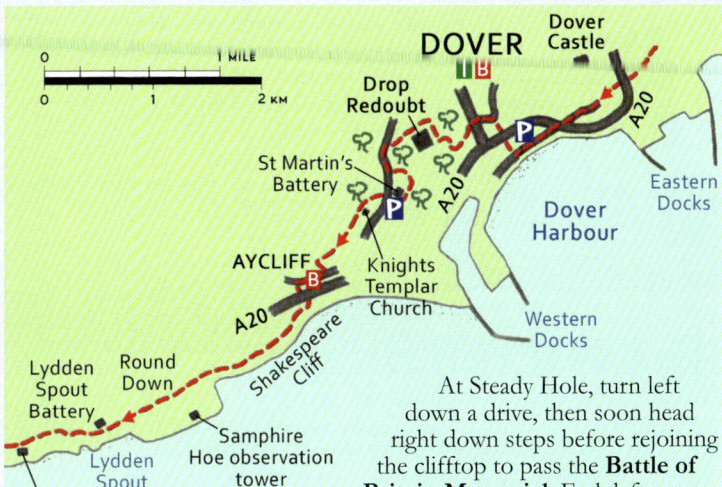

DOVER

Dover Castle

Drop Redoubt

St Martin's Battery

AYCLIFF

Knights Templar Church

Dover Harbour

Eastern Docks

Western Docks

A20

Shakespeare Cliff

Round Down

Lydden Spout Battery

Lydden Spout

Samphire Hoe observation tower

Abbot's Cliff Sound Mirror

0   1 MILE
0   1   2 KM

At Steady Hole, turn left down a drive, then soon head right down steps before rejoining the clifftop to pass the **Battle of Britain Memorial**. Fork left beyond, leaving the North Downs Way to descend steadily into Folkestone. After the first **Martello Tower**, keep to the left off the grassy sward then climb towards a second tower on **Copt Point**. Keep left down the grass to pick up a rough concrete track that soon joins the road. Bear left down steps to join the end of Coronation Parade, which leads around Sunny Sands to **Folkestone Harbour**. Folkestone was a small fishing village around the mouth of the Pent Brook before the harbour and pier were built by Thomas Telford in 1807. Even then it took the arrival of the railway in 1843 to transform the town into a fashionable resort and major cross-channel port.

Beneath the arches, keep left along the front to round the ship-shaped **Grand Burstin Hotel**, built on the site of the old Royal Pavilion Hotel in 1984. Soon turn left across the shingle beach to pick up a lovely railway-sleeper path across the heart of the otherwise slow-going beach.

The Channel Tunnels

The modern Channel Tunnel leaves its indelible mark at Samphire Hoe as it sets off for the continent, but a smaller tunnel entrance beneath Shakespeare Cliff reveals the workings of the first attempt to link Britain and France. Though it had been suggested to Napoleon as early as 1802, work first began on a tunnel in 1880, using a circular burrowing machine. It was stopped in 1882 with a little over a mile dug at either end as it had been decided on both sides that it posed too great a threat to national security.

Abbot's Cliff Sound Mirror

Join the long promenade behind **Mermaid Beach** and round the corner of **Mill Point** to be presented with a great arc of golden sand leading all the way round Romney Bay to Dungeness. It is a straightforward stroll along the front to Hythe from here, passing the mini-resort of **Sandgate** soon after the 16th-century castle that was built by Henry VIII at the same time as those around Deal.

Join the road soon after Sandgate, the promenade continuing alongside until just before the two **Martello Towers** at the far end of Hythe. These lie within Hythe Ranges, which forces the coast path inland along St Leonards Road and whose gunfire provides a soundtrack to the town. Reaching the green, bear left on the tarmac pathway and head straight across the road at the end to join the **Royal Military Canal**. This was built in the early 19th century as a defensive barrier against an invasion from France. The centre of **Hythe** is reached by turning right at the next road; it is a charming town whose historical significance as one of the Cinque Ports is no longer evident. Hythe means 'haven' and its original port was a few miles west at Port Lympne and later West Hythe, but these silted up as the coastline took its current shape. The harbour moved east, but by the 16th century this too had silted up and is now buried beneath the shingle on which the modern seafront resort stands.

SONG OF THE DAY

Baby Queen – *Dover Beach*
A 2021 single by South African-born pop singer Bella Latham inspired by the 19th-century poem *Dover Beach* by Matthew Arnold. It is about seeing someone everywhere you look, and the video features the cliffs around Dover and Samphire Hoe.

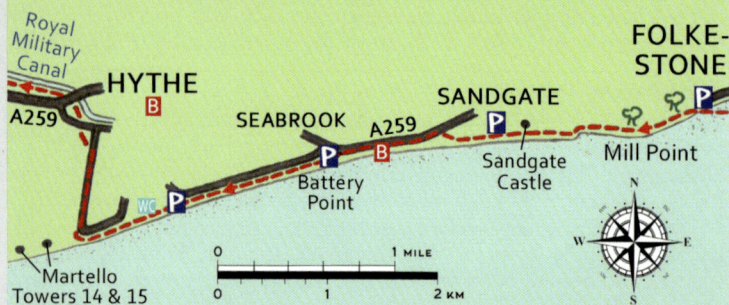

Section 2.5 – Hythe to Lydd-on-Sea

Distance: 20km (12½ miles)

Height Gained: 10m

Parking: Pay parking in Hythe, Dymchurch and Greatstone Beach. Small free seafront car park at the Lade, Lydd-on-Sea.

Public Transport: The Wave (Bus 102, Stagecoach South East, towards Dover) runs regularly from Lydd-on-Sea to Hythe 7 days a week, with its furthest stop towards Dungeness at the Pilot Inn. At weekends and holidays you can also ride the steam train along the Romney, Hythe & Dymchurch Railway from Lydd-on-Sea or Dungeness back to Hythe.

Refreshments: Various cafes, pubs and snack bars by the seafront in Dymchurch.

Accommodation: Rooms are available at the Castaways B&B (01797 320017) in Lydd-on-Sea, as well as a number of other places on Airbnb. There is camping right by the route a further 5 miles on at Herons Park Campsite (07585 316316) near Lydd.

Overview: A straightforward, almost tedious day along the lengthy sea wall that protects Romney Marsh. A short initial section along the Royal Military Canal provides the only variety to the broad sands and endless resorts of the Romney Bay seafront.

Route Description

From the centre of **Hythe**, rejoin the coast path on the south side of the Royal Military Canal by the former Dukes Head pub. It soon passes the terminus of the **Romney, Hythe and Dymchurch Railway**, a narrow gauge railway built in the 1920s that has long been held to be the smallest public railway in the world. The path is sandwiched between the railway and canal for over a mile before emerging on the road. Follow this right, then turn left along Kingfisher Avenue. Turn left again on Heron's Way to return to the side of the railway, crossing it at the second opportunity to join an industrial track that leads to the main road on the edge of **Palmarsh**. Follow the road right for over a mile, passing the Martello Lakes estate and **Dymchurch Redoubt**, the main barracks associated with the Napoleonic defences along this stretch of coastline.

Beyond the redoubt, bear left up onto the new sea wall at the far end of **Hythe Ranges**. Though there has been a sea wall here since the Romans, and Dymchurch Wall was first built in the 13th century, this promenade was only built in 2011. It continues for 4 miles all the way to

Martello Towers

Between 1804 and 1812 a chain of 104 Martello Towers were constructed between Aldeburgh in Suffolk and Seaford in Sussex to defend against invasion by France. Their circular design and thick walls were based on the Genoese Tower on Mortella Point in Corsica, which repelled a British bombardment in 1794 and after which they are named. Dozens of others were built around the world, particularly on the Irish coast, and the oldest Martello Tower is in Halifax, Nova Scotia.

Littlestone-on-Sea, though in particularly severe weather or at spring high tides, the flood gates may be shut and necessitate following the road through Dymchurch and St Mary's Bay. A trio of Martello Towers bookend **Dymchurch**, the second (Tower 24) having been restored and opened as a museum, but in between it is a garish resort promoting itself as 'Children's Paradise'. The town was home to Edith Nesbit, author of *The Railway Children*, and the setting for the Dr Syn books by Russell Thorndike, which are celebrated locally with a biennial Day of Syn. The name Dymchurch relates to *deme*, an Old English word for a judge, as it was the medieval residence of the governors of law on Romney Marsh.

At **Littlestone-on-Sea**, with its prominent brick **water tower**, join Coast Road, which runs all the way along the front to Lydd-on-Sea. Half a mile offshore and exposed at low tide, lies part of the **Mulberry harbours** that were used during the D-Day landings in 1944. The 200ft-long concrete Phoenix caissons (large watertight chambers) were left at locations around the south coast before being refloated when they were needed, but this section was damaged and could not be lifted, so it was abandoned here. The coast path branches off the road across the green soon after, passing Littlestone's beacon pan and **lifeboat station**. Continue through the warren of paths in the dunes beyond until you join the sandy part of the beach. In case of adverse weather, there is an alternative path up to the road in **Greatstone-on-Sea**, differentiated from Littlestone by the size of the shingle on their respective beaches. Greatstone, like Lydd-on-Sea, is a 20th-century collection of bungalows and prefabs, whereas Littlestone was laid out by Sir Robert Perks in the 1880s as an upmarket resort around the now-demolished Grand Hotel.

The coast path continues on the beach for another ½ mile before cutting across the shingle near the Romney Tavern. It is a further 2 miles to the Pilot Inn at the far end of **Lydd-on-Sea**, where the road bends away from the sea and there is the last bus stop on Romney Bay.

Royal Military Canal

HYTHE

PALMARSH

Hythe Ranges

A259

Canal Cutting

Martello Tower 19

Martello Towers 14 & 15

Dymchurch Redoubt

Martello Tower 23

Romney Marsh

Dymchurch Wall

DYMCHURCH

Martello Towers 24 & 25

St Mary's Bay

ST MARY'S BAY

New Sewer

A259

Jesson Outfall

water tower

NEW ROMNEY

Mulberry harbour

LITTLESTONE -ON-SEA

lifeboat station

GREATSTONE -ON-SEA

LYDD- ON-SEA

Pilot Inn

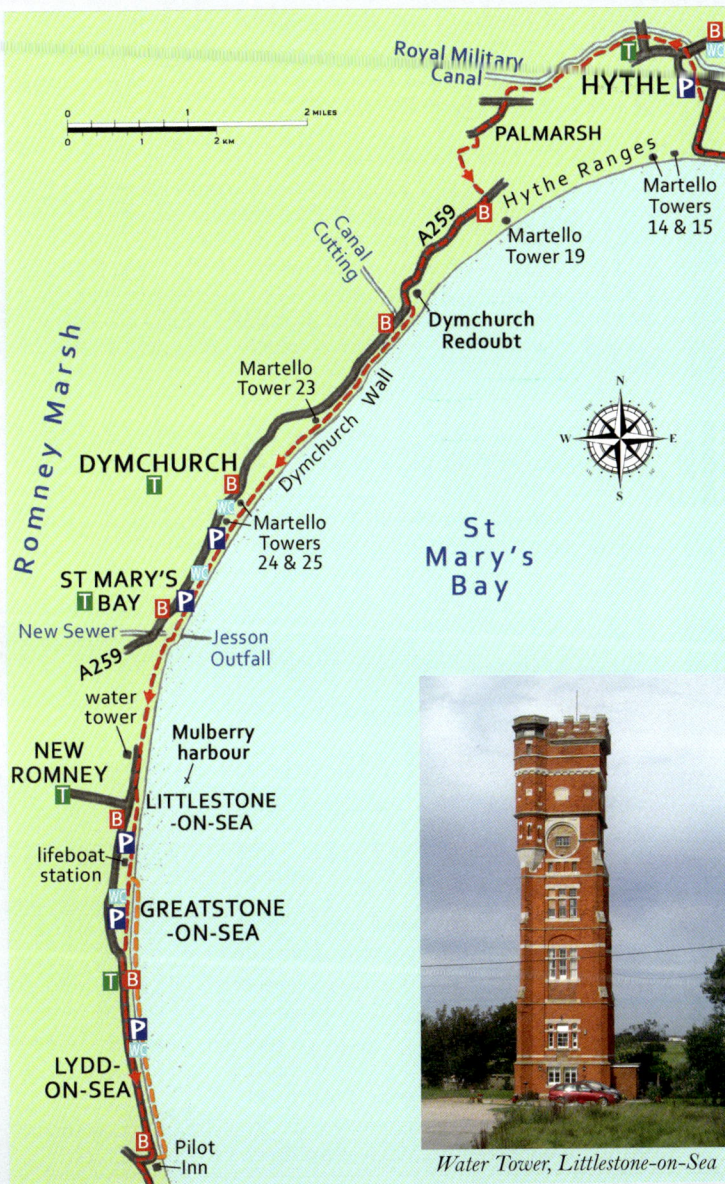

Water Tower, Littlestone-on-Sea

ALTERNATIVE ROUTE: *Though it is possible to stay on the beach all the way, this is only possible when the tide is out and there are only a couple of places you are permitted to cross the protected shingle bank above. One of these routes heads across the shingle to rejoin the route by the Pilot Inn.*

Smuggling on Romney Marsh

The remote beaches on Romney Marsh are said to have been the birthplace of smuggling in the south of England after export taxes were introduced in the late 17th century. It began with the illegal export of wool to the continent by local fishermen, but by its height smugglers in the area traded in everything from tin and tea to silk and lace. The whole area and its authorities were ruled by ruthless gangs, and only with the eventual abolition of most government import duties in the mid 19th century did the smuggling trade diminish.

SONG OF THE DAY

Terry Gilkyson – *The Scarecrow of Romney Marsh*

Recorded in 1963, this was taken from one of the earliest Disney films, which would later reach the big screen as *Dr. Syn, Alias the Scarecrow*. Dr Syn was created by Dymchurch author Russell Thorndike and lived a double life as a country vicar and the greatest smuggler in the region. The stories were based on a real character who became a Robin Hood-like hero on Romney Marsh, giving all the money from his trade to the poor and needy.

Section 2.6 – Lydd-on-Sea to Rye

Distance: 25.4km (16 miles)
Height Gained: 20m
Parking: Pay car parks in Rye and Camber. Small free car parks at the Lade in Lydd-on-Sea and Dungeness Nature Reserve.
Public Transport: The Wave (Bus 102, Stagecoach South East, towards Dover) runs regularly from Rye to Lydd-on-Sea 7 days a week.
Refreshments: There is nothing directly on the route between Dungeness and Camber, but on the way through Lydd the New Moon & Stars Cafe and the Royal Oak are within ½ mile.
Accommodation: Various accommodation is available in Rye, with an Information Point (01797 223902) at the Town Hall. The nearest

Overview: A long flat day around Dungeness and the Denge and
Walland Marshes, with Lydd Ranges necessitating a substantial
diversion inland to Lydd. The desolate and other-worldly shingle
landscape of Dungeness and its power stations gives way to the cosier
beaches of Camber Sands and the gentile charms of Rye. Though the
official route ends 2 miles short of Rye, there is an obvious informal
continuation into the town.

Route Description

Prospect Cottage

At the **Pilot Inn**, follow the road
as it bends inland, then turn left
out towards Dungeness, known
locally simply as the Ness. The
landscape is suddenly bleak and the
scattered houses perch uncertainly on
the shingle peninsula, many of them
former fishermen's huts. One of these
dwellings, **Prospect Cottage**, is
highlighted by its bright yellow window
frames and famous for the driftwood garden laid out by the film-maker
Derek Jarman before his death in 1994.

It is 1½ miles to the end of the road and the only alternative is to
cross the shingle at one of a couple of permitted routes to follow the
shore round to the power station, although this may be unwise given the
length of the day ahead. Follow the road round past the **new
lighthouse**, then turn left in front of the **old lighthouse**. Actually the
fourth built on Dungeness, it was closer to the shore when constructed
in 1904 and was superseded when the first nuclear power station
obscured it in the 1960s. This reactor is still in the process of being
decommissioned, while Dungeness B, which was developed alongside in
the 1980s, is now itself at the start of the decommissioning process.

Keep left around the **nuclear power stations** and follow a path along
the perimeter fence. At the far end, bear left up onto the artificial
shingle bank and follow it for over ½ mile – these stones are regularly
replenished to protect the power station. Signage is poor here, but keep
going until you pass the brick **lookout tower** by the edge of **Lydd
Ranges** and pick up a vehicle track heading inland along the perimeter
fence. The desolate shingle landscape gives way to the vast expanse of
Denge, Walland and Romney Marshes, whose wetlands developed over

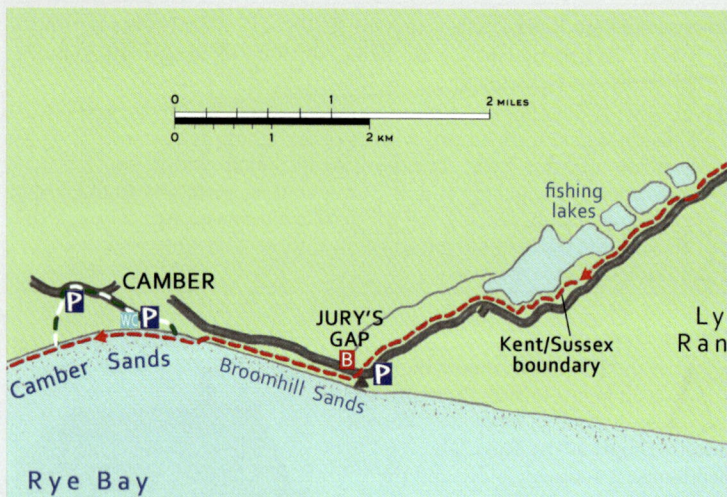

many centuries behind the shingle bank of Dungeness. After 1½ miles, turn left beyond **Brickwall Farm** on a track towards Herons Park. Keep left and follow the edge of the range to an entrance point, where you turn right along the perimeter fence all the way into Lydd.

Lydd is an intriguing garrison town, centred around a prominent Saxon church known as 'the cathedral of the marshes', parts of which date from the 5th century. It was here that the explosive Lyddite was first tested in 1888 – made of picric acid, it would be widely used in shells during World War I. However, the coast path reveals little of Lydd, as the route turns left at the edge of town along Tourney Road. Reaching the edge of town beyond the camp, join a cycleway running parallel to the right side of the road. This continues all the way to Jury's Gap, skirting around the large fishing lakes created in Scotney Court's former

The Camber & Dungeness

Until the Great Storm of 1287, the geography of the coast between Romney and Rye was greatly different. The River Rother flowed into the sea at New Romney and Lydd stood on island between this and the River Brede, their mouths forming the great natural harbour of the Camber, similar to those around Portsmouth or Chichester. The storm threw shingle across the mouth of the Rother and diverted its course past Rye, creating the Dungeness headland. However, the smaller Camber was still home to the ports of Rye and Winchelsea before succumbing to siltation and land reclamation by the 16th century.

Map labels:

LYDD

LYDD-ON-SEA

Lydd Camp

Aqua Park

d d g e s

Denge Marsh

Brickwall Farm

Pilot Inn

Prospect Cottage

Dungeness Power Stations

new lighthouse

lookout tower

old lighthouse

Dungeness

Dungeness old lighthouse

gravel pits and crossing the boundary from Kent into Sussex.

Reaching the seafront at **Jury's Gap**, cross the road to join the promenade above Broomhill Sands. Jury's Gap is a corruption of Jew's Gate, referring to the area's use for landing goods by Jewish merchants. Follow the seafront into **Camber**, where the route crosses the famed **Camber Sands**, initially over gravel but quickly becoming sandy to pass the main car park, toilets and cafes. The broad sands are popular with kitesurfers and landboarders, and the village takes its name from the Camber, a bay that once covered large parts of the marsh around the mouth of the River Rother.

ALTERNATIVE ROUTE: *Dogs are banned from the central section of the*

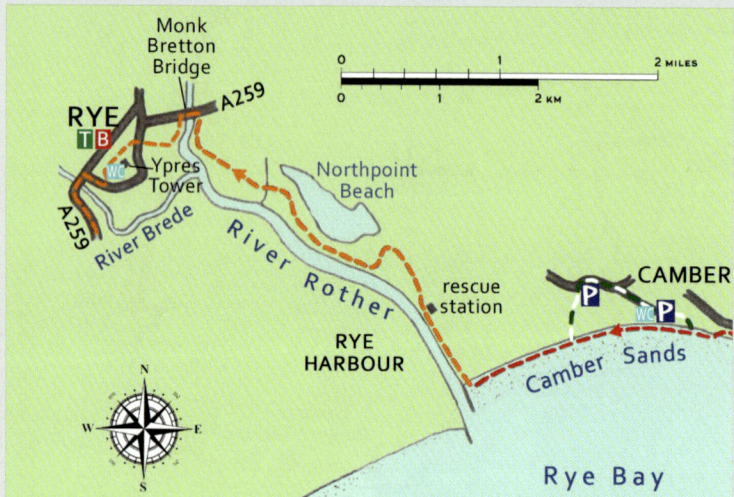

Map labels

Monk Bretton Bridge

A259

RYE

T B

WC

Ypres Tower

A259

River Brede

River Rother

Northpoint Beach

rescue station

RYE HARBOUR

CAMBER

P

WC P

Camber Sands

Rye Bay

0   1   2 MILES

0   1   2 KM

N   E   S   W

---

beach, so dog walkers will need to follow a partially signed alternative route inland from zone K. Turn left at the first junction and follow a sandy path behind the dunes to pick up a vehicle track that emerges at the main car park. Now follow the access road through the village and join the main road. Almost at the edge of the village, turn left through a gate and follow the car park edge to zone B. A path through the dunes emerges on the beach again beyond the restricted area.

The routes converge to follow the beach all the way to its end by the entrance to the **River Rother**, which is where the official route ends because of problems creating a safe route through Rye. However, the long distance walker will need to continue inland and there is already a

Camber Sands and the mouth of the River Rother

Rye

Rye was a place of great importance and one of the Cinque Ports when it stood on the coast, but the vast harbour of the Camber gradually silted up to leave the town stranded inland. It was burnt to the ground by the French in 1377 and under French rule for several periods in its history, hence its great town walls and defensive towers, like the 13th-century Ypres Tower. Yet the town slumbered for centuries, economically abandoned until its charming warren of cobbled streets was rediscovered by tourists as a glimpse into the past and what Jonathan Raban called 'a representation of Britain at large'.

Mermaid Street, Rye

fairly simple and pleasant path that can be followed along the river to Rye. Join a path along the right side of the channel and fork right of the rescue station at **Rye Harbour** to join the access track. At the first bend, bear left onto an embankment across the marshes. This continues all the way into Rye, which looms on a rise above the confluence of the Brede and Rother. At the road, cross **Monk Bretton Bridge** into the town, then turn immediately left on a path, before turning right past the bowling green. Head straight across the main road to climb up some steps to reach the High Street, following it left through the beautiful heart of **Rye** and turn right then left to head up into the town centre. Turn right at Market Road to reach the rail and bus station.

SONG OF THE DAY

Trembling Bells – *Devil in Dungeness*
The title song from the Scottish band's 2018 *Dungeness* album, this wonderful dose of folk psychedelia was inspired by a trip to Kent and the strange atmosphere that pervades the landscape of this end of Romney Marsh.

THE SEVEN SISTERS

Part 3:

The Sussex Coast

Part 3 – The Sussex Coast

Start: Rye
Finish: Emsworth
Total Distance: 202.7km (126 miles)
Total Ascent: 1,530m (5,020ft)
Days: 9

Little tarred bungalows with tin roofs paraded backwards, gardens scratched in the chalk, dry flower-beds like Saxon emblems carved on the downs. Notices read: 'Pull in Here ', 'Mazawattee tea ', 'Genuine Antiques', and hundreds of feet below the pale green sea washed into the scarred and shabby side of England.

Graham Greene, *Brighton Rock*

Sussex (referring to the land of the South Saxons) is a long blade stretching across a large chunk of the south coast. Its coastline is one of the most varied in the country, cutting across various distinct landscapes, particularly in East Sussex. The levels of Winchelsea and Pevensey contrast with the Wealden Hills, which meet the sea at

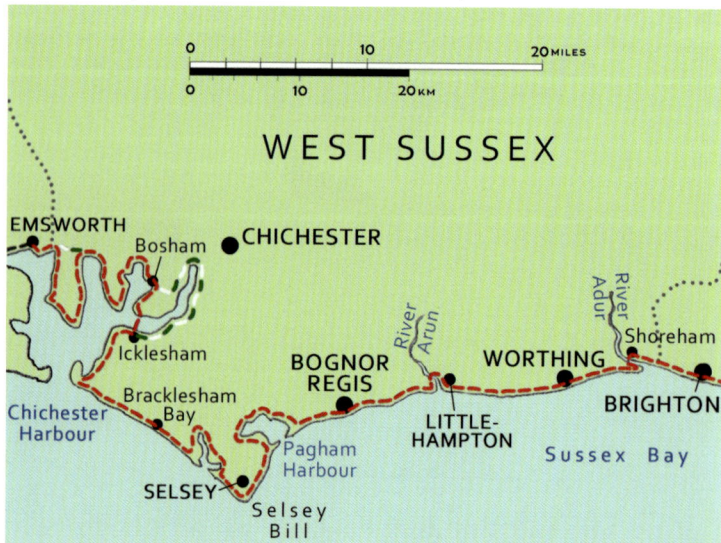

Fairlight and Hastings, and the South Downs, whose searing chalk faces form the famous cliffs of Beachy Head and the Seven Sisters. The coast flattens out in West Sussex and there are miles of shingle beaches and promenades through Brighton, Worthing, Littlehampton and Bognor Regis. Around Selsey and beyond, the myriad estuaries of Pagham Harbour, RSPB Medmerry and Chichester Harbour provide some beautiful walking and great bird-watching opportunities.

Sussex's geology mirrors its shape, with the chalk ridge of the South Downs running east-west through the middle of it. To the north are the older rocks of alternating clays and sandstones that make up the Weald, while to the south are the younger gravels and clays of the coastal plain. Flint is a hard crystalline type of quartz that forms irregular nodules within the chalk and has been widely used as a cheap and durable

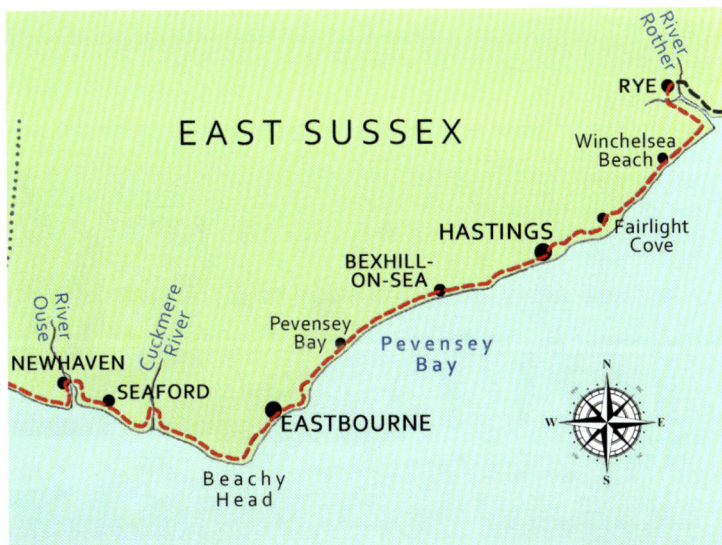

building material in Sussex. It also forms most of the shingle that is a defining characteristic of the Sussex coast, its jumble of orange stones lining the county's shore everywhere other than the surprising expanse of sand at West Wittering.

When you hit the seafront promenade in Sussex, the bright stones beckon you towards the sea, and you can even have a quick dip without getting covered in sand or mud. However, the shingle quickly proves painful to walk across with bare feet, uncomfortable to picnic on without sufficient padding, and most of all a slog to cross on a long distance walk. There are mercifully few places you have to walk on the shingle, but it is a shame as the perfect arc of the beach is alluring any time you don't have to set foot on it. It is interesting to note that, in the 19th and early 20th centuries, local people crafted a type of shoe from wood to work like a snowshoe, enabling them to cross the shingle.

Historically the Sussex coast was defined by its river mouths, with the only ancient ports being at Chichester and Rye, as the Ouse, Adur and Arun regularly shifted course and, dangerous to approach, were used largely by local trade. In between these ports, the shingle shore was home to small fishing villages and smugglers' hideaways that only developed further when seawater bathing became fashionable in the late 18th century. Its proximity to London and miles of safe shoreline meant Sussex's resorts took off remarkably quickly though, and have continued to expand to the point where it seems like every gap on the coast will soon be filled in. From Hastings to Eastbourne and Seaford to West Wittering, there is little open ground other than the estuarine nature reserves at Pagham Harbour and Medmerry. The glens of

A groyne on Rye Beach

Hastings Country Park and the chalk downs of Beachy Head and the Seven Sisters provide the only real open countryside before Chichester Harbour, although these spectacularly beautiful areas more than make up for some of the more tedious promenades encountered elsewhere.

Sussex was divided into the two counties of East and West Sussex as late as the Local Government Act of 1972, though the two halves had been administered separately from the twin county towns of Lewes and Chichester since the 19th century because the county was so long. Most of the coast's real drama is contained within East Sussex, which ends at Portslade just west of Brighton, but the whole county is treated as one for the purposes of this chapter.

The Sussex coast is pretty much a straight line east to west though, so you do make quick progress, crossing more than a third of the south coast as the crow flies in just nine days. Only upon reaching the myriad inlets of Chichester Harbour does the route become convoluted as it winds around Chichester, Bosham, Thorney and Emsworth Channels, to reach the Hampshire border at Emsworth. The coast path through Sussex makes use of a few short sections of existing promoted paths – the South Downs Way, Monarch's Way, Lipchis Path and Sussex Border Path – but is a largely new long distance route that makes use of existing footpaths, beaches and promenades. Even before all sections of the route are officially open and signed, it is accessible and generally easy to follow.

Useful Information

Tourist Information – *www.visitsoutheastengland.com*

Southern Rail – 0345 1272920 *(www.southernrailway.com)*

Brighton & Hove Buses – 01273 886200 *(www.buses.co.uk)*

Stagecoach South & South East – 0345 2418000 *(www.stagecoachbus.com)*

Train Times – *traintimes.org.uk*

Bus Times – *bustimes.org*

Traveline – *www.traveline.info*

COUNTY ANTHEM — **Bad Manners** – *Sussex by the Sea*

Written in 1907 by Lancashire-native William Ward-Higgs for his sister-in-law's wedding, this march has become Sussex's unofficial anthem. The title is thought to have been inspired by Rudyard Kipling's poem *Sussex* and versions have been adopted by Sussex County Cricket Club and Brighton & Hove Albion, including this version recorded by the legendary two-tone ska band, some of whose members were Seagulls fans.

Section 3.1 – Rye to Hastings

Distance: 22.9km (14 miles), or 19.5km (12 miles) from Rye Harbour
Height Gained: 440m
Parking: Various pay car parks in Rye and Hastings. Large free car park at Rye Harbour and several places to park free along the seafront between Winchelsea Beach and Pett Level.
Public Transport: The Wave (Buses 100/101, Stagecoach South East, towards Rye) runs regularly from Hastings railway station to Rye 7 days a week.
Refreshments: C-Side Cafe and Cockles & Dreams are close to the route at Pett Level, while the Cove pub in Fairlight Cove and excellent Coastguard Cafe in Fairlight are less than ½ mile from the route.
Accommodation: There are many accommodation options in Hastings, with a Visitor Information Centre (0303 003 8265) by the railway station. Camping is available at Shear Barn Holiday Park (01424 423583) just a few yards off the route at Ecclesbourne Glen.
Overview: A great day of two distinct halves. Once the official route is rejoined at Rye Harbour, it crosses great shingle expanses past Winchelsea Beach and Pett Level to reach the foot of the towering Wealden cliffs. These crumbling sandstone faces form a dramatic series of ridges and glens the rest of the way to Hastings, providing great coast walking even if the views are limited much of the way.

Route Description

There is no official route through Rye, with the England Coast Path restarting at Rye Harbour. It is simple enough to walk out along the road from Rye, though you may prefer to catch the 313 bus to Rye Harbour and save the dull 2-mile trudge. *To reach Rye Harbour, continue along RYE's High Street until it drops down to emerge by the Strand, beyond which lies the River Tillingham. Turn right along the A259 by Rye Heritage Centre and follow the road over Tillingham Bridge. You can follow a riverside path along STRAND QUAY, but after 200m you need to cut right through the garden of the River Haven Hotel to rejoin the main road. Turn next left on Harbour Road, a busy route to Rye Harbour – there is no pavement for the first few yards and this is the reason that no official route exists through Rye. Cross where you can to pick up a pavement along the far side, heading over the RIVER BREDE at Brede Sluice and bending round past the marina. It is now a bit of a slog through the industrial estates and business parks into Rye Harbour, which is reached by the neat Church of the Holy Spirit and the former navigational buoys by Rye Wharf.*

RYE

A268
A259

River Tillingham

B T

P
P

Rye Heritage
Centre

B P

Ypres
Tower

A259

River Brede

River Rother

buoys

Church of
the Holy Spirit

RYE
HARBOUR

B WC
P

Martello
Tower 28

Discovery
Centre

hide

hut

pillboxes

Rye Harbour
Nature Reserve

hide

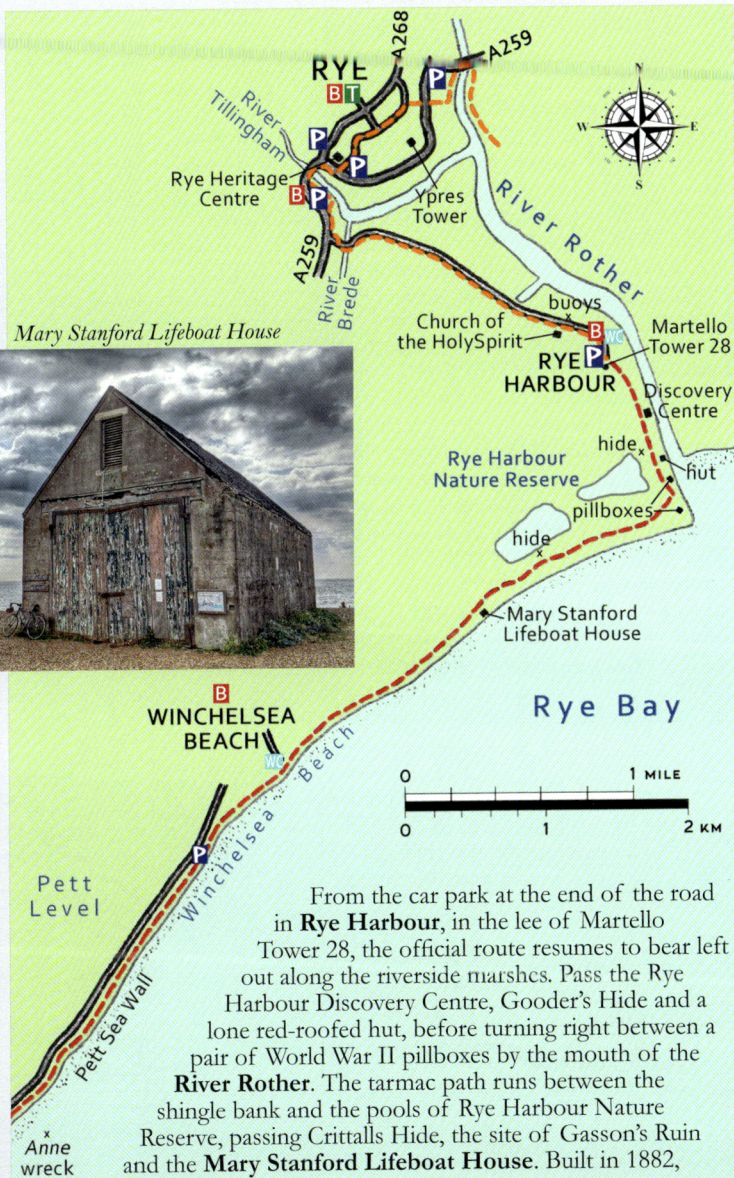

Mary Stanford Lifeboat House

Mary Stanford
Lifeboat House

B
WINCHELSEA
BEACH
WC

Winchelsea Beach

R y e   B a y

0   1 MILE

0   1   2 KM

Pett
Level

Pett Sea Wall

P

Anne
wreck

From the car park at the end of the road
in **Rye Harbour**, in the lee of Martello
Tower 28, the official route resumes to bear left
out along the riverside marshes. Pass the Rye
Harbour Discovery Centre, Gooder's Hide and a
lone red-roofed hut, before turning right between a
pair of World War II pillboxes by the mouth of the
River Rother. The tarmac path runs between the
shingle bank and the pools of Rye Harbour Nature
Reserve, passing Crittalls Hide, the site of Gasson's Ruin
and the **Mary Stanford Lifeboat House**. Built in 1882,

Old Winchelsea

The original settlement of Old Winchelsea stood on a shingle spit now lost beneath the sea, its name relating to the Saxon word *chesil* for a shingle embankment. With a population of thousands, it became one of the Cinque Ports in 1190, but the sea gradually swallowed the town during the 13th century before it was completely destroyed by a storm in 1287. By then, Edward I had granted a charter for the new walled town of Winchelsea that was laid out on a grid pattern on higher ground inland. With a tidal harbour on the River Brede, it retained its Cinque Port status and grew to a population of 6,000, before the harbour began to silt up in the 15th century, leaving it with just 600 inhabitants today.

when the building was 50m further from the sea, the lifeboat house hasn't been used since the *Mary Stanford* was lost in 1928 along with all 17 of its crew, the RNLI's single greatest disaster.

Stay along the back of the shingle bank to reach the edge of **Winchelsea Beach**, where you can bear left up onto the sea wall in a number of places. Stay along the top past the collection of holiday parks that makes up this small settlement, the older port of Winchelsea standing on a sandstone bluff a mile inland. The route follows **Pett Sea Wall** parallel to the road all the way across the reclaimed land of Pett Level, passing the wreck site of the *Anne*, which was burned deliberately after being damaged fighting the French in 1690. Continue past the village of **Pett Level** towards the foot of the sandstone cliffs, then turn right over some steps beyond the caravan park. A path cuts through to join the road by the western end of the defensive line of the **Royal Military Canal**, which you last encountered back near Hythe *(see page 113)*.

Follow the road left for 100m, then turn left into a track just beyond the road junction, following a narrow fenced path between the gardens of **Cliff End** to emerge on the clifftops. Though you don't get a particularly good sense of the cliffs from above, it is a

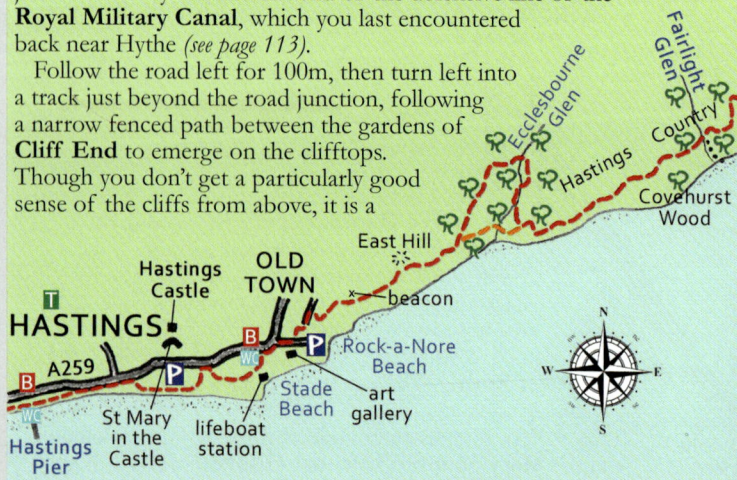

lovely path down towards the edge of **Fairlight Cove**, a series of estates laid out since the 1920s that are in imminent danger of falling into the sea. Follow the fence right, then turn left on a path that joins the end of Lower Waites Lane. After ¼ mile, turn left on Cliff Way, then right on a footpath at its end to cut through to Rockmead Road. Follow this left as it continues round the clifftop estates as a rough track; at its end, the centre of the village is reached to the right, while the route continues left to join Channel Way along the clifftop. A path continues from its end into **Hastings Country Park**, where it is simplest to keep left along the lower path even if the coast path is eventually signed elsewhere. The path climbs steadily towards the radar tower at Fairlight Coastguard Station on **Fairlight Head**, finally offering views over the crumbling sandstone cliffs around Covehurst Bay.

Keep left below the radar tower and descend steeply through the bracken and gorse towards **Warren Glen** (lower), where Exmoor ponies and Belted Galloway cattle graze among the trees. Follow the main path up

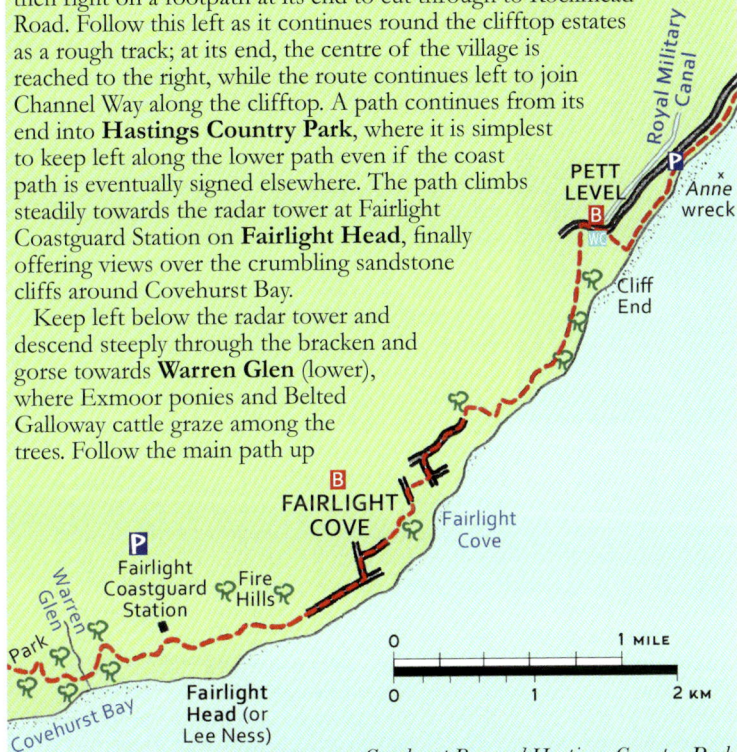

Royal Military Canal

PETT LEVEL

P

Anne wreck

Cliff End

FAIRLIGHT COVE

Fairlight Cove

P Fairlight Coastguard Station

Fire Hills

Warren Glen

Park

Covehurst Bay

Fairlight Head (or Lee Ness)

0   1 MILE

0   1   2 KM

Covehurst Bay and Hastings Country Park

through a gate the other side, ascending the steps to cross a meadow on the next spur, before turning left and descending once more into **Fairlight Glen** (lower). At the bottom, a rough path leads left down to the beach at **Covehurst Bay**, the only place to reach the shore or admire the cliff geology along this section of coast – be aware that this is also a naturists' beach.

The coast path continues on up through the trees towards Ecclesbourne Glen, the steps cutting through a band of sandstone before joining a path along the clifftops. Keep left to reach a viewpoint overlooking the dramatic cliffs around the mouth of **Ecclesbourne Glen**, then cut right and head down the steps, part of the Victorian pathways that were laid out in these glens when visitors flocked to hunt for dinosaur footprints after the first known Iguanodon footprint was found here in 1825.

Fairlight Glen

It is currently possible to follow the steps all the way to the bottom of the glen and climb steeply up the other side, but the possibility of further landslips means the formal coast path will be signed inland. Turn right part way down the steps towards Ecclesbourne Glen (upper) and wind through the dense trees. Cross the stream a couple of times, then climb to a junction, where you turn left and keep left to recross the glen. At the next junction of paths, turn left on a smaller path through the scrub, keeping left to wind around the top of the landslip and rejoin the other route at the top of the steps.

Keep left as the path opens out to climb around the edge of **East Hill**, which has fine views over Hastings and the coast beyond. The banks of a medieval settlement site can be seen in the picnic area on the highest ground, before you descend past the beacon pan to the top of East Hill Cliff Lift and a bird's-eye view over **Hastings Old Town**. Follow the steps down to the town, turning left on the first road to continue down Tamarisk Steps and emerge on the seafront at **Rock-a-Nore** amid the black weatherboarded net shops, where fishermen stored their nets vertically due to a lack of space on the beach. Rock-a-Nore is a contraction of 'Rock against the north', which was not a regional musical alliance but the name given to a shop below the cliffs.

Follow the road right past **Hastings Contemporary Gallery**, then turn left towards the lifeboat station and join a path along the far side of the miniature railway and through the chaos of Hastings' busy beachfront. Rejoining the road, turn immediately left again to follow a walkway along the back of Pelham Beach. **Hastings Castle** stands on the top of West Hill's rocky eminence up to the right, with the former church of **St Mary in the Castle** the centrepiece of a fine crescent built into the cliff below. Rejoin the roadside as far as a subway, which leads under the main road and into the centre of **Hastings**, its railway station just over ¼ mile away.

Hastings

There is much more to Hastings than 1066 – indeed Britain's most famous battle was fought over 5 miles inland at Senlac Hill, near what would become known as Battle. Hastings itself is thought to have been a medieval small market town, though it may originally have been located further west near Bulverhythe and only moved when the Normans built their first castle on West Hill in the years following the battle. They created a 'new burgh' at what is now confusingly Old Town and, with a small harbour protected by the White Rock, it would become one of the Cinque Ports. The town was devastated by the great storm of 1287 and the port never recovered, though attempts were made to create a vast new harbour in the 1890s. By then the town had once again extended westwards along the seafront, following its development as a seaside resort around the railways, which reached St Leonards in 1846 and Hastings in 1851.

SONG OF THE DAY   **John Martyn** – *Dreams By The Sea*

After visiting for several years, Martyn and his wife Beverley moved into a house in Cobourg Place in Hastings Old Town from 1971 to 1976. He released several songs from his most popular albums about his life here, including this song from 1973's *Solid Air* album, as well as hosting his good friend Nick Drake on occasions before his tragic death in 1974.

Hastings Old Town from East Hill

Section 3.2 – Hastings to Eastbourne

Distance: 24.8km (15½ miles)

Height Gained: 70m

Parking: Several pay car parks in Hastings, Bexhill, Pevensey Bay and Eastbourne. Free parking along the seafront at West St Leonards and Cooden Beach.

Public Transport: Buses 98/99 (Stagecoach South East, towards Hastings/Silverhill) run regularly from Eastbourne to Hastings 7 days a week, with the latter stopping opposite Eastbourne Pier.

Refreshments: Various options in Bexhill and Pevensey Bay, with the Cooden Beach Hotel and the Star Inn in Normans' Bay in between.

Accommodation: Eastbourne has a plethora of accommodation options, with a Visitor Centre (01323 415415) at the Welcome Building just inland from the Wish Tower. YHA Eastbourne (0345 3719316) is located on the edge of the downs nearly 2 miles inland, while the closest campsite is at Cannon Camping & Caravan Park (07899 651612), 3 miles before Eastbourne near Pevensey Bay.

Overview: A day of long promenades and shingle beaches that is a taster of things to come in West Sussex. Much of the seafront is built up between Hastings and Bexhill, and between Pevensey and Eastbourne, but there are still quieter sections around Bulverhythe and Normans' Bay. Beyond the low bluffs around Bexhill, the coast flattens out across the Pevensey Levels, but there is plenty of interest along the way, including elegant piers, Martello Towers, Regency architecture and historic wrecks.

Route Description

Rejoin the **Hastings** seafront to reach **Hastings Pier**, which opened in 1872 but was close to being lost before its recent renovation, particularly after much of the structure was damaged by fire in 2010. The promenade beyond divides into a unique twin deck, created in the 1930s and dubbed **Bottle Alley** for the 15 tons of broken bottles used to create the mosaic patterns on the interior walls. It is worth following the lower deck until the routes converge opposite Warrior Square in **St Leonards**, a Regency resort laid out in the 1830s by developer James Burton and centred around the Royal Victoria Hotel. The promenade continues past the bright Goat Ledge cafe and the Art Deco **Marine Court**, built in the 1930s and modelled on the shape of the *Queen Mary* liner. Almost opposite the Royal Victoria Hotel stood St Leonards Pier, but nothing remains of this once-grand structure after it was intentionally severed during World War II to prevent its use by the enemy and removed entirely soon after.

The promenade continues along **Marina Beach** past a Banksy mural of sandcastles made of Tesco bags (on the far side of some steps leading down to the beach from the Marina car park) and the site of the Old Bathing Pool in **West St Leonards**, thought to be the largest in Europe when it opened in 1933. Keep left beyond, joining the Bulverhythe Coastal Link cycleway over the **Combe Haven** stream and through the beach huts beyond. Follow the side of the railway and, opposite the first footbridge, you may see the wreck of the *Amsterdam* in the sand at low tide – this Dutch East India cargo ship was driven aground in a storm in 1749 and sank completely into the sand before slowly re-emerging over the last 50 years.

Stay alongside the railway over a low sandstone bluff to reach **Glyne Gap** (by Ravenside Retail Park on the edge of Bexhill-on-Sea), then ascend the low cliffs once more to pass the coastguard station on **Galley Hill** (the site of a Martello Tower that has fallen into the sea). Follow the road down to join the end of the long Bexhill promenade, keeping left to stay along the seafront past the **De La Warr Pavilion**, a modernist structure that opened as a 'people's palace' in 1935 and was the first building in the country to use a welded steel frame. Bexhill was a small enough village not to have its own station when Earl De La Warr built the first sea wall here in the 1880s and developed **Bexhill-on-Sea** as a high-end

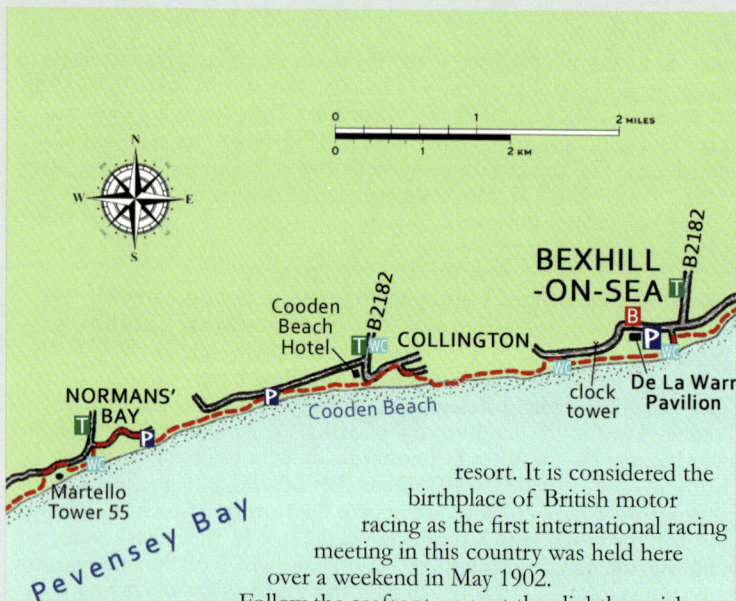

NORMANS' BAY · Cooden Beach Hotel · COLLINGTON · BEXHILL-ON-SEA · B2182 · Cooden Beach · Pevensey Bay · Martello Tower 55 · clock tower · De La Warr Pavilion

resort. It is considered the birthplace of British motor racing as the first international racing meeting in this country was held here over a weekend in May 1902.

Follow the seafront on past the slightly garish **clock tower**, a memorial to the Coronation of Edward VII in 1902. The road starts to head away from the seafront and, just before the bend, the route turns left to join the onward promenade below the low cliffs of **Collington**. At the end of the promenade, briefly join the shingle beach, before heading up the steps to Beaulieu Green and following the road left. Turn left at the end to reach **Cooden Beach Hotel**, in front of which the route rejoins the shingle beach for ½ mile. At low tide, there is firmer sand lower down the beach, but at high tide it can be slow going until you join the side of Herbrand Walk alongside the railway. In summer this area is lined with vans, the route picking its way along the firmer shingle to the seaward side of some

---

The Normans in Sussex

Normans' Bay is disappointingly not the place where the Normans landed 700 ships unopposed on September 28th 1066. This was instead closer to Pevensey, though the coastline would have looked very different then, with extensive marshes instead of the shingle bank that has since built up with eroded material from Beachy Head. William I had built three wooden castles on the coast between Pevensey and Hastings by the time the Battle of Hastings took place just over two weeks after his landing, forever changing the course of English history.

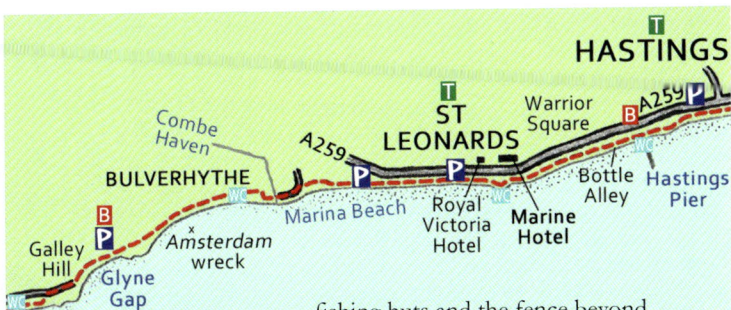

The map at top shows: HASTINGS, ST LEONARDS, BULVERHYTHE, Combe Haven, A259, Warrior Square, A259, Galley Hill, Glyne Gap, Amsterdam wreck, Marina Beach, Royal Victoria Hotel, Marine Hotel, Bottle Alley, Hastings Pier

fishing huts and the fence beyond.

Reaching the houses of **Normans' Bay**, bear right through the small car park to join the road. The tiny hamlet of Normans' Bay is said to have its own railway station because a whale was stranded here in the 19th century and so many people visited from London that a halt had to be created.

At the end of the road, bear left alongside Coast Road past the toilet block, unless you want to rejoin the shingle beach past **Martello Tower 55**. Beyond the next cluster of buildings, the route bears left off the road up onto a firmer shingle bank that ends by the first houses of Pevensey Bay. The beach beyond is private, so you have to drop back down to the road and follow it for a mile past the modernist bungalows of **Beachlands**, an estate laid out in Art Deco style in the 1930s. Finally turn left on Bay Avenue, then follow the Parade right, before joining the back of the shingle beach past the main car park at Pevensey Bay. **Pevensey Bay** is a modern seaside resort a mile seaward of Pevensey Castle and the Roman fort of Anderita, which stood on a limb of land that was once surrounded by saltmarshes.

Beyond the next garden jutting out prominently across the beach, you can head right to join Norman Road, then bear left at its end to round the **Sandcastle** (a large house that has hogged yet more of the beach). *At spring high tides, it may be necessary to follow the alternative route inland along Val Prinseps Road, then keep left on Innings Drive, at the far corner of which a path cuts back through to the beach.* Follow the firm shingle bank for another ½ mile, then bear right beyond Pevensey Bay Sailing Club to join its access road. Keep straight on to join a surfaced path along the back of the broad beach as it passes **Martello Tower 64**. Just beyond lies the wreck of SS *Barnhill*,

Bexhill Clock Tower

a Dutch merchant ship that was bombed near Beachy Head in 1940 by German planes in the first aerial attack of the war, before being dragged aground here.

Reaching **Sovereign Harbour**, turn right around the outer harbour and follow it round to the left to reach the double lock gates at the entrance to the inner harbour. You can usually cross one of the footbridges here, but if the lock is impassable for a while, you'll have to circumnavigate the inner harbour, which can also require waiting for one or more of three further bridges to be lowered. Sovereign Harbour's five basins (Inner, Outer, North, South and West) have all been dug since 1991 on an area of beach formerly known as the Crumbles, providing over 800 moorings and 3,500 homes.

Beyond the lock, follow the promenade round to the harbour entrance by **Martello Tower 66**

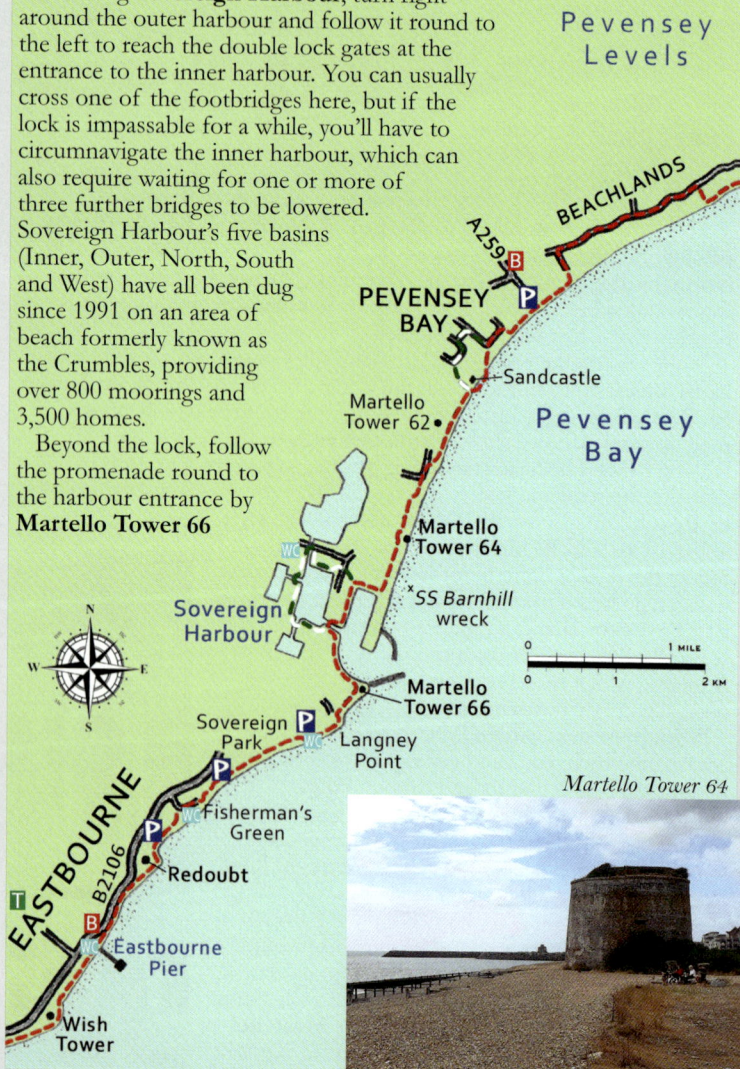

Pevensey Levels

BEACHLANDS

A259

PEVENSEY BAY

Sandcastle

Martello Tower 62

Pevensey Bay

Martello Tower 64

WC

SS Barnhill wreck

Sovereign Harbour

N

0   1 MILE
0   1   2 KM

Martello Tower 66

Sovereign Park

Langney Point

Fisherman's Green

EASTBOURNE

B2106

Redoubt

T

Eastbourne Pier

Wish Tower

Martello Tower 64

and head along the shingle bank beyond. You soon join the end of Eastbourne's promenade at **Langney Point**, passing the redbrick water works and Sovereign Park. After 1 mile a ramp leads down to the road past the huts of Fisherman's Green. Keep left to stay on the cycleway along the busy beachfront past the **Redoubt**, a circular Napoleonic fort built in 1805. The promenade joins the side of Marine Parade to reach Eastbourne's recently renovated **Pier**, a fine structure that was rebuilt in the 1870s after the first effort was swept away. The centre of **Eastbourne** is reached by turning next right on Terminus Road, with the railway and bus stations about ½ mile away.

Eastbourne

Eastbourne was for a long time just a large village at the foot of the downs, from which its stream (the Bourne) rose. Standing a mile inland and with no natural harbour, it only grew substantially after the railway arrived in 1849. The landowners William Cavendish (later to become the Duke of Devonshire) and John Davies Gilbert laid it out as a new town on a grid plan and marketed it as a resort 'for gentlemen by gentlemen'. Eastbourne retains plenty of the elegance and gentility they imagined, with no shops being permitted on the seafront to this day.

SONG OF THE DAY

Kevin Coyne – *Eastbourne Ladies*
From the Derbyshire-born blues rocker's 1973 album *Marjory Razorblade*, this is a scathing portrait of the wealthy older generation in Eastbourne with their hair done nice – 'You're always on your own, sitting on those seaside chairs on your own, nobody seems to care if you flash your underwear'.

Section 3.3 – Eastbourne to Seaford

Distance: 21km (13 miles)

Height Gained: 650m

Parking: Several pay car parks in Eastbourne and along the popular route beyond. Free parking along the Esplanade in Seaford.

Public Transport: Coasters 12A & 12X (Brighton & Hove Buses, towards Eastbourne) run frequently from Seaford town centre to Eastbourne 7 days a week, with a stop on the Eastbourne seafront near the Wish Tower.

Refreshments: The National Trust cafe at Birling Gap is well placed for lunch, with the Saltmarsh Farmhouse Cafe and Cuckmere Inn at Exceat closer to the day's end.

Accommodation: There are various hotels and guest houses in Seaford, with a Tourist Information Centre (01323 897426) on Church Street. Camping is available close to the seafront near the far end of town at Buckle Holiday Park (01323 897801).

Overview: Quite simply the finest day's walking on the south coast, the dizzying chalk cliffs of Beachy Head and the Seven Sisters providing ever-changing dramatic backdrops to this undulating route. Though it is inevitably busy, the long distance walker can usually escape the crowds away from the car parks.

Route Description

Follow **Eastbourne**'s promenade beyond the pier and leave the road to skirt around the seaward side of the **Wish Tower**, one of the only Martello Towers in public ownership. The promenade continues towards the foot of the first white cliffs of the day, before which you bear right up a road to rejoin Duke's Drive. Follow this left past the **Helen Garden** and head straight on at the end, but rather than climbing directly towards Beachy Head, follow a path left along the edge of the heath. Keep left to descend and cross some sports pitches, then continue along the top of the cliffs. A short diversion leads left down some steps to emerge on the pebble shore at **Cow Gap** (the only way to see Beachy Head from below), but the only safe onward route stays on the grass clifftop to climb steeply up to one of the highest points on the English coast. Turn left past the World War II memorial and reach the dizzying cliffs of **Beachy Head** by the site of an old watchtower.

The route is straightforward from Beachy Head, following the broad grassy swathe along the top of the cliffs towards the decommissioned

Beachy Head

Beachy Head

At 531ft Beachy Head is the highest chalk sea cliff in the UK, formed where the steep escarpment of the South Downs meets the sea. Its name is a corruption of the French *beau chef*, meaning 'beautiful headland', and its cliffs are actually far whiter than the White Cliffs of Dover, because they have been allowed to erode naturally rather than being protected by defences (hence becoming discoloured by pollution). The first suicide was recorded here as early as the 7th century, and it still claims around 20 lives a year despite the efforts of regular patrols. Beachy Head also features in the opening and closing scenes of The Who's rock opera *Quadrophenia*, in which Jimmy's bike plunges over the cliffs to be dashed on the rocks below.

lighthouse at **Belle Tout**. Bear right around its walls, then keep left of the gorse to rejoin the cliff-line as it descends steadily towards **Birling Gap**, with the fine outline of the Seven Sisters laid out beyond. At the bend in the road, bear left up a vehicle track past the toilet block and follow the obvious path from its end as it climbs Went Hill, the first of the **Seven Sisters**. It is a joyous romp up and over each of these rolling downland ridges, though by the end you will be cursing the fact that there are eight and not seven hills. This striking landmark was named by mariners and legend has it that the sisters each had a house in one of the valleys, which may explain the apparent miscounting. On the second, Bailey's Hill, there is an obelisk and on the fourth, Flagstaff Brow, there is a sarsen stone memorial to commemorate the purchase of this land by the National Trust in 1926.

Reaching the final hilltop (**Haven Brow**), overlooking the pebble beach and marshy pools of Cuckmere Haven, the route forks right and descends gently across the side of the down. *Though it is possible in most weather to continue straight on down the steeper ground and cross the beach, the shallow Cuckmere River does have to be waded across.* The signed route reaches a large track along the valley bottom, then bears immediately right through the next gate to ascend the side of **Exceat Hill**. Though apparently unnecessary, this climb provides a great view across the meandering Cuckmere River, before gently angling back down to the lower track by the Seven Sisters Country Park Visitor Centre at **Exceat**.

Turn left along the A259 and follow it to cross Exceat Bridge, then turn left in front of the **Cuckmere Inn**. A path continues beyond the car park; bear right where it forks and follow the bottom of the slope back out to **Cuckmere Haven**. Above the buildings, pick up a grassy path along the top of Short Cliff to **Hope Gap** and one of the finest views on the English coast. Continue straight on up the hollow of Cliff Bottom and follow the path along the top of Buckle Church, a curious name possibly related to the Earls of Chichester or the existence of a 14th-century hermitage here.

Beyond **Seaford Head** the land drops down steeply around crumbling chalk cliff faces to the end of Seaford's promenade. Follow it round **Martello Tower 74**, the final one of these Napoleonic defences to be constructed in 1810. After a ¼ mile, Seaford town

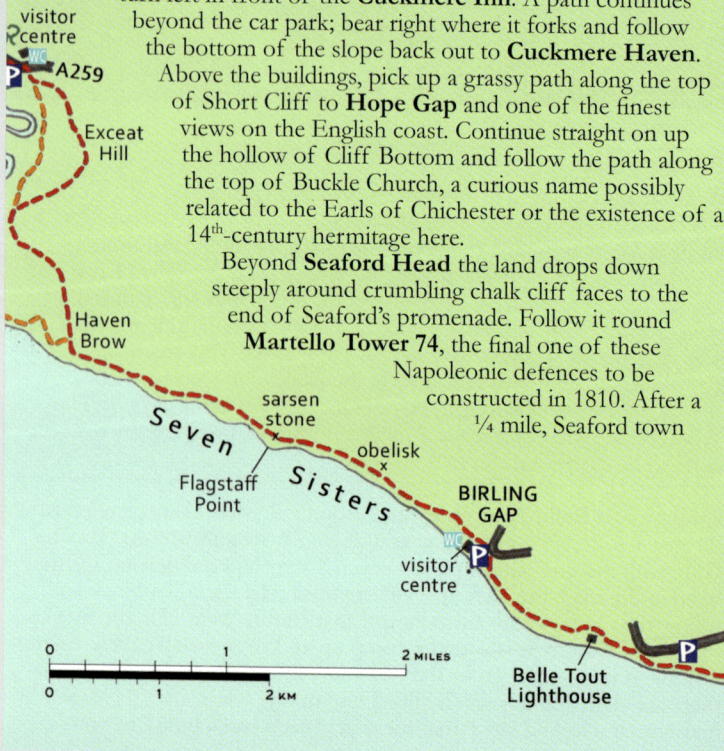

The Seven Sisters from Cuckmere Haven

centre is signed right along West View, with the bus stops and train station just 300m away. **Seaford** was briefly one of the Cinque Ports, giving it enough power to return two Members of Parliament - it subsequently became a rotten borough and was represented by two Prime Ministers, William Pitt (the Elder) and George Canning. It also stood in for the fictional resort of Walmington-on-Sea in the 1971 film spin-off of *Dad's Army*.

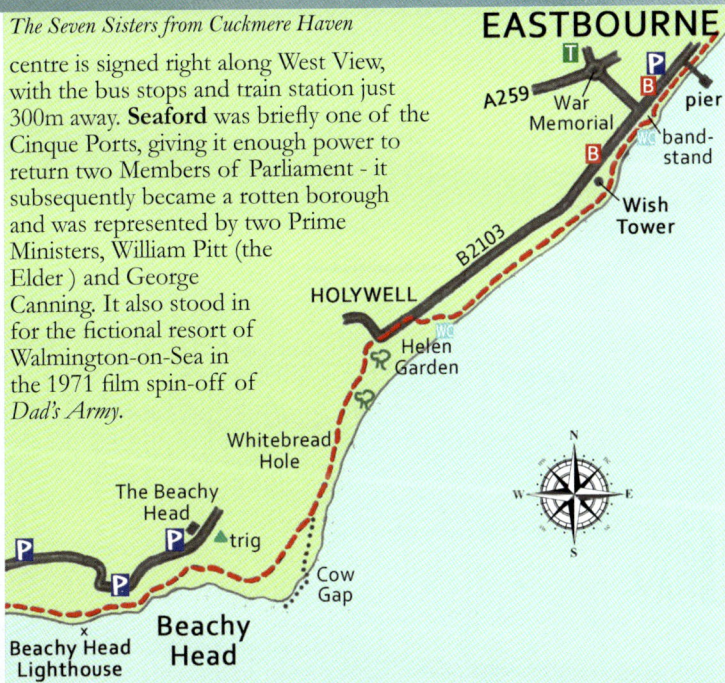

EASTBOURNE

A259

War Memorial

pier

band-stand

Wish Tower

B2103

HOLYWELL

Helen Garden

Whitebread Hole

The Beachy Head

trig

Cow Gap

Beachy Head Lighthouse

Beachy Head

The approach to Seaford from Seaford Head

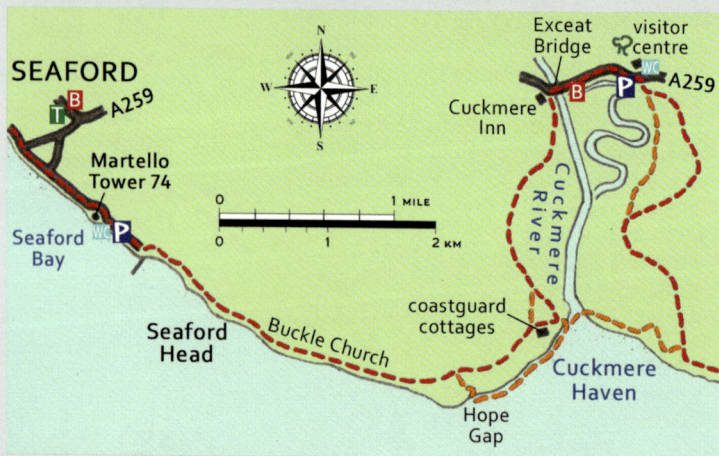

SONG OF THE DAY

Veronica Falls – *Beachy Head*

This 2010 single from the short-lived London indie band is a wonderfully harmonious accompaniment to the dizzying chalk cliffs near Eastbourne. Unlike many of the tragic stories associated with this suicide hotspot, it has a happy ending – 'They're not dead, They saw the waves below, That's no way to go.'

Section 3.4 – Seaford to Brighton

Distance: 20.5km (12½ miles)

Height Gained: 260m

Parking: Various pay car parks in Brighton. Free parking along the Esplanade in Seaford.

Public Transport: Coasters 12/12A/12X (Brighton & Hove Buses, towards Eastbourne/Seaford) run frequently from Brighton seafront to Seaford town centre 7 days a week. Half-hourly trains also run from Brighton station to Seaford.

Refreshments: The Whitecliffs Cafe at Saltdean, Smugglers Rest at Telscombe Cliffs and various places in Peacehaven and Rottingdean are well placed along the route for lunch.

Accommodation: There are numerous hotels and guest houses in Brighton, including dorm rooms at YHA Brighton (0345 3719176), HAPPY Brighton (01273 676826), the Grapevine (07916 775086) and Seadragon Backpackers. The closest campsite is at Brighton Caravan and Motorhome Club Campsite (01273 626546) in Whitehawk, a mile from Brighton Marina. Brighton Visitor Information Point (01273 290337) is near Shelter Hall, 500m beyond Palace Pier.

Overview: What looks like quite an urban day is actually very varied and interesting due to the rolling chalk cliffs from Peacehaven to Black Rock. There are places you can opt to follow the Undercliffs Walk along their foot, though the Greenwich Meridian monument, Rottingdean Windmill and Newhaven Fort provide plenty of interest along the clifftops.

Route Description

Seaford's promenade stays alongside the seafront road until bearing left past the sailing club. Fork left along the line of an old railway behind the beach to reach **Tide Mills**, the footings of whose buildings and mill pond remain among the pebbles. This was a small village that developed around a tidal corn and flour mill, built in 1761. Rundown by the 1930s, its last residents were evicted to allow street fighting training in the lead up to World War II and to accommodate Canadian troops during the war itself.

Continue along the main concrete pathway until the fencing of Newhaven Docks, where the path is forced round to the right. Cross **Mill Creek** (the old course of the River Ouse) and the railway before joining the road through **Newhaven**. Turn left at the end (in the lee of

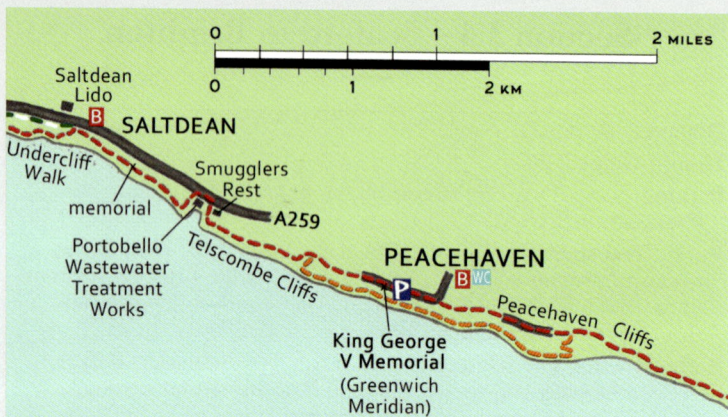

0   1   2 MILES
0   1   2 KM

Saltdean
Lido
B **SALTDEAN**
Undercliff Walk
memorial
Smugglers Rest
A259
Portobello
Wastewater
Treatment
Works
Telscombe Cliffs
PEACEHAVEN
P
B **WC**
Peacehaven Cliffs
King George
V Memorial
(Greenwich
Meridian)

the A259 flyover), crossing the railway by Newhaven Town Station and following the main road over the swing bridge across the **River Ouse**. Keep left beyond (towards West Quay), a footway continuing along the harbour beyond the end of the road. At the end you reach a roundabout and turn left towards **Newhaven Fort**. Bear right off this up Fort Rise and double back sharply just before the entrance to the fort, one of the Palmerston Forts built in the 1860s to defend against a potential attack from France. The **Port of Newhaven** only developed after the arrival of the London, Brighton and South Coast Railway in 1847, the railway company dredging the harbour to allow the cross-channel ferry to Dieppe to be established here.

Pass through the higher car park and join a road briefly, before bearing left through the scrub to emerge high on the natural ramparts of **Castle Hill**, site of a Bronze Age hillfort. There is a series of World War I batteries in the lee of the **Coastwatch lookout**, a great vantage point across Newhaven Harbour and Seaford Bay. The coast path continues along the crumbling cliff edge past the chalets of Newhaven Heights. Keep left along the grassy crest towards the sheer chalk faces and houses of **Peacehaven**. *Though steps lead down the cliffs here and at a couple*

Peacehaven

Peacehaven was laid out on land purchased by entrepreneur Charles Neville in 1916 and was originally known as New Anzac-on-Sea, a name chosen by the public via a competition in the *Daily Express*. With plots offered for just £50, the resort was intended for World War I veterans and many working-class people moved here from London. Initially much of the accommodation was in temporary railway carriages and old army huts, a handful of which survive.

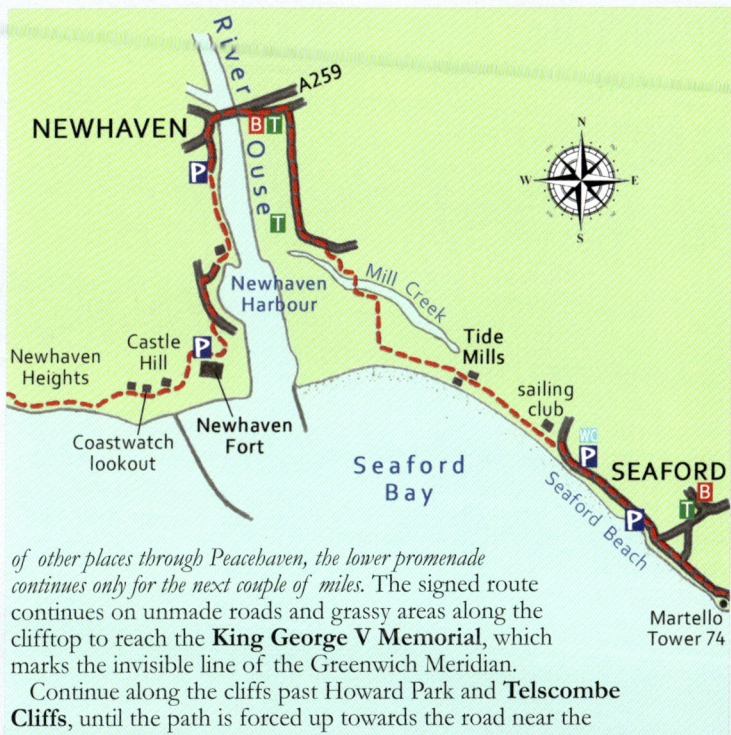

NEWHAVEN

A259

River Ouse

B T

P

Newhaven
Harbour

Mill Creek

Tide
Mills

Castle
Hill

P

Newhaven
Heights

sailing
club

Coastwatch
lookout

Newhaven
Fort

Seaford
Bay

WC
P

SEAFORD

B

Seaford Beach

P

T

Martello
Tower 74

N
W E
S

of other places through Peacehaven, the lower promenade
continues only for the next couple of miles. The signed route
continues on unmade roads and grassy areas along the
clifftop to reach the **King George V Memorial**, which
marks the invisible line of the Greenwich Meridian.

Continue along the cliffs past Howard Park and **Telscombe
Cliffs**, until the path is forced up towards the road near the

Rottingdean Windmill

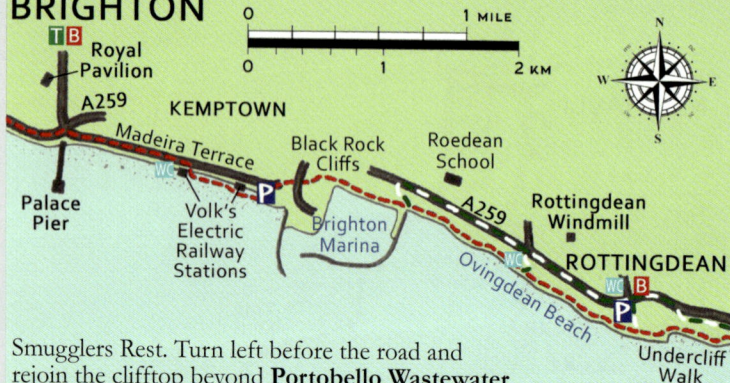

BRIGHTON

Royal Pavilion

A259 **KEMPTOWN**

Madeira Terrace

Black Rock Cliffs

Roedean School

A259

Palace Pier

Volk's Electric Railway Stations

Brighton Marina

Rottingdean Windmill

ROTTINGDEAN

Ovingdean Beach

Undercliff Walk

Smugglers Rest. Turn left before the road and rejoin the clifftop beyond **Portobello Wastewater Treatment Works**, built in 1874 as Brighton's main sewage outfall. After the next memorial, the path descends steadily to **Saltdean**, where steps lead down past the Whitecliffs Cafe to the **Undercliff Walk**, a broad concrete promenade that leads all the way along the foot of the chalk cliffs to **Brighton Marina**.

ALTERNATIVE ROUTE: *If the weather is bad or you prefer to stay along the top of the cliffs for better views, an alternative route climbs back up onto the next clifftop rise. This joins the main road to descend into* ROTTINGDEAN, *before picking a path up again just beyond the car park. Rottingdean's main feature is* ROTTINGDEAN WINDMILL *(or Beacon Mill), which was built on Beacon Hill in 1802 to grind flour and has been restored from a dilapidated state since the 1920s – it is well seen from the higher route and is just a short diversion from it. The cliffs continue to rise and fall as the alternative route follows the A259 past Ovingdean and Roedean, the latter dominated by* ROEDEAN SCHOOL's *grand buildings. Soon after, turn left opposite Roedean Cafe and follow a concrete track down the cliff to rejoin the lower route by Brighton Marina.*

Stay along the bottom of the cliffs to the far end of the marina, where **Black Rock Cliffs** mark the abrupt end of the chalk cliffs and younger rocks take over. Bear left beneath the road out to the marina, then join the start of Brighton's long promenade. Initially there is a path along the beach side of **Volk's Electric Railway**, the oldest operational electric railway in the world, built by Magnus Volk in 1883. At the second station, cross the tracks and join the road along the foot of the beautiful but dilapidated arches along Madeira Terrace, created in the 1890s to attract tourists to Brighton.

You soon reach the iconic **Brighton Palace Pier**, built as a pleasure pier but nearly destroyed before it opened by the 1896 storm that took out Brighton's first pier, the Royal Suspension Chain Pier. Turn right

The Royal Pavilion

This remarkable building began life as a modest farmhouse, which was rented as lodgings by the Prince of Wales (the future George IV). In 1787, after his debts were wiped out by Parliament, it became one wing of a far larger classical villa known as the Marine Pavilion. Once he had become Prince Regent, George employed John Nash to transform this into the lavish Oriental-inspired edifice we see today. It took seven years to complete from 1815-1822 and was widely ridiculed as 'a little Kremlin', but it was frequently used by royals until Queen Victoria sold it to the town as she found it cramped and ostentatious.

opposite the pier to head into the centre of Brighton via the **Royal Pavilion** and its famous Lanes shopping area. The station is about ⅔ mile from the seafront. **Brighton**, its name referring to an Old English name Beorhthelm, was a declining fishing settlement when the health benefits of drinking, and dipping in, seawater were popularised in the late 18th century. It quickly developed into a fashionable Georgian resort that was frequented by royalty and many of the celebrities of the day.

SONG OF THE DAY

Queen – *Brighton Rock*

Recorded in 1974 for their third album *Sheer Heart Attack*, this is a song for the seaside about a doomed holiday romance in Brighton between Jenny and Jimmy. It is most famous for Brian May's guitar solo, which predated the song and is considered one of the greatest of all time.

The Royal Pavilion, Brighton

Section 3.5 – Brighton to Worthing

Distance: 21.4km (13½ miles)

Height Gained: 20m

Parking: Various pay car parks in both Brighton and Worthing, as well as several seafront places in between.

Public Transport: There are regular trains between Worthing and Brighton, though the 700 Bus (Stagecoach South, towards Brighton), running every 15 minutes 7 days a week, stops right on the seafront in both towns and saves the additional walk to/from the railway stations.

Refreshments: Carats Café Bar at Southwick, or various cafes and pubs either side of the Adur Ferry Bridge in Shoreham.

Accommodation: There are numerous hotels and guest houses in Worthing, which has a Visitor Information Line (01903 221066). The closest camping is at the Barn Caravan Park (07801 694064), close to the seafront in South Lancing, 3 miles before Worthing.

Overview: The most urban day on the Sussex coast, linking the two grand regency resorts of Brighton and Worthing. There are some fine sections of Victorian promenade through Hove and Worthing and long expanses of shingle beach, but the route becomes more industrial as you negotiate Portslade and Shoreham Harbour.

Route Description

From **Brighton Palace Pier** follow the roadside until a path leads down to the shingle beach to pass the rebuilt Shelter Hall, originally a Victorian rotunda. Very little remains of Brighton's **West Pier** in an area now dominated by the 450ft-high British Airways i360 experience. The 1150ft-long pier was constructed three decades before the Palace Pier but, after a long period of neglect, two fires in 2003 destroyed the pavilion and concert hall. Only a skeleton remains, around which starlings dance beautifully at dusk.

The promenade widens to a motorway as it passes **Hove Lawns**, part of the Victorian esplanade that was laid out partly as a coastal defence. The beach here had been much broader and more sandy before ferocious storms removed much of the material in the 19th century. **Hove** was a small fishing village with a reputation for smuggling and, when its first large Regency houses were built, developers were loath to use the name Hove. Ironically it is now famed for the phrase 'Hove, actually', used to distinguish it from Brighton and reputed to have been coined by resident Laurence Olivier.

Brighton Palace Pier

Continue along the Western Esplanade to **Hove Lagoon**, beyond which you turn right and join the road leading left through the industrial estates of **Portslade**. As the road follows a more remote part of the seafront, there are a couple of sections where you can walk along rough ground above the beach. You pass uneventfully from East to West Sussex as **Shoreham Power Station** dominates the scene, a gas-fired station opened in 2000 on the site of an earlier coal-fired station.

The promenade returns beyond the power station but, as you near the wind turbines at the entrance to **Shoreham Harbour**, you turn right off it and follow a footway over a series of bridges across the harbour. Emerging from the industrial estate, follow the main road left through **Southwick**. It is over 1½ miles into Shoreham, with the only break from this ugly road being a brief detour left by Kingston Beach to pass

---

River Adur

The River Adur, once navigable as far inland as Bramber and Steyning, originally joined the Arun to enter the sea at Lancing. In the 15th century the shingle bank shifted and the two rivers diverged to break through separately at Shoreham and Littlehampton, but the entrance to Shoreham Harbour was only firmed up in the mid 19th century and its breakwaters built in the 1950s. Originally known as the River Bramber or River Sore (from which Shoreham is derived), its current name is thought to have arisen after a misinterpretation of the location of the Roman port of Portus Adurni (now thought to have been Portchester).

Map labels (reading across the map):

N

River Adur

🅃 SHOREHAM
-BY-SEA

Shoreham
Lighthouse

🅱

🅿

🅿

🅿 WC

Brooklands
Pleasure
Park

🅃 SOUTH
LANCING

Widewater
Lagoon

🅃 WORTHING

A259

🅿
🅱 WC

🅱 🅿

Onslow
Court

Lancing
Sailing
Club

WC

Church
of the Good
Shepherd

Shoreham Beach

Shoreham
Fort

Steyne
Gardens

Worthing
Pier

Shoreham Power Station © Paul Gillett

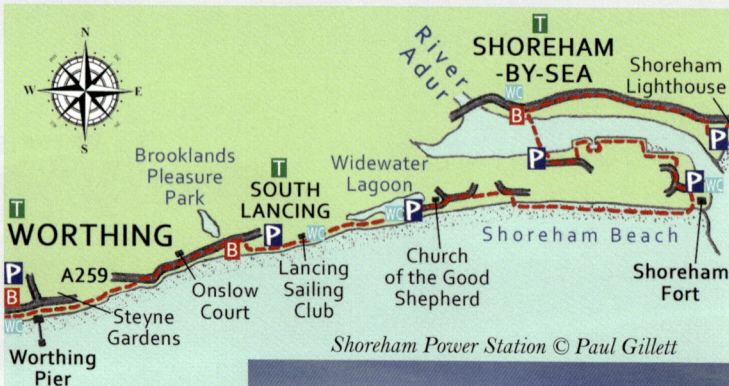

**Shoreham Light-
house** and the lifeboat
station at the mouth
of the River Adur.

Reaching the busy
centre of **Shoreham-
by-Sea**, turn left over
the **Adur Ferry
Bridge**, a new
structure built in 2013 to replace the original 1921 footbridge to
Shoreham Beach. Bear left along Riverside Road for 300m, then turn
left at Emerald Quay to join a walkway alongside the river. After
winding around the small marina, it continues along Sussex Wharf
before bending inland. Cut left through a gap to follow another
shorefront walkway until it ends by Shoreham Sailing Club. Join the
road bending round to the right here, then turn left along Forthaven and
keep right of **Shoreham Fort** to join a plastic boardwalk across the
beach. The fort was built in 1857 as part of the Palmerston Defences
and features a Carnot wall, a separate defensive wall behind which
soldiers could hide and fire upon invaders.

The boardwalk continues along **Shoreham Beach** for over a mile as
the coast arcs round towards Worthing Pier. By the start of a line of
rocky groynes, the path joins Beach Road briefly and keeps left to
continue along the back of the beach and pass the Church of the Good
Shepherd. West Beach Road ends by **Widewater Lagoon**, which was
part of the original course of the River Adur but is now separated by a
man-made shingle bank to protect the area from flooding.

A lovely promenade continues along the shingle bank, with great

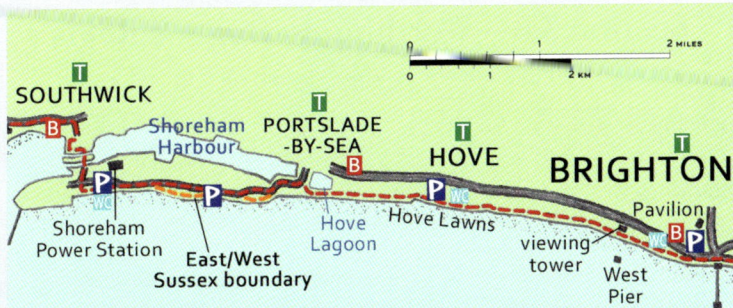

views across the water towards the extravagant chapel of Lancing College. Follow it past Lancing Sailing Club and along the back of **Lancing Beach**, before joining the A259. Pass Brooklands Pleasure Park, originally a 1950s leisure complex with boat rides and a miniature railway, and the houses of **East Worthing**, before bearing left on a broad promenade. This continues alongside Marine Parade past Steyne Gardens to reach **Worthing Pavilion Theatre** and **Pier** at the heart of **Worthing**'s grand regency seafront, the town having become a fashionable resort in the early 19th century. Buses stop at Worthing Lido just beyond and the town centre is reached to the right, with the railway station just under a mile inland.

SONG OF THE DAY

The Kooks – *Seaside*

The Kooks formed in Brighton in 2004 and were signed to Virgin Records within 4 months. This innocent song about falling in love at the seaside forms the prologue to the band's debut album *Inside In / Inside Out*.

The remains of Brighton's West Pier

Section 3.6 – Worthing to Bognor Regis

Distance: 24.8km (15½ miles)

Height Gained: 20m

Parking: Pay car parks in Worthing, Bognor Regis, Littlehampton and most places in between. Free parking along Marine Drive by Goring Greensward.

Public Transport: There are regular trains from Bognor Regis to Worthing but you have to change trains at either Barnham or Littlehampton. The 700 Coastliner (Stagecoach South, towards Littlehampton) runs regularly 7 days a week from Bognor Regis High Street to Worthing seafront, though you change buses to another 700 service (towards Brighton) in Littlehampton and it is generally slower than the train.

Refreshments: Various places on the way into Littlehampton or West Beach cafe on the west side of the River Arun.

Accommodation: There are various options in Bognor Regis, with the information centre at Love Bognor (01243 778600) in the Arcade. Rowan Park Caravan and Motorhome Club Site (01243 828515) is 1½ miles from the centre of Bognor, but only a short bus ride away.

Overview: Another day of long promenades and shingle beaches, but with rather more variety than the last. The greenery of Goring Gap and Climping Gap breaks up the urban walking, while the private estates of Kingston, East Preston and Middleton-on-Sea provide generous greenswards along the back of the beaches. There is a brief detour from the shore to cross the River Arun in Littlehampton, but otherwise this is a direct line from one grand pier to the next.

Route Description

Rejoin the promenade at **Worthing Pier** and continue past the **Lido**, which was open from 1925 to 1988 and is now a family amusement attraction. The broad promenade continues past West Worthing to Goring-by-Sea, where a lovely greensward lies inland and the path picks its way through the tamarisk behind the shingle beach. The **Goring Gap** represents the first break in development along the seafront this side of Brighton and is an important feeding site for migrating birds.

As the houses resume at **Ferring**, the route joins Patterson's Walk along Ferring Beach. Keep right of the Bluebird Cafe to enter the Kingston Gorse Estate, following a pleasant grassy sward on into the

West Kingston Estate, one of the private residential enclaves that dominate this part of the West Sussex coast. A stone commemorates the 12th-century **Kingston Chapel**, which was lost to the sea by the early 17th century along with part of the village of Kingston; its bells are said to still toll far out beneath the waves.

By public toilets at the far end of the greensward you have to join **East Preston Beach** for almost ½ mile, until you can cut right and join South Walk, another broad grassy path past the Willowhayne Estate. Keep along the left side of this until a concrete walkway resumes and leads round to join the B2140 along the **Rustington** seafront. Follow the road past Rustington Convalescent Home, a neo-Caroline mansion built in 1897 for working men to recover after accidents or illnesses. Beyond Mewsbrook Park, the promenade bears left away from the road along Littlehampton's **East Beach**. Pass Britain's longest bench to reach

---

Worthing Pier

The 960ft-long pier opened in 1862, with a pavilion added at its end in 1889, and paddle steamers from Brighton regularly stopped alongside it. When a storm severed the pier on Easter Monday 1913, the stranded pavilion was nicknamed Easter Island. After reopening, the pavilion was burnt down in 1933 and the pier partially blown up during World War II to prevent the Germans using it as a potential landing stage. The 1926 Pavilion Theatre and the restored Art Deco Southern Pavilion now bookend this fine structure.

Worthing Pavilion Theatre and Pier

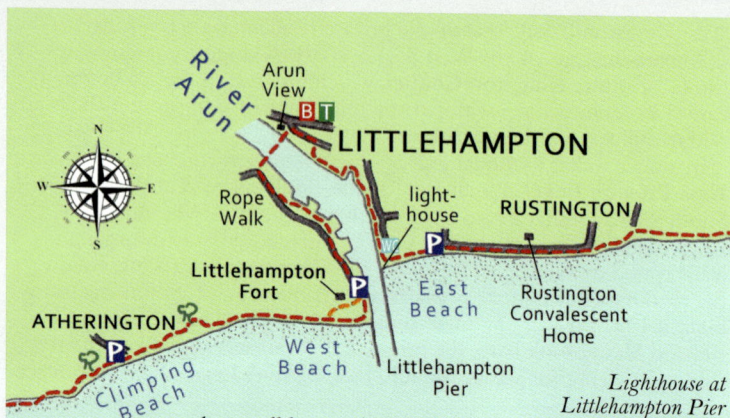

River Arun

Arun View

B T

LITTLEHAMPTON

Rope Walk

light-house

RUSTINGTON

P

Littlehampton Fort

P

ATHERINGTON

P

East Beach

Rustington Convalescent Home

West Beach

Littlehampton Pier

Climping Beach

Lighthouse at Littlehampton Pier

the small but striking lighthouse at Littlehampton Pier. The walkway bends right to run alongside the River Arun into **Littlehampton**, which developed as a port after the silting up of the River Arun towards the ancient port of Arundel. It was known as Hampton until the 17th century, when it was renamed to distinguish it from Southampton, but only grew from a small settlement after the late 18th century.

Stay along the river bank until you are forced to join the road alongside. Follow this to the Arun View Inn, where a footbridge crosses the **River Arun**, having replaced a swing bridge on this site in 1981. Prior to this, a notoriously rickety chain ferry was the only way to cross the river to the shipyards and former ropewalk on the west bank. Follow the road left and then bear left onto a footpath by the start of the private road to **West Beach**. Pass the various wharves along the riverside before rejoining the road by Arun Yacht Club to reach the car park at its end. The route continues straight

The March of the Sea

The West Sussex coast is more fragile than it appears but, even though there are no crumbling cliffs, the flux of its constantly shifting shingle has wreaked havoc on many coastal villages. The small port of Cudlow (near the breakwater at Poole Place) and the hamlet of Islham were lost by the 17th century, with the old church in Middleton surviving until the 19th century. Much of the hamlet of Atherington has also disappeared and the high wooden groynes along Climping Beach were badly damaged during storms in winter 2020.

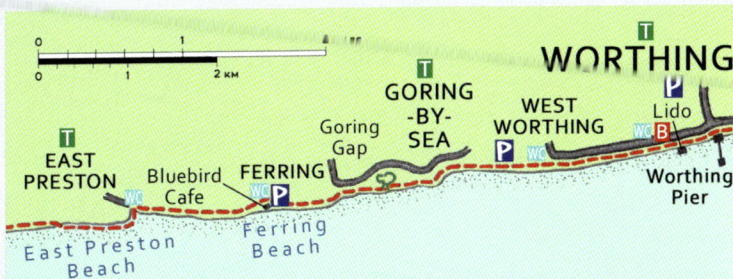

WORTHING

GORING
-BY-
SEA

WEST
WORTHING

Lido

Goring
Gap

FERRING

EAST
PRESTON

Bluebird
Cafe

Worthing
Pier

East Preston
Beach

Ferring
Beach

on to join the back of the beach, *but a walkway right climbs through the dunes to give good views of the Napoleonic redoubt of* LITTLEHAMPTON FORT *before joining the beach.* The next couple of miles are known as the **Climping Gap**, a broad undeveloped part of the coast that was used to practice for the D-Day Landings and is now important for migrating birds. A path soon runs through the grass behind the beach to reach a vehicle track, which you follow left to reach the car park at **Climping Beach** by the hamlet of Atherington.

At the far end of the car park, pick up a path through the trees, then keep left along the edge of a long field before dropping down to join the back of the beach. If you continue to the far end you'll have to scramble over the concrete sea defences to get onto the beach. Follow **Elmer Beach** past the first few of a series of offshore rock break-waters that protect this fragile coast, before the path bears right down to the road. Follow Manor Way left through **Elmer** and turn left on a narrow path beyond the Cabin pub to rejoin the beach. At first the going is good, but then you have to plod heavily through the shingle past the houses of **Middleton-on-Sea**. Shortly before Middleton Point, turn right on a pathway back to the road and keep left to return to the beach beyond the point. A good path follows the back of the beach

The River Arun in Littlehampton

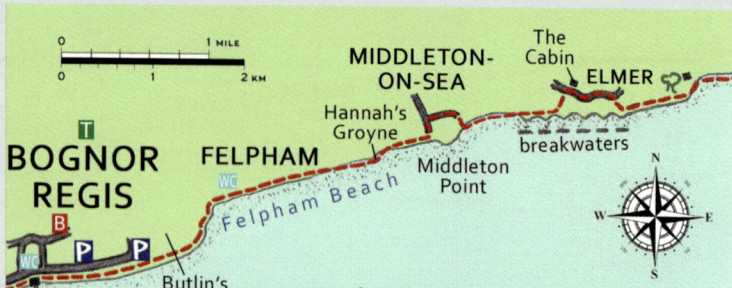

BOGNOR REGIS — FELPHAM — MIDDLETON-ON-SEA — ELMER — The Cabin — Hannah's Groyne — Middleton Point — Felpham Beach — breakwaters — Butlin's Bognor — Bognor Pier

round to the next point on the Summerley Estate, where the breakwater of **Hannah's Groyne** marks the site of a Napoleonic signal station. Continue along the pathway to soon join Bognor Regis Promenade, which runs for nearly 2 miles into the centre of the town. It is a pleasant route that is free of traffic as it passes **Felpham** and a collection of fascinating bungalows near the point that are built around railway carriages. Continue past the large Butlin's camp to reach **Bognor Pier**, which opened in 1865 but is now 80ft shorter, having been badly damaged by storms in the 1960s and 1999. The centre of **Bognor Regis** is reached by turning right here or by the beacon just before, the railway station reached ½ mile away and buses stopping on the High Street. Bognor (the Regis only appended in 1929) is named after a female Saxon chieftain called Bucga, but was a relatively insignificant place until Sir Richard Hotham developed it as a fashionable Regency bathing place known as Hothampton in the late 18th century.

Butlin's Bognor

Butlin's in Bognor Regis began in 1932 as an amusement park near the town centre called Butlin's Recreation Shelter, with a zoo added nearby the following year. The far larger holiday camp opened in 1960 at a new site to the east, with what were considered the 'unsightly' zoo and amusement park moved out of the town centre. It has since been revamped several times and is one of only three remaining Butlin's, its helter skelter water slide the only one of its kind in the world.

SONG OF THE DAY

Luke Haines – *Bugger Bognor*

An epic seaside song from The Auteurs and Baader Meinhof songwriter, taken from his 2003 album *Das Capital*. Rather than being King George V's dying words, the phrase is thought to have been uttered by him after he was asked to bestow the suffix Regis upon the town after he had been taken there to recover from lung surgery in 1929.

Section 3.7 - Bognor Regis to Selsey

Distance: 18.2km (11½ miles)

Height Gained: 20m

Parking: Pay car parks in Bognor Regis, Selsey and several places in between, with free car parks at RSPB Pagham Harbour, Church Norton and the end of Grafton Road in Selsey.

Public Transport: Bus 51 (Stagecoach South, towards Chichester) runs from Selsey to Chichester bus station, from where you can catch the Coastliner 700 (Stagecoach South, towards Littlehampton/Flansham) to Bognor Regis High Street. Both buses run regularly 7 days a week.

Refreshments: Pagham Beach Cafe and other nearby outlets in Pagham, but there is little between here and Selsey other than the Crab & Lobster at Sidlesham Quay.

Accommodation: Rooms are available in Selsey at Vincent Lodge (01243 602985), the Seal (01243 608989), the Coast Yard Hotel (01243 606899) and Greenacre (01243 602912). The closest campsite is not far off the route at Warner Farm Touring Park (01243 606080), just beyond Selsey near RSPB Medmerry.

Overview: A shorter but more varied day, with the long shingle beaches of Bognor and Selsey divided by the great inlet of Pagham Harbour. This offers an abundance of wildlife and lots of historical interest at Sidlesham Quay, Church Norton and the former Selsey Tramway.

Route Description

The promenade continues west along the **Bognor** seafront, passing the Royal Norfolk Hotel, a striking Georgian edifice built in 1829. It eventually runs out as you join the road alongside to enter **Aldwick** and a series of private residential estates. Turn left along High Trees and follow the road round to a footpath leading left alongside Aldwick Hundred. Follow the shingle of **Aldwick Beach** for a mile, the going being easier on the sand lower down when the tide is out. You can continue along the beach past **Pagham**, but the route heads inland level with the second pipe outfall on the beach to join the end of East Front Road. After bearing left on a dead-end road after ½ mile, you cut through to another rough road and follow it right to join Harbour Road, which leads left out of Pagham to the car park at **Pagham Harbour**.

Turn right near the far end of the car park and follow a gravel path between the sea and **Pagham Lagoon**, formed by shifting shingle around the mouth of the former harbour. Keep left around the shore

Map labels

Halsey's Farm

SIDLESHAM QUAY

Cod & Lobster

North Wall

Bremere Rife

Pagham Rife

Salthouse

PAG

Pagham Lagoon

B2145

hide

Selsey Tramway

Mill Channel

Ferry Channel

Ferry Pool

P a g h a m   H a r b o u r

Pagham Spit

Pagham

Church Norton Spit

St Wilfrid's Church

Church Norton Mound

hide

CHURCH NORTON

Norton Priory

Greenlease Farm

EAST BEACH

WC

SELSEY

B2145

WC

lifeboat station

WC

Bill House

Selsey Beach

Selsey Bill

Scale

0   1   2 MILES

0   1   2 KM

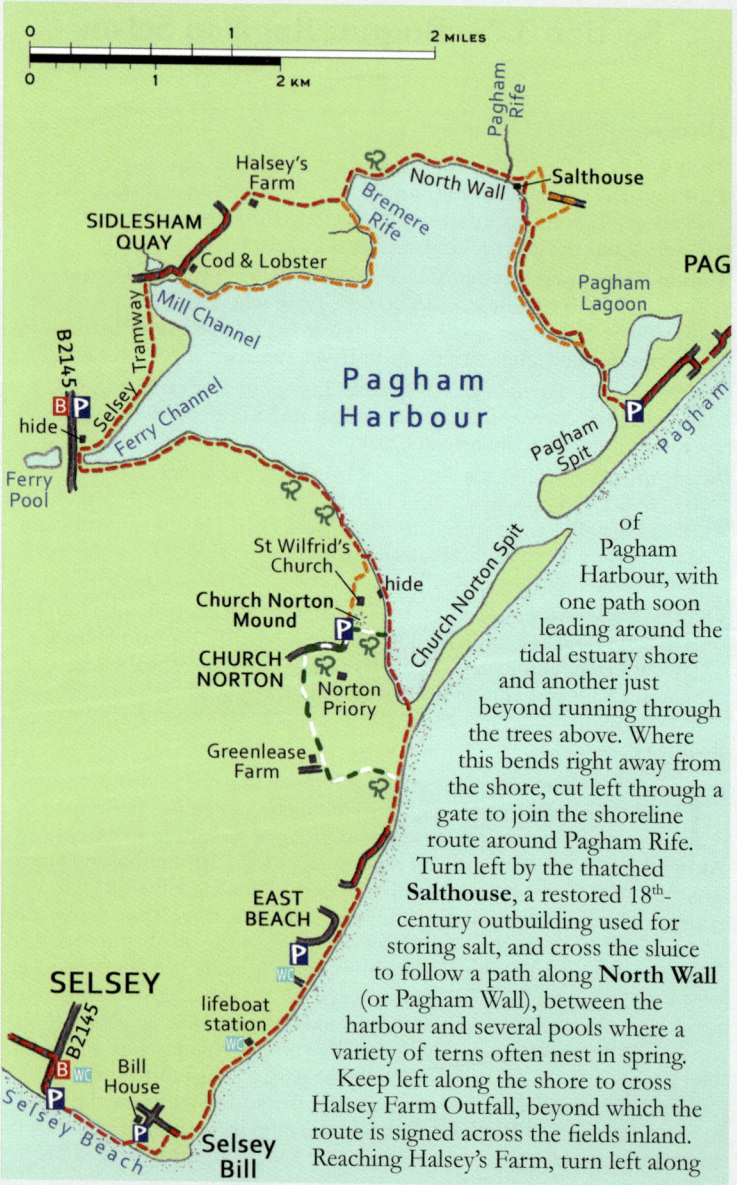

of Pagham Harbour, with one path soon leading around the tidal estuary shore and another just beyond running through the trees above. Where this bends right away from the shore, cut left through a gate to join the shoreline route around Pagham Rife. Turn left by the thatched **Salthouse**, a restored 18th-century outbuilding used for storing salt, and cross the sluice to follow a path along **North Wall** (or Pagham Wall), between the harbour and several pools where a variety of terns often nest in spring. Keep left along the shore to cross Halsey Farm Outfall, beyond which the route is signed across the fields inland. Reaching Halsey's Farm, turn left along

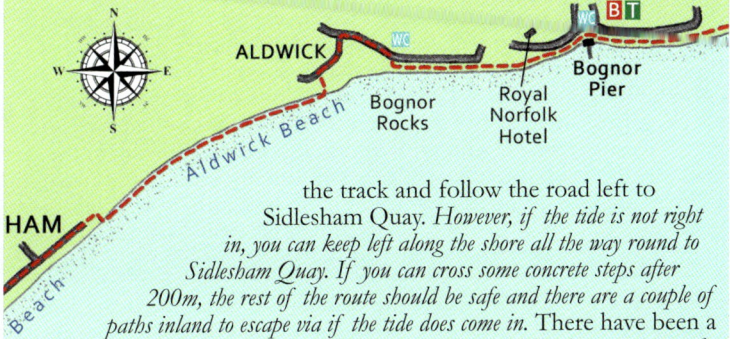

ALDWICK

Bognor
Rocks

Royal
Norfolk
Hotel

Bognor
Pier

HAM

Aldwick Beach

Beach

the track and follow the road left to Sidlesham Quay. *However, if the tide is not right in, you can keep left along the shore all the way round to Sidlesham Quay. If you can cross some concrete steps after 200m, the rest of the route should be safe and there are a couple of paths inland to escape via if the tide does come in.* There have been a series of mills at **Sidlesham Quay** since the Middle Ages, powered by the tidal mill pond on the other side of the road, with the last mill building pulled down after the harbour was sealed off in the 1870s.

Follow the road briefly beyond the quay, then turn left along the shore, following the only raised section of the **Selsey Tramway** line, a notoriously rickety light railway. At the end, turn left by one of the hides for RSPB Pagham Harbour, crossing the sluice by Ferry Pool and following a path left alongside **Ferry Channel**. The path winds around the western shore of Pagham Harbour, briefly joining the shingle before bearing right on a path through the trees alongside. The route then cuts left down some steps to follow the shore past **Church Norton Hide** and reach the broad shingle spit at the far end of Pagham Harbour.

ALTERNATIVE ROUTE: *The high tide alternative continues inland towards Church Norton past ST WILFRID'S CHURCH, a tiny chapel of ease that was in use until 1990. Alongside you can see the impressive earthworks of a Norman castle known as CHURCH NORTON MOUND. Follow the road from the car park, passing Norton Priory before turning left on Pigeon House Farm Lane. Follow the track past the farm and, where it bends right by Greenlease Farm, continue straight on for 100m, then turn left across the open field. The path cuts through the trees to rejoin the main route on the shingle beach.*

Follow the most defined route through the shingle until it joins the end of a road on the edge of Selsey. Stay on the gravel road until a tarmac promenade begins alongside, following the beautiful sheltered shore on this side of the headland. Continue past **Selsey Lifeboat Station** and round the

St Wilfrid's Church in Church Norton

Pagham Harbour

Pagham Harbour is a large tidal inlet whose shelter was an important Roman harbour, with three separate ports developing subsequently at Pagham (known as Wythering), Sidlesham Quay (known as Wardur) and Church Norton (known as Charlton and the site of the original fishing community of Selsey). Wythering had silted up by the 14th century and now forms Pagham Lagoon, with the other ports succumbing to the mud much later. An attempt was made to turn the area into farmland in 1876 by creating an embankment across the seaward side, but this was broken by a storm in 1910 and the tidal flats have since been abandoned to the birds, the site becoming an RSPB reserve in 2012.

front towards Selsey Bill, where the swirling tide races past dangerously.

Follow a path right before the headland to join Oval Lane, then cut left alongside the park to rejoin the shore the other side. Follow the shingle beach round the corner from near the Arts and Crafts-style **Bill House** to reach the car park at Selsey Beach. The route follows the B2145 inland, soon passing a bus stop; the small town centre is reached beyond. **Selsey** was cut off from the mainland at high tide until land reclamation in the 18th century and reached only by a 'wadeway' across the tidal marshes. Its name meaning 'island of seals', Selsey is thought to have been an important settlement site in the Palaeolithic era and Iron Age, before becoming the capital of the Kingdom of Sussex in the Dark Ages.

SONG OF THE DAY — **Eric Coates** – *By the Sleepy Lagoon*

This song was composed by Eric Coates in 1930 and was inspired by the view from the beach at Selsey towards Bognor Regis. Already a popular orchestral tune, it became the theme song to the BBC's *Desert Island Discs* for its first programme on the Forces Network in 1942, and continues in use to this day.

The tranquil Selsey scene that inspired 'By the Sleepy Lagoon'

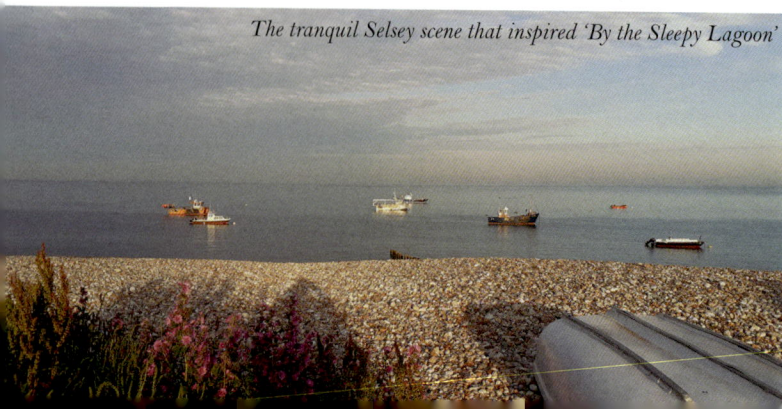

Section 3.8 – Selsey to Bosham

Distance: 25.4km (16 miles), or 35.3km (22 miles) via alternative route if the Itchenor Ferry isn't running

Height Gained: 20m, or 60m via alternative route

Parking: Pay car parks in Selsey, Bosham and several other places along the route. Small free car parks at RSPB Medmerry near Almodington, and close to the alternative route at Apuldram.

Public Transport: Bus 56 (Stagecoach South, towards Chichester) runs every 1½ hours Mon-Sat from the car park in Bosham to Chichester Cathedral, where you can catch the more regular Bus 51 (Stagecoach South, towards Selsey) to Selsey. For a more regular service and on Sundays you can continue a mile beyond Bosham to the A259 and catch the Coastliner 700 (Stagecoach South, towards Chichester).

Refreshments: Various options in Bracklesham Bay, East Wittering and West Wittering Beach, as well as the Quarterdeck cafe and Ship Inn in West Itchenor.

Accommodation: Rooms are available in Bosham at the Millstream Hotel (01243 573234) and Windward House (01243 574929). If following the alternative route, rooms in Fishbourne can be found at the Bull's Head (01243 839895) and Ingleside B&B (01243 780160). The closest campsites to Bosham are on the alternative route, at the Under the Stars Campsite (07340 011834) and Applegarth Camping & Caravaning (01243 782043) in Fishbourne.

Overview: A long but rewarding exploration of the Manhood Peninsula and parts of Chichester Harbour. Beyond the newly created RSPB reserve at Medmerry, the beaches of Bracklesham Bay, East and West Wittering take over until East Head at the mouth of Chichester Harbour. The route along the wooded estuary shore beyond is magical, with the main route continuing via the Itchenor Ferry to the picturesque village of Bosham. When the ferry isn't running (weekdays from Oct-Apr), the alternative route has several further beautiful sections, blending the estuary shore with open fields, but it is a long way round via Fishbourne. If following this route, I would advise shortening the day slightly by ending at Fishbourne, extending the previous day considerably to Bracklesham Bay or East Wittering, or even splitting this section in two at West Wittering.

Route Description

Rejoining the route on the B2145 away from the seafront at **Selsey**

The map shows the area around East Head, Ella Nore Spit, West Wittering, East Wittering, Cakeham Manor House, and Brackles Bay, with the coast path marked.

Labels on map:
- Ella Nore Spit
- East Head
- Ella Nore Lane
- WEST WITTERING
- The Hinge
- West Wittering Beach
- Cakeham Manor House
- EAST WITTERING
- East Wittering Beach
- BRAC
- Brackles Bay
- 0 1 MILE
- 0 1 2 KM

Medmerry Windmill

Beach, turn first left along Clayton Road and follow it round to its end. Turn left along West Street, then go right along a track beyond the coastguard lookout tower to pick up a path along the low cliffs. Carry straight on, with the early 19th-century **Medmerry Windmill** away to the right, then join the shingle beach past West Sands

RSPB Medmerry – RSPB Medmerry represents the largest coastal realignment on a section of open coastline in Europe, the shingle bank here being intentionally breached to create an intertidal area of 183 hectares. During its creation, a Bronze Age cemetery and settlement, and a 14th-century fish weir were unearthed. As well as providing flood mitigation, the newly created saltmarshes were quickly settled by black-winged stilts, avocets and little terns. In places, the trees that once grew here are being turned to elegant skeletons by the brackish waters.

Avocets at RSPB Medmerry

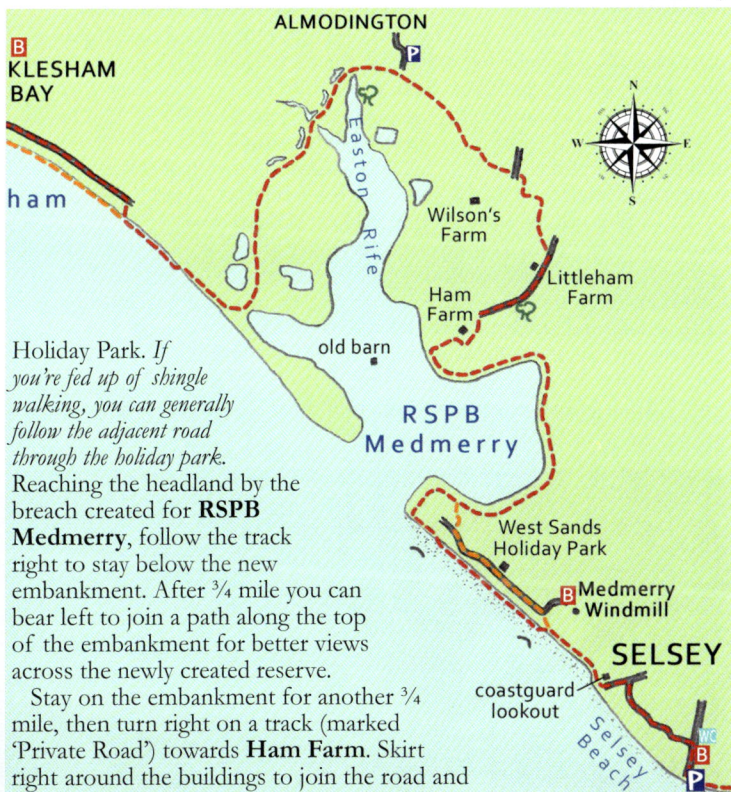

Holiday Park. *If you're fed up of shingle walking, you can generally follow the adjacent road through the holiday park.* Reaching the headland by the breach created for **RSPB Medmerry**, follow the track right to stay below the new embankment. After ¾ mile you can bear left to join a path along the top of the embankment for better views across the newly created reserve.

Stay on the embankment for another ¾ mile, then turn right on a track (marked 'Private Road') towards **Ham Farm**. Skirt right around the buildings to join the road and keep right to follow Ham Road past Littleham Farm. Bear left onto a track that winds across the fields to cross another road by the entrance to Wilson's Farm. At the next junction head straight on to rejoin the embankment, following it past the small RSPB car park and on round **Easton Rife** (*rife* being a West Sussex word for a stream). The route stays on the embankment between a series of further inlets and small pools where little terns and other birds breed in spring, until eventually you are forced to join the adjacent track as it reaches the beach on the far side of the Medmerry breach.

Follow a path alongside the fragile shingle bank behind the beach, before joining its crest towards the houses of **Bracklesham**, the old settlement here, as well as that of East Thorney, long lost to the sea. Although the shingle beach can generally be followed, the formal route gives you a break by turning right at the first opportunity to join East Bracklesham Drive. At its end, by the heart of **Bracklesham Bay**, continue straight on along West Bracklesham Drive, then turn right on Kimbridge Road. Turn left at its end, then left again into Charlmead, at the end of which a path cuts back through to the broader East Wittering Beach. Stay behind the pebbles to join Barn Walk, then keep left by the end of Shore Road in **East Wittering** to follow a narrow walkway behind the beach. A broader path soon resumes between the houses and a tamarisk hedge, before a brief section of fields opens up around **Cakeham Manor House**, which contains parts of a 13th-century palace of the Bishops of Chichester.

A broad greensward continues past the private estate, before the path weaves through the sand dunes to drop down to Sussex's greatest expanse of sand at the ever-popular **West Wittering Beach**. The route follows the line of beach huts along the back of the beach until forced into the adjacent car park near the far end. The constantly shifting sandy spit of **East Head** extends into the mouth of Chichester Harbour,

The wooded shore of Chichester Harbour

although the route follows a path right along the mainland shore. Pass the sheltered mooring on the edge of **West Wittering** village and pick up an onward path that winds through the scrub to **Ella Nore Spit**, which is particularly rich in birdlife at low tide.

Continue through the trees, then keep left at the end of Ellanore Lane to follow the shore round to **Rookswood House**. Turn left where the path emerges amid the houses, then keep straight on to follow another path back to the shoreline beyond. There are great views across Chichester Harbour and its myriad channels, before the path ducks into the trees beyond Horse Pond. Beautiful oak trees shroud the shore round to **Chalkdock Point**, beyond which the path skirts around the

The Anchor Bleu in Bosham

saltmarsh of Chalkdock Marsh. Follow the shore past a dockyard to emerge by the Harbour Office in West Itchenor. The **Itchenor Ferry** crosses the Chichester Channel regularly from the adjacent jetty from 9am-6pm every day from May to September and at weekends only for the rest of the year. Now often simply called Itchenor and famed as the most expensive village in England, **West Itchenor** lost its twin at East Itchenor, a hamlet and manor house that was abandoned after the Black Death. In the 18th and early 19th centuries Itchenor was a major shipbuilding centre, launching a series of naval warships, a tradition that is continued on a smaller scale at Itchenor Shipyard.

Across the estuary, join the tidal shoreline leading left round the headland and alongside **Bosham Channel** (if the tide is high you can follow the path of Smugglers Lane straight on from the ferry to join Lower Hone Lane for ½ mile). The main route stays on the shore all the way round to the road, where you turn right then immediately left on a path alongside the driveway to the Saltings. Turn left at the end and follow the field edge round to skirt along the edge of a garden, then cut left across the road. Rejoin Shore Road before following a path to the right of a tidal section of the road. Bear right again on another path that squeezes behind the houses before joining a track to reach the road again. Head straight on along Shore Road, passing the **National School** before bearing left onto a path above the shore. This winds around the shorefront before cutting through to join the road in the middle of the

BROADBRIDGE
B

Berkeley
Arms

BOSHAM

Holy
Trinity
Church
P B
WC

Bosham
Quay

Anchor
Bleu

National
School

Bosham Channel

The
Saltings

N
W E
S

BOSHAM
HOE

ferry

Chalkdock
Point

Harbour
Office
WC

Longmore
Point

Chichester
Harbour

Ship Inn
P

WEST
ITCHENOR

Horse
Pond

Westlands
Copse

BIRDHAM
B

Rookswood
House

Ella Nore
Lane

0   1   2 MILES

0   1   2 KM

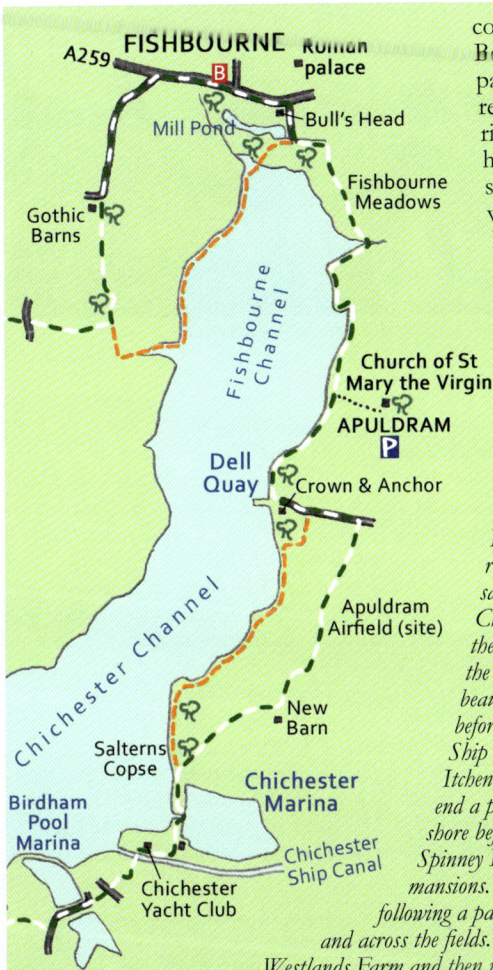

Map labels:
- A259
- **FISHBOURNE**
- Roman palace
- B
- Bull's Head
- Mill Pond
- Fishbourne Meadows
- Gothic Barns
- Fishbourne Channel
- **Church of St Mary the Virgin**
- **APULDRAM**
- P
- Dell Quay
- Crown & Anchor
- Apuldram Airfield (site)
- Chichester Channel
- New Barn
- Salterns Copse
- **Chichester Marina**
- Birdham Pool Marina
- Chichester Ship Canal
- Chichester Yacht Club

comely village of Bosham with the car park and bus stop reached by keeping right. **Bosham** was a historically significant settlement; its church was depicted in the Bayeux Tapestry, and it is thought that Vespasian had a villa here before he became emperor. In addition, the first church is thought to have been built on the site of a Roman basilica.

ALTERNATIVE ROUTE: *If the Itchenor Ferry isn't running or you want to savour the beauty of Chichester Harbour further, the alternative route follows the road briefly up through beautiful WEST ITCHENOR, before turning left opposite the Ship Inn on a private road to Itchenor Sailing Club. At the end a path continues along the shore before cutting up to join Spinney Lane, which is lined with mansions. Turn right at the end, following a path past Westlands Copse and across the fields. Bear right around Westlands Farm and then join the road into BIRDHAM. Soon after this becomes tarmacked, turn left on a path to join an estate road at Westlands, before bearing left on the second bend on a path along the shoreline. This soon bends right to follow a field edge and you join a track, before turning left on the road through Birdham Pool Marina. At the far end, keep straight on along Lock Lane and the path that continues beyond, which winds around the houses to cross a bridge over the CHICHESTER SHIP CANAL. Built as part of the Portsmouth and Arundel Canal in the 1820s, this 4-mile section into Chichester is*

The approach to Bosham across the fields on the alternative route

one of the few parts of it still in use.

Follow the canal right past Chichester Yacht Club, then turn left in front of the buildings beyond to cross a bridge over the lock by the entrance to CHICHESTER MARINA. The path continues left beyond to enter Salterns Copse, where the formal route follows the right fork along the edge of the wood and the large field beyond. Follow a large track past New Barn and the site of Apuldram Airfield, where two temporary runways were built during World War II. Turn left on the road at the end to reach DELL QUAY, a 16th-century wharf and the principal port for the important medieval town of Chichester. There is a slightly shorter and more pleasant informal alternative route that follows the left fork through Salterns Copse, then follows the field edge along the estuary shore to emerge on the road just before Dell Quay.

Pass the Crown and Anchor at Dell Quay, then follow a path right along the shoreline, cutting through the trees before emerging in open fields, at which point the pretty 12th-century CHURCH OF ST MARY THE VIRGIN in Apuldram is reached just 250m inland. The route keeps left along the shore of Fishbourne Channel, then crosses Fishbourne Meadows to reach a bridge over Fishbourne Stream. Turn left and follow the mill stream to the end of Mill Lane, where the formal route heads right up to the main road in the middle of Fishbourne. It is possible (and shorter) at most states of the tide to keep straight on past the marshes by the Mill Pond and

Roman Fishbourne

The largest Roman home found in Britain, the palace at Fishbourne was only discovered in 1960 by a workman laying pipes. It most likely belonged to the fantastically named Cogidubnus, King of the Regni tribe and a major supporter during the Roman occupation of Britain in the 1st century, but may also have been the residence of a later governor of Britain. Lying close to what would have been a port on the then-navigable Fishbourne Channel, the palace burnt down around 270 CE and is renowned for its elaborate mosaics and formal garden.

King Cnut and Bosham

Holy Trinity Church in Bosham is said to be the burial place of both King Cnut's daughter (who drowned in the Roman mill stream here in 1020 and is buried at the foot of the chancel steps) and King Harold (whose remains disappeared after his defeat at the Battle of Hastings). Cnut, who is thought to have had a palace here, is also said to have unsuccessfully commanded the tide to turn back at Bosham (though Southampton also makes this claim), exclaiming 'Let all men know how empty and worthless is the power of kings'.

stay round the estuary shore, before turning right at the fields to rejoin the main route.

The formal route follows the A259 left through FISHBOURNE, with the remains of the Roman palace sadly invisible behind buildings. Turn left on Old Park Lane for ½ mile, then bear left onto a path before Gothic Barns. This crosses a couple of fields before turning right at the first junction, where the unsigned shortcut approaches from the opposite direction. Head straight across Old Park Lane again and follow the field edge to join a vehicle track at Churchfield Cottage. Bear right off this on the bend, crossing a bridge and the open field towards the edge of Bosham. Head straight across the road, cutting between the houses to rejoin the main route along the shore into BOSHAM.

The Jam – *Saturday's Kids*

Taken from the Surrey mod band's 1979 *Setting Sons* album, this is a song about ordinary people who 'Save up their money for a holiday, to Selsey Bill or Bracklesham Bay'.

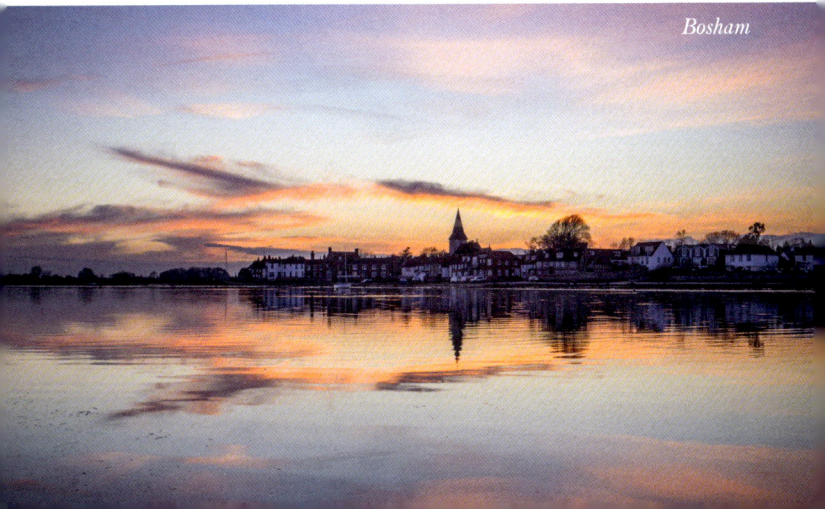

Bosham

Section 3.9 – Bosham to Emsworth

Distance: 23.7km (15 miles), or 14.3km (9 miles) if Thorney Island route closed

Height Gained: 30m

Parking: Pay car parks in Bosham and Emsworth, with small free car park on the shore in Prinsted.

Public Transport: Bus 700 (Stagecoach South, towards Chichester/Littlehampton) runs regularly 7 days a week from Emsworth bypass to the White Swan in Broadbridge, from where you can catch the more irregular Bus 56 (Stagecoach South, to Bosham) to Bosham car park, though the White Swan itself is only a mile off the route.

Refreshments: Rooms in Emsworth at the Crown Inn (01243 372806), 36 on the Quay (01243 375592), the Railway Inn (01243 372351), Millers House B&B (01243 378222), and the Brookfield Hotel (01243 373363). The closest campsite is at Chichester Camping and Caravanning Club Site (01243 373202), 1½ miles away at Southbourne, but easily reached by bus.

Accommodation: There is nothing on the route between Bosham and Emsworth, but the Traveller's Joy pub and a couple of Chinese takeaways are ½ mile off the route in Southbourne.

Overview: The north side of Chichester Harbour is riven by several further channels, with the coast path making its way around the broad headlands of Cobnor Point and Thorney Island, hugging the estuary shore most of the way. Thorney Island is a Ministry of Defence military base, so an alternative route cuts out the headland in the unlikely event it is closed, but it would be a great shame to miss the island's delights. These quiet peninsulas are great for watching birds, seals and other wildlife.

Route Description

The route continues through **Bosham** by following High Street parallel to the shore, passing the Anchor Bleu and **Holy Trinity Church**, part of which is Saxon in origin, representing the oldest known place of worship in Sussex. Turn right at **Bosham Quay Meadow**, then fork left along a private drive to join the tidal shore, crossing a couple of small streams to reach the far end of the village. *There are a couple of escape routes to reach the high tide alternative, which follows Bosham Lane inland through the village. This route turns left on Moreton Road, before bearing left onto a path at the next junction, then continuing straight on to* *rejoin the main route.*

Follow the shore of **Colner Creek** to the second junction, where the official route turns right to join the A259, though it is possible to stay on the path round the shore to join the road further on. Turn left off the road immediately beyond **Cutmill Creek**, following a path along its shore and round the adjacent fields. Turn left alongside Chidham Lane to cross Chidham Creek and briefly join the road, before turning left along Harbour Way. At its end a hedged path leads out to the shore and soon joins the low embankment, rounding an inlet and passing a pond before nearing the pier at **Cobnor Hard**. The well signed path heads inland and cuts through a Christian activity centre before rejoining the shore to follow Chidham Walkway around **Cobnor Point**.

The old coast path soon drops down some steps to join the **Cobnor Foreshore**, which can be under water at high tide but is generally pleasant walking. The new route continues straight on along the edge of the field overlooking the striking line of **Stakes Island**, a failed dam across the mouth of the Thorney Channel. Bear right of a couple of small copses before rejoining the shore, where seals can sometimes be seen basking on the mudflats. The path soon bears right along an embankment and drain to cross the fields, before rejoining the shore beyond **Chidham Point**. An increasingly well defined path leads round

Poppies on the shore of Bosham Channel

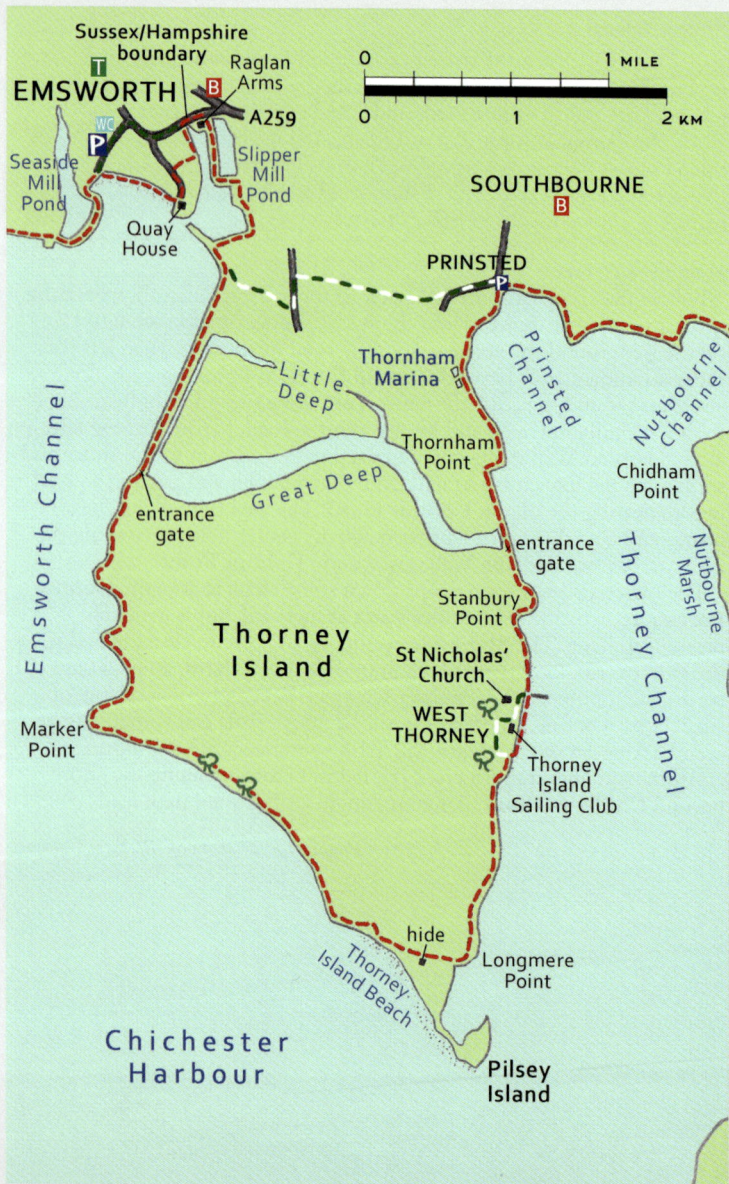

Sussex/Hampshire boundary

Raglan Arms

EMSWORTH

A259

Slipper Mill Pond

Seaside Mill Pond

Quay House

SOUTHBOURNE

PRINSTED

Thornham Marina

Prinsted Channel

Nutbourne Channel

Little Deep

Thornham Point

Chidham Point

Emsworth Channel

Great Deep

entrance gate

Nutbourne Marsh

Thorney Island

entrance gate

Thorney Channel

Stanbury Point

St Nicholas' Church

WEST THORNEY

Marker Point

Thorney Island Sailing Club

hide

Thorney Island Beach

Longmere Point

Chichester Harbour

Pilsey Island

0   1 MILE

0   1   2 KM

NUTBOURNE   A259   BROADBRIDGE

Cutmill Creek

B   B T

Colner Creek

Chidham Creek

BOSHAM

CHIDHAM

Holy
Trinity
Church

P B
WC

Bosham
Channel

Bosham
Quay

Anchor
Bleu

Cobnor
Hard

Cobnor
Activities
Centre

N

W   E

S

Stakes
Island

Cobnor
Point

Chichester
Harbour

Chichester
Channel

Chalkdock
Point

the shore of Nutbourne and Prinsted Channels.
Reaching the road end at **Prinsted**, the main route keeps
left along the shore towards **Thorney Island**, the whole of
which is owned by the Ministry of Defence.

ALTERNATIVE ROUTE: *In the unlikely event that access to this land is restricted,*

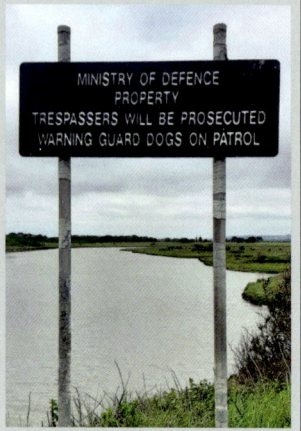

Thorney Island Military Base

Thorney Island was joined to the mainland by land reclamation in the 1870s, but it was still very remote when a plane crashed here in 1933. Their attention drawn to the site, the RAF constructed barracks and an airfield on Thorney Island in the 1930s and it was used by fighter planes in both the Battle of Britain and Normandy Landings. After the RAF left in 1976, it was used to temporarily house asylum seekers from Vietnam (the so-called 'boat people'), before being taken over by the Royal Artillery as Baker Barracks (named after Field Marshal Sir Geoffrey Baker).

there is an alternative route across the neck of the island, continuing straight on along the private lane then bearing right on a gravel track on the bend. A path follows the field edge through to Thorney Road, 150m left along which a path continues right to emerge on the main route on the edge of Emsworth.

Resuming the main route in Prinsted, the path continues along the shore past Payne's Boatyard and **Thornham Marina** to round Thornham Point, once the end of the mainland before land reclamation in the 1870s. Keep left along the sea wall to cross the sluice over **Great Deep** and reach the entry point to the military base. You need to press

St Nicholas' Church, West Thorney

the buzzer on the gate, which should automatically be opened for you (if not there is a phone number for the main gate). The path hugs the shore beyond and the signage makes it clear you shouldn't stray from the route. Beyond Stanbury Point, join the shore by Thorney Island Sailing Club, though it is worth following the high tide alternative up some crude steps by the slipway. This passes the 12th-century Norman church of St Nicholas, which served the village of **West Thorney** and the armed forces. The church retains a civilian congregation, who still call the island home, and is worth a look around, particularly for the 14th-century oak screen.

The high tide route stays inland of the sailing club, then turns left through the car park to follow a path back to the shore, where the main route ascends some steps to rejoin the sea wall. Follow a lovely path along the shore to Longmere Point, where Pilsey Island continues into the mouth of Chichester Harbour and the route bends right to pass around the back of the fine sands of **Thorney Island Beach**. Barring a very brief diversion inland, the broad path hugs the shore, becoming fenced in before following the back of the shingle beach round to **Marker Point** at the entrance to Emsworth Channel.

The path winds pleasantly along the open embankment on the west side of the island to leave the base at another gate by the far end of Great Deep. The embankment continues high above the marsh to join the alternative route at the deckhouses by **Emsworth Yacht Harbour**. Turn left then right to pass through the boats, then turn left along the far side of the marina. Follow the shore round to cut through a gap the far end, then turn left beyond the next building to circle round **Slipper Mill Pond**. Along with the marina and Seaside Mill Pond, these striking tidal ponds powered Emsworth's flour mills, which milled wheat from the surrounding area. Reaching the road by the Lord Raglan, the town centre is reached to the left and the bus stop on the main road is 100m to the right. **Emsworth** is an attractive little town, which was known for rope-making, shipbuilding and its oyster beds.

SONG OF THE DAY

Iron Maiden – *Aces High*

Thorney Island Military base was heavily used by fighter planes during the Battle of Britain and Normandy Landings, and the chaos of these duels is well captured by Maiden's 1984 classic rock single.

Approaching Emsworth past Slipper Mill Pond

ASHLETT MILL, SOUTHAMPTON WATER

Part 4:

The Hampshire Coast

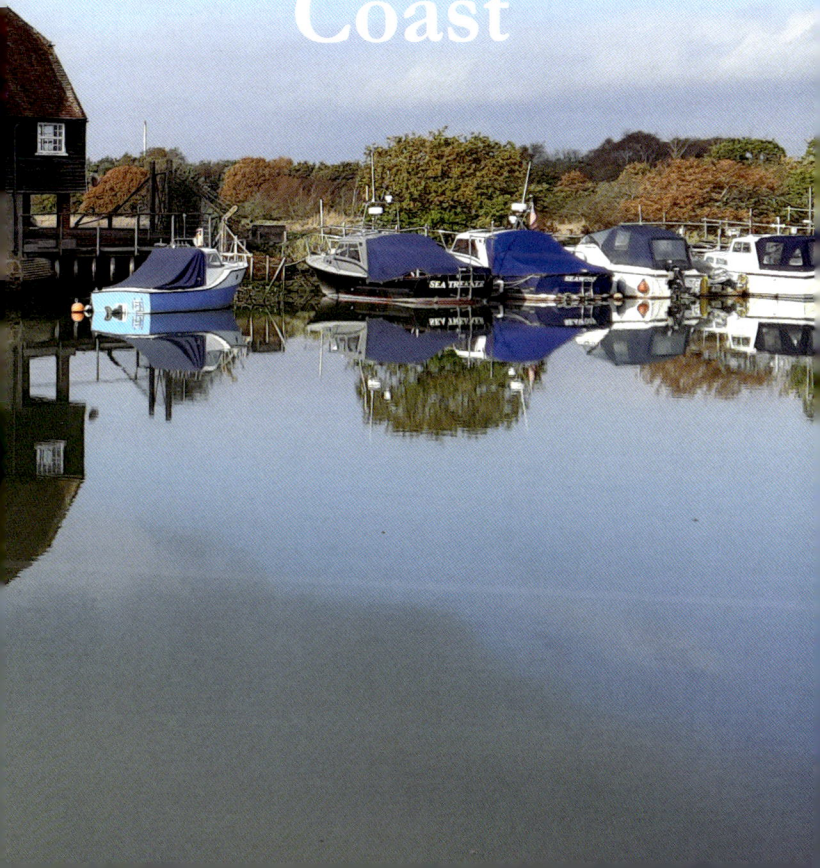

The Hampshire Coast

Start: Emsworth
Finish: Mudeford
Total Distance: 197.7km (123 miles)
Total Ascent: 620m (2,030ft)
Days: 10

To the left lay the green Island of Wight, with its long, low, curving hills peeping over each other's shoulders to the sky-line; to the right the wooded Hampshire coast as far as eye could reach; above a steel-blue heaven, with a wintry sun shimmering down upon them, and enough of frost to set the breath a-smoking. 'By St. Paul!' said Sir Nigel gayly, as he stood upon the poop and looked on either side of him, 'it is a land which is very well worth fighting for'.

Sir Arthur Conan Doyle, *The White Company*

The Hampshire coast looks relatively modest on the map, but the intricacies of Portsmouth Harbour, Langstone Harbour and the Solent shore provide it with substance. Though the estuaries around Portsmouth can be cut off by using the Hayling and Gosport Ferries, the main route traces the true coastline all the way, only relying on ferries to cross the River Hamble and Southampton Water. With most of the route following the sheltered shore of the Solent, there are barely any cliffs on this section of the route, but the ancient woods of the New Forest, the various marshes of the estuarine shore, the beaches of Hayling Island, Lee-on-Solent and Christchurch Bay, and the historic docks of Portsmouth, Gosport and Southampton provide a great variety of interest.

Though Winchester is its county town, Hampshire is a contraction of Hamptonshire, referring to the settlement of Southampton, which was originally *Hamtun* (meaning 'town on the bend in the river'). It was the administrative heart of the Anglo-Saxon kingdom of Wessex (the land of the West Saxons), which extended from here to Cornwall and survived as a political unit until 1066. The most powerful kingdom in the country, with Alfred the Great and his grandson Æthelstan (who united England as a single kingdom) among its kings, Wessex gave us the shire system that still divides much of the country.

As trade with the continent became more important, the well placed ports of Southampton and Portsmouth developed under the Normans. Southampton took over from Winchester as the county's most important town by the 16th century and became renowned for shipbuilding, sending soldiers off to war, and departures to the New World, including most notoriously the *Titanic*. Henry VII made Portsmouth the country's first Royal Dockyard in the 1490s, building warships for the British Navy, and it became the world's greatest naval port by the 18th century. The Solent remains one of the busiest stretches of water in England, and the marinas that line the rivers around it and the tidal harbours to the east are like floating boat shows, with thousands of expensive yachts clustered around the sheltered waterways of this affluent part of England.

In Hampshire, the chalk ridge of the South Downs runs inland of the coast, meaning most of the shoreline is composed of clays and sands laid down more recently, at a time when woolly mammoths were roaming the land. The coastline itself was completely re-formed during the Neolithic era; when sea levels rose greatly at the end of the last ice age, the Isle of Wight was cut off and the Solent formed along a former river valley that continued through Poole Harbour up into the hills of Dorset. Most of the modern coastline of Hampshire is made up of a series of flooded river valleys, with shallow basins making up the Solent and the harbours to the east. Despite a very low tidal range, vast mudflats open up along much of the shoreline. The Solent is famous for its double high tides due to its position at the midpoint of the south coast and further impacted by the position of the Isle of Wight – as a

Portsmouth Harbour © Jack Pease Photography

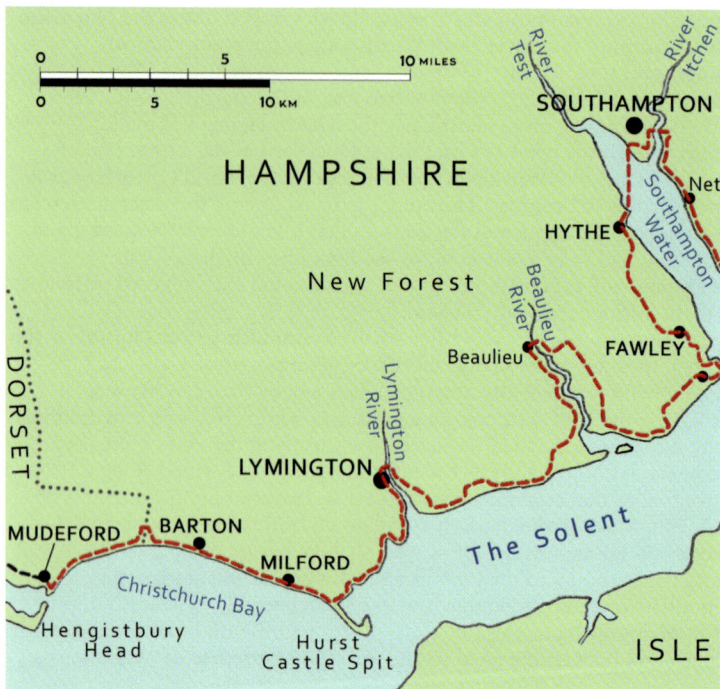

result the high tide stands for up to 3 hours and has a second lower peak and a shorter ebb.

The Hampshire coast is split in two by Southampton Water and, if you are including the Isle of Wight on a complete circuit of the English coast, it probably makes most sense to reach the island via the Southampton to Cowes ferry, though there are also ferries and hovercraft from Portsmouth to Ryde and Fishbourne.

The two halves of the Hampshire coast have very different characters. To the east, a string of settlements run into each other all the way from Emsworth to Southampton, with many of the gaps in between being rapidly filled with new developments. This part of the south coast has among the highest densities of new housing in the country and the infrastructure has not necessarily kept up, resulting in remarkable blooms of algae *(page 187)* across many of the beaches around the Solent and the harbours to the east. The coast path itself manages to find some quiet corners in this landscape, picking an intricate route around Hayling Island, Langstone Harbour and Portsmouth Harbour,

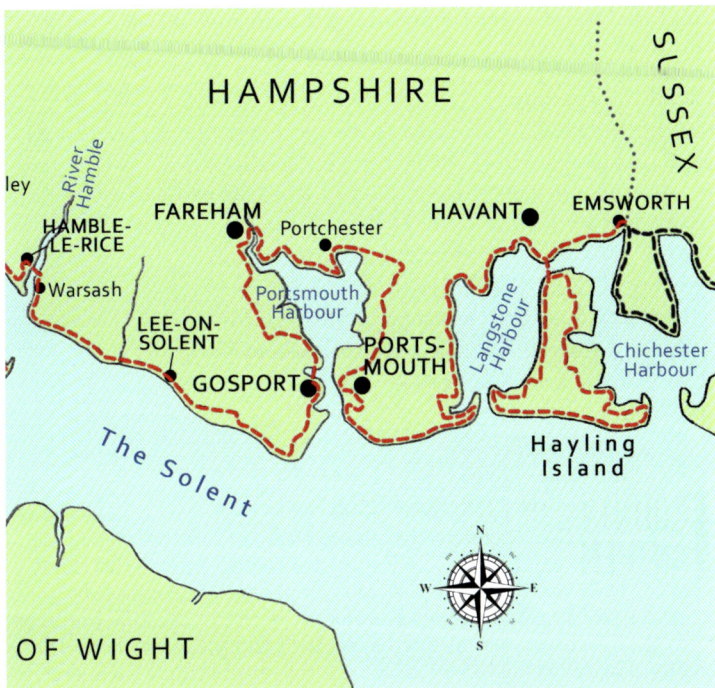

Map labels:
HAMPSHIRE
SUSSEX
River Hamble
...ley
HAMBLE-LE-RICE
FAREHAM
Portchester
HAVANT
EMSWORTH
Warsash
LEE-ON-SOLENT
Portsmouth Harbour
Langstone Harbour
Chichester Harbour
PORTS-MOUTH
GOSPORT
The Solent
Hayling Island
OF WIGHT

before following the Solent shore towards Southampton. Apart from on Portsea Island (home to Portsmouth) and through Gosport, there is far less tarmac than the long promenades of Sussex, and even in these places the rich naval history means the route is rarely dull. This section of the route follows the existing Solent Way for most of its course.

West of Southampton Water, you quickly enter the New Forest National Park, whose coastal fringe is largely free of the open woodland and heath that has given this area its designation. Instead the coast is a gentle mix of fields, marshes and copses, but the existence of several grand houses and estates means access to the shore is limited. The new coast path does its best to provide glimpses of the sea not afforded by the existing Solent Way and traces the shoreline as much as it can either side of the Beaulieu River, but there is still a lot of road walking. Beyond Lymington the shore is easier to follow, the route soon leaving the Solent behind at Hurst Castle Spit and rounding the broad sandy arc of Christchurch Bay to reach Dorset. The western part of Hampshire is far less built up, but as a result can be more unreliable for public transport. Like all of the county's coast, though, the walking is largely flat and straightforward.

Useful Information

Tourist Information – *www.visit-hampshire.co.uk* and *www.thenewforest.co.uk*

Stagecoach South – 0345 241 8000 *(www.stagecoachbus.com)*

First Portsmouth, Fareham & Gosport – 0345 646 0707 *(www.firstbus.co.uk)*

Bluestar – 01202 338421 *(www.bluestarbus.co.uk)*

morebus – 01202 338420 *(www.morebus.co.uk)*

Hampshire Community Transport – 01962 846785

Hampshire Travel – *www.hants.gov.uk/transport/trafficandtravel*

Train Times – *traintimes.org.uk*

Bus Times – *bustimes.org*

Traveline – *www.traveline.info*

COUNTY ANTHEM

Brian T Parks – *Hampshire Born*

This hymn to the county made it to the semi-final stage for the UK's 2019 Eurovision song, though this is not saying a lot as our entry by Michael Rice famously finished dead last. Parks, who was ironically born just over the border in Surrey, says the song was inspired by James Taylor's *Carolina in my Mind*, singing 'The salty tang of the Solent sea, the only perfume there ever need be'.

Millennium Beacon, Lepe Beach

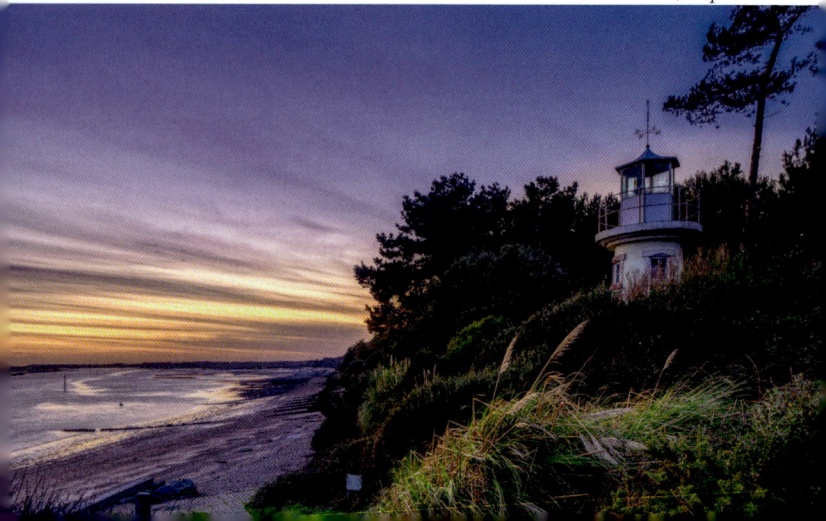

Section 4.1 – Emsworth to South Hayling

Distance: 23.0km (14½ miles)

Height Gained: 90m

Parking: Pay car parks in Emsworth and along the beachfront in South Hayling. Free car parks along the route at either side of Langstone Bridge and North Common in North Hayling.

Public Transport: Buses 30/31 (Stagecoach South, towards Havant) run regularly from Beachlands in South Hayling to Havant bus station, from where Coastliner 700 (Stagecoach South, to Flansham) runs every 20 minutes to Emsworth.

Refreshments: The Ship Inn is passed at one end of Langstone Bridge and a Costa Coffee at the other, as well as Salt Shack Café at Northney Marina, and the Yew Tree Inn and Maypole in Fleet.

Accommodation: There are various accommodation options along the beachfront through South Hayling, with the Visitor Information Centre (023 9246 7111) by the bus stop at Beachlands. The closest campsite to the route on Hayling Island is Fishery Creek Touring Park (023 9246 2164) at Eastoke, but the Oven Campsite (023 9246 4695) is also well-placed at the heart of the island.

Overview: A varied day around the western part of Chichester Harbour and the eastern side of Hayling Island. The route strays from the shoreline for long sections, with the fields of Warblington and North Hayling providing great contrast to the estuary shore of Emsworth, Langstone and Mengham. There are some beautiful villages, most notably at Langstone, and the day finishes along the sunny shingle beach of South Hayling. It is possible (though not recommended) to miss out the circular route around Hayling Island and continue to Anchorage Park, or you may prefer to complete the circuit of the island in a single day, though this is a long trek of over 17 miles.

Route Description

In **Emsworth** the route continues past the Lord Raglan, before turning left opposite the Old Flour Mill onto a path alongside the creek, which marks the boundary between Sussex and Hampshire. After the path bends right, turn left along King Street to its end by Quay House, where you turn right along the tidal shore. *At high tide you'll have to retrace your steps along King Street into the town centre, joining the High Street before turning left at the small triangle in the centre.* The routes converge on the quay, where you keep left past Quay Mill and follow the walkway

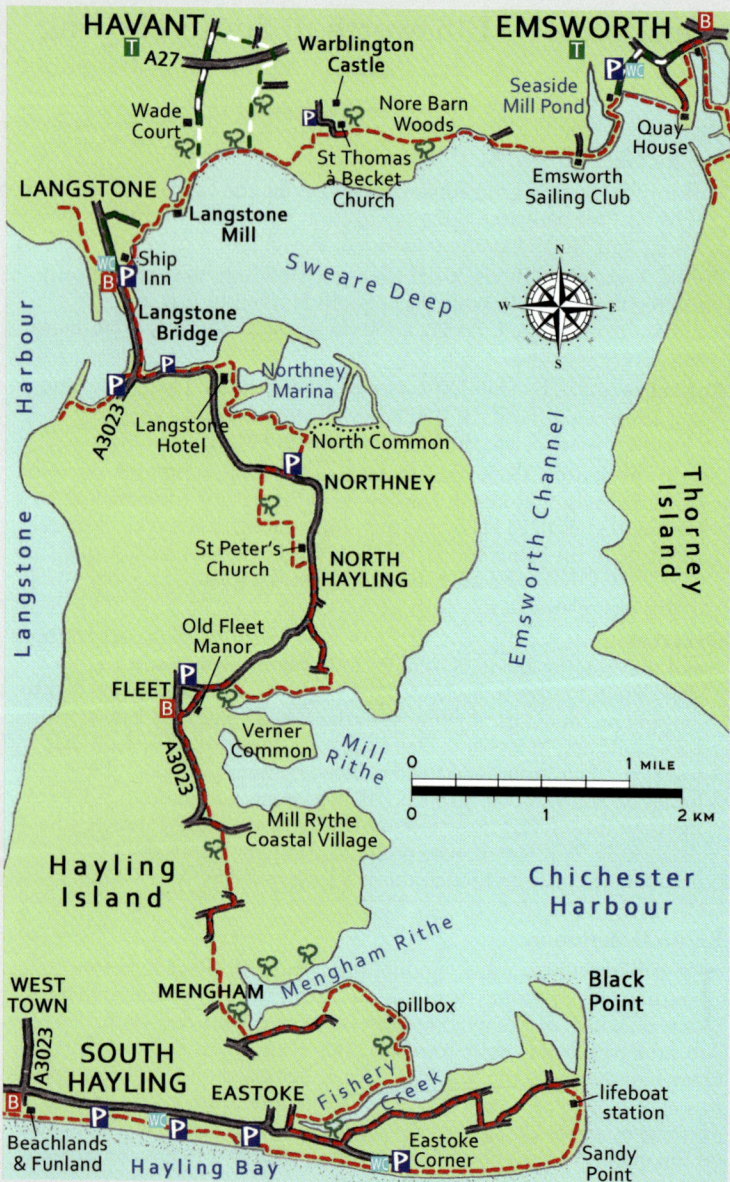

HAVANT

A27

Warblington Castle

Wade Court

Nore Barn Woods

St Thomas à Becket Church

EMSWORTH

Seaside Mill Pond

Quay House

Emsworth Sailing Club

LANGSTONE

Langstone Mill

Ship Inn

Langstone Bridge

A3023

Langstone Hotel

Northney Marina

North Common

NORTHNEY

St Peter's Church

NORTH HAYLING

Old Fleet Manor

FLEET

A3023

Verner Common

Mill Rithe

Mill Rythe Coastal Village

Hayling Island

Harbour

Langstone

Sweare Deep

Emsworth Channel

Thorney Island

Chichester Harbour

MENGHAM

Mengham Rithe

pillbox

Black Point

WEST TOWN

A3023

SOUTH HAYLING

EASTOKE

Beachlands & Funland

Hayling Bay

Eastoke Corner

Fishery Creek

lifeboat station

Sandy Point

Langstone Harbour

0   1 MILE

0   1   2 KM

around **Seaside Mill Pond**. Fisherman's Walk snakes out through the mud to some of the oyster beds that used to cover the harbour. Emsworth produced over three million oysters a year at the industry's height in the late 19th century.

Continue straight on at the end of the mill pond, passing Emsworth Sailing Club to pick up a concrete path along the shore. Keep left past a series of road-ends and rejoin the shore, before following the main track straight on along the right side of **Nore Barn Woods**. The historic Church Path continues straight on across the fields to reach **St Thomas à Becket Church** in Warblington, the parish church until St James' Church was built in Emsworth in 1839. Beyond the churchyard you can see the crumbling tower of **Warblington Castle**, a 14th-century moated manor house; though it was largely destroyed in the Civil War, the tower was retained as a navigational aid for ships.

The route follows the track left of the church, before cutting straight on through the cemetery, zigging left then right to reach a gate into the field beyond. The path rejoins the shoreline and soon drops down to the tidal shingle itself to follow it round towards the prominent windmill at Langstone. *There is a 1-mile high tide alternative along the tree-lined*

Langstone Mill and village

Langstone Bridge & the Wadeway

Langstone Bridge now connects Hayling Island to the mainland, although you can see traces of the medieval Wadeway, by which horses and carts once crossed the flats at low tide. It leaves the shore soon after the Royal Oak Inn and, though still technically a bridleway, it is severed by the New Cut, a dredged channel created for the Portsmouth and Arundel Canal in the 1820s. The first bridge was constructed in 1824, a wooden swing bridge that remained in use until the current Langstone Bridge was built in the 1950s.

path inland; keep left to cross the A27, then follow a narrow pathway between the houses and turn left at its end along North Close. Having passed beneath the dual carriageway, follow a path straight on by the extravagant turret of Wade Court to reach the shore again. A tarmac pathway leads on past **Langstone Mill Pond** and the 18th-century mill buildings, which contain both a windmill and water mill. Skirt around the beautiful village of **Langstone**, whose quay once served as the port for nearby Havant. Another high tide route cuts through the village, but you can generally stay along the shore to join the main road by the Ship Inn.

Reaching **Hayling Island**, turn left along Northney Road, passing the end of the Wadeway by the lay-by. Bear left past the Langstone Hotel, then cut right across the car park to follow a road behind it and keep left to pick up a path along the estuary shore. This winds round to reach a gravel path at **North Common**, which you follow right back to the road (the route left is a dead-end loop). Turn right along the road only as far as a path left along the edge of the large field beyond the recreation ground. The path eventually cuts through the graveyard of St Peter's Church in **North Hayling**, before joining a track that leads back to the road. There is no pavement but you follow this road right for ½ mile, before bearing left on Woodgaston Lane. Turn left at its end, then right on a footpath between the houses to rejoin the estuary shore by Brenton House. The path continues past the new development at Yachthaven, before bearing inland to rejoin the road. Keep left along Yew Tree Road, passing the 16th-century timber and thatch of **Old Fleet Manor** to reach the main road in Fleet.

The coast path follows the A3023 left for over ½ mile, then bears left past the school, following the road towards Mill Rythe Coastal Village. Turn right along the cycleway past the golf course and follow the second road right at the end. Turn second left on Beech Grove and keep straight on at the end to pick up a path alongside the fields. Head straight on along the track at the end, then bear left on a path through to the road in **Mengham**. Follow Salterns Lane left, then keep straight on into Marine Walk and join a path by the entrance to Wilson's Boatyard. Rejoin the shore by Mengeham Rythe Sailing Club and follow it round to the next inlet past a World War II pillbox. Continue along the shore past the boating lake and all the way up **Fishery Creek** to the road at its end. Keep left on the roads, following Eastoke Avenue until it becomes a rough track between holiday parks. Turn left on Bosmere Road, then left at its end and left again along Bracklesham Road. Keep straight on towards Hayling Island Sailing Club and follow a footpath right to reach the beachfront by **Hayling Island Lifeboat Station**. The peninsula of Black Point finally marks the western end of Chichester Harbour, reached after two days of circuitous walking.

Follow a path behind the beach through **Sandy Point Nature Reserve**, before it turns to shingle above the new coastal defences. You soon pick up a tarmac promenade behind the mountain of shingle that protects this end of Hayling Island. At **Eastoke Corner** the view opens out across Hayling Bay and the path cuts right to run alongside the line of Hayling Seaside Railway, a narrow-gauge railway opened in 2003. There are various car parks along the seafront and the route meanders between them, sometimes well defined, sometimes not at all. Pass a memorial to the Combined Operations Pilotage Parties, a top-secret unit based on Hayling Island that gathered information on proposed landing beaches for D-Day. Follow the railway towards the Funland Amusement Park at **Beachlands**, the official route staying along the top of the beach here, although you can bear right to reach the bus stop and toilets by the car park entrance. **South Hayling** is a broad name for the collection of settlements along the beachfront, with the village centre of West Town being reached ½ mile inland.

———————— •◆• ————————

SONG OF THE DAY

Mark Handley – *Sweet Home Hayling Island*
A 2014 song about the island by the singer from local band The Bone Idols that takes off Lynyrd Skynyrd's famous song about Alabama.

Fishery Creek near Eastoke

Section 4.2 – South Hayling to Anchorage Park

Distance: 21.4km (13½ miles)

Height Gained: 20m

Parking: Free parking along the route along the Hayling Billy cycleway, at either end of Langstone Bridge, Broadmarsh Park and Farlington Marshes, with pay car parks along the seafront in South Hayling.

Public Transport: Bus 21 (Stagecoach South, towards Havant) runs regularly from Anchorage Park to Havant bus station, from where Buses 30/31 (Stagecoach South, towards Hayling Island) run regularly to Beachlands in South Hayling. Both services run 7 days a week.

Refreshments: The Ferryboat Inn and Beach Café are passed on the route at Sinah Beach, as are a Costa Coffee at one end of Langstone Bridge and the Ship Inn at the other, with a Greggs just a few yards from the route in Stoke.

Accommodation: Anchorage Park is little more than a collection of industrial estates and new housing developments, but the Holiday Inn Express Portsmouth North (0371 9021580) is close to the route by the A27 roundabout before Ports Creek, while the Farmhouse & Innlodge Portsmouth (023 9265 0510) is passed less than a mile further along the route. There are no campsites nearby.

Overview: The bulk of the day's route from Hayling to Portsea Island is spent circumnavigating Langstone Harbour, which is more industrial and less intricate than Chichester Harbour, although it still has its moments. The beaches of Hayling Island peak at its western end with the remarkable shells of Sinah Beach; there is a lovely section along the old Hayling Billy railway; and Farlington Marshes provide the best view of the harbour and its wildlife. The harbour can be cut off entirely by catching the Hayling Ferry to Portsea Island, although by using this and the Gosport Ferry from Portsmouth to Gosport is to miss out much of the varied charm of this fascinating part of the coastline.

Route Description

Rejoining the Hayling Island beachfront at **Beachlands**, you can follow either the beach, or the road past the various car parks, or the green swathe in between, to reach **West Beach**. Beyond the Inn on the Beach (a former lifeboat station), the road runs along the

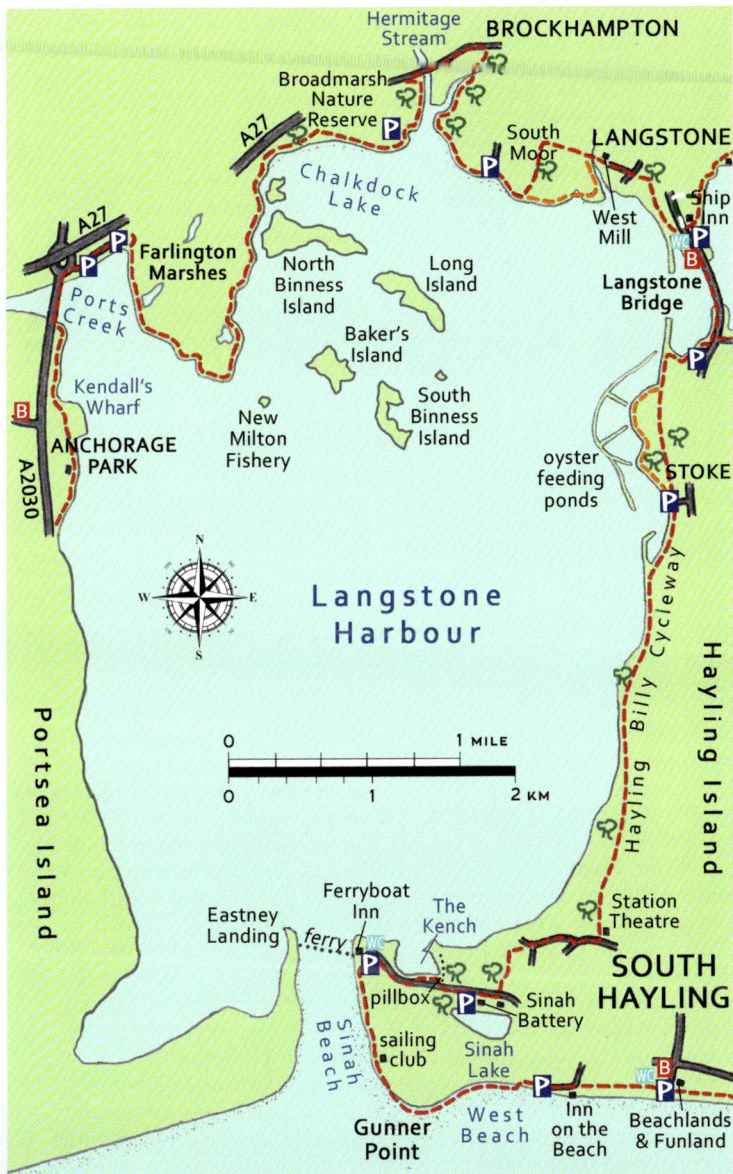

BROCKHAMPTON

Hermitage Stream

Broadmarsh Nature Reserve

A27

South Moor

LANGSTONE

Chalkdock Lake

West Mill

Ship Inn

A27

Farlington Marshes

North Binness Island

Long Island

Langstone Bridge

Ports Creek

Baker's Island

Kendall's Wharf

New Milton Fishery

South Binness Island

oyster feeding ponds

STOKE

ANCHORAGE PARK

A2030

Langstone Harbour

Hayling Billy Cycleway

Hayling Island

N

W   E

S

0   1 MILE

0   1   2 KM

Portsea Island

Ferryboat Inn

The Kench

Eastney Landing

ferry

Station Theatre

SOUTH HAYLING

pillbox

Sinah Battery

sailing club

Sinah Lake

Sinah Beach

Gunner Point

West Beach

Inn on the Beach

Beachlands & Funland

The shells of Sinah Beach

back of the beach until the fence of Hayling Golf Club forces you on to the beach itself. The shingle crest can be hard work, but as long as the tide isn't in you can follow the sandier portion of the beach round **Gunner Point** and alongside the entrance to Langstone Harbour, a particularly powerful tidal race. The remarkable bank here is formed not of shingle but millions of shells, which were used in the mortar of the ancient St Mary's Church at the heart of the island. Beyond the sailing club, a path runs along the back of the beach and leads past the car park to the Ferryboat Inn at **Ferry Point**. Hayling Ferry regularly crosses the channel to Portsea Island during the summer months, an obvious shortcut that cuts out the circuit of Langstone Harbour.

Mulberry Harbours & Wartime Hayling

A concrete ramp to the south of the Ferryboat Inn was used to launch parts of the two Mulberry harbours that were constructed in the lead up to the Normandy Landings. These vast floating harbours were designed to protect larger ships from storms and attack, but one was destroyed in a storm after just a few days. Hayling Island's beaches were used to simulate Gold Beach in Normandy during Exercise Fabius in May 1944, which was presided over by Winston Churchill. Hayling Island was also used for a large decoy site, designed to distract bombers aiming for Portsmouth Docks, which it successfully did in April 1941.

Follow Ferry Road inland past the **Kench**, a natural cove that was renowned for its cockles, winkles and oysters, and whose name refers to a deep container in which fish and animal skins were salted. A path runs briefly along the left side of the road before rejoining it by a pillbox (the path continuing left is a dead end). Stay on the road past the remains of the **Sinah Heavy Anti Aircraft Battery** by Sinah Lake, then turn left on a path behind the houses. Head straight on along the road, following Sinah Lane into **West Town**, before turning left before the Station Theatre to join a cycleway along the former line of the **Hayling Billy Railway**.

The cycleway is a lovely route along the western shore of Hayling Island, in places wooded and elsewhere offering great views across Langstone Harbour. Beyond **North Hayling Halt**, the cycleway stays away from the shore and it is possible to bear left and follow a good path along the shoreline, passing a series of well preserved oyster feeding ponds. Oysters were brought here during the winter months, before being taken to the rich grounds of Whitstable in the summer.

Aerial view of the west end of Hayling Island

The route turns right before the old signal at the site of the railway bridge across to the mainland, following the shore round to the main road, which leads back over **Langstone Bridge**.

Turn left opposite the **Ship Inn** in Langstone and briefly rejoin the line of the railway, before turning left and following Mill Lane. Cross the stream beyond West Mill and, *though it is currently possible to follow the shore left*, plans to allow a breach in the sea wall here to develop into an intertidal habitat mean the official route bears right across the marsh of **South Moor**. Aim for a gate the far side, turning left through the trees before it to return to the path along the shore. This continues past a small parking area and briefly joins the shingle shore, before bending

---

Hayling Billy

The Hayling Island Branch Line opened in 1865, though the original route across the mudflats had to be abandoned after the embankment quickly eroded (part of this can be traced through the oyster beds near North Hayling Halt). The original road bridge was weak, meaning the railway was the only way to transport heavy goods to the island and became well used to carry freight and summer holidaymakers. The railway swing bridge could still only carry lighter 'Terrier' trains, which were affectionately known as Hayling Billies. These Victorian engines remained in use until the line's closure in November 1963.

round to the right at the mouth of the **Hermitage Stream**. The path crosses a side stream before joining the road to head left through the industrial estates and cross the broad stream. Double back left to join a path along the far side of the stream and pass a slipway by the car park for **Broadmarsh Coastal Park**.

A path hugs the shore to join the cycleway alongside the A27 for ⅓ mile, before bearing left onto a path around the perimeter of **Farlington Marshes**. Jutting some way out into the harbour, with a series of low islands off its shore and pools inland, this is a great place to see wading birds and overwintering wildfowl, particularly at low tide. The path stays along the embankment throughout, passing a couple of wartime pillboxes and the pools of a former tidal creek. At the end turn left through the car park and follow a small road alongside the busy A27. Keep left to join the A2030 and cross the bridge over **Ports Creek** to Portsea Island, which has the greatest population density of any British island. A path rejoins the embankment beyond and, where it crosses the road to Kendall's Wharf, you can turn right off the route and cross the main road to reach the bus stop in **Anchorage Park** (with Hilsea railway station reached ½ mile beyond).

———————— ◆◆ ————————

SONG OF THE DAY

FC Kahuna – *Hayling*
A beautiful sunset song, this 2003 single features vocals from Icelandic singer Hafdis Huld and music by the short-lived London-based electronic duo of Jon Nowell and Daniel Ormondroyd. It is built around an electronic bass sample from Tangerine Dream's 1976 track *3am at the Border of the Marsh from Okefenokee*.

A little egret at Langstone Harbour © Andy Morffew

Section 4.3 – Anchorage Park to Cosham (Portsea Island Circuit)

Distance: 23km (14½ miles)

Height Gained: 40m

Parking: Free car parks along the route at Great Salterns Quay, Fort Cumberland, Mountbatten Centre and Hilsea Lido, as well as various pay parking through Eastney, Southsea and Portsmouth.

Public Transport: It is possible to take a convoluted bus/train route from one side of Portsea Island to the other, but far quicker to complete the circuit of the island by following the path along Ports Creek for just over a mile.

Refreshments: Many seafront options through Eastney, Southsea and Portsmouth.

Accommodation: The Village Hotel Portsmouth (023 9200 6199) is passed on the route just beyond the A27 roundabout, and the Premier Inn Port Solent (0333 3218334) and Portsmouth Marriott Hotel (023 9238 3151) are a mile further along the route, while the Red Lion (023 9238 2041), in Cosham, is under ¾ mile from the route. There is no camping anywhere nearby.

Overview: Portsea Island, home to Portsmouth and its outlying suburbs, is a very urban part of the route, but this is a fascinating day's walking around arguably the UK's most important maritime city. Though there are inevitably road sections and industrial estates, you also pass muddy estuary shores, shingle beaches, intricate harbours, vast dockyards and military fortifications from various eras.

Route Description

The shoreline path resumes beyond **Kendall's Wharf**, skirting along the western shore of Langstone Harbour, but until the coastal defence work is completed it may be necessary to stay inland of Tudor Sailing Club and the Watersports Centre and follow the A2030. Continue past Harbourside Park and **Great Salterns Mansion** (now a Harvester restaurant), before bearing away from the road at Milton Common. The path passes the **People's Memorial** and a trio of lakes (Frog, Duck and Swan), then hugs the shore round to **Milton Sea Lock**, where the Portsea Canal once reached the sea.

The main route crosses the lock and keeps left to join the tidal estuary shore via some crude steps by the (no longer) Thatched House. Stay

Horsea
Island

*Sails of the
South*

M27

Tipner Lake

Tipner
Point

Mount-
batten
Centre

P

P

TIPNER

Portsmouth
Harbour

M275

Whale
Island

International
Ferry Terminal

Naval
Base

A3

A3

Portsmouth
Historic Dockyard

St John's Cathedral

HMS Warrior ×

P

PORTSMOUTH

T B

Gosport Ferry

Spinnaker
Tower

No. 1 Gunwharf
Quay

Gunwharf
Quay

P

Isle of Wight
Ferry terminal

GOSPORT

Spice
Island Inn

WC

Spice Quay

OLD
PORTSMOUTH

Fort
Blockhouse

Round
Tower

B

Square
Tower

Royal Garrison
Church

SOUTHSEA

Canoe
Lake

P

Clarence
Pier

Naval War
Memorial

Clarence Esplanade

Southsea
Castle

WC

A288

B

WC

Southsea Pier

COSHAM

Ports Creek

A2030

WC B
Hilsea
Lido

A3

HILSEA

Kendall's
Wharf

B

ANCHORAGE
PARK

Watersports
Centre

Great Salterns
Mansion

A2030

P Great
Salterns
Quay

B

People's
Memorial

Portsea
Island

Milton
Common

Swan
Lake

Milton
Sea Lock

MILTON

P

Thatched
House

Eastney
Landing

*Hayling
Ferry*

B

lifeboat
P station

Eastney Lake

Southsea
P Marina

EASTNEY

Fort
P Cumberland

Eastney
Pier

Eastney
Fort W.

Gunners
Row

Eastney
Fort E.

WC

Lumps
Fort

P

Eastney Beach

Eastney Esplanade

Langstone
Harbour

Hayling
Island

0   1 MILE

0   1   2 KM

The Portsmouth and Arundel Canal

Devised as part of an inland route between Portsmouth and London when Napoleon was terrorising shipping on the English Channel, this ambitious canal was built in stages during the 1820s but never turned a profit. The Portsea Canal section opened in 1822 between a basin at Langport and a pair of locks at Milton, only one of which is still evident. However, the canal had to be drained in 1827 as salt water was seeping into several wells in Portsmouth and, by the late 1820s, Ports Creek was made navigable. Part of the route was later used for the line of the railway between Portsmouth and Fratton.

along the shore round **Eastney Lake**, whose lowest point at the far end can be avoided by an informal path up the bank. Soon after this, pick up a path above the shore that continues round the other side of the inlet. *A high tide alternative heads inland at Milton Sea Lock to follow Locksway Road for ½ mile, then turns left along Ironbridge Road and continues straight on across the park at its end. Turn left on the road, then left again on Ferry Road, before bearing left to rejoin the main route along the shore.* The route soon rejoins Ferry Road, following it left before bending right inland.

The new route of the coast path will turn left at the end of Ferry Road to pass **Southsea Marina**, before turning right to the large public car park by Southsea Sea Angling Club. A concrete walkway follows the perimeter fence of Fort Cumberland along the shore, a short section of which is being modified to allow the new route to continue all the way to Eastney. The largest of its kind remaining in the country, Fort Cumberland was a pentagon-shaped bastion rebuilt in the late 18th century to defend the entrance to Langstone Harbour. A path continues beyond to follow the back edge of the naturist part of Eastney Beach and join **Eastney Esplanade**.

ALTERNATIVE ROUTE: *Until this walkway is open, it is possible to follow the road all the way to the lifeboat station at Eastney Landing, the disembarkation*

The walls of Old Portsmouth

point for the Hayling Ferry. However, you'll have to return the same way, so you may simply choose to turn right at the T junction at the end of Ferry Road. Bear left off this road at the bend, following a cycleway to cut through to the Eastney Esplanade.

The esplanade continues past the grand **Gunners Row**, built as Eastney Barracks in 1867 and formerly home to the Royal Marines Museum, as well as a series of fortifications. The **Eastney Forts** were built in the 1860s and later expanded during World War II, while **Lumps Fort** was a Napoleonic defence. Reaching Southsea, the esplanade passes **South Parade Pier**, which opened in 1879 and has been damaged by fire three times, and stays along the shore past **Southsea Castle**. Built by Henry VIII in 1544 to protect against French invasion, this fort was expanded after 1859 as part of the Palmerston defences, which were laid out across the eastern entrance to the Solent. Of the four sea forts in the channel, **Spitbank Fort** (once a museum, now a luxury hotel) is closest, less than a mile offshore, while No Man's Land Fort and Horse Sands Fort are more substantial.

Pinball Wizard

Most of Ken Russell's 1975 film of The Who's rock opera *Tommy* was shot around Portsmouth and features Eastney Beach Huts, Hilsea Lido, Southsea Castle, Kings Theatre, and Warblington Castle and Church. A couple of sequences were filmed on South Parade Pier, including the ballroom dance between Ann-Margret and Oliver Reed, during which a serious fire broke out and caused £500,000 damage to the pier, but throughout which Russell kept filming.

The **Clarence Esplanade** (now rebranded as the Millennium Promenade) continues alongside Southsea Common, passing the mammoth **Naval War Memorial** to reach the amusement park of **Clarence Pier**, alongside which hovercraft depart for the Isle of Wight. Continue along the shore past the Spur Redoubt to cross a bridge to the harbour walls of **Old Portsmouth** – further coastal defence work here may require another diversion past the Royal Garrison Church inland. It is a dramatic walk along the **Hotwalls** (named for the habit of heating cannon balls to make them more deadly) past the Square Tower to the **Round Tower**, with wonderful views across the entrance to Portsmouth Harbour. Retrace your steps a few yards from the tower to head down some steps and cut through another wall to reach Capstan Square. Follow narrow Tower Street out to Bath Square on the Point, where the iconic **Spinnaker Tower** stands out across the water – this 170m landmark was created in 2005 to resemble a billowing sail.

Head back down the other side of the Spice Island Inn, then turn left on East Street and keep left around the waterfront. Pass the Bridge

HMS Warrior

Tavern and keep left around the wharf until an arch leads right through from **Spice Quay** to the road. Follow this left only as far as a path leading left along the other side of the quay. A port was established here by Jean de Gisors in the 12th century to trade with Normandy, making this area (the **Camber**) Portsmouth's original harbour. Turn left at the end, passing the terminal for the ferry to Fishbourne on the Isle of Wight, then turn left along the wall to cut through to a walkway around the new developments of **Gunwharf Quays**. Reaching the waterway at the heart of this area, follow it inland past the tower at No. 1 Gunwharf Quay to reach the road again. Turn left along the road, heading under the railway and follow its side to Portsmouth Harbour station, from where the Gosport Ferry departs.

Follow the road past **HMS Warrior**, launched in 1860 as Britain's first iron warship, and continue past the entrance to **Portsmouth Historic Dockyard**, staying alongside the high 18th-century walls to the dockyard. Beyond the HMS Nelson naval base, bear left before the Catholic church of **St John's Cathedral**, continuing around the dockyard walls even as it turns left before Morrisons supermarket. Carry on to the bottom, before turning right and then heading left alongside the main road. Follow the cycleway as it cuts across the various lanes approaching the international ferry terminal and then joins the approach

---

Portsmouth Dockyard

The first docks were built here in 1212 and, by the 15th century, Portsmouth was England's only Royal Dockyard. The oldest surviving dry dock in the world dates from Henry VIII's reign and the city continued to grow in importance until it was the world's largest industrial complex and greatest naval port at the height of the British Empire in the 18th century. Today the dockyard is a museum housing both *HMS Victory* and the *Mary Rose*. *HMS Victory* is the oldest warship still in commission anywhere in the world, having been Lord Nelson's flagship at the Battle of Trafalgar on 21st October 1805. It was built in Chatham dockyards from 1759 to 1765 from approximately 6,000 oak trees, and was so broad the docks had to be widened to put it to sea. The *Mary Rose* was a 16th-century wooden warship that was salvaged from the bottom of the sea in 1982.

road. Follow it round to the roundabout at the beginning of the M275, turning left just before on a road towards **Whale Island**. This is largely reclaimed land composed of the spoil dredged out of Portsmouth docks and built by convict labour in the 1860s. It became home to the Navy's *HMS Excellent* training school and now houses the Navy Command Headquarters.

Before the causeway out to this private island, turn right along the cycleway to hug the shore beside the motorway. At the next motorway roundabout turn right and follow the road past the entrance to the Park & Ride. Turn right at the end and follow it round to the left, before turning left along Target Road, at the end of which the cycleway continues through to Twyford Avenue. Follow this left and join the broad cycleway along the shore of **Tipner Lake** by the Mountbatten Centre. Keep left along the shore, with views of the Sails of the South sculpture, to reach **Hilsea Lido**, opened in 1935 and used for Olympic training in the lead up to the Munich Games in 1936. Turn left beyond the lido to reach the large roundabout where the A3 meets the M27, the route continuing straight on along the A27, while **Cosham** can be reached along the A397 via a subway beneath the dual carriageway.

To complete the circuit of Portsea Island and return to your start point, continue straight on past the lido and bend round to the right to reach a footbridge over the A3. At the far side, paths lead along either side of the moat parallel to Ports Creek, before rejoining briefly to cross a road-end. Where the two paths converge again beneath a railway bridge, you should take the left fork and follow the widening shore of Ports Creek to reach the A2030 on the other side of the island. The coast path is joined along the shore opposite.

The Spinnaker Tower

Mike Oldfield – *Portsmouth*
A traditional English country dance tune that was first recorded in the 17th century, this version was released as a single in 1976. Remarkably this two-minute instrumental folk ditty reached number 3 in the UK charts, Oldfield's highest chart placing. Other versions have been used as the theme tune for the BBC TV series *Billy Bunter* and in Ralph Vaughan-Williams' *Sea Songs* arrangement.

Section 4.4 – Cosham to Gosport

Distance: 22.7km (14 miles)

Height Gained: 50m

Parking: Pay car parks in Gosport, with free car parks along the route at Portchester Castle and Wicor Recreation Ground.

Public Transport: The quickest way back to Cosham is take the Gosport Ferry across to Portsmouth Harbour, from where there are regular trains to Cosham. You can also catch the E2 Bus (First, towards Fareham) to Fareham bus station, then Bus 3 (First, towards Southsea) to Cosham. All these services run 7 days a week.

Refreshments: Salt Café is passed on the shore at Wicor, along with various pubs and cafes in Fareham.

Accommodation: Various accommodation is available in Gosport or across the water in Portsmouth, with Gosport Tourist Information Centre (023 9252 2944) near the ferry terminal. The nearest camping is at Kingfisher Caravan Park (023 9250 2611), right by the route 3½ miles further on near Browndown.

Overview: A surprisingly rewarding day around the shores of the broad haven of Portsmouth Harbour. Despite how built up the area is, the shoreline remains quiet and beautiful, particularly between Portchester and Fleetlands. Other than a couple of long road sections, the walking is pleasant throughout and Portchester Castle, Fareham Creek and the well preserved naval buildings of Gosport provide plenty of interest.

Route Description

The route resumes along the **A27**, following the cycleway along its left side away from the junction with the M27. After a mile the path leads through a subway beneath the road, then doubles back left to cross the A3 and continue alongside the A27. Cross back to the left side at any of the pedestrian crossings and continue beneath the motorway, before joining the shore just beyond by the road to Port Solent. A path winds along the shore of **Paulsgrove Lake** before you are forced to rejoin the main road by Mother Kelly's. The chalk ridge of **Portsdown Hill** towers over this part of the coast and is lined with six large forts, which were among the first built by Lord Palmerston in the 1860s – they were known as **Palmerston Follies** as they faced inland, imagining a French attack on Portsmouth from inland, having landed further along the coast.

Turn first left along Hamilton Road and, at its end by a huge

Portchester Castle

Portchester Castle began life as the Roman fort of Portus Adurni and is the best preserved of a series of forts built by the Romans along the south coast. Its shape and walls were retained when the Norman baronial keep was built in the 11th century, before becoming a favourite of King John. From the 17th century it was used as a prison, and in the late 18th century it housed over 2,000 former slaves captured fighting for the French in St Lucia, some of whom would go on to enlist in the British Army or Navy.

underwater carbon fibre reel, keep straight on along a footpath. This winds along the shore to pass Portchester Sailing Club and then circle around the grand edifice of **Portchester Castle**. The main route keeps left beyond the castle to briefly follow the estuary shore, but an alternative high tide route cuts inland to join the approach road to the castle. In the heart of old **Portchester**, turn left along Hospital Lane to rejoin the main route as it resumes along a walkway past Turret House.

Continue along the beautiful shore of Portsmouth Harbour past the estates of Portchester and Wicor to reach another short section along the tidal shore of **Wicor Lake** by Salt Café. *The high tide alternative crosses a field to join a path heading left to the entrance to the marina; follow the road right then left, and keep left through the Wicor Recreation Ground car park to return to the shore.* Beyond Wicor Lake the route winds along the edge of the

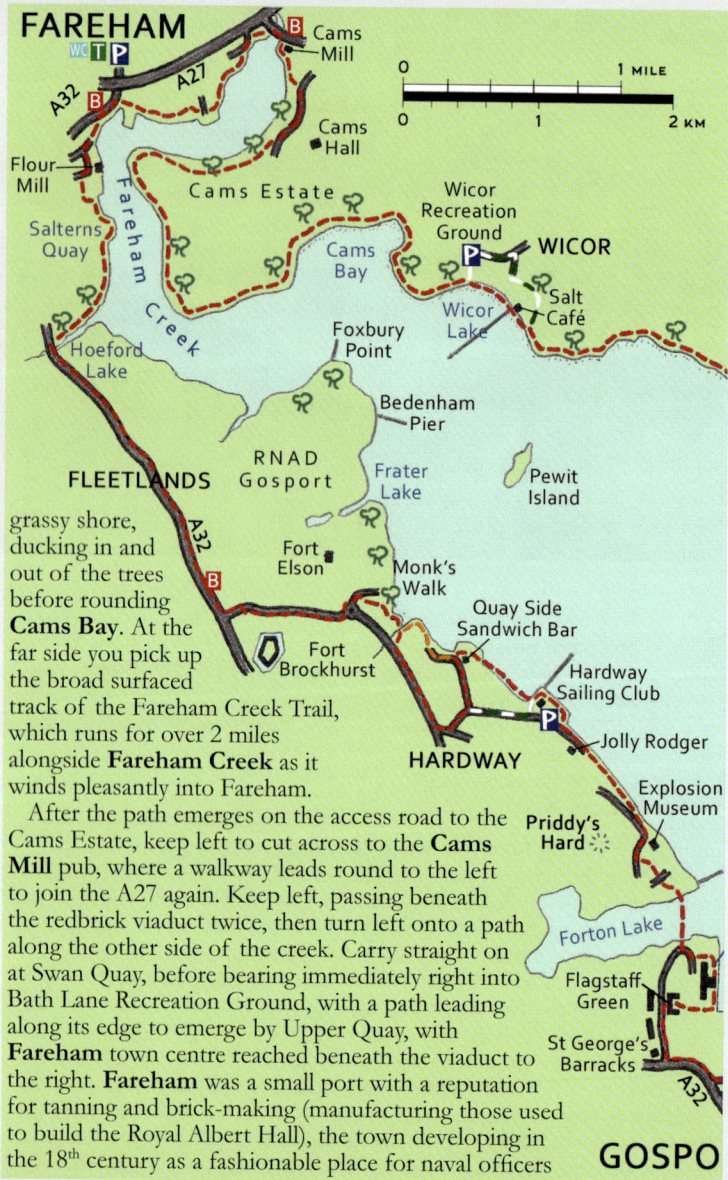

FAREHAM

WC T P

A32　A27

B　Cams Mill

B

Cams Hall

Flour Mill

Cams Estate

Salterns Quay

Fareham Creek

Cams Bay

Hoeford Lake

Foxbury Point

Bedenham Pier

Wicor Recreation Ground

P

WICOR

Salt Café

Wicor Lake

Pewit Island

R N A D Gosport

Frater Lake

FLEETLANDS

A32

B

Fort Elson

Monk's Walk

Quay Side Sandwich Bar

Fort Brockhurst

Hardway Sailing Club

P

Jolly Rodger

HARDWAY

Explosion Museum

Priddy's Hard

Forton Lake

Flagstaff Green

St George's Barracks

A32

GOSPO

0 ___ 1 MILE
0 ___ 1 ___ 2 KM

grassy shore, ducking in and out of the trees before rounding **Cams Bay**. At the far side you pick up the broad surfaced track of the Fareham Creek Trail, which runs for over 2 miles alongside **Fareham Creek** as it winds pleasantly into Fareham.

After the path emerges on the access road to the Cams Estate, keep left to cut across to the **Cams Mill** pub, where a walkway leads round to the left to join the A27 again. Keep left, passing beneath the redbrick viaduct twice, then turn left onto a path along the other side of the creek. Carry straight on at Swan Quay, before bearing immediately right into Bath Lane Recreation Ground, with a path leading along its edge to emerge by Upper Quay, with **Fareham** town centre reached beneath the viaduct to the right. **Fareham** was a small port with a reputation for tanning and brick-making (manufacturing those used to build the Royal Albert Hall), the town developing in the 18th century as a fashionable place for naval officers

Portsdown Hill

Mother Kelly's

PAULSGROVE

A27 B

carbon fibre reel

M27

A27

T

COSHAM

PORT-CHESTER

Paulsgrove Lake

Port Solent

Hilsea Lido

M27

B WC

Cormorant

P WC

P

Horsea Island

Tipner Lake

HILSEA

Turret House

Portchester Castle

Portsea Island

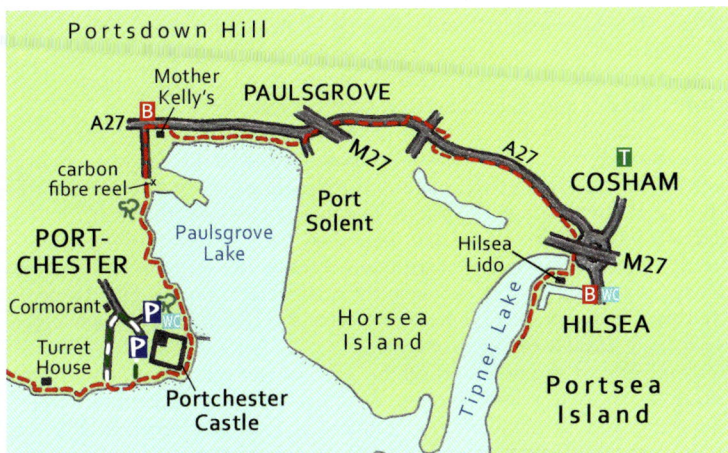

Portsmouth Harbour

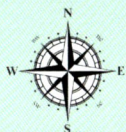

N
W   E
S

Royal Clarence Marina

Burrow Island

PORTSMOUTH

Castle Tavern

RT

P B

Gosport Ferry

Spinnaker Tower

The Bedenham Pier Explosion

The Explosion Museum in Gosport is dedicated to naval firepower, but in 1950 a different sort of explosion occurred at the Royal Naval Armament Depot in Fleetlands. As several barges were being loaded with ammunition, a depth charge set fire and two massive explosions destroyed the pier, barges, several buildings and 5,000 tons of explosives. Shells landed across the water in Wicor and a locomotive wheel in Landport, while Cams Hall's roofs and windows were damaged, yet remarkably no one was killed. It has always been suspected it was an act of sabotage by Communists at the height of the Cold War.

away from the grime of Portsmouth.

The route continues left alongside the road, before turning left towards the striking redbrick **Flour Mill** at Lower Quay. Follow the road round to the right here, then turn left on a footpath to cut through to the open shore of Salterns Quay. The path hugs the shore all the way round to the inlet of Hoeford Lake, where it cuts through the trees to reach the A32. Follow this right for 1½ miles past the Royal Naval Armaments

Depot (**RNAD Gosport**) and former RAF helicopter repair site at Fleetlands. Finally turn left on Heritage Way towards Priddy's Hard, soon crossing to the opposite pavement and continuing past **Fort Brockhurst** (a moated Palmerston fort) for another ¾ mile.

At a roundabout, bear left towards **Monk's Walk**, then follow a path right through the trees to rejoin the shore. The signed route turns right before the industrial estate, but an informal shortcut continues along the shore and cuts through the estate. The main route joins the road, keeping left on Priory Road and then Quay Lane to return to the same point. On the bend, a fenced path cuts through the shoreline side of the Quay Side Sandwich Bar to follow the tidal shore round to **Hardway Sailing Club** and joins the road just beyond. *The high tide alternative stays along Priory Road to reach the same point.*

At the end of the road beyond the Jolly Rodger pub, a path continues along the shore to rejoin Heritage Way. Continue past the entrance to the Explosion Museum and the ramparts of **Priddy's Hard**, an 18th-century fort and gunpowder magazine. Turn left between the blocks of flats and follow a walkway right to recross the road and approach the Millennium Bridge, which crosses Forton Lake towards the naval buildings of **Royal Clarence Yard**, a victualling yard supplying the Royal Navy from 1831. Turn left on the road and left again on a footway between Galleon Place and Ledwell Court to reach the waterside. Pass beneath the Granary and go right at the end to make your way round to the entrance gate at the far end of the bright white buildings and fountain of **Flagstaff Green**.

Follow the road left past the various offices and quarters, before turning left onto the A32 by **St George's Barracks**. Turn left on Harbour Road, keeping left to reach a footpath out to the yacht marina. You are soon forced back from the shore at **Endeavour Quay**, keeping left to pass the Castle Tavern and rejoin the waterfront by the Gosport Ferry Terminal, from where ferries run across the water to Portsmouth Harbour every 15 minutes. The bus station is just beyond and **Gosport** town centre reached to the right. As Portsmouth grew rapidly from the 17th century, Gosport (its name referring to wild geese) developed on the other side of the harbour to supply goods to the Navy and in 1627 it was even proposed to transfer the whole dockyard across the water.

SONG OF THE DAY

Bellowhead – *Gosport Nancy*

A traditional drinking song that was sung by sailors in the port at Gosport, suggesting the town's women 'like a drink and dancing the Can Can', is given Bellowhead distinctive brass-infused treatment.

Section 4.5 – Gosport to Warsash or Hamble-le-Rice

Distance: 22.2km (14 miles)

Height Gained: 50m

Parking: Pay car parks in Gosport. Free car park at Warsash, as well as various places along the route between Lee-on-the-Solent and Meon.

Public Transport: Bus X5 (First, towards Gosport) runs regularly 7 days a week from Warsash village centre to Gosport, though it can actually be quicker to change for Bus E2 (First, towards Gosport) at Fareham bus station.

Refreshments: Various cafes and pubs in Lee-on-the-Solent, as well as Titchfield Haven Tea Rooms at Hillhead Harbour.

Accommodation: Hamble-le-Rice has various accommodation, while there are rooms in Warsash at Howerts House (07958 584714). Mercury Yacht Holiday Park (023 8045 3220) offers camping a mile off the route at Hamble-le-Rice.

Overview: A lovely walk along the Solent shore with great views across the water to the Isle of Wight. Between the busy marinas of Gosport and the River Hamble, there are lovely sections of promenade around Stokes Bay and Lee-on-the-Solent and, at Brownwich and Chilling, the first cliffs passed on the route since Brighton. The day can be ended on either side of the River Hamble, which is crossed by a distinctive pink ferry.

Route Description

Rejoin the waterfront path by Gosport Ferry Terminal to pass **Haslar Marina**, before joining the road as it crosses Haslar Bridge. Follow Haslar Road between the impressive redbrick

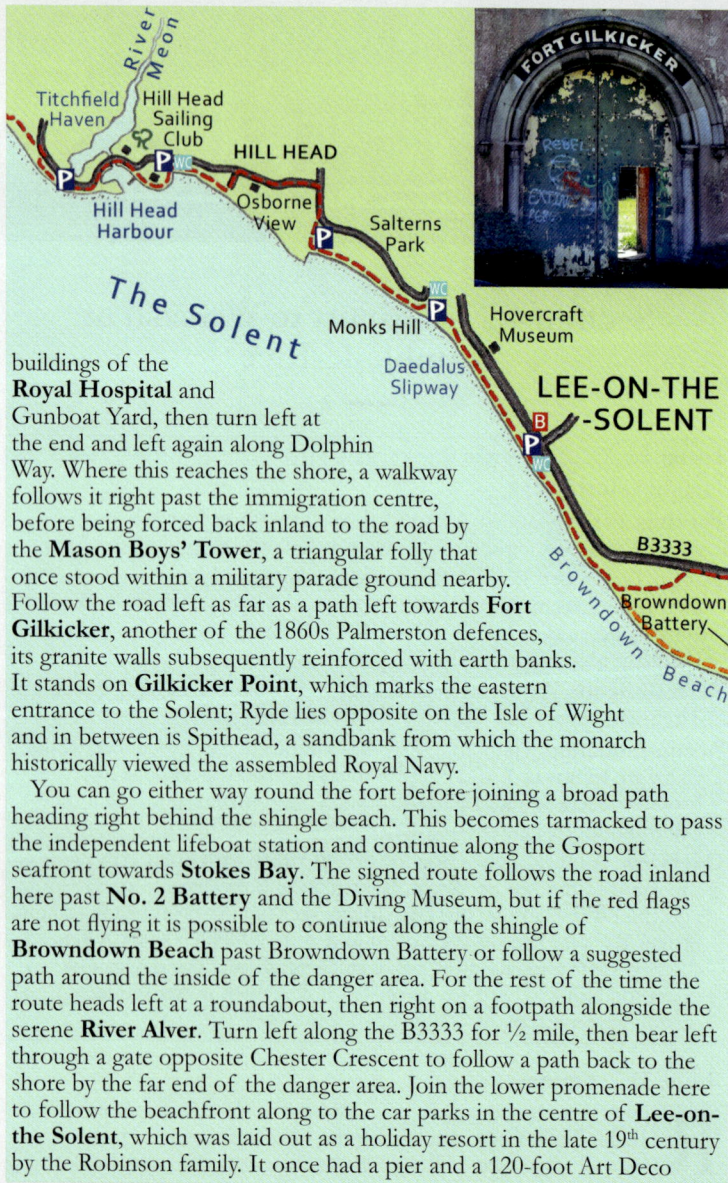

Map labels:

River Meon

Titchfield Haven

Hill Head Sailing Club

HILL HEAD

P WC

Hill Head Harbour

Osborne View

P

Salterns Park

The Solent

Monks Hill

WC P

Daedalus Slipway

Hovercraft Museum

LEE-ON-THE -SOLENT

B P WC

B3333

Browndown Beach

Browndown Battery

FORT GILKICKER

buildings of the **Royal Hospital** and Gunboat Yard, then turn left at the end and left again along Dolphin Way. Where this reaches the shore, a walkway follows it right past the immigration centre, before being forced back inland to the road by the **Mason Boys' Tower**, a triangular folly that once stood within a military parade ground nearby. Follow the road left as far as a path left towards **Fort Gilkicker**, another of the 1860s Palmerston defences, its granite walls subsequently reinforced with earth banks. It stands on **Gilkicker Point**, which marks the eastern entrance to the Solent; Ryde lies opposite on the Isle of Wight and in between is Spithead, a sandbank from which the monarch historically viewed the assembled Royal Navy.

You can go either way round the fort before joining a broad path heading right behind the shingle beach. This becomes tarmacked to pass the independent lifeboat station and continue along the Gosport seafront towards **Stokes Bay**. The signed route follows the road inland here past **No. 2 Battery** and the Diving Museum, but if the red flags are not flying it is possible to continue along the shingle of **Browndown Beach** past Browndown Battery or follow a suggested path around the inside of the danger area. For the rest of the time the route heads left at a roundabout, then right on a footpath alongside the serene **River Alver**. Turn left along the B3333 for ½ mile, then bear left through a gate opposite Chester Crescent to follow a path back to the shore by the far end of the danger area. Join the lower promenade here to follow the beachfront along to the car parks in the centre of **Lee-on-the Solent**, which was laid out as a holiday resort in the late 19th century by the Robinson family. It once had a pier and a 120-foot Art Deco

The Solent

The Solent is a 20-mile strait between the Isle of Wight and the mainland and, like the harbours to the east, represents a drowned river system. The bed of the River Solent lies about 40m below sea level as it flows round the east side of the Isle of Wight, meaning the whole basin is relatively shallow. It gathers the waters of the Test, Itchen and Hamble (merging as the Southampton Water) and is now the most popular yachting and dinghy sailing area in the country. Possibly named after the solans goose (or northern gannet) that is found here, it has also been suggested the Solent is derived from an ancient word for 'free-standing rock', referring to the Needles at its western entrance.

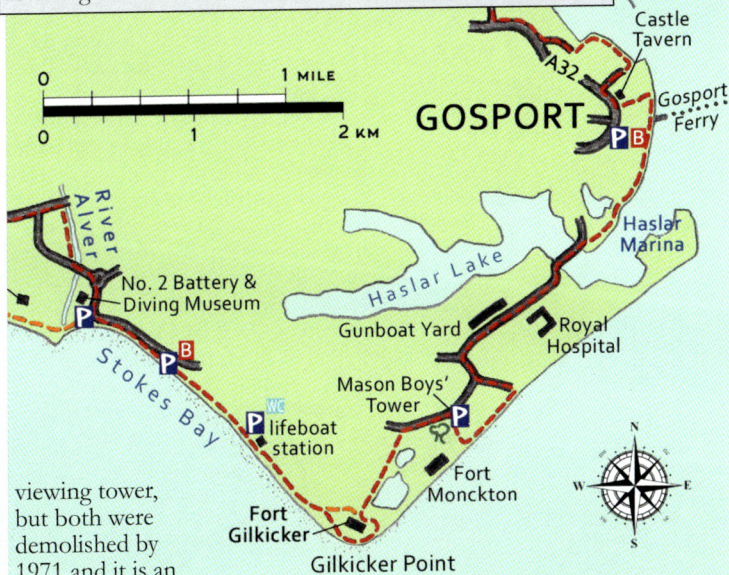

viewing tower, but both were demolished by 1971 and it is an unassuming place now.

Continue along the seafront promenade, passing the **Daedalus Slipway**, which was created in 1917 for launching seaplanes from the Naval Seaplane Training School (now used as Solent Airport, as well as housing the Hovercraft Museum). The route passes through the large car park at Monks Hill, before resuming along the seafront past **Salterns Park**. At the next car park, the route that continues along the shingle shore is both tidal and requires scrambling over several groynes, so the coast path is signed up to the road. Keep left to rejoin the promenade along Hill Head Beach and continue round Hill Head Sailing Club before rejoining the road around **Hill Head Harbour**. This marks the end of the Titchfield Canal, created in the early 17th century as the country's second canal. It blocked off the mouth of the River Meon and created the freshwater pools that now form the nature reserve over the road at **Titchfield Haven**.

You can join the shingle beach at **Meon Shore**, but the signed route follows the road before bearing left on the bend to pass through the chalets. At the end a path climbs above the low clay cliffs of **Brownwich Cliffs**. After ½ mile the path drops down to **Brownwich Beach**, staying along the back of the shingle to cross one of a pair of bridges and climb back to the clifftops. Follow the field edge past a low trig point to reach **Chilling Cliffs**, where coastal erosion has removed the old path (as well as some of the chalets) and the route is forced inland. Follow the field edge round to join a track by Chilling Barn, then turn left along the road. Bear right onto a track before the entrance to Solent Breezes Holiday Park and turn left beyond the substation to return to the low shore.

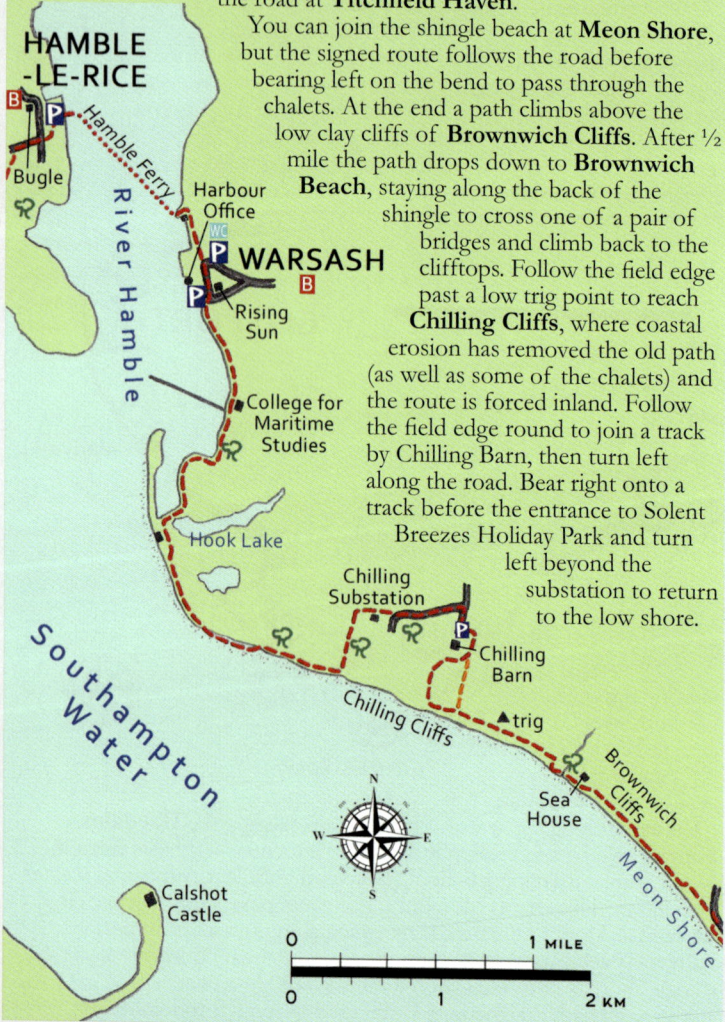

HAMBLE-LE-RICE
Bugle
Hamble Ferry
River Hamble
Harbour Office
WARSASH
Rising Sun
College for Maritime Studies
Hook Lake
Southampton Water
Chilling Substation
Chilling Barn
Chilling Cliffs
trig
Sea House
Brownwich Cliffs
Meon Shore
Calshot Castle

0   1 MILE
0   1   2 KM

Brownwich Cliffs and the Meon Shore

The path intermittently joins the shingle beach past the local nature reserve here, before reaching a concrete building by the spit at the mouth of the **River Hamble**. Bear right to join a gravel path across Hook Lake Control Gates and along the sea wall. Keep left to pass the College for Maritime Studies and skirt along the edge of Strawberry Fields into **Warsash**. The village centre is reached by turning right by the Rising Sun, but the route continues along Shore Road before bearing left onto a path on the bend to reach the bright pink Hamble Ferry, which runs regularly across the river to **Hamble-le-Rice**. The ferry has run since at least the 16th century, but the pink colour only arrived in 2002, and the shelter on the Warsash side was built by one of the pubs in the early 20th century. The sheltered River Hamble has long been popular for shipbuilding and is now a centre for yachting, an extensive array of fancy boats lining its course.

SONG OF THE DAY **Ralph Vaughan Williams** – *The Solent*

Composed in 1902 when Vaughan Williams was just 30, this wonderful evocation of the sea was among his first orchestral pieces, yet ranks among his finest achievements. It was introduced with the words of poet Philip Marston 'Passion and sorrow in the deep sea's voice, a mighty mystery saddening all the wind.'

The bright Hamble Ferry

Section 4.6 – Warsash or Hamble-le-Rice to Southampton

Distance: 12.5km (8 miles)

Height Gained: 70m

Parking: Pay car parks in Hamble-le-Rice and Southampton, with free car parks at Warsash and along the route at Hamble Common Beach, Netley Hard and Weston Promenade.

Public Transport: Bus 6 (First, towards Hamble) runs regularly from Houndwell Park in the centre of Southampton to Hamble-le-Rice, with an hourly service at weekends.

Refreshments: Various pubs and cafes along the route through Netley and Woolston.

Accommodation: There are plenty of accommodation options in Southampton, but no campsite nearby or across the water in Hythe.

Overview: An exceptionally short day that has the benefit of providing plenty of time to look around Southampton or take the ferry either to Hythe or the Isle of Wight to continue the route. Alternatively it can be combined with the subsequent section to Calshot. It is a fine approach to this pleasant city, the greenery of Hamble Common and Royal Victoria Country Park giving way to the mudflats of Weston Shore and the marinas of the River Itchen.

Route Description

Having crossed the **River Hamble**, follow the shore left past the Hamble Lifeboat station, then bear right to head up the lane beside the pink cottage (the path on along the shore continues only as far as the sailing club). Turn left across the green to enter the woods of **Hamble Common** and keep left to return to the shore. Turn left again to cross a couple of tidal streams, then keep left along the muddy estuary shore until forced into the trees by Hamble Point Marina. Beyond the gate, fork right to join the edge of the open common and then keep left to reach the road opposite the car park by **Hamble Common Beach**. The Bofors anti-aircraft gun mounted here was used to protect the nearby oil terminals in World War II and was moved from the concrete emplacement that is now behind fencing at the other end of the car park due to coastal erosion.

The route follows a path along the shore past the emplacement and the site of **St Andrew's Castle**, another of Henry VIII's defensive structures along the south coast. Turn left beyond to briefly cross the

Pillbox near Hamble Cliff

shingle shore and pick up a pathway around the oil terminal, whose jetty was extended in 1943 to supply fuel to ships involved in the D-Day Landings. Rejoin the beach for ¼ mile before bearing right to pass beside a **pillbox**, which was linked to a line of mines laid across Southampton Water and has a lookout post above.

A path winds between the car parks and through the trees above **Hamble Cliff**, before dropping down to rejoin the beach for ⅓ mile. *This section is tidal, so a high tide alternative bears right to join the road, then keeps right of Hamblecliff House to follow a path round Netley Sailing Club and into* ROYAL VICTORIA COUNTRY PARK. *Turn left to return to the main route*, which heads up some steps to follow a broad path along the edge of the country park. **Royal Victoria Chapel** stands proudly on the hill and is the only remaining section of the ¼-mile long Royal Victoria Hospital, which was the British Army's first purpose-built hospital in 1863 and had over 1,000 beds. The 570ft pier that once stood here was used to land patients from large hospital boats, and Queen Victoria was also a regular visitor from Osborne House on the Isle of Wight.

The path soon joins the access road to leave the country park by the slipway at **Netley Hard**. Continue along the road through Netley, before turning left down Beach Lane to follow a path along the shore past **Netley Castle**. This 16th-century fort was converted into a Gothic mansion in the late 19th century, but the ruins of Netley Abbey, a Cistercian monastery founded c1239, stand in the grounds beyond.

Royal Victoria Chapel

SOUTHAMPTON

B Bargate

T

God's
House
Tower

Itchen
Bridge

A3025

P

B T
WOOLSTON

P A33
Water-
gate

W

Ocean
Village
Marina

River Itchen

Centenary
Quay

Water
Treatment
Works

Town
Quay

Southampton
Docks

Weston
Point

WESTON

Weston Shore

Hythe Ferry

Southampton
Water

P

Netley
Castle

Weston
Sailing Club

P NETLEY

B

Netley
Hard

Hythe
Pier

HYTHE

0   1 MILE

0   1   2 KM

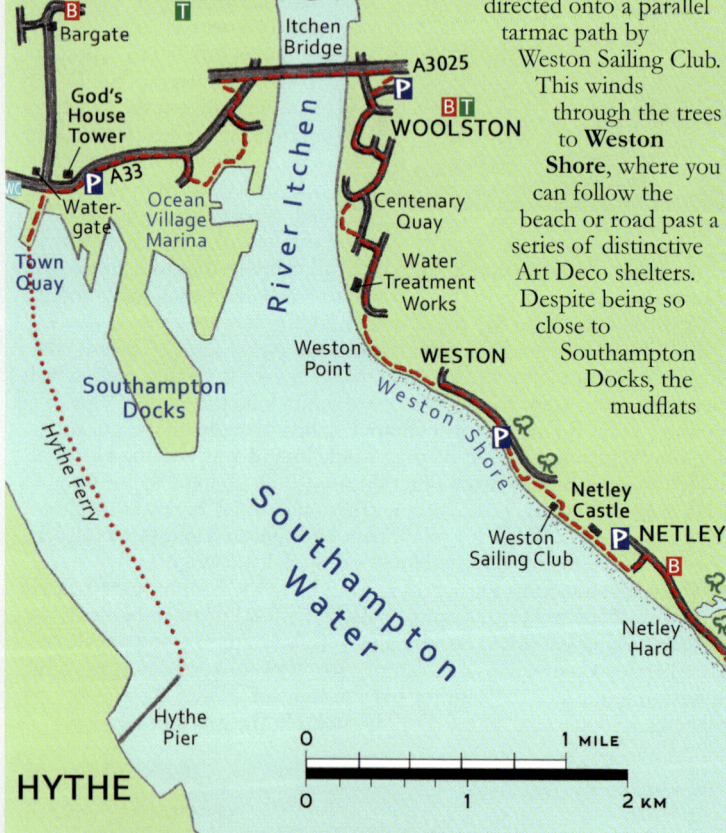

Follow the shore until
directed onto a parallel
tarmac path by
Weston Sailing Club.
This winds
through the trees
to **Weston
Shore**, where you
can follow the
beach or road past a
series of distinctive
Art Deco shelters.
Despite being so
close to
Southampton
Docks, the
mudflats

*Bargate,
Southampton*

along this shoreline are one of the most popular areas in the UK for overwintering wading birds and wildfowl like dunlin, plover, curlew, turnstone and brent geese.

A tarmac path continues along the shore to reach Victoria Road, where the route bears left past the futuristic Woolston Wastewater Treatment Works. Turn left along Oswald Road, then head straight on along Denyer Walk at **Centenary Quay**, where regeneration work is ongoing. Turn right to join a road and head straight on at the roundabout, before heading left down Keswick Road and keeping left. Bending round to reach Hazel Road through the heart of **Woolston**, bear left to reach some steps leading up onto the **Itchen Toll Bridge**. Cross high above the River Itchen with great views across this part of Southampton. The bridge opened in 1977, replacing a chain ferry known as Woolston Floating Bridge and the earlier Itchen Ferry, which had been used by Jane Austen on her regular trips to Southampton.

Turn sharply left down some steps at the first opportunity, turning right along Canute Road and then turn immediately left on Channel Way. On the bend a walkway leads right to Admiral's Quay and emerges on **Ocean Village Marina**, whose quayside you follow right. On the bend bear right and right again to rejoin Canute Road, following it left into the city across a railway crossing. Continue past Queen's Park and **God's House Tower**, a 15th-century artillery blockhouse built in preparation for Henry V's war with France. Soon after, you turn left at **Town Quay** to reach the

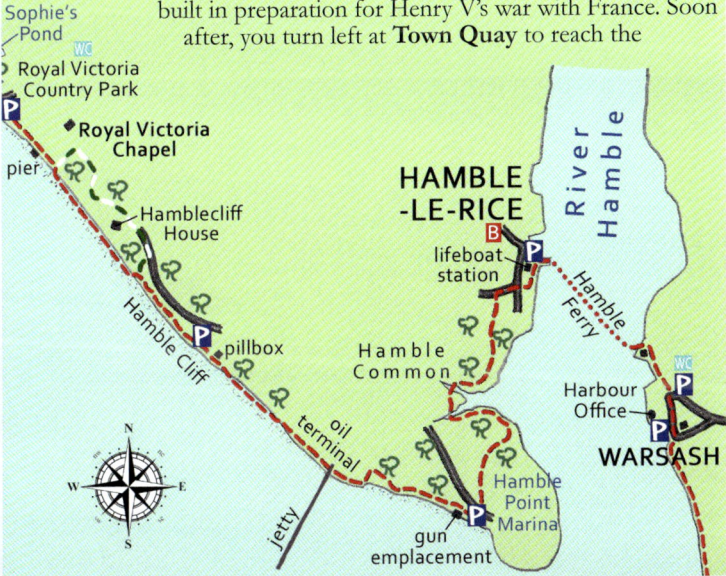

Sophie's Pond

WC

Royal Victoria Country Park

P

Royal Victoria Chapel

pier

Hamblecliff House

Hamble Cliff

pillbox

P

Hamble Common

oil terminal

jetty

gun emplacement

HAMBLE -LE-RICE

B

lifeboat station

P

River Hamble

Hamble Ferry

Harbour Office

WC P

P

WARSASH

Hamble Point Marina

N
W E
S

passenger ferries to both Cowes on the Isle of Wight and Hythe across the estuary. The centre of **Southampton** and its central bus stops are reached by turning right by the ruins of Watergate, an entrance through Southampton's medieval city walls.

Southampton

Southampton began life as the principal port for the city of Winchester, which was the capital of England until the early 12th century. The Normans used it as their primary link with France, but after a French raid in 1338 destroyed much of the town, its defensive walls were created. As well as an important port, it became a fashionable spa town in the 18th century and was the embarkation point for the *Titanic*, with over a third of those lost when it sank hailing from Southampton. Although much of the city was destroyed by bombing in World War II, parts of the city walls remain, including at Bargate and Arundel Tower on the far side of the Old Town.

SONG OF THE DAY **Craig David** – *One More Time*
David was born in Southampton in 1981, growing up on the Holyrood housing estate near the city centre, which is referenced in the lyrics of this 2016 single – 'Southampton I was raised in the days, Remember when you used to pick me up from raves in the days, When I was selling mixtapes instead of getting grades'.

Southampton Docks

Section 4.7 · Southampton to Calshot

Distance: 14.3km (9 miles)

Height Gained: 80m

Parking: Pay car parks in Hythe and Calshot, with small free car park along the route at Ashlett.

Public Transport: Bus 9 (Bluestar, towards Southampton) runs hourly from Calshot to Hythe Pier 7 days a week. The same bus continues all the way to Southampton, though it is probably quicker to return on the ferry from Hythe.

Refreshments: Meals at the Jolly Sailor in Ashlett or the Falcon in Fawley, while KFC and Holbury Fish Bar are passed in Holbury.

Accommodation: There is no accommodation in Calshot, the closest rooms being at Walcot Guest House (023 8089 1344) and the Falcon Inn (023 8184 4467) a short bus ride away in Fawley, or Holbury B&B (07585 605560) in nearby Holbury. Lepe Beach Campsite (0330 1000842) is located 3 miles further along the route towards Beaulieu, though it is only open during holidays and weekends May-August.

Overview: A short and very straightforward day that could be easily combined with either of the days either side. Although half of it is on roads and only short sections follow the shore due to the presence of Fawley Refinery, there is plenty of variety around the edge of the New Forest and the final section from Ashlett to Calshot is delightful.

Route Description

The Hythe Ferry runs hourly 7 days a week from Town Quay in Southampton to **Hythe Pier**, which is nearly ½ mile long and home to the world's oldest electric pier railway. Turn left at its end to join the pedestrianised High Street through **Hythe**, then turn left to reach the riverside promenade. Follow this right only briefly, before following the road inland past St John the Baptist's Church and the information centre. Beyond the shipyards of Hythe Marine Park, Shore Road opens out on the shore by **Spartina Marsh Nature Reserve**, named after a type of cordgrass commonly found on saltmarshes.

Hythe waterfront

Stay on the road to cross the railway, then bear left on Hart Hill to pass the **Travellers Rest** in Frostlane and join a path straight on into the woods beyond. This ancient route, lined with beech, oak and chestnut trees, gives a first taste of the beautiful woodlands of the New Forest. Briefly join a vehicle track, before continuing straight on along the bridleway to round the site of Esso's Hythe Terminal. The coast path runs inland here because the shore is dominated by the vast site of **Fawley Refinery**, the largest oil refinery in the UK, processing around 270,000 barrels of oil a day.

Follow the access road, then head straight on at its end, before turning immediately left on a track through the trees to emerge on the A326 just beyond the Lighthouse Community Church. Follow the main road left, then cross at the first pedestrian crossing to stay on its right side for a mile through Hardley and **Holbury**. Stay on the cycleway as it bears right at the roundabout, then turn left after 100m onto a path that cuts through to follow the side of the B3053. This opens out along the edge of the park, passing Gang Warily Fishing Pond before rejoining the roadside into **Fawley**. Gang Warily (translating as 'go carefully') is the motto of the Drummond Clan, a Scottish family who moved to Hampshire in the 18th century and acquired large tracts of land here

Turn left into Church Lane and soon join a pleasant path through the trees to its left. Continue into the old village, then turn right through the graveyard of **All Saints' Church**, parts of which date from the 12th century or possibly earlier. Follow the path out of the far end of the graveyard, bearing left in the field to join a narrow path behind the houses that emerges on Copthorne Lane. Follow the road right, then turn left as Copthorne Lane continues around the edge of the village.

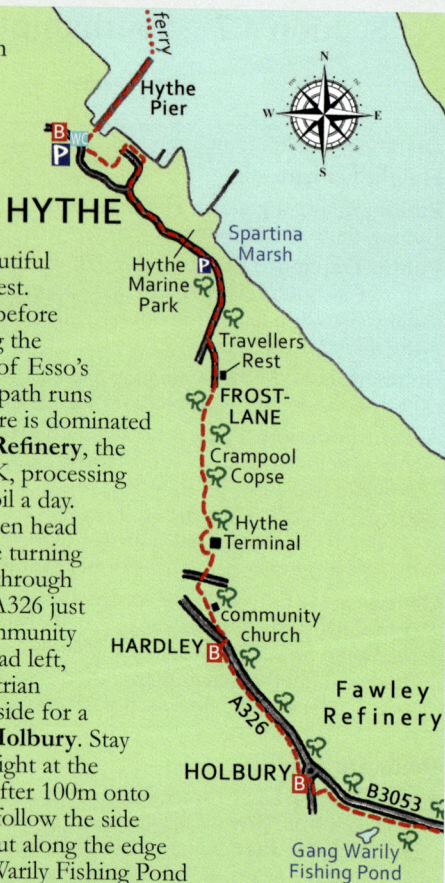

Turn sharply left to enter the New Forest National Park for the first time and keep left to drop down to the Jolly Sailor pub and picturesque Victoria Quay in Ashlett. **Ashlett Tide Mill**, an early 19th-century flour mill with a fine mansard roof, stands between Ashlett Creek and its tidal mill pond. The name **Ashlett** is thought to refer to a custom of Viking invaders who erected an ash post where they came ashore.

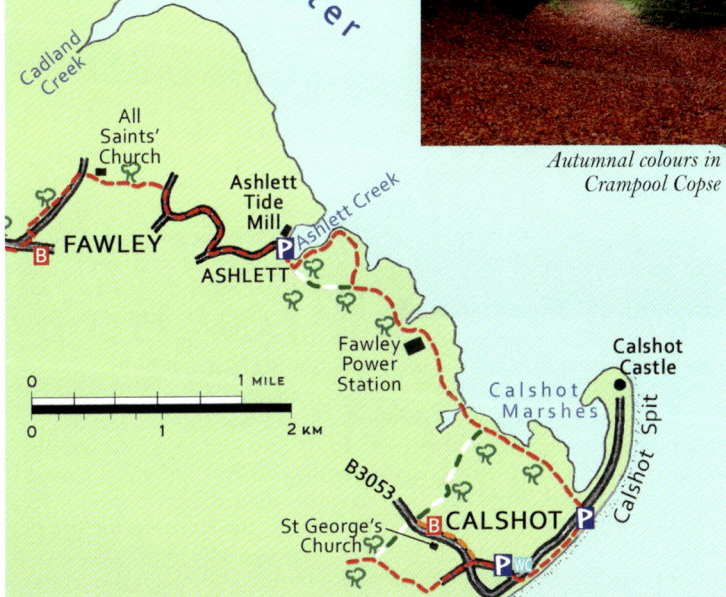

Autumnal colours in Crampool Copse

Calshot Tower and Castle on Calshot Spit

A lovely path follows the shore round the creekside past Ashlett Sailing Club and into the trees beyond – at particularly high tides it may be necessary to follow the alternative route through the trees inland to this point. Wind along the wooded shore to **Fawley Power Station**, the route skirting the shoreline side of the perimeter fence all the way round to the swing bridge at the entrance to its small quay. When the bridge is being opened, red flags are raised and you may have to wait up to 45 minutes for it to be closed again. The oil-fired power station was decommissioned in 2013, the site since being used by an offshore energy firm to assemble wind turbines and is soon to become a new housing estate. The 650ft-high chimney stack was pulled down in 2021

and the brutalist **control centre** (which is known as 'the Flying Saucer' and has featured in *Rollerball*, *Solo: A Star Wars Story*, *Mission Impossible* and *Red Dwarf*) will soon go the same way.

Shortly after the swing bridge, the route divides again, with the main route continuing along the edge of **Calshot Marshes**, with the buildings of Calshot Spit laid out across the water. Henry VIII built **Calshot Castle** at the mouth of Southampton Water in 1539, and alongside it stand the Coastwatch's Calshot Tower and a World War II hangar for flying boats that now houses the country's oldest velodrome. You can explore the spit, but the route turns right along the road or the shingle beach, whose beach houses look across the Solent to the Isle of Wight. At the point where the beach becomes private, preventing access to the coast for the next couple of miles, turn right through the car park and follow the road into **Calshot**. A new section of the coast path will continue straight on into Castle Lane at the first junction, before crossing the fields from its end, but until that is open you need to stay on the road through Calshot to rejoin the alternative route at the far end of the village. The hourly bus can be caught from outside St George's Church to Fawley or Hythe.

ALTERNATIVE ROUTE: *Parts of the path across Calshot Marshes can be inundated at high tide, so you may need to follow a route right along the perimeter fence of the former power station site. Bear left to reach a bridge over the drain by a brick bunker and follow a grassy path up to the main road through Calshot.*

Calshot and Tristan da Cunha

Though unprepossessing, the former council houses of Tristan Close link Calshot with one of Britain's most remote Overseas Territories. It was on a former RAF base here that the 268 residents of Tristan da Cunha were evacuated when the South Atlantic island was threatened by a volcanic eruption in 1961. Though finding work at the electric blanket factory in Hythe, many struggled with infections, particularly through the harsh winter of 1962. Most islanders were repatriated once their home was declared safe to return to, renaming their main port Calshot Harbour, but a handful remained in Calshot.

SONG OF THE DAY

Pink Floyd – *Southampton Dock/The Final Cut*
A 1983 song about the departure of soldiers for the Falklands War just as they had from the same dock four decades earlier. Marchwood Military Port on the west side of the River Test was built for the D-Day assault during World War II and would not be used again until the Falklands War. The song here runs seamlessly into *The Final Cut* at the end of the album of the same name.

Ashlett Tide Mill & Victoria Quay

Section 4.8 – Calshot to Beaulieu

—◆◆—

Distance: 15.3km (9½ miles)

Height Gained: 60m

Parking: Pay car parks at Calshot, Lepe Beach and in Beaulieu. Free car park along the route at Moonhills Car Park on Beaulieu Heath.

Public Transport: Bus 112 (morebus, towards Hythe) runs at 1426 from Beaulieu to Hythe Pier on weekdays during the summer, and on Tuesdays and Thursdays in winter. The Hythe Taxishare (Hampshire Community Transport, 01962 846785, pre-booking essential) does the same route at 0925 on Tuesdays and Fridays. Bus 9 (Bluestar, towards Calshot) then runs hourly 7 days a week from Hythe to Calshot, but this service can also be picked up on Rollestone Road in Holbury, just 2 miles off the route across Beaulieu Heath.

Refreshments: The Lookout cafe is at Lepe Beach, while both Mr Eddy's Tea Rooms and VGF's Vegan & Gluten Free Food can be found in Exbury Gardens.

Accommodation: There are expensive rooms at the Montagu Arms Hotel (01590 624467) in Beaulieu, or more affordable options at the Turfcutters Arms (01590 612331), 1½ miles away in East Boldre, or the Master Builder's House Hotel (01590 616253), 2 miles further along the route in Buckler's Hard. There is also a pop-up campsite (*www.caravanclub.co.uk*) in the Beaulieu Estate during the summer.

Overview: A frustratingly road-dominated section, with access to the coast and Beaulieu estuary restricted by the Cadland House and Exbury House estates and their clever use of nature reserve designations. The one coastal section around Lepe is lovely, but also tidal, so be careful to avoid passing two hours either side of high tide and being left with nothing but tarmac all day. This is particularly true until the few off-road sections of the new coast path are opened up and give a little more taste of the rich woodland of the New Forest, most of which remains behind fences on its southern fringe.

Route Description

Leave the main road through **Calshot** to follow Elmfield Lane to its end, where a path continues into the woods beyond and rejoins the new section of coast path once it has opened. Head straight across a private road, then turn left on Stanswood Road for 1½ miles. Pass **Stanswood Farm** and the drive to Stone Farm, before another new section of the route turns left on the next vehicle track, following it

The Watch House at Lepe

for a mile down to the beach near **Stansore Point**. It is possible to follow the beach past the Spit and below the low cliffs here, although the route turns right on the broad track through **Lepe Country Park**. Beyond the Coastwatch lookout on Stone Point, turn left down a walkway to the cafe and toilets by the lower car park, before joining the road along the shore beyond. *Until this new section is open, you'll have to stay on the road throughout, keeping left to reach the Lepe shore.*

Follow the road along the **Lepe** seafront and, after crossing Lepe Outfall over the Dark Water, bear left on a footway past the **Watch House**, a boathouse built in 1828 and used by the coastguard, whose former cottages stand nearby. Until the 18th century, and possibly as far back as Roman times, there was a harbour at Lepe by the original mouth of the Dark Water to the east of Stone Point – its name is thought to refer to a leap for deer, possibly across the water itself.

At the end of the walkway the route joins the back of the shingle beach for a mile, but there is a section in the middle that is likely to be impassable for around 2 hours either side of high tide. *If the tide is in, you can rejoin the road by the* Millennium Beacon *(a modern lighthouse built to guide boats into the treacherous Beaulieu River) or at a footpath ¼ mile further on.* The main route tiptoes along the foot of the crumbling gravel cliffs to pass the **Inchmery House** estate and continue along the wooded shore beyond. Inchmery House was used during World War II for training a group of Polish parachutists, who were dropped behind enemy lines in Operation Bardsea during the build up to the D-Day Landings.

Another path leads up to the road, but the route continues along the edge of the saltmarshes at the mouth of the **Beaulieu River** to reach the road near a small private quay. This river was originally the River Exe (from a Celtic word for water) before being renamed by the Normans after the hunting estate they founded here. The road leads inland past **Three Stones** and is followed for the next 3 miles, as the Exbury House estate and North Solent National Nature Reserve prevent access to the shore. Bear left onto a larger road in **Exbury** by a redbrick water tower, passing St Katherine's Church and the entrance to **Exbury Gardens**. Exbury was originally sited closer to the river at Lower Exbury, but it was moved to its current location in the early 19th century to house workers

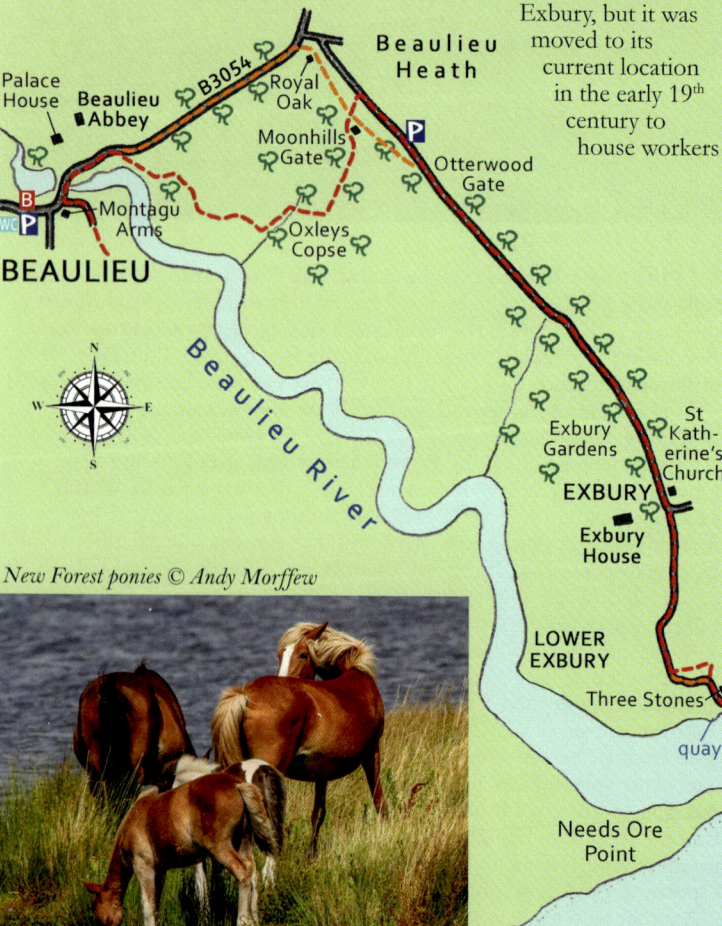

Beaulieu Heath

Palace House

Beaulieu Abbey

B3054

Royal Oak

Moonhills Gate

P

Otterwood Gate

Montagu Arms

Oxleys Copse

BEAULIEU

Beaulieu River

N W E S

Exbury Gardens

St Katherine's Church

EXBURY

Exbury House

LOWER EXBURY

Three Stones

quay

Needs Ore Point

New Forest ponies © Andy Morffew

New Forest Heaths

The New Forest was established around 1079 by William I as a new royal forest for hunting, although it is not, and never was, entirely composed of woodland. Though it represents the greatest concentration of ancient trees in Western Europe, over half of its area is made up of heathland. There is a long history of grazing by ponies and cattle, which are free to roam across the area but are owned by those with commoners' grazing rights,. It has produced a unique landscape of woodland pasture that is probably closer to the ancient wildwood that once covered Britain than our dense modern woodlands. The heaths themselves are particularly rich in wildlife and maintained by a mix of grazing and annual burning.

at Exbury House. The Rothschild family bought **Exbury House** in 1919 and created its exotic gardens, which have been open to the public since 1955 and are famed for their rhododendrons and azaleas.

Follow the road through the mixed woodland to reach a cattle grid at Otterwood Gate that marks the start of **Beaulieu Heath**. Though the route continues along the road for another ½ mile, you'll probably be fed up of it by now and can bear immediately left on a path into the trees along the edge of the heath. Briefly join a vehicle track by the next houses, then continue straight on to rejoin the main route where it turns left on a track towards **Moonhills Gate**.

Once opened, the coast path will

keep left beyond the house to follow a path along the edge of Moonhills Copse, then it will fork right after nearly ½ mile to drop down to a small stream. Just beyond, a new section of path will turn left and skirt along the edge of **Oxleys Copse** down to Dock Lane. Follow this rough road right for ⅓ mile to a narrow footpath leading left just beyond Bignalls. This opens out on a grassy area alongside the Beaulieu River before joining the B3054, which leads left past **Beaulieu Abbey** and the Palace House, before crossing the river into the chocolate-box village of **Beaulieu**. A corn mill has stood here since the 13th century, with the tidal mill pond created by Beaulieu Abbey's monks in the 14th or 15th century and still in use until the early 20th century. The focal point of the perfectly preserved estate village is the **Montagu Arms**, which was originally the Ship Inn before being renamed in 1742.

ALTERNATIVE ROUTE: *Until the new section opens and the route is signed through Moonhills Copse, you will have to continue along the edge of Beaulieu Heath from Moonhills Gate, crossing a number of driveways to reach the ROYAL OAK. Keep left across the heath to reach the busy B3054, which leads left down through the woods to rejoin the main route across the bridge into Beaulieu.*

———————◆◆◆———————

SONG OF THE DAY

Frank Turner – *English Curse*
A 2011 a cappella folk song by the Hampshire-born songwriter Turner about the Blacksmith's Curse, which is said to have been put on William I following the Norman Conquest. Though it would take over 30 years to bear fruit, the new king's son William Rufus (crowned as William II) would die in 1100 while hunting in the New Forest, one of the royal hunting parks he created by seizing English land.

Beaulieu entrance lodge and Palace House

Section 4.9 – Beaulieu to Lymington

Distance: 18.4km (11½ miles)

Height Gained: 90m

Parking: Pay car parks in Beaulieu, Buckler's Hard and Lymington.

Public Transport: Bus 112 (morebus, towards Beaulieu/Hythe) runs 4 times a day from Lymington to Beaulieu on Tuesdays and Thursdays. No service at weekends and only one bus a day at 1515 on Mondays, Wednesdays and Fridays.

Refreshments: There is nothing on the route between Buckler's Hard and Lymington, though the East End Arms is just ¾ mile off the route in East End.

Accommodation: There are various options in Lymington, with a Visitor Information Point at St Barbe's Museum (01590 676969). Embers Camping (0345 2572267) in Pylewell Park is passed along the route 2 miles before Lymington, and Lymington Camping (07764 603073) is 1½ miles from the route on Sway Road.

Overview: Another frustrating day around the edge of the New Forest will be improved by new sections of path being created for the England Coast Path, but the North Solent Nature Reserve at Needs Ore Point and wildfowlers' shooting rights along Boldre Foreshore mean that access to this part of the Solent shore is limited. There are, however, some lovely sections along the Beaulieu River to Buckler's Hard and through Pylewell Park, plenty of points of interest along the way and some surprisingly pleasant road walking.

Route Description

In **Beaulieu**, turn left off the B3054 just before the Montagu Arms, following Fire Station Lane past the fire station to join a gravel path

Beaulieu Abbey and Estate

Formerly the site of a royal hunting lodge, the Beaulieu estate was granted by King John to Cistercian monks to found Beaulieu Abbey in 1204. After the abbey was reduced to ruins during the 16th-century Dissolution, the estate passed to the Montagu family, who converted the former gatehouse into a manor house. It would be transformed into the current Palace House in the 1860s and became one of the first stately homes opened to the public in 1952. Since 1972 it has also been home to the National Motor Museum and houses the *Bluebird* car, with which Donald Campbell set the land speed record.

The Beaulieu River

from its end. Continue past the water works and ancient woodland in Jarvis's Copse to reach Brickworks House by **Bailey's Hard**. This quay served the brickworks, whose domed kilns are still present in the private woods alongside and produced cream-coloured Beaulieu Buff bricks from the late 18th century.

Follow the track round to the right, then turn left onto a dead straight gravel path into **Keeping Copse**. Two short sections of path branch off to the left and follow the beautiful shore of the Beaulieu River – when the coast path is complete, these will be linked to provide a continuous riverside path. Rejoining the gravel path near the Keeping Marsh hide, follow it past the boatyards into **Buckler's Hard**. Head straight across the access road to join the shore past the thatched **Duke's Bath House**, built in 1760 for bathing in a tidal pool alongside. Follow the track up past the

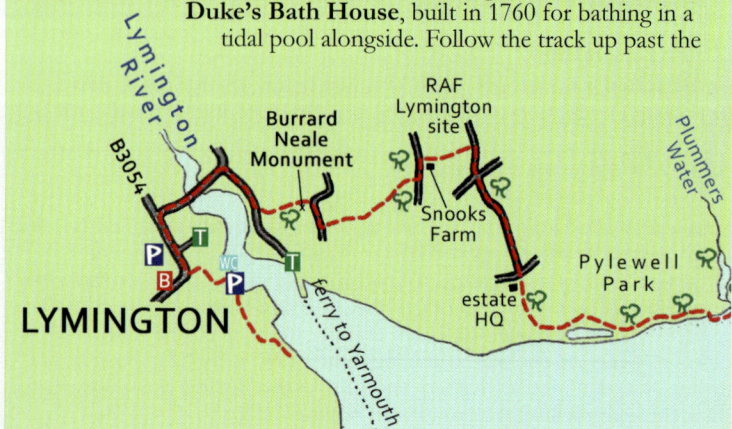

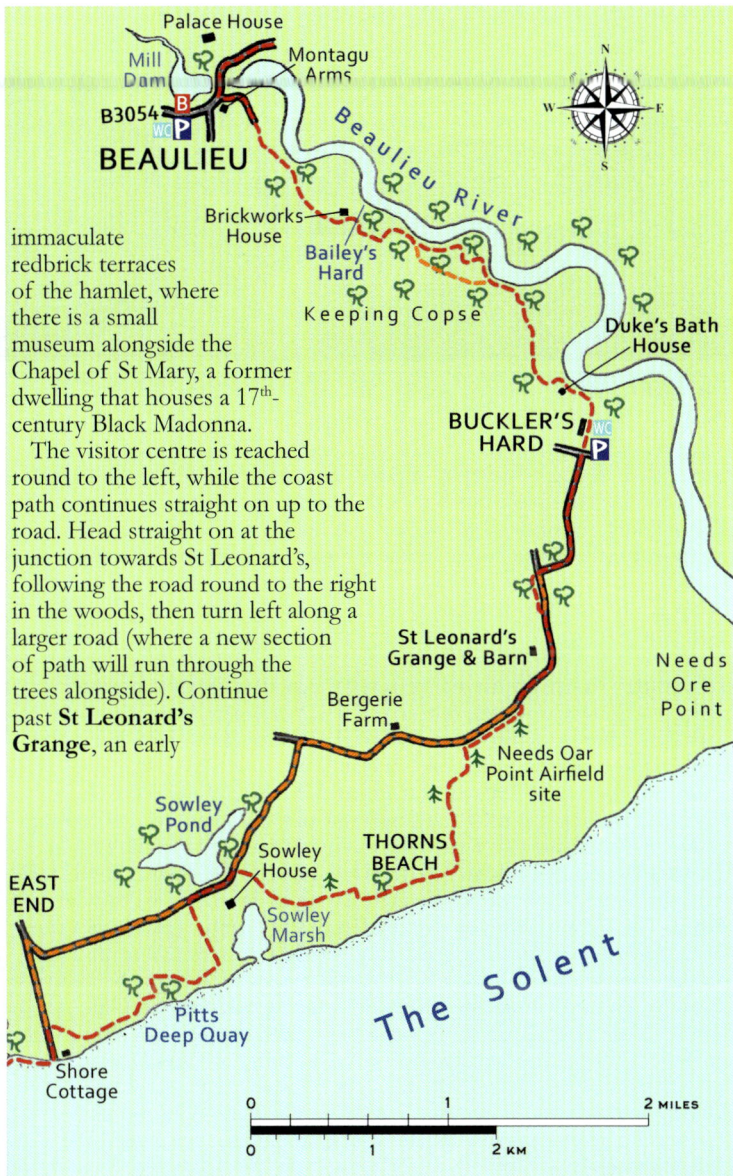

Palace House
Montagu Arms
Mill Dam
B3054
BEAULIEU
Beaulieu River
Brickworks House
Bailey's Hard
Keeping Copse
Duke's Bath House
BUCKLER'S HARD
St Leonard's Grange & Barn
Needs Ore Point
Bergerie Farm
Needs Oar Point Airfield site
Sowley Pond
Sowley House
THORNS BEACH
Sowley Marsh
EAST END
Pitts Deep Quay
Shore Cottage
The Solent

0   1   2 MILES
0   1   2 KM

immaculate redbrick terraces of the hamlet, where there is a small museum alongside the Chapel of St Mary, a former dwelling that houses a 17th-century Black Madonna.

The visitor centre is reached round to the left, while the coast path continues straight on up to the road. Head straight on at the junction towards St Leonard's, following the road round to the right in the woods, then turn left along a larger road (where a new section of path will run through the trees alongside). Continue past **St Leonard's Grange**, an early

> **Buckler's Hard**
> Buckler's Hard (named after the local Buckle family) was a small landing place on the Beaulieu River when the Duke of Montagu founded a free port called Montagu Town to import sugar from the West Indies. The trade quickly collapsed, but Buckler's Hard developed as a centre for shipbuilding, making use of wood from the New Forest to supply over 50 ships for the Royal Navy. As the industry declined, the neat rows of Georgian cottages that had been built for shipyard workers became popular with day-trippers, particularly via the Gosport Steam Launch Company.

18th-century house on the site of one of Beaulieu Abbey's monastic granges. Alongside are the remains of a 13th-century chapel and tithe barn, the latter standing beside the road and thought to have been one of the largest barns in medieval England.

Beyond the site of **Needs Oar Point Airfield** (a World War II advanced landing ground), the England Coast Path will turn left on the gravel of Park Lane and follow it round past the exclusive piles of **Thorns Beach**. Soon after Thorns Lane bends right, the route will turn left on a new section across the fields to rejoin the road past **Sowley Pond**. The stream here was dammed in the 14th century by monks from Beaulieu Abbey to create a fishery and would later serve an ironworks on the opposite side of the road. Beyond Sowley House and Sowley Farm, you'll turn left again on Browns Lane towards Sowley Gate House. Near its end, turn right onto a new path through the trees along the Solent shore, then stay inland of the buildings at **Pitts Deep**. Turn left briefly on Pitts Deep Lane, then cut through the trees to the right to follow the field edge along the shore before bending right to reach Tanners Lane, whose name relates to the tanpits that once lined the Solent shore.

ALTERNATIVE ROUTE: *Until this part of the coast path is open, the section from Park Lane to Tanners Lane is inaccessible and you will have to stay on the road throughout. It is, however, one of the most delightful sections of road walking in the area, as the road past BERGERIE FARM is lined with ancient trees and surrounded by a narrow strip of New Forest pasture that is often grazed by horses. Bergerie (meaning 'sheep pen' in French) was the site of Beaulieu Abbey's medieval sheep station, where their wool would have been gathered. Turn left on Sowley Lane and follow this all the way past SOWLEY POND, ignoring the private lanes off to the left until Tanners Lane doubles back sharply left.*

The routes converge on Tanners Lane to follow it down to the Solent shore by **Shore Cottage**. Follow the beach right round to a footbridge across Plummers Water, 200m beyond which a fenced permissive path leads right into the woods along the edge of **Pylewell Park**. This faint path will be improved when the England Coast Path is opened, but is a little overgrown in places at the moment and in the meantime is rejoined in several places from the Boldre Foreshore. There are also some broken boardwalks and stiles, but the path still remains useable as it winds delightfully through the trees, before keeping right of a lagoon to open out into a field used for Embers Camping in the summer. Bear diagonally right to a gap, then angle back towards the shore to join Shotts Lane at a crude gate.

Follow Shotts Lane up to the road by the **Pylewell estate HQ**, then head straight on along the lane past Shotts Copse. Continue straight across a larger road, then turn left on a track by the site of **RAF Lymington**, which was laid out in 1943 for use as an advanced landing ground in the lead up to D-Day. At the end, turn left on the road by Snooks Farm, then turn right after 100m on a narrow path through Walhampton Wood. Bear left by the farm shop to continue down to its access road, then bear right on a path through the scrub beside the golf course. Join a driveway, then turn right on the road to reach the **Burrard Neale Monument**, a 76ft obelisk erected on Walhampton Hill in the 1840s to Sir Harry Burrard Neale,

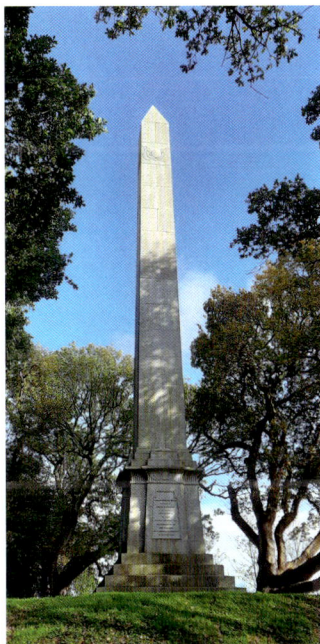

Burrard Neale Monument

Lord of the Admiralty during the Napoleonic Wars and a former Mayor of Lymington.

Turn left and follow a path to the monument's right to drop down through the trees to the main road. Follow the shore of **Lymington River** right, then turn left on the B3054 to cross the river into Lymington. Turn left at the roundabout to reach the town centre and bus stops. **Lymington** is an attractive market town, renowned for its Georgian architecture, cobbled streets and busy riverside marina. Until the mid 19th century its major industry was salt-making, but its busy port also supported shipbuilding and had strong trade links with the French, who had twice razed the town during the Hundred Years War.

SONG OF THE DAY **Birdy** – *Surrender*
Jasmine van den Bogaerde (a relation of Dirk Bogarde) was born in Lymington and brought up on the family estate at Pylewell House, which is passed on today's route. She took her stage name from the nickname her parents gave her as a baby. The video for this sumptuous 2021 single was filmed during the Covid-19 pandemic on the coast at St Leonards in Sussex.

Section 4.10 – Lymington to Mudeford

Distance: 24.9km (15½ miles)

Height Gained: 70m

Parking: Several pay car parks in Lymington and Mudeford, as well as various places in between.

Public Transport: Buses X1/X2 (morebus, towards Lymington) run regularly from Mudeford to Lymington. Limited service on Sundays.

Refreshments: Various seafront options in Milford on Sea and Barton on Sea.

Accommodation: Rooms are available in Mudeford at Bure Lodge (01425 277260), Avon Beach B&B (07973 660025) and Bub Lane Cottage (07739 026357) in Stanpit, while Christchurch Harbour Hotel & Spa (01202 483434) is passed along the route. The closest campsite is Sionna Camping (07768 117974) in Burton, just over a mile from the route through Christchurch. Christchurch Information Centre (01202 499199) is at the Regent cinema on the High Street.

Overview: A long but very gentle day around the last marshes of the Solent, whose western entrance is marked by the striking shingle spit on which Hurst Castle perches. Thereafter the route skirts above or below the fragile cliffs of Christchurch Bay past Milford on Sea, Barton on Sea and Highcliffe, before following the long beach into Mudeford at the entrance to Christchurch Harbour.

Route Description

Opposite the foot of **Lymington High Street**, turn left down Quay Hill past the King's Head Inn and bend right along Quay Street to reach Lymington Quay. Continue along the road past Berthon Marina, then bear left through Bath Road Recreation Ground to rejoin the shore. Beyond Royal Lymington Yacht Club, keep left around **Lymington Sea Water Swimming Baths** – the oldest lido in the country, this opened in 1833 and is renowned for the minerals provided by the local estuarine mud. The footpath leaves the waterside to cut right then left through the boat/car park at Lymington Yacht Haven, before joining a shingle path onto **Normandy Marsh**. Turn left to

Quay Hill, Lymington

pick up the shoreline path and follow the circuitous route around Normandy Lagoon and the inlet of Maiden Dock. After crossing a footbridge, double back left and skirt around Oxley Marsh, passing various pools and salterns that are the remains of the extensive

Saltworkings

Salt pans were recorded around Lymington in the Domesday Book and, at the industry's peak in the early 18th century, there were 200 salt pans between Lymington and Milford, each producing around 3 tonnes of salt a week. Seawater was allowed to evaporate for three weeks, before the remaining water was boiled off in a coal-fired boiling house. The primary production area for sea salt in the country, Lymington salt fetched a high price in London until high taxation and the arrival of the railways hastened the industry's demise, the last saltern closing in 1866.

saltworkings between Lymington and Milford.

Continue along the broad shore-line path around Pennington and **Keyhaven Marshes**, with Hurst Castle looming ahead across the water. At the road turn left over the Avon Water into **Keyhaven**, then double back left along the shoreline and pass the ferry to Hurst Castle. Follow the shore round to rejoin the road until a footbridge leads left onto the great shingle bank of **Hurst Spit**, which stretches for over a mile across the western entrance to the Solent. It was formed by the longshore drift of pebbles along the beaches of Christchurch Bay, but has been artificially replenished after recent storms, hence its rather unnatural profile. **Hurst Castle** was built in the 1540s as part of Henry VIII's defences along the south coast and enlarged in the 19th century, but it too is being undermined by erosion.

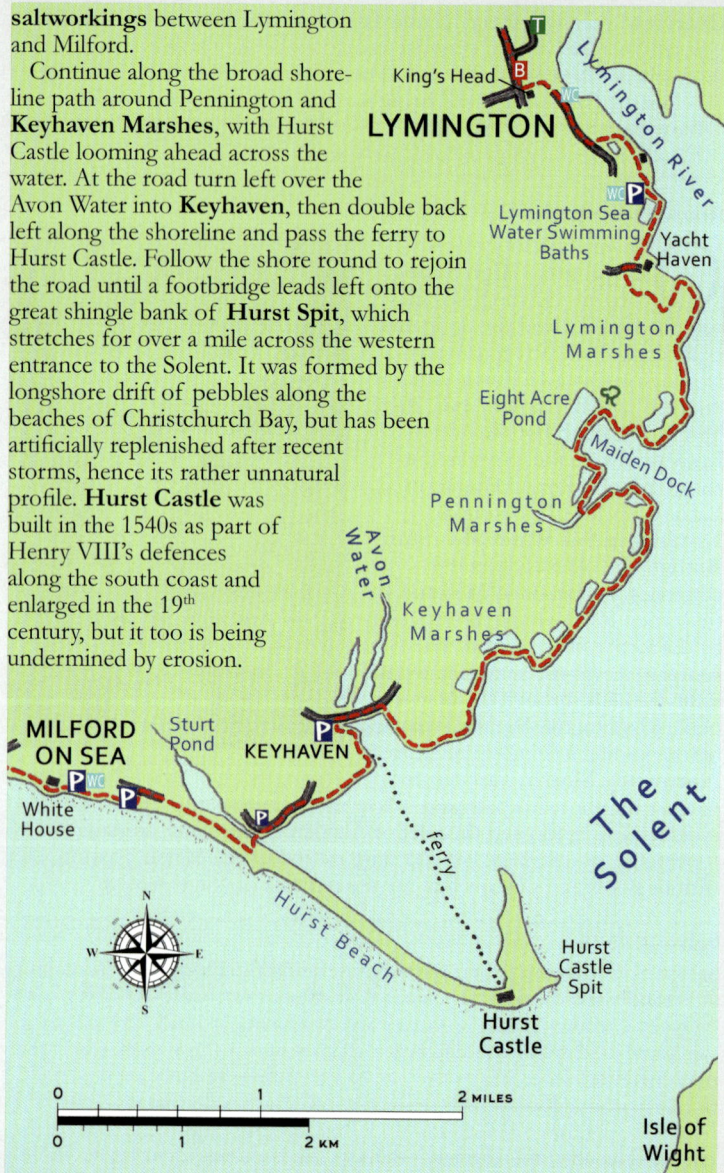

King's Head

LYMINGTON

Lymington River

Lymington Sea Water Swimming Baths

Yacht Haven

Lymington Marshes

Eight Acre Pond

Maiden Dock

Pennington Marshes

Avon Water

Keyhaven Marshes

MILFORD ON SEA

Sturt Pond

KEYHAVEN

White House

Hurst Beach

ferry

The Solent

Hurst Castle Spit

Hurst Castle

N
W   E
S

0   1   2 MILES

0   1   2 KM

Isle of Wight

Keyhaven Marshes

The Needles on the Isle of Wight cut a striking outline as you turn right along Hurst Beach and follow the shingle bank into **Milford on Sea**, where you join the promenade by the first car park. Keep left of the White House and climb above the low cliffs, continuing along the promenade until a footpath resumes along a section of precarious but fossil-rich clays on **Hordle** and **Rook Cliffs**, notable for their crocodile beds, in which the remains of many crocodiles, sharks and mammals have been found. Drop down to cross the gentle hollow of Taddiford Gap (a corruption of 'toad ford'), then pass the golf course before keeping left through the scrub around **Becton Bunny** (*bunny* being a local name for a narrow ravine). The crumbling cliffs rise steadily towards the edge of **Barton on Sea**, where the path crosses the broad greensward until being forced to join the road by Fisherman's Walk. At the heart of Barton stands the **Indian Memorial Obelisk**, which commemorates the Indian soldiers who recovered at a convalescent camp here after fighting on the Western front during World War I.

At the next car park bear left back towards the clifftops, then keep to the left of the Cliff House to continue along the greensward. Reaching the fence around **Naish Holiday Village**, you are forced right along a narrow footpath beside the houses. This leads onto a tarmac cycleway that winds through the pine trees around the estate beyond. Stay on the cycleway until it reaches the A337, which you follow left for 500m past the entrance to the holiday camp. At **Chewton Bunny Nature Reserve** turn left into the trees and wind down Walkford Brook, which marks the boundary between Hampshire and Dorset. Turn left at the next road, which soon becomes a path, with all routes leading down to the sea at the foot of the ravine. Highcliffe can be reached up the slope here, but the route follows a firm walkway along the back of **Highcliffe Beach**, soon passing beneath **Highcliffe Castle**. Invisible from below,

Barton Cliffs and Becton Bunny

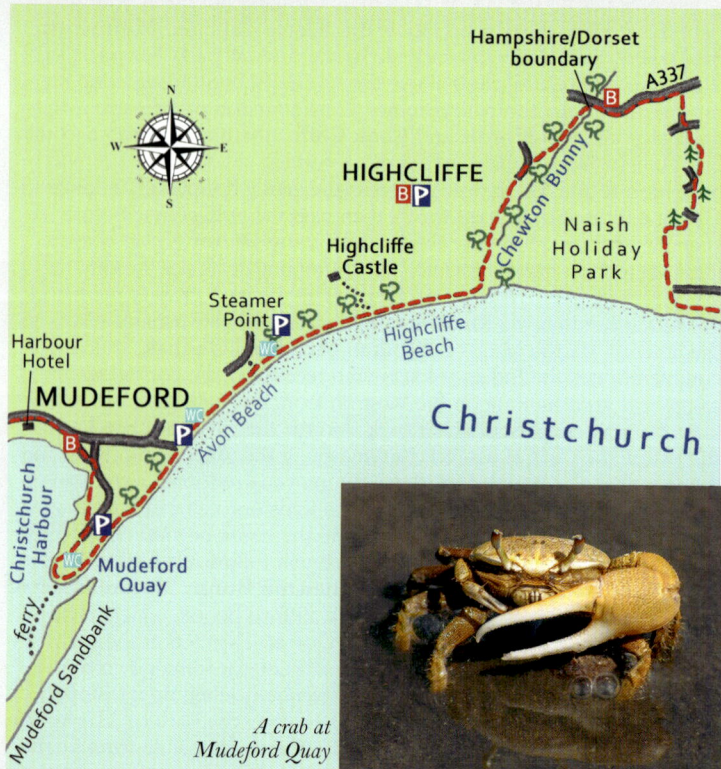

Hampshire/Dorset boundary

A337

HIGHCLIFFE

Highcliffe Castle

Naish Holiday Park

Chewton Bunny

Steamer Point

Highcliffe Beach

Harbour Hotel

MUDEFORD

Avon Beach

Christchurch

Christchurch Harbour

ferry

Mudeford Quay

Mudeford Sandbank

A crab at Mudeford Quay

this extravagant Gothic Revival mansion was built in the 1830s by Lord Stuart de Rothesay.

Continue along Highcliffe Beach beneath the towering sandstone cliffs, before following the concrete sea wall that soon joins the busy promenade around **Avon Beach**. Stay along the beach to reach Mudeford near the far end; though the village can be reached to the right here, unless you are particularly tired or using the ferry across Christchurch Harbour, you are generally better off continuing around **Mudeford Quay**. The promenade continues to the headland at the narrow entrance to Christchurch Harbour, an area that is popular for crabbing. **Mudeford Ferry** runs seasonally from here to Hengistbury Head, but the main route continues round the shore and joins the road back towards **Mudeford**, before keeping left to reach the main road by a bus stop. A former fishing village at the mouth of the River Mude (passed invisibly near the Harbour Hotel), there is little focus to modern Mudeford other than the beach and quay.

SONG OF THE DAY

State of Undress – *Mudeford Mood*
A mellow folk song from 2009's *Livin' It Lovin' It* album by the Christchurch-based Celtic roots band, fronted by Charlie and Alan Rose.

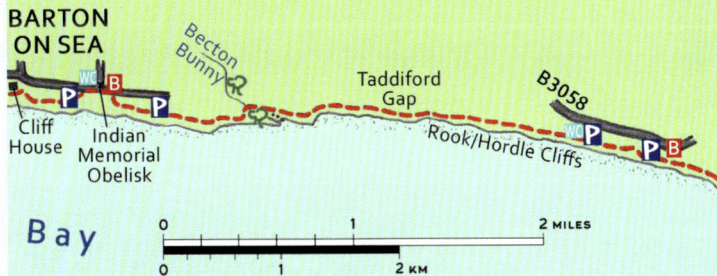

BARTON ON SEA

Becton Bunny

Taddiford Gap

B3058

Rook/Hordle Cliffs

Cliff House

Indian Memorial Obelisk

Bay

0   1   2 MILES

0   1   2 KM

The Battle of Mudeford

Mudeford and Christchurch were notorious for engaging in 'the free trade', with smugglers landing contraband on Avon Beach and storing it at the Haven House Inn at Mudeford Quay. On 15th July 1784, while liquor and tea were being unloaded from a pair of boats from France, excise men and the Royal Navy exchanged prolonged fire with the smugglers at Mudeford Quay. Though they escaped with their wares, one smuggler called George Coombes was hanged for murder and his body suspended in chains outside the Haven House Inn.

ATHERFIELD POINT, CHALE BAY

Part 5:

The Isle of Wight

The Isle of Wight

Start: East Cowes
Finish: East Cowes
Total Distance: 138.3 km (86 miles)
Total Ascent: 2,060m (6,760ft)
Days: 7

(Take it and come) to the Isle of Wight;
Where, far from noise and smoke of town,
I watch the twilight falling brown
   All round a careless-order'd garden
Close to the ridge of a noble down.

For groves of pine on either hand,
To break the blast of winter, stand;
   And further on, the hoary Channel
Tumbles a billow on chalk and sand...

Alfred Tennyson, *Maud, and Other Poems*

The Isle of Wight is England's largest island and one of its smallest counties – indeed it is said that at high tide it becomes smaller than Rutland. Historically it was part of Hampshire, but since 1890 has been its own county, with Newport as its county town. Its climate is the sunniest in the country, particularly in the south of the island, and produces many species of subtropical plant, including the county flower, the pyramidal orchid. The island gained a reputation for being behind the times, both for better and worse, as it was so cut off from the rest of the country, though this is increasingly less true. Islanders call themselves caulkheads, which was originally a derogatory term given to them, as their heads were said to be so stuffed with caulk (a sealing material) that they could float across the Solent.

   Although you might think the island's name relates to the chalk cliffs, its etymological origins are more complicated. The Romans called it Vectis (possibly meaning 'nether sea'), but it is thought a form of Wight predates this, either a Celtic reference to a place divided between the

two limbs of the Solent, or a name given by the Beaker folk for 'what rises over the sea'. Its outlook was more continental than most of England, with Julius Caesar referring to its Belgic culture upon his arrival. Following the Romans' withdrawal, the island was settled by Jutes, before becoming part of Wessex and later England. It took the brunt of several French attacks in the 14th and 16th centuries, and was greatly fortified in the 19th century as fears of fresh invasion gripped the country. By then it had become a fashionable holiday retreat, particularly once Queen Victoria had her summer home at Osborne House built in the 1840s. The island's winter population of 140,000 is now doubled during the summer months.

The Isle of Wight has a particularly fascinating geology. It was first separated from the mainland by repeated sea level changes around 125,000 years ago that flooded the Solent valley, though its most recent inundation was at the end of the last ice age around 9,000 years ago. The northern half of the island is composed of various clays from the London basin, a cross-section of whose layers is seen most impressively at Whitecliff Bay near Bembridge. A line of chalk cuts across the heart of the island between the Needles and Culver Cliff, with high downs rolling southwards. Greensand cliffs are exposed beneath the chalk, but the Gault (or Blue Slipper) clay that underlies this has resulted in a complex series of landslips across the southern end of the island. Like the greensand and Gault clay, the island's oldest rocks from the Wessex Formation are part of the Wealden Group. Formed 145 to 126 million years ago in the early Cretaceous period, they are exposed along its south west coast. The island's sedimentary rocks are full of fossils, including so many dinosaur bones and fossilised footprints that it has been dubbed 'Dinosaur Island'.

The island already has its own coast path, the 67 mile-long Isle of Wight Coastal Path being generally well signed. However, the new England Coast Path will open up some new areas for coastal access and,

Shanklin seafront

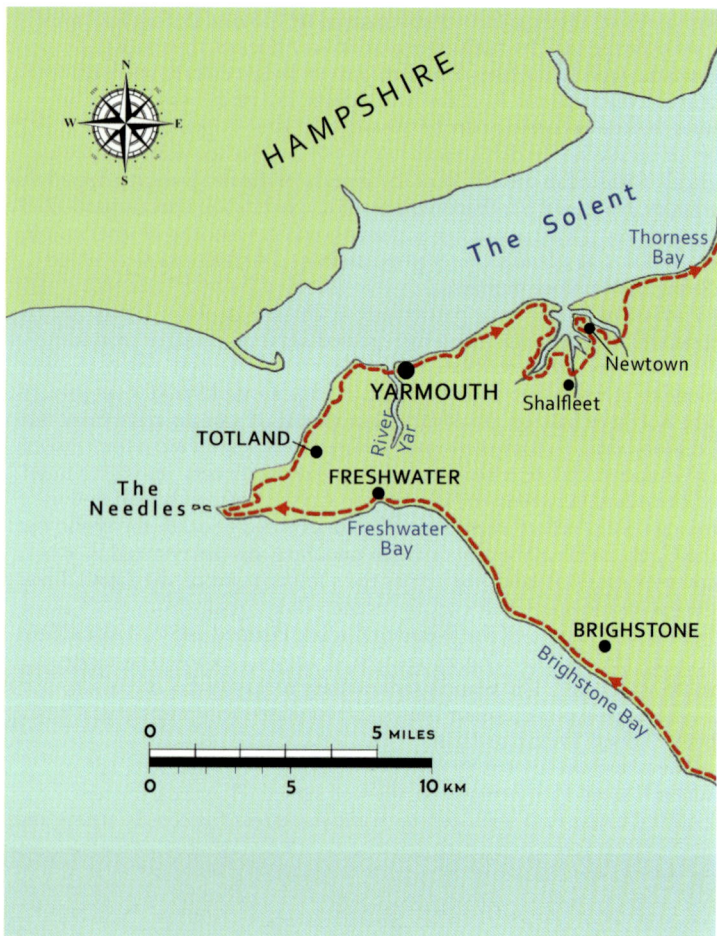

though some of these sections are not yet accessible, the existing path can be used until the new route is in place. The England Coast Path around the Isle of Wight is a circuit, so can naturally be started anywhere; though I have described it from East Cowes, where the ferry arrives from Southampton, it could equally be started at Fishbourne or Ryde, where other ferries disembark from Portsmouth. The first section from East Cowes to Wootton is still in negotiation due to complications through the Osborne House estate, so the existing coastal path will have

Map labels:

PORTS-MOUTH

The Solent

ferry from Southampton

ferry from Portsmouth

EAST COWES

COWES

Fishbourne

River Medina

WOOTTON

RYDE

Seaview

NEWPORT

ST HELENS

Fore-land

BEMBRIDGE

River Yar

ISLE OF WIGHT

SANDOWN

Culver Cliff

SHANKLIN

Sandown Bay

Dunnose

Chale

Chale Bay

NITON

VENTNOR

St Lawrence

St Catherine's Point

to be followed along the roads inland. Beyond Ryde, though, the route largely clings to the coast, the low Solent shore making way for dramatic chalk and greensand cliffs beyond Bembridge. After picking its way through the intricate undercliffs and landslips around Ventnor and Niton, high-level cliffs lead all the way along the south west of the island to the spectacular chalk of Freshwater Bay and the Needles. The return along the Solent shore is gentler, passing historic Yarmouth and picking its way around the estuaries of Shalfleet and Newtown to reach the beaches of Cowes. One last optional day around the Medina estuary via Newport completes this thorough tour of the island.

In all, this is one of the finest weeks of walking you can do anywhere in the country, distilling the different landscapes of the entire south coast into one manageable package. Chalk cliffs, shingle beaches, long promenades and piers, wooded estuaries, busy boatyards, subtropical undercliffs – it's all here in just a few satisfying miles. There is a reason Tennyson, Dickens and so many artists and writers flocked to this unique diamond-shaped island adrift from England's south coast.

Useful Information

Official Isle of Wight Tourism site – *www.visitisleofwight.co.uk*
Ferry information – *www.redfunnel.co.uk* and *www.wightlink.co.uk*
Train times – *traintimes.org.uk*
Bus times – *bustimes.org*
Southern Vectis – 01983 827000 *(www.islandbuses.info)*
Traveline – *www.traveline.info*
Isle of Wight Luggage Transfers – 01983 281662 *(www.wight-walks.co.uk)*

COUNTY ANTHEM

Derek Sandy – *Welcome to the Isle of Wight*
This 2008 reggae anthem is absolutely unforgettable – a true earworm – and was introduced to the nation when the 56-year-old took *Britain's Got Talent* by storm in 2013. Originally from Tobago, Sandy has become an official ambassador for the island, likening it to a Caribbean paradise.

Alum Bay and the Needles from Headon Hill

Section 5.1 – East Cowes to Bembridge

Distance: 22.6km (14 miles)

Height Gained: 250m

Parking: Pay car parks in Ryde, Seaview and at the Duver near St Helens. Free car park at Bembridge Point and on the seafront ½ mile off the route in East Cowes.

Public Transport: Bus 8 (Southern Vectis, towards Ryde) runs hourly from Bembridge to Ryde, from which Bus 4 (Southern Vectis, towards East Cowes) runs hourly to East Cowes. Both buses run 7 days a week all year round.

Refreshments: There are many options in Ryde, as well as the Sloop Inn at Wootton Bridge and the Creek Café and Fishbourne Inn by the ferry terminal in Fishbourne.

Accommodation: The Pilot Boat Inn (01983 872077) and Harbourside View houseboat (01983 339084) are ideally placed by the route in Bembridge, and there are also rooms at the Birdham (01983 872840) and the Crab & Lobster Inn (01983 872244). The closest camping is at Nodes Point Holiday Park (0330 1234907) right by the route 2½ miles before Bembridge, Carpenters Farm Campsite (01983 874557) just over a mile from the route through St Helens, or Whitecliff Bay Holiday Park (01983 872671) 2½ miles beyond Bembridge.

Overview: The first section of the Isle of Wight coast is complicated by the Osborne House estate, with whom negotiations to establish a new coast path have stalled, leaving a gap in the dedicated England Coast Path. It is hoped this will change, but for now the existing coastal path can be followed for 4 miles along rather busy roads to Wootton Bridge, or a bus taken from East Cowes. From Wootton Bridge the route along the gentle north-eastern shore of the island is very pleasant, linking the busy hubs of Ryde, Seaview and the Duver via some charming seafront promenades and tree-lined paths inland.

Route Description

Having disembarked the vehicle ferry from Southampton in **East Cowes** (the passenger service stops the other side of the estuary in Cowes), the existing coast path follows the main road straight on at the roundabout. It bypasses the town centre and continues up the hill past the recreation ground and the main entrance to **Osborne House** by Prince of Wales Lodge. Stay on the A3021 out of town, keeping left at the next roundabout, before turning second left along

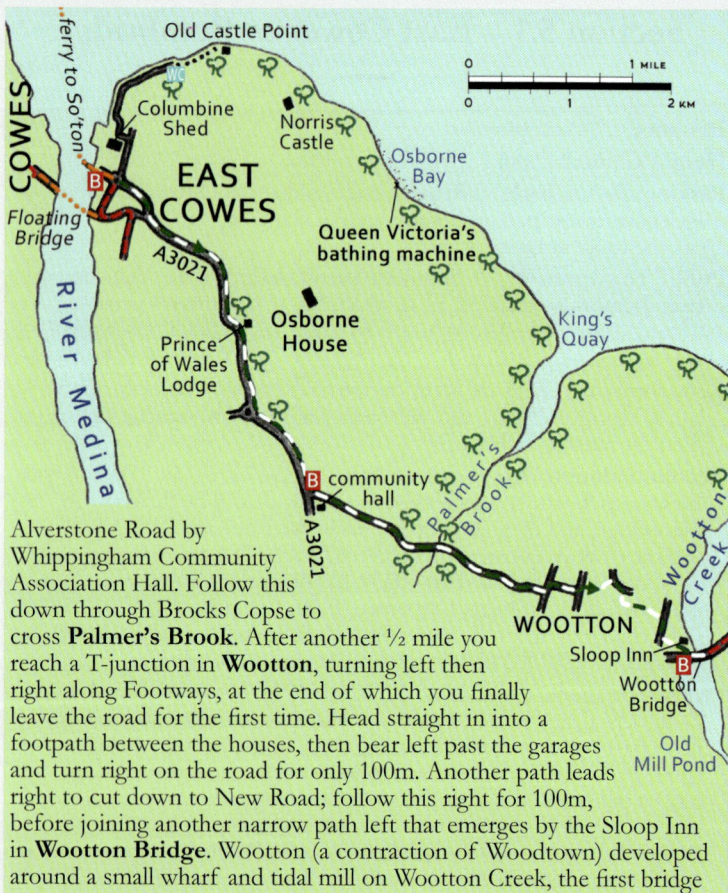

Old Castle Point

ferry to So'ton

COWES

Columbine
Shed

Norris
Castle

Osborne
Bay

EAST
COWES

Floating
Bridge

B

A3021

Queen Victoria's
bathing machine

River Medina

Prince
of Wales
Lodge

Osborne
House

King's
Quay

Palmers Brook

B community
hall

A3021

Wootton Creek

WOOTTON

Sloop Inn

B

Wootton
Bridge

Old
Mill Pond

0   1 MILE
0   1   2 KM

Alverstone Road by Whippingham Community Association Hall. Follow this down through Brocks Copse to cross **Palmer's Brook**. After another ½ mile you reach a T-junction in **Wootton**, turning left then right along Footways, at the end of which you finally leave the road for the first time. Head straight in into a footpath between the houses, then bear left past the garages and turn right on the road for only 100m. Another path leads right to cut down to New Road; follow this right for 100m, before joining another narrow path left that emerges by the Sloop Inn in **Wootton Bridge**. Wootton (a contraction of Woodtown) developed around a small wharf and tidal mill on Wootton Creek, the first bridge

Osborne House

Osborne House was built on the site of a modest earlier edifice in the 1840s for Queen Victoria and Prince Albert as a seaside retreat from London. The Italianate style extended to the gardens, with extensive drives and pleasure grounds laid out across the 2,000-acre estate. Queen Victoria died here on 22nd January 1901 and her successor, Edward VII, gave the estate to the nation, part of it being used for a new Royal Naval College. Today it is owned by English Heritage and Queen Victoria's private beach was finally opened to the public in 2012, her restored bathing machine taking centre stage.

Osborne House

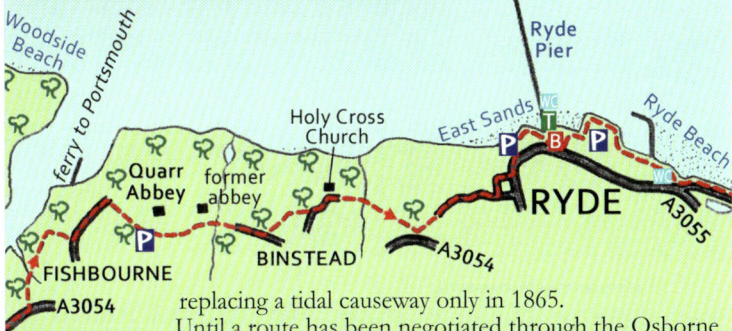

Woodside Beach

ferry to Portsmouth

ferry and hovercroft to Portsmouth

Ryde Pier

Holy Cross Church

East Sands

Ryde Beach

Quarr Abbey

former abbey

RYDE

A3055

BINSTEAD

A3054

FISHBOURNE

A3054

replacing a tidal causeway only in 1865.

Until a route has been negotiated through the Osborne House estate, this is where the England Coast Path officially restarts, following the main road across Wootton Creek and up through **Fishbourne**. After a ¼ mile turn left down Ashlake Copse Lane, which soon becomes a path cutting through to Ashlake Copse Road. Keep straight on until a narrow path leads right through to the B3331. Follow this left past the ferry terminal (for the vehicle ferry to Portsmouth) and the **Fishbourne Inn**, then turn right on the bend along Quarr Lane.

The Isle of Wight Festival

One of the most famous music festivals in the UK was held on the Isle of Wight between 1968-70, with 1969 held at Woodside Bay near Wootton. This festival took place just 11 days after the Woodstock Festival and an estimated 150,000 people descended on the area for what was deemed Britain's own version of Woodstock. It was headlined by Bob Dylan, playing his much-anticipated first gig for 3 years following his motorcycle accident, and it was rumoured the Beatles would join him on stage. After an even bigger festival at another site the following year, the Isle of Wight County Council Act of 1971 prevented outdoor gatherings of more than 5,000 people and ensured this brief era would go down in island lore.

This broad path leads past **Quarr Abbey**, a modern Benedictine monastery constructed in the early 20th century from a plan by one of the French monks. Built using red brick from Flanders, its striking outline incorporates Byzantine and Moorish influences. As you continue past Quarr Abbey Farm, the almost-forgotten ruins of the original 12th-century Cistercian abbey can be seen, named after a nearby stone quarry.

The path joins a road into **Binstead**, the coast path soon bearing left to cut through to Church Road, which leads left to **Holy Cross Church**, parts of which date from the 12th century. An arch just beyond the church has a rare carving of a *sheela na gig* (a female grotesque touching herself to ward off evil spirits), referred to in the 18th century as 'the Saxon Idol' and thought to have been brought from Quarr Abbey after the Dissolution.

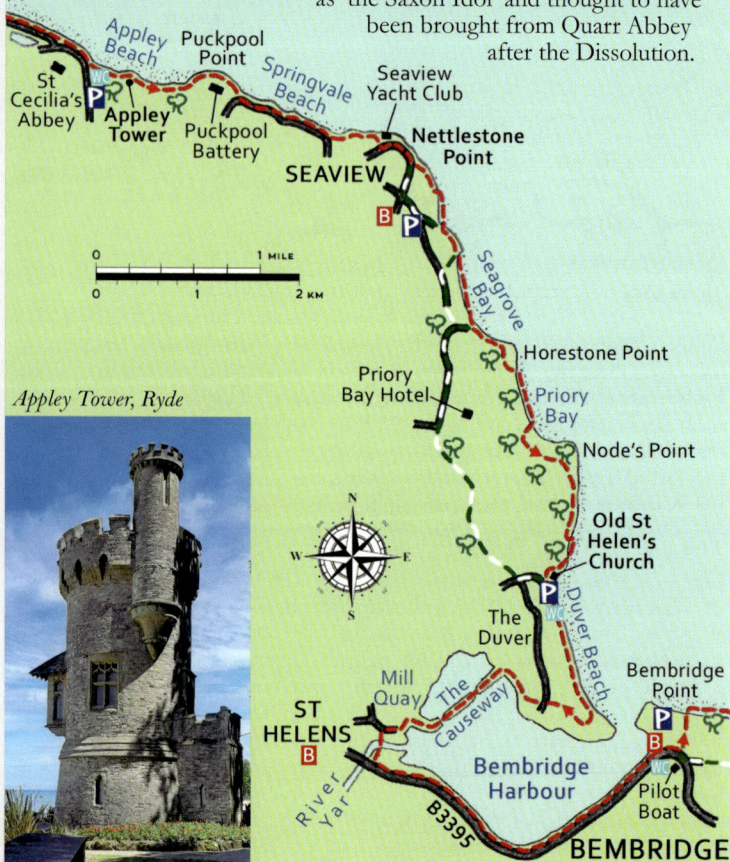

Appley Tower, Ryde

The broad path of **Ladies' Walk** continues from the end of the road, crossing a small creek and passing Ryde Golf Club to emerge back on the main road on the edge of Ryde. Bear left immediately on a path that cuts between the houses to join the end of Spencer Road. Follow this all the way to its end, then turn left down the hill towards the seafront. Cut through the first car park on the left to join a walkway along the shore to reach the end of **Ryde Pier**, the second longest pleasure pier in the UK after Southend but also the oldest, having opened in 1814. **Ryde** began life as a village with the Norman name La Rye, before the French razed it in 1377 during the Hundred Years War. The villages of Upper and Lower Ryde merged in the 19th century to form a fashionable seaside resort that became a favourite of Queen Victoria.

Follow the road past the railway and bus stations, then turn left on a footbridge over the railway. Rejoin the seafront beyond the terminus for the hovercraft from Portsmouth and follow it round the small marina and past the broad beach of **Ryde Sands**. The promenade continues past the canoe lake and alongside Appley Beach, whose centrepiece is **Appley Tower**, a Gothic revival folly built in 1875 in the grounds of the Appley Towers mansion, part of which now forms Appley Park. The pleasant promenade hugs the sea wall around **Puckpool Point**, where mortar emplacements defended the Solent as part of the Palmerston defences in the 1860s. Join the road round Springvale Beach into **Seaview**, where a path bears left along the shore to emerge by Sea View Yacht Club. From **Nettlestone Point** there are fine views of the Palmerston sea forts – No Man's Land Fort and Horse Sand Fort – in the entrance to the Solent.

Just beyond the point, a footpath (R92) leaves the road to follow the sea wall, before dropping down steps onto the back of the beach for 200m. *This route is not accessible for a couple of hours either side of high tide, so an alternative route stays on the High Street up through* SEAVIEW, *then turns left at the mini-roundabout. Keep left to rejoin the shore.* At **Seagrove Bay** the route cuts along the back of the beach – this section is inaccessible only for a short period around high tide, but a signed alternative follows the rough road behind to rejoin at the foot of Ferniclose Road. Here, the England Coast Path eschews the existing coastal path and follows the promenade round the bay to a wooden walkway. Steps lead up the slope before Horestone Point, before dropping straight back down to the beautiful sands of **Priory Bay**. Over halfway along the beach, steps lead up into the trees again, a rough and muddy path winding through the landslipped ground above. After climbing over Node's Point, the path runs just above the beach beyond, before bending round to join it for the last 100m and emerge by the striking tower of **Old St Helen's Church** at the end of **the Duver** beach. This 13th-century tower is all

Old St Helen's Church

that remains of a Norman church linked to the nearby Benedictine priory of St Helens. A *duver* is Isle of Wight dialect for a low-lying coastal area, usually composed of sand dunes, and is thought to be derived from the French word *duvair* for a 'dividing line'. It is the site of one of England's first golf courses; the club was founded in 1882 and had its own set of rules that vied with the Royal & Ancient in St Andrew's for prominence in golf's early history.

ALTERNATIVE ROUTE: *Though the route along the beach at Priory Bay is only affected by spring high tides, the path beyond is currently rough, unsigned and closed due to a small landslip that is fairly simple to pass but enough to put many people off. Once the England Coast Path is opened here, this path should be greatly improved, but until then you may be better sticking to the existing coastal path. Follow the road up from Seagrove Bay, keeping straight on up Ferniclose Road until its end by the entrance to the PRIORY BAY HOTEL. Continue straight on, then immediately turn left down through the trees. Turn right on the road at the bottom, then keep straight on past Nodes Point Holiday Park, before turning left onto a path that leads down to Duver Road. Keep left to rejoin the main route by OLD ST HELEN'S CHURCH.*

The routes converge to follow the promenade along the beach to the mouth of **Bembridge Harbour**, before bending right around the first building to cut back along the landward side of the boatyards. Rejoin the existing coast path by the end of the road to follow the shore round to the **Causeway**, which tiptoes across the harbour and encloses a former mill pond. Follow the edge of Mill Quay to pick up the road the far side, then cut left to cross a footbridge over the **Eastern Yar** (the

---

The Isle of Bembridge

The area between Bembridge and Yaverland was once an island cut off from the Isle of Wight by Brading Haven, an estuary which extended along the River Yar beyond the port of Brading, and an area of marshes to the west. Yarbridge provided the earliest crossing to the Isle of Bembridge in the 14th century, while the name Bembridge may be a contraction of Beam-bridge, suggesting another early form of crossing. Only when the embankment and railway were constructed along the south side of the estuary in 1880 was the Bembridge Harbour we see today created, allowing land reclamation along the former estuary.

---

longest river on the island, with its source in Niton) and reach the main road on the edge of **St Helens**. Follow the B3395 left around the harbour for 1 mile to reach **Bembridge** by the Palmer Memorial, a drinking fountain dedicated to Revd James Nelson Palmer, and the **Pilot Boat Inn**, a historic inn now housed in a modern ship-like building.

SONG OF THE DAY

The Beatles – *Ticket to Ride*

Paul McCartney claims this was inspired by a train trip he and John Lennon took to the Isle of Wight to visit John's aunt Betty in Ryde, though Lennon would later say it was a reference to Hamburg prostitutes and their receiving a clean bill of health. It is possible they had both meanings in mind, and the song is the obvious accompaniment as you reach the town – try catching the bus without wanting to ask for 'a ticket to Ryde'!

Section 5.2 – Bembridge to Ventnor

Distance: 19.5km (12 miles)

Height Gained: 350m

Parking: Free car park by Bembridge Point and on Culver Down. Pay car parks at Bembridge Lifeboat Station and along the seafront through Sandown, Shanklin and Ventnor.

Public Transport: Bus 3 (Southern Vectis, towards Ryde) runs twice hourly from Ventnor to Sandown, from where Bus 8 (Southern Vectis, towards Ryde) runs hourly to Bembridge. Both buses run 7 days a week all year round.

Refreshments: Various options along the route in Sandown and Shanklin.

Accommodation: There are various options in Ventnor, with a Tourist Information Point at Occasions & Ventnor Post Office (01983 852131). The only camping is in glamping yurts at Bank End Farm (01983 852649), just off the route beyond Ventnor Botanic Garden, 1½ miles after Ventnor.

Overview: A fine and varied day around the south-eastern corner of the island. After rounding the Foreland on Bembridge's fascinating foreshore, the long promenades of Sandown, Shanklin and Ventnor are set against the high chalk cliffs of Culver Down and the richly vegetated landslips around Bonchurch.

Route Description

In **Bembridge** the England Coast Path again diverges from the existing coastal path, turning left into Beach Road opposite the Pilot Boat Inn (Footpath BB32). Pass the Watch House to join the beach near **Bembridge Point** and follow it right along the wooded shore. Dead trees emerge from the sand and Tyne Ledge houses some fantastic rockpools in the limestone shore, while less than a mile offshore stands St Helen's Fort, the nearest of the Palmerston sea forts. A walkway soon leads on towards the pier for **Bembridge Lifeboat Station**, where the England Coast Path returns to the beach to round the **Foreland**, the easternmost tip of the Isle of Wight. Stay on the shore past the buildings of Bembridge Coast Hotel to reach a slipway, beyond which a path follows the low sea wall.

ALTERNATIVE ROUTE: *Parts of the main route round this headland are impassable around high tide, so an alternative route stays inland through the edge of Bembridge. This follows the existing coastal path at first, leaving the main road by the PILOT BOAT INN to follow a track up the hill past Old Bembridge House (Footpath BB34). Head straight across the first road, then turn left to follow Love Lane, a path continuing on from the end. At the next junction, ignore the existing coastal path and continue straight on along the rough track of Swains Lane. Follow the road left at the end for 100m, then turn right into Forelands Farm Lane (Bridleway BB39). Rejoin the coastal path briefly, before heading straight on along Poplar Close, then follow a path from the end that cuts through to Paddock Drive. Turn left to reach the slipway leading down to the onward path along the sea wall.*

The routes converge to follow the sea wall round the point below the **Crab & Lobster**, before turning right before the Beach Hut cafe and heading up the steps to a small car park. Turn left and follow the path around the landslipped shore above the rocky flats of Black Rock Ledge. Keep left to wind through the trees around the edge of the grounds of **Bembridge School**, which was founded in 1919 in a former hotel and is now part of Ryde School.

The route soon emerges on the grass by Sandhills Holiday Park, but ignores a couple of paths down to the beach at **Whitecliff Bay**, instead following the top of the slope round

Yarborough Monument

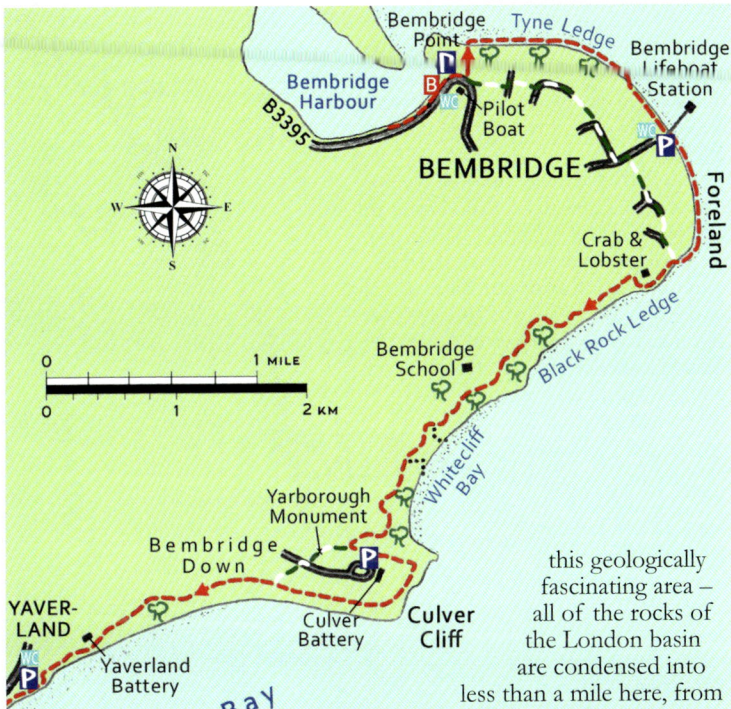

Bembridge Point

Tyne Ledge

Bembridge Lifeboat Station

Bembridge Harbour

B3395

Pilot Boat

BEMBRIDGE

Foreland

Crab & Lobster

Bembridge School

Black Rock Ledge

N W E S

0 1 MILE
0 1 2 KM

Whitecliff Bay

Yarborough Monument

Bembridge Down

Culver Battery

Culver Cliff

YAVER-LAND

Yaverland Battery

Sandown Bay

this geologically fascinating area – all of the rocks of the London basin are condensed into less than a mile here, from marl and limestone through the clays and sands to reach the soaring chalk faces of Culver Cliff. At the far end of the bay the path emerges from the trees to climb diagonally up onto Culver Down, where the existing coastal path continues straight on past the **Yarborough Monument** (a granite obelisk erected in 1849 to the 1st Earl of Yarborough), but the England Coast Path turns sharply left. The path continues from the far left corner of a car park, heading out to the fence above the precipice of **Culver Cliff**, from which there are great views over Bembridge and its harbour.

Follow the fenceline round the headland towards the great sweep of Sandown Bay, hugging the cliffs below the Culver Haven Inn and the Yarborough Monument, before descending gradually across the graceful sweep of **Bembridge Down**. A lovely grassy path continues all the way past Yaverland Battery to join the seafront promenade by Yaverland Beach. Pass the rebranded **Isle of Wight Zoo** (housed in the former Granite Fort and where the TV show *Tiger Island* was shot) and the

faded grandeur of the 1930s Art-Deco Grand Hotel
as you head into Sandown. **Sandown** is aptly
named, its miles of sand and good bathing
ensuring its rapid development as a
resort after the arrival of the railway
in 1864.

Shortly before reaching the roundabout in the centre of Sandown, turn
left down some steps to join the lower
esplanade, which leads past the war
memorial and **Sandown Pier**, which
opened in 1879 but was later extended
significantly so that paddle steamers
could land here. The existing coastal
path (via the Ferncliff Path)
follows the top of the
greensand cliffs arcing
round the bay all the
way past Lake to
Shanklin, while the
England Coast Path
stays on the esplanade
that follows the
revetment built to protect
these crumbling cliffs.
After **Small Hope
Beach**, the path joins the
road along the busy
Shanklin seafront,
with the bulk of
the town hidden

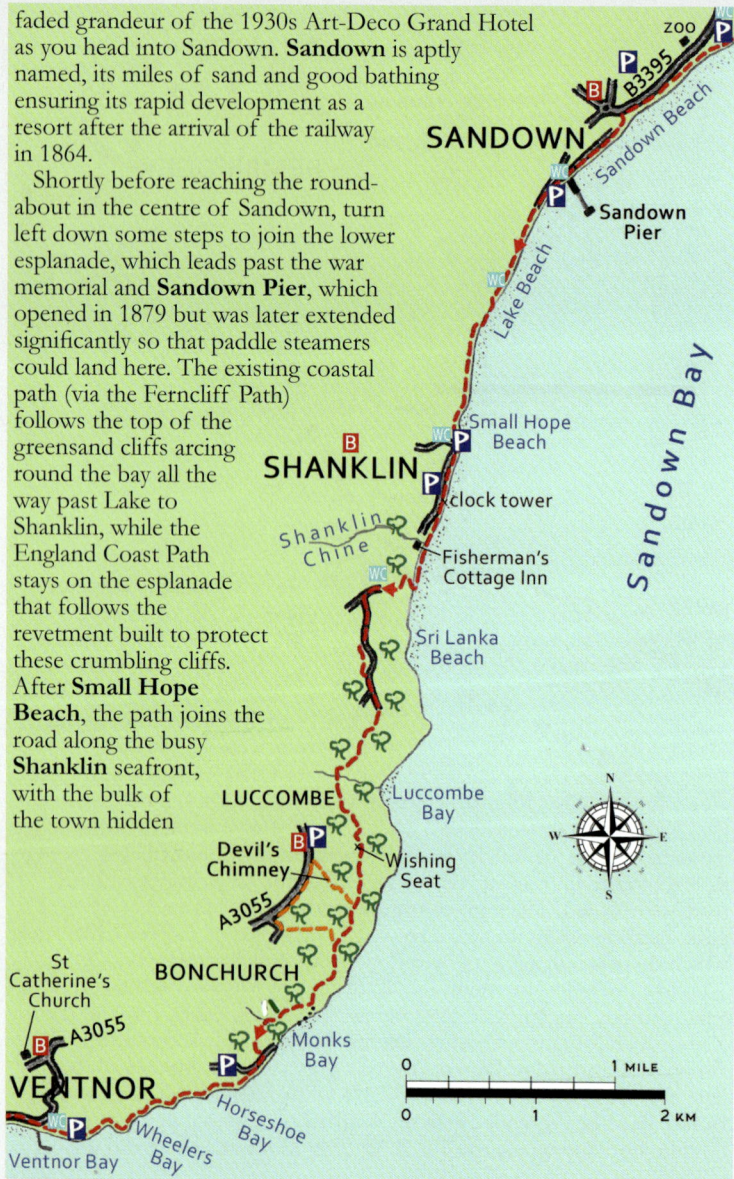

ZOO

SANDOWN

B3395

Sandown Beach

Sandown Pier

Lake Beach

Sandown Bay

SHANKLIN

Small Hope Beach

clock tower

Shanklin Chine

Fisherman's Cottage Inn

Sri Lanka Beach

LUCCOMBE

Luccombe Bay

Devil's Chimney

Wishing Seat

A3055

St Catherine's Church

BONCHURCH

A3055

Monks Bay

VENTNOR

Horseshoe Bay

Ventnor Bay

Wheelers Bay

N
W E
S

0   1 MILE

0   1   2 KM

behind the high cliffs above. Shanklin Pier once stood in the heart of the seafront opposite the Royal Spa Hotel, but the latter was destroyed during World War II and is now a car park, while the pier was demolished following a storm in 1987.

Pass the **Clock Tower**, celebrating Queen Victoria's Diamond Jubilee, then join a path along the back of the beach from the end of the promenade. Pass the Fisherman's Cottage Inn at the foot of the gorge of **Shanklin Chine**, then turn right up Appley Steps to climb steeply to the clifftop. Join the road at the top, then turn left into Luccombe Road and climb steadily above the crumbling sandstone cliffs. A path briefly runs along the edge of the field to the right before rejoining the road. Keep left on the road, then follow a path through the trees from the road's end to Luccombe Chine, where a path leads down to the beach at **Luccombe Bay**. The route continues straight on, joining a vehicle track to its end by Rosecliff Lodge, then following a path into the jumbled ground beyond that is the result of a major landslip in 1810. Fork left past the **Wishing Seat** and some wonderful oak trees engulfed in dense subtropical vegetation.

The coast path continues along Footpath V65a, even where it claims to be closed because of landslips – the collapsed section is reached after only a short distance and the ground is easy to cross (or assess for yourself). *The only alternative is to climb steeply up to the road through the Devil's Chimney, a dramatic Victorian pathway, before turning left at Bonchurch Chute to return to the path just 200m further on.* **Bonchurch** was popular with artists and writers in the mid 19th century and a regular haunt of Charles Dickens, who is said to have based some of his characters on local residents, including Miss Havisham in *Great Expectations* and Mr Dick in *David Copperfield*.

The path continues down through the trees to emerge on a track by Carrigdene Farm. Turn right just beyond, then go left off the existing

The esplanade between Shanklin and Sandown

coastal path to descend across a small stream and keep left down a tarmac path to join the end of the seafront promenade in Bonchurch. This leads beneath the bright chalk cliffs to **Wheelers Bay** and on round the shore into **Ventnor**, the promenade soon reaching the foot of Shore Hill, which winds steeply up the hill into the centre of this beautifully situated town.

> **Ventnor**
> Perching perilously on steep slopes on the south of the island, **Ventnor** was once a small fishing village noted for its crab and lobster. It quickly grew after Dr James Clark published a book in 1830 recommending the town as the best place in the country to recover from chest infections because of its warm microclimate. As people flooded to the town for convalescence, a railway and pier were built in what became known as the 'English Mediterranean'. The town's fortunes waned once drugs to treat tuberculosis were developed in the 1960s, with the railway closing soon after and the pier being removed in 1993 following fire damage.

SONG OF THE DAY

The Bees – *Wash in the Rain*
This catchy number is taken from Ventnor-based psychedelic band The Bees' 2004 album *Free The Bees*. The video features an animated section with seafront scenes from the south coast of the island.

Section 5.3 – Ventnor to Brighstone

Distance: 24.8km (15½ miles)
Height Gained: 560m
Parking: Pay car parks in Ventnor. Free car parks along the route at the end of Old Blackgang Road, Blackgang Viewpoint and Whale Chine.
Public Transport: The Island Coaster bus (Southern Vectis, towards Ryde) runs seasonally just once a day from Grange Chine to Ventnor at 1701. Alternatively Bus 12 (Southern Vectis, towards Newport) runs 6 times a day from Brighstone village to Newport bus station, from where Bus 3 (Southern Vectis, towards Ryde) runs twice hourly to Ventnor. All services run 7 days a week.
Refreshments: The Beach Cafe at Castlehaven is passed on the route near St Catherine's Point, while the Buddle Inn at Niton Undercliff and the Wight Mouse Inn in Chale are just off the route.

Accommodation: Grange Farm Camping (01983 740296) and Brighstone Holiday Centre (07562 772528) are perfectly placed right on the route and with great sea views. There are rooms in Brighstone village at Homelea B&B (01983 740718) and the Three Bishops Inn (01983 740226), and closer to the route at Chilton Farm (01983 740338). There is a Tourist Information Point (01983 740843) at the village shop in Brighstone.

Overview: A fabulous if rather complicated day's walking around the geologically and botanically fascinating southern tip of the island. There are several places where the England Coast Path differs from the existing coastal path, all accessible to some degree at present but currently entirely unsigned. It is a wonderful route out of Ventnor, taking in both shoreline undercliffs and towering inland precipices, before a new section explores St Catherine's Point, its lighthouse and the various landslips. There is a lot of up and down, but beyond Blackgang the route becomes easier, following the gradually descending clifftops around Chale and Brighstone Bays.

Route Description

Follow the promenade around **Ventnor Beach**, then bear right up the hill before the Spyglass Inn. A path continues below La Falaise car park, passing the letters Ventnor spelled out in chalk. Fork right beyond, then keep left to descend some wooden steps and cross Flowers Brook by a small pond. A new concrete path leads on round the shore of Castle Cove to reach the beautiful unspoilt fishing hamlet of **Steephill Cove**. Follow a path right up the hill before the Beach Shack, then double back left to climb steps to a higher path into the varied trees surrounding **Ventnor Botanic Garden**. This houses a rare collection of subtropical plants that thrive in the unique

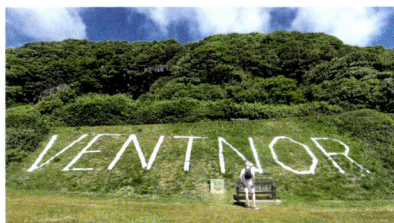

microclimate on the south-facing slopes around Ventnor. It was founded in 1970 in the grounds of the Royal National Hospital, a convalescent home for those with tuberculosis and other chest diseases that opened a century earlier.

The path soon opens out to pass Orchard Bay House and join the clifftops around an area of fascinating undercliffs. Beyond Mount Bay and Sir Richard's Cove the path climbs to Woody Point, before heading inland of the houses at **Woody Bay**. Turn left to reach a point where the existing coastal path turns right, while the new England Coast Path

Steephill Cove

continues straight on to a kissing gate. It follows a fenced path along the crumbling cliffs around Binnel Point to **Binnel Bay**, where a couple of paths drop down to the back of the beach. Turn immediately right beyond a stream (where a rope aids you up the bank, though it is far from necessary) and wind up through the trees to join a better path along a fenceline. In time the England Coast Path will turn left and wind through the scrub alongside the adjacent landslip, but until it is signed and widened it is easier to continue ahead, then fork left to climb past a fallen tree. After ¼ mile, bear left again to keep climbing through the scrub above the **Old Park Hotel**, a 19th-century mansion that once housed a tropical bird park.

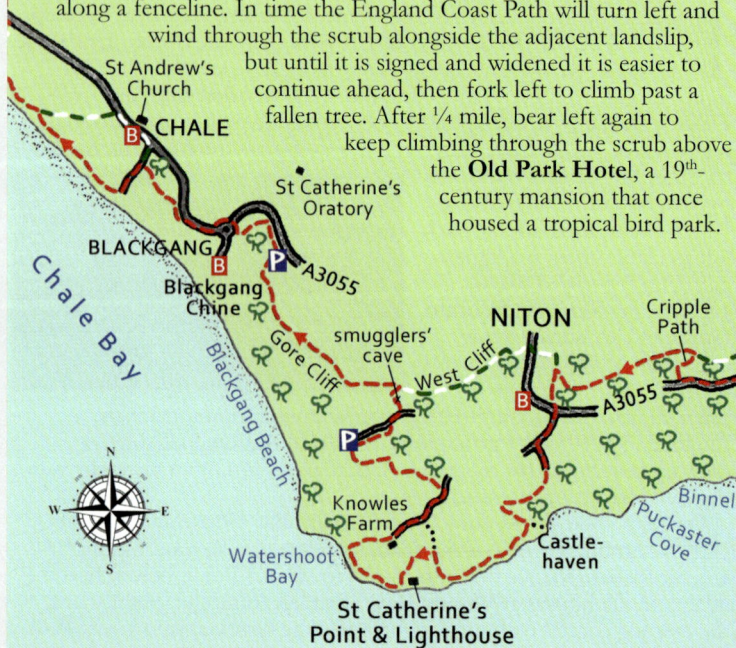

The Undercliff

Ventnor, St Lawrence and Bonchurch all stand on an area known as the Undercliff, a 7-mile-long shelf that has slumped dramatically since the end of the last ice age in one of Europe's largest landslip events. The island's highest chalk downs rest on top of layers of softer greensand and Gault clay, which the islanders call 'blue slipper clay' as it continues to cause regular landslips across the area, particularly at Blackgang and Bonchurch, and most recently severing the main road through St Lawrence. There is evidence of prehistoric occupation on the Undercliff, doubtless taking advantage of the unique climate that would later attract substantial Victorian settlement.

Keep left as the path bends round to join the end of Undercliff Road, which was the main road around the southern end of the island until a short section collapsed in a landslip in 2014. A path continues past the landslip and onto the road's continuation the other side. Follow it for ¾ mile, then turn right up the **Cripple Path** (Footpath NT117), which climbs steeply beneath an impressive greensand crag to rejoin the existing coastal path along the crest. This ancient route is said to have been used by smugglers and pilgrims, as well as Charles II when his boat was forced to anchor off the island in bad weather in 1675.

ALTERNATIVE ROUTE: *The route described above is accessible but awkward and overgrown in places and entirely unsigned, so you may prefer to keep to the existing coastal path here until the England Coast Path is fully open. Heading inland from* WOODY BAY*, you reach Woolverton Road, turning left then right up the hill at the end. At the main road, head straight across into Spindlers Road, then turn left at the top. After 100m,*

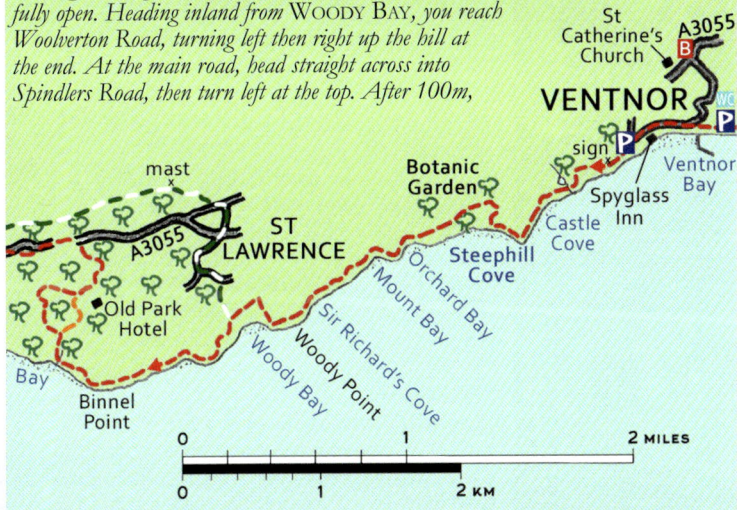

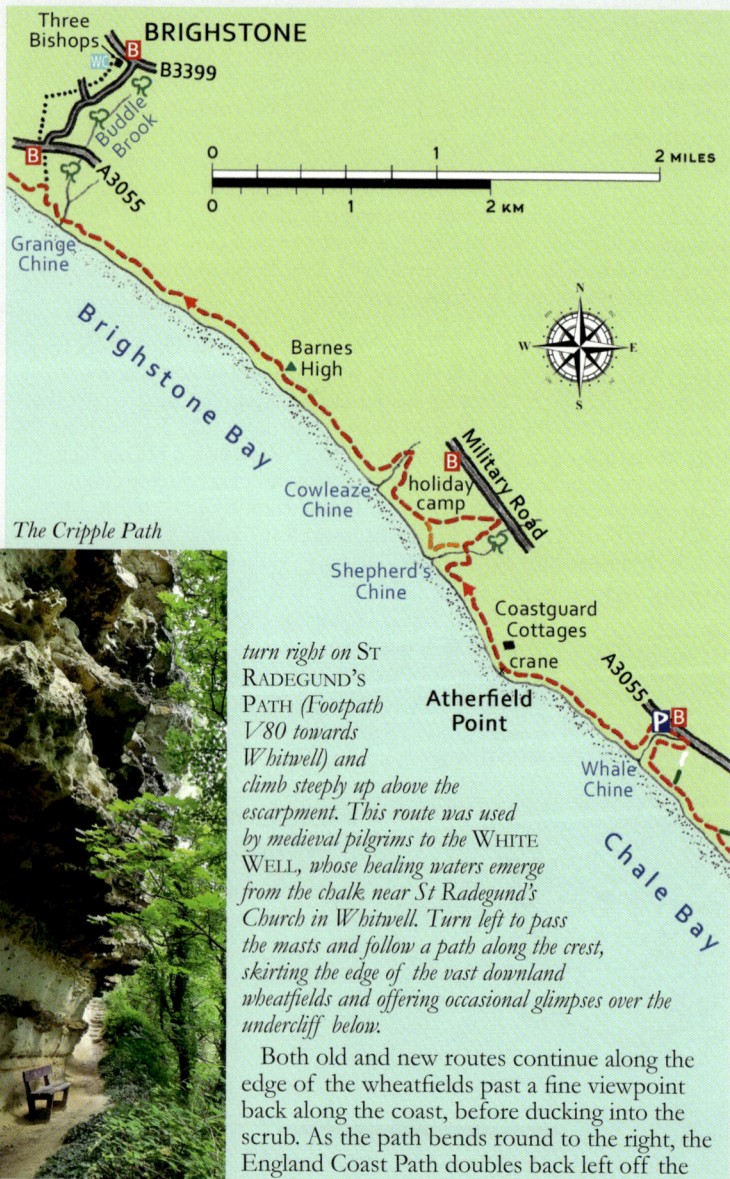

Map labels:
- Three Bishops
- WC
- BRIGHSTONE
- B
- B3399
- Buddle Brook
- B
- A3055
- Grange Chine
- Brighstone Bay
- Barnes High
- 0 ... 1 ... 2 MILES
- 0 ... 1 ... 2 KM
- N W E S
- Cowleaze Chine
- B
- holiday camp
- Military Road
- Shepherd's Chine
- Coastguard Cottages
- crane
- Atherfield Point
- A3055
- P B
- Whale Chine
- Chale Bay

The Cripple Path

turn right on ST RADEGUND'S PATH *(Footpath V80 towards Whitwell)* and climb steeply up above the escarpment. This route was used by medieval pilgrims to the WHITE WELL, whose healing waters emerge from the chalk near St Radegund's Church in Whitwell. Turn left to pass the masts and follow a path along the crest, skirting the edge of the vast downland wheatfields and offering occasional glimpses over the undercliff below.

Both old and new routes continue along the edge of the wheatfields past a fine viewpoint back along the coast, before ducking into the scrub. As the path bends round to the right, the England Coast Path doubles back left off the

St Catherine's Lighthouse

existing coastal path, following Footpath NT30 through a pair of small tunnels back down to Undercliff Drive. *Staying on the existing coastal path around the edge of Niton saves 1½ miles and a fair amount of climbing, but misses out on the drama of St Catherine's Point.* Reaching the main road on the new route, head straight on along St Catherine's Road, then turn second left down Castlehaven Lane. Follow the bridleway all the way down to the Beach Cafe just above **Castlehaven**, turning right before it to rejoin the low clifftops leading towards the lighthouse at **St Catherine's Point**, the notoriously foggy southernmost tip of the island. **St Catherine's Lighthouse** began operation in 1840, replacing the landmark of the 14th-century St Catherine's Oratory on the downs inland. It became one of the first electric lighthouses in 1888 and its fog horn stands alongside, having been moved away from the cliffs in 1932.

The route bends round to the right of the buildings, before turning left to some steps over a wall and heading back to the cliffs beyond the lighthouse. Stay on the low shore round to **Watershoot Bay**, then turn right along a fenceline and follow a path up to Knowles Farm, where Gugliemo Marconi conducted radio transmission experiments before moving to the Lizard Peninsula in Cornwall. Follow the rough road up from the farm until it ducks into the trees, then turn left onto a path and keep left as it climbs up onto a ridge of landslipped chalk. Follow the crest until a path bears off right to follow a dry grassy hollow to reach the car park at the end of **Old Blackgang Road**, where the former main road was severed by a major landslip in 1928. A path follows the right side of the road for ¼ mile, before joining it through a gate. Soon after, turn left on Footpath NT36 and climb steps which were cut by the

Blackgang Chine

Blackgang Chine is the country's oldest theme park, opened in 1843 by Alexander Dabell next to a new roadside hotel. It centred around the dramatic ravine of Blackgang Chine and landscaped clifftop gardens, and featured many curios, including the skeleton of a whale that washed up near the Needles and is still in situ. The chine itself was destroyed by a series of landslips, but the theme park has gone from strength to strength and is still owned by Dabell's family.

venture scouts in the late 1970s, passing the entrance to a partially flooded **smugglers' cave**.

Rejoin the existing coastal path on top of the escarpment to head along the dramatic edge of **Gore Cliff**, with St Catherine's Point and the colourful sands of Blackgang Beach laid out far below, then the great sweep of Chale Bay opening up beyond Blackgang Chine. Reaching a gravel path, turn right to Blackgang Viewpoint car park, from which a path continues down through the scrub, passing a bench which lays out the geology of the landslip. Turn left down Footpath C12 to the vast car park at **Blackgang Chine theme park**, then turn right up some steps to the A3055. Follow the main road left for ¼ mile beyond the roundabout, then turn left on a bridleway down to **Chale**. At the end, the existing coastal path turns right, while the England Coast Path goes left along the lane to its end. A grassy path follows the cliff edge right and keeps left along the crumbling greensand and chalk faces above **Blackgang Beach**, which are retreating at a rate of 1m per year. *The existing coastal path follows the A3055 through Chale, passing St Andrew's Church before turning left opposite the entrance to the Wight Mouse Inn to return to the clifftops.*

Rejoining the existing coastal path, the path bounds along the edge of the fields to **Whale Chine**, where you can either cross the field, or hug the edge of this dramatic sandstone gorge. Both paths converge to follow the main road to Whale Chine Car Park, at the far end of which the path resumes along the clifftops. This road is part of what is known as the **Military Road**, which was constructed to defend against the threat of a French invasion in 1860 – its original line actually ran closer to the cliff edge, much of it now lost to the sea, and this new road was created in 1930.

It is a lovely high level walk to **Atherfield Point**, where a series of reefs run offshore and a wooden crane stands on the clifftop by

Coastguard Cottages. The cliffs between here and Compton Bay are composed of the oldest rocks on the Isle of Wight, a collection of Wealden mudstones and sandstones laid down on an extensive floodplain. Reaching **Shepherd's Chine**, don't be tempted to scramble straight down into the gorge, but bend round to the right for 100m before following an unsigned path down some steps to the bottom. A new section of the England Coast Path will turn right here, before doubling back left at the road to skirt around the edge of the **Atherfield Bay Holiday Camp**, but in the meantime you need to follow the existing but unsigned route left. This skirts along the edge of the gorge, then climbs to rejoin the grassy clifftop path. After bending right around Cowleaze Chine, turn left on a vehicle track and resume the pleasant coastal yomp through the fields. Climb steadily to the trig point at **Barnes High**, then wind along the gradually diminishing cliffs for another mile to **Grange Chine**. Drop straight down to cross Buddle Brook and follow the track up through Grange Farm Campsite the other side. Where the route continues left, carry straight on to reach the main road and simple routes along footpaths or roads into **Brighstone**, less than a mile away. The **Three Bishops** inn stands at the heart of the village, named after three parish rectors who went on to become Bishops of Salisbury, Winchester and Bath & Wells.

SONG OF THE DAY

Wet Leg – *Angelica*

The island's most recent breakout musical act shot to prominence in 2021 with their kooky, catchy slices of pop. The band hails from West Wight and all their videos feature sumptuous rural landscapes around the area. This single from February 2022 namechecks singer Rhian Teasdale's best friend and was filmed on a beautiful day around St Catherine's Lighthouse near Niton. The band's name is said to be a reference to outsiders to the island, who would once have got a wet leg after stepping off the ferry.

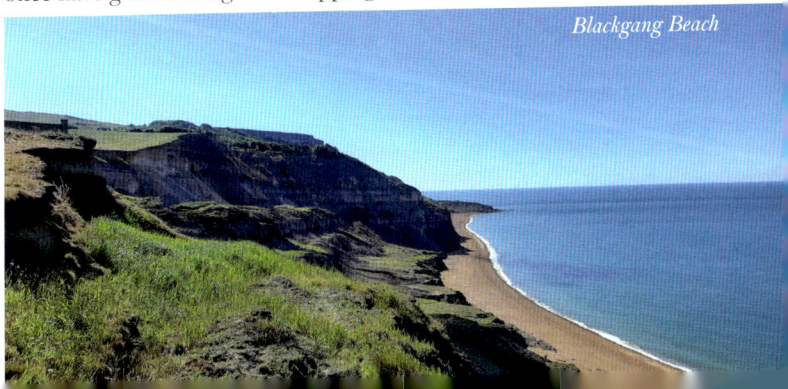

Blackgang Beach

Section 5.4 – Brighstone to Totland

Distance: 19.3km (12 miles)

Height Gained: 450m

Parking: Pay car parks at Brook Chine, Compton Bay, Freshwater Bay, Alum Bay and Totland. Small free car park on the route at Chilton Chine.

Public Transport: The Island Coaster (Southern Vectis, towards Yarmouth) runs seasonally from Totland to Grange Chine 3 times a day (all during the afternoon). Bus 12 (Southern Vectis, towards Newport) runs 6 times a day year round from Totland to Brighstone village. Both services run 7 days a week.

Refreshments: Dimbola Tea Room and Piano Cafe are ¼ mile off the route in Freshwater Bay at the midpoint of the day's walk, while there are other options further on at the Needles Landmark Attraction.

Accommodation: The Hermitage B&B (01983 752518) is passed along the route on the way into Totland, while Sentry Mead (01983 753212) and Chart House (01983 755193) are closer to the centre of the village. There is also accommodation a mile further along the route in Colwell Bay. Totland Youth Hostel (01983 752165) is just ½ mile off the route, while the closest campsites are at Stoats Farm (01983 759608), not far from the hostel, and Heathfield Farm (01983 407822), near the route through Colwell Bay.

Overview: Another wonderful day's walking through the dramatic cliff scenery of West Wight. The crumbling cliffs from Brighstone to Compton Bay are the oldest rocks on the island and home to some fascinating fossils, while the route beyond is dominated by the towering chalk faces of Tennyson Down and the Needles. Though always busy, there is much to see around the Needles Headland and Alum Bay, before you drop into the sheltered haven of Totland Bay, a fine place for a swim at the end of the day.

Route Description

Rejoin the route at **Grange Farm** and follow the cliff edge through the campsite into the adjacent holiday park. The England Coast Path will cut through the colourful chalets of Brighstone Holiday Centre to pass the faded swimming pool building and stay along the cliff edge beyond, but this is currently closed due to the unstable cliffs and has become very overgrown. Instead, a diversion follows the edge of the camping field up the side of a vehicle track to reach the A3055.

Stay on the roadside verge for ½ mile to rejoin the main route and pass **Isle of Wight Pearl**, home to the country's largest collection of pearl jewellery, before turning left through the Chilton Chine car park (Footpath

Chalets at Brighstone Holiday Centre

BS72). Rejoin the crumbling clifftops to pass **Sudmoor Point**, before dropping gently down to **Brook Green**, where the lifeboat station that was in use until 1937 stands in ruins.

Follow the track briefly right, then cut left across a meadow to the Brook Chine car park, rejoining the clifftop path as it runs parallel to the road. Pass the striking outline of **Hanover Point**, below which several dinosaur footprints can be found on the beach, fossilised imprints of three-toed Iguanodons being the most obvious. Continue past the next car park and hug the fragile shore around a couple of landslips above **Compton Bay**, before dropping down to Compton Chine. Keep left of the fenceline until forced to bear right to skirt around the narrow chine itself, then climb above the chalk cliffs to rejoin the road cutting across the face of **Compton Down**. Beyond the highest point, you can bear left on either of a pair of paths skirting above the high cliffs. Pass a memorial to a 15-year old child who fell from the cliff here in 1846 as you descend steadily to **Freshwater Bay**, which is guarded by a pair of chalk stacks – Mermaid Rock and Stag Rock, onto which a stag is said to have leapt to avoid capture.

Drop down to join the beachfront promenade, then turn right before the Albion Hotel to join the road briefly. Turn left by the public toilets

The stacks of Freshwater Bay

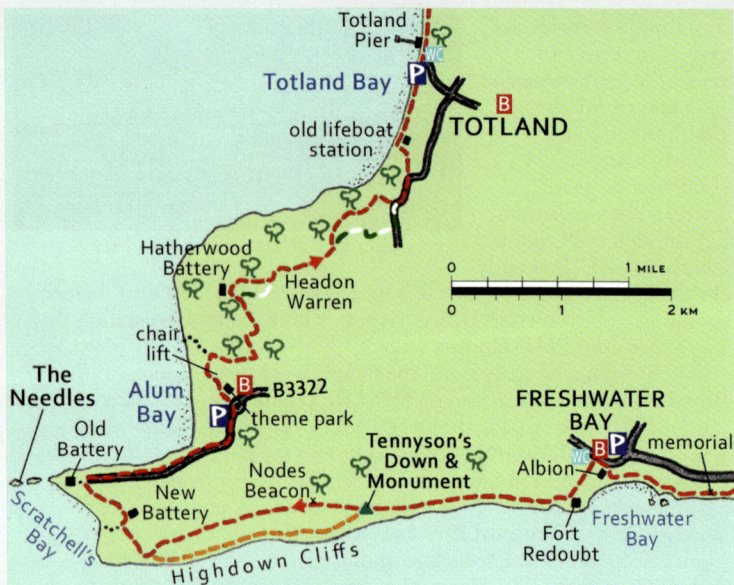

to follow the track towards **Fort Redoubt**, a Palmerston fort in use until 1928, then follow any of the paths up onto Tennyson Down (previously known as Beacon Down). It is a long steady climb above the highest cliffs on the island to reach **Tennyson's Memorial**, a granite cross erected in 1897 in memory of the poet who spent the last 40 years of his life in Freshwater. You can follow any of the paths across the downs beyond, but the route bears right away from Highdown Cliffs to a gate by a half-size replica of the **Nodes Beacon** navigational marker that once stood on top of Tennyson Down.

Tennyson's Monument

   Fork left beyond the gate to stay along the crest of West High Down, then bear left past the entrance to a bunker to reach another gate near the mast on the **Needles Headland**. Round the mast and pass above High Down Rocket Testing Site to drop down to the Needles Viewpoint, a small platform that is one of the few places on land from which it is possible to get a good view of these iconic chalk landmarks, seen across Scratchell's Bay. **The Needles** are composed of a series of narrow spiny sea stacks, but the name related to a fourth 120ft-high needle-like stack called Lot's Wife, which fell into the sea in the 18th century.

Head back up the hill from the viewpoint to the **New Battery**, where a path leads left down the hill towards the tip of the headland, on which the **Old Battery** perches – this was built along with Hatherwood Battery in the 1860s, with the New Battery added in the 1890s. You can pay to look around this National Trust property, for another

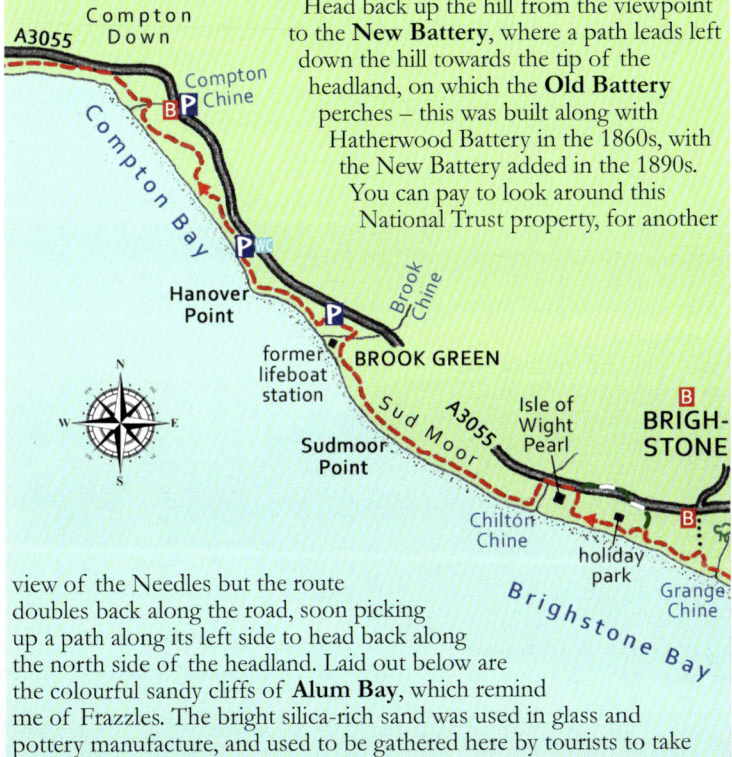

view of the Needles but the route doubles back along the road, soon picking up a path along its left side to head back along the north side of the headland. Laid out below are the colourful sandy cliffs of **Alum Bay**, which remind me of Frazzles. The bright silica-rich sand was used in glass and pottery manufacture, and used to be gathered here by tourists to take home in vials, but now has to be imported from elsewhere for sale in the gift shops.

Follow the road round to reach the **Needles Landmark Attraction** (previously the Needles Pleasure Park), then turn left at the roundabout through the theme park. Bear right past the entrance to the **chair lift**, which takes people down to Alum Bay for boat trips to the Needles, then turn right beneath the pylons and head down some steps. It is a brief detour left to Alum Bay, while the route turns right up Footpath T22, then next left on a path into Headon Warren. Turn right just before the open ground of **Hatherwood Battery** and head up onto the top of Headon Hill, with great views across West Wight. **Headon Warren**, now a heather-covered common, was created as a rabbit warren in the 15th century, when it is estimated that up to a third of the island's income came from exporting rabbit skin and meat.

Keep left along the crest of Headon Hill, then follow the main path down through the bracken to emerge on a hedged path around Warren Cottage. In time it is hoped the England Coast Path can be reinstated on the old coastal path to the left, but landslips mean this is currently

impassable. Follow the track down to the road and head left for ¼ mile down the hill into Totland, before bearing left on a footpath into **Widdick Chine**. Wooden steps lead down to the end of the promenade in Totland Bay by the 19ᵗʰ-century **Old Lifeboat House**. Follow the quiet seafront round to Totland Pier, from which it is less than ½ mile up the hill into the heart of the small village. **Totland** (a corruption of Tout-land, referring to a lookout) featured in J.M.W. Turner's *Isle of Wight Sketchbook*, produced in the 1790s, before being laid out as a new resort in the 1870. The imposing Totland Bay Hotel was pulled down in 1972 to leave a pleasingly low-key seafront.

———————————•❖•———————————

SONG OF THE DAY **Richard M. & Robert B. Sherman** – *Chitty Chitty Bang Bang* A famous scene from the 1968 film, showing the car driving over the cliff and plunging towards the sea before it takes flight, features the Needles and the cliffs of West Wight. The film's music was composed by the Sherman Brothers, who also wrote Oscar-winning songs for *Mary Poppins* and *The Jungle Book*.

The Needles

Section 5.5 – Totland to Shalfleet

Distance: 18.9km (12 miles)

Height Gained: 170m

Parking: Pay car park on the seafront at Totland, Colwell Bay, Fort Victoria and Yarmouth. Small free car park at Bouldnor Viewpoint.

Public Transport: Bus 7 (Southern Vectis, towards Alum Bay) runs hourly 7 days a week from Shalfleet to Totland.

Refreshments: There are various pubs and cafes in Yarmouth, but nothing between there and Shalfleet.

Accommodation: The only accommodation in Shalfleet is listed on Airbnb, otherwise you are as well to get the hourly bus into either Yarmouth or Newport. The closest campsites are at Camp Wight (07748 844242), ½ mile off the route in Ningwood, or the Orchards Holiday Caravan and Camping Park (01983 531331) in Newbridge, just over a mile inland from Shalfleet.

Overview: A gentler day along the Solent shore takes in the beaches of Totland and Colwell, the charming streets of Yarmouth and the rich landslipped woods of Fort Victoria Country Park and Bouldnor Cliff, before rounding the myriad creeks of the Newtown estuary. Beyond Bouldnor, the path is much quieter among the secluded heaths, copses and meadows of Hamstead.

Route Description

Rejoin the promenade at **Totland Pier** to reach Warden Point, where a landslide destroyed the sea wall in 2012. The promenade resumes around **Colwell Bay**, where the main route continues across the sandy beach, before heading inland up the next slipway at

Sunset over Yarmouth Green

Colwell Bay and Fort Albert

Brambles Chine. There are steps over the groynes, but at high tide the route may not be passable and the slipway is currently closed due to erosion, though it is simple enough to duck under the barriers. *The alternative route turns right up some steps shortly before the end of the promenade, then follows Madeira Lane right to reach the main road. Follow this left for 300m, then turn left on a track past Brambles Farm.* On the bend by Brambles Chine, bear left off the main route (or right off the alternative route) to follow a narrow path through to **Linstone Chine Holiday Village**. Turn right to follow the road out to the entrance, then turn left along Monks Lane. Turn right before the barrier to another part of the holiday village, following a fenced path around its perimeter and into **Fort Victoria Country Park**. Stay straight on along the main path through the woods unless you want to drop down towards the water for a view along the Solent shore towards **Fort Albert**, which stands prominently on the headland opposite Hurst Castle, and Sway Tower, a distinctive concrete folly visible 5 miles away on the mainland.

After ½ mile turn left towards **Fort Victoria** and drop down through the trees to emerge on the shore by the vast 19th-century fort on Sconce Point, built on the site of Henry VIII's Sharpenode Bulwark. Follow the walkway round the point, then join the back of the shingle beach until the sea wall resumes past Norton Grange Coastal Village. Turn right beyond to join the A3054 across the **Western Yar** estuary, whose breadth is misleading as the river is only 3 miles long. Over the bridge, bear left through the bus park by Yarmouth Harbour, then turn left towards the Isle of Wight Ferry Terminal, from where vehicle ferries depart for Lymington. Follow the road round into the centre of **Yarmouth**, a charming little town with a Tudor castle in the lee of its 19th-century timber pier. First recorded in the 10th century, Yarmouth is the oldest town on the island and retains its Norman grid layout of streets from a time when it was among the most prominent ports on the south coast.

Bear right in the square, then turn left along High Street to reach **Yarmouth Green**, where the England Coast Path leaves the existing coastal path to follow the promenade along the shore to **Bouldnor**. Take one of two paths up to the main road before the walkway is fenced off for private gardens, then follow the road left for 500m. Turn left on a vehicle track, at the end of which a path continues to the low wooded shore. Turn right on a narrow path through the woods behind this precarious muddy coast, where trees are continually falling onto the tidal shore and in the submerged mud just beyond lies one of the most significant prehistoric settlement sites in the country.

After crossing a boardwalk, the path opens out in gorse heathland and starts to climb steadily above the great landslips of **Bouldnor Cliff**.

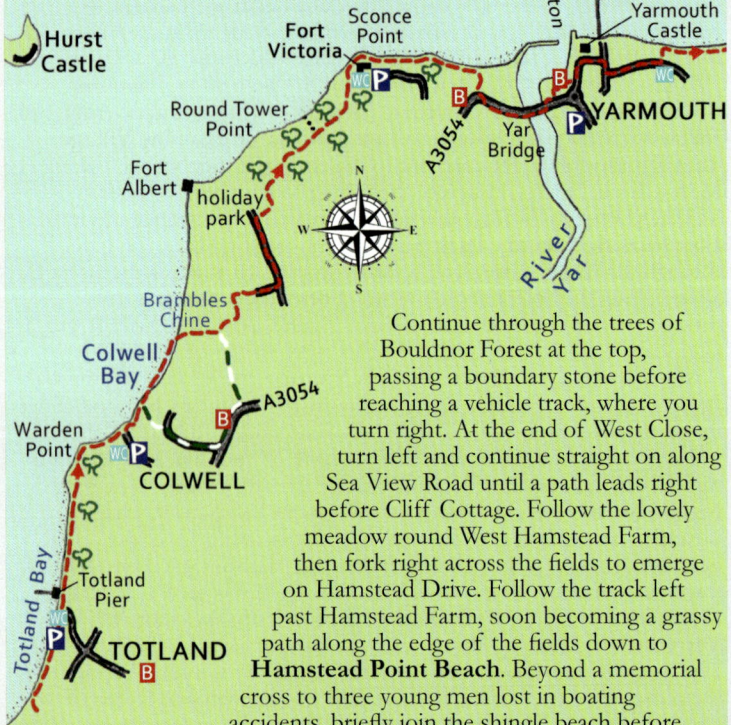

Continue through the trees of Bouldnor Forest at the top, passing a boundary stone before reaching a vehicle track, where you turn right. At the end of West Close, turn left and continue straight on along Sea View Road until a path leads right before Cliff Cottage. Follow the lovely meadow round West Hamstead Farm, then fork right across the fields to emerge on Hamstead Drive. Follow the track left past Hamstead Farm, soon becoming a grassy path along the edge of the fields down to **Hamstead Point Beach**. Beyond a memorial cross to three young men lost in boating accidents, briefly join the shingle beach before turning right up some steps. After a long

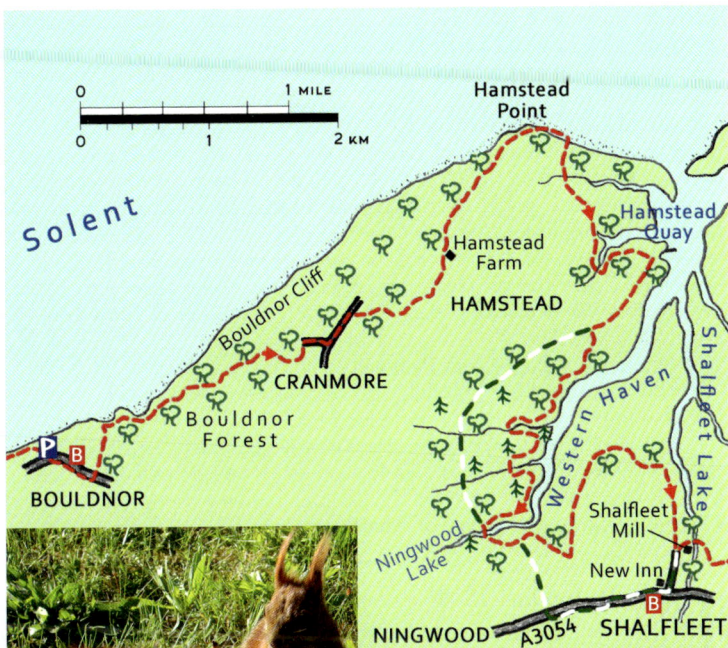

The forests of the Isle of Wight are among the few places in England where you can still find the red squirrel

boardwalk over a creek, cross a couple of fields before joining the edge of another muddy creek. Cross a bridge and return along the other side of the creek, before cutting right on a gravel path to emerge by **Hamstead Quay**, a small wharf on the bank of Newtown River that was served by the Hamstead Tramway, the first railway on the island, opened in 1832.

Bouldnor Cliff

Just off the shore of Bouldnor Cliff, a unique submerged Mesolithic landscape has been discovered beneath the waters of the Solent since the 1980s. Dating to 6,000 BCE, its scattered settlements stood on the edge of a fertile valley before the Solent was flooded to create the Isle of Wight. Wooden implements, burnt nuts and charcoal, and evidence of boat-building have been preserved at a series of sites along the foot of the cliff by the sea level's subsequent rise, and exhibits from these excavations can be seen displayed at Fort Victoria.

Follow the vehicle track right past Lower Hamstead Farm to a bend in the track. The England Coast Path will turn left here on a brand new path across the meadows to join the intricate wooded shore of **Western Haven**, before returning to the track along the muddy creek of Ningwood Lake. *However, until that is opened and during the winter months (when this route will be closed) you'll have to follow the existing coastal path along the main track through the varied plantations.* Keep left to drop down to rejoin the new route at a bridge over **Ningwood Lake**, just beyond which you bear left into the trees. *The current coastal path follows the edge of the field round to head up to the A3054, which you have to follow left into **Shalfleet**. At first there is a path along the far side, then there is a pavement or verge on the left as you pass St Michael's Church to reach the centre of the village by the **New Inn**, which dates from 1743.*

In time the England Coast Path will avoid this road section by cutting left at the corner of the first field and circling round Woodslade Coppice to join the right edge of a long field along the other side of Western Haven. At the far corner, you'll turn right past a small copse and skirt along the edge of a couple more fields to reach Shalfleet Quay Lane. Follow this right to rejoin the existing coastal path beyond Crab Cottage, with the tiny village of **Shalfleet** reached 300m further on.

———— ◆◆◆ ————

SONG OF THE DAY

Redpoint – *The Weather in Shalfleet*
Andrew Lowe and Ian Boffin make electronic music about the English coast 'inspired by natural splendour, 80s arcade games and Cold War cold sweats'. This is a suitably sombre piece of estuarine disquiet from their 2009 album *Sense of Summer*.

Ningwood Lake

Section 5.6 – Shalfleet to Cowes

Distance: 17.9km (11 miles)

Height Gained: 180m

Parking: Pay car parks in Cowes and Newtown, with free parking along Prince's Esplanade between Gurnard and Cowes.

Public Transport: Bus 1 (Southern Vectis, towards Newport) runs every 10 minutes from various places in the centre of Cowes to Newport bus station, from where the hourly Bus 7 (Southern Vectis, towards Alum Bay) runs to Shalfleet. Both services run 7 days a week, but make sure you get the right Bus 7, as alternating services run via Calbourne instead of Shalfleet.

Refreshments: Food is available at the Sportsman's Rest in Porchfield and the Fish & Chip Shop in Thorness Bay Holiday Park.

Accommodation: There are various options in Cowes, with a Tourist Information Point at Aqua Marine Gifts (01983 303050). The closest campsite is 2 miles inland at Comforts Farm (01983 293888), though you can camp along the route at Whippance Farm (07872 612873) or Thorness Bay Holiday Park (0330 1234895) some 3-4 miles before Cowes, or at the Riverside Paddock Touring Park (01983 821367), 3 miles along the route beyond Cowes towards Newport.

Overview: Another quiet section of walking around the Newtown River estuaries and the gentle Solent shore, which gets busier only around Newtown and Cowes. The route is complicated by several new sections, only parts of which are currently accessible, with a result that, until the England Coast Path has been fully opened, there is more road walking than ideal early on.

Route Description

From the centre of **Shalfleet**, follow Mill Road left past the New Inn to the second fork, where the onward route follows the continuation of Mill Road right past **Shalfleet Mill**. Cross the Caul Bourne stream, which drove a waterwheel here since before the Domesday Book and powered a bakery on the site until the 1920s. The path soon joins a track up to Corf Road, which can be busy at times and has little in the way of a verge. After ½ mile turn left towards Newtown on Town Lane and cross **Causeway Creek** at Cassey Bridge, before turning left off the existing coastal path on Footpath CB16a. Briefly follow the creek shore, then bear right up the field to reach the road in **Newtown** village. Head straight on along the road to its end, from

Newtown

After Yarmouth, the next two ports that developed on the Isle of Wight were Newtown and Newport. Originally known as Francheville, meaning 'free town' as its inhabitants were free men, Newtown was renamed upon receipt of its charter in 1256. The Newtown River was considered the safest harbour on the island and the town was laid out on a ridge with strip fields running down to the water. It had become the island's hub by the time the Black Death and a French raid in 1377 razed the place, and it never recovered. With Newport becoming pre-eminent, Newtown's harbour silted up, and by the 19th century it was a rotten borough, returning two MPs with an electorate of just 39.

where a path follows the left edge of Coastguard Meadows to join a causeway around the estuary shore to the medieval **Newtown Quay**, which is surrounded by saltern reservoirs where salt was once made.

The causeway bends back towards the village and crosses a long boardwalk, just beyond which you turn left across a meadow to reach the Seabroke bird-watching hide. The various creeks of the **Newtown River** are all part of Newtown National Nature Reserve and are rich in

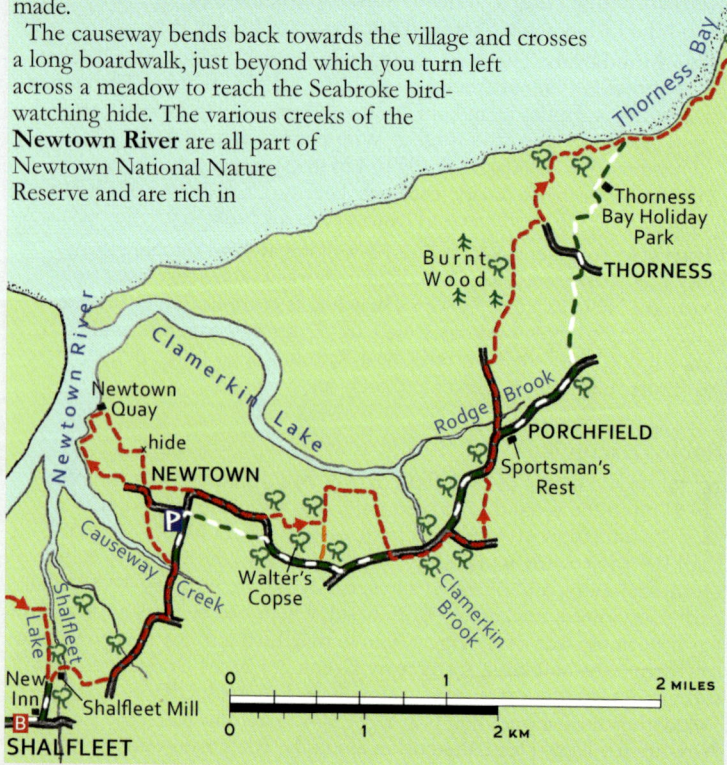

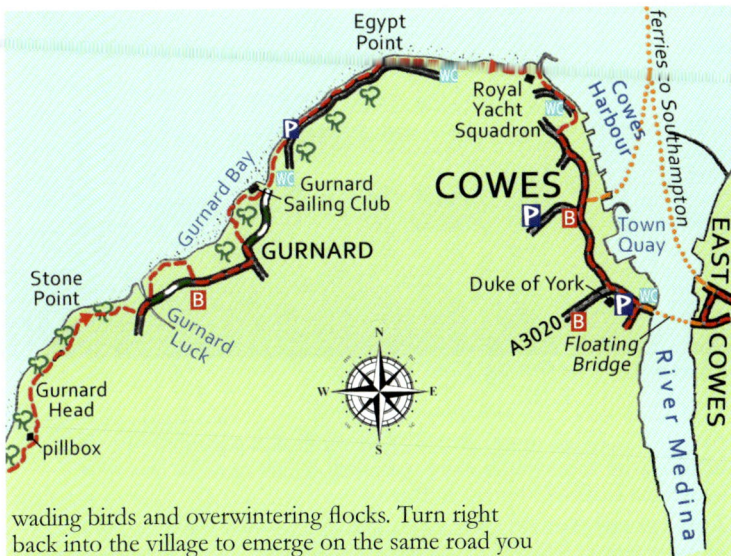

wading birds and overwintering flocks. Turn right back into the village to emerge on the same road you trod earlier, then turn immediately left over a stile to follow a pleasant footpath behind the church and houses. Join the quiet road to head out of the village, then head straight on at the bend into **Walter's Copse**. Follow the path round to the right, then turn next left and keep straight on to the far edge of this ancient woodland. Here the England Coast Path will turn left and follow a new path leading through the meadows alongside Clamerkin Creek, before turning right to head up past **Clamerkin Farm** to the road. *Until it is opened up though, you will need to turn right here and follow a narrow path through the trees back to the road. Follow the road left and keep left to join a busier vergeless road.*

The new England Coast Path will improve the walking along this road by providing a path alongside it either side of the crossing of **Clamerkin Brook**. Leave the existing coastal path again at the next junction, turning right on Colemans Lane for 300m, then turn left on Footpath CB8 towards Porchfield. Follow the right edge of the fields, before following a track left to rejoin the road, which leads right into the village of **Porchfield**.

At the war memorial, the England Coast Path will, once open, bear off left along Elmsworth Lane, crossing **Rodge Brook** and skirting along the edge of the danger area around Newtown Rifle Range. Beyond the last cottage, it will turn right into the field on a brand new footpath, skirting the edge of the fields as it climbs up the hill past the edge of **Burnt Wood** to reach Thorness Bay Holiday Park. Turn left on

Thorness Bay from Gurnard Head

the main access road and follow it through the chalets for ¼ mile until a path leads off left into the trees. This winds down through the woods between the shore and holiday park, before emerging in a meadow above the cliffs of **Thorness Bay**.

ALTERNATIVE ROUTE: *Until the England Coast Path is fully open, this route will remain inaccessible and the existing coastal path will have to be followed. It stays on the main road through* PORCHFIELD, *passing the Sportsman's Rest and climbing out of the village for ½ mile, then turns left into a field at the top. Stay along the right side of the meadows before cutting right around South Thorness Farm. Follow the road left briefly, then bear right around part of the* THORNESS BAY HOLIDAY PARK. *At the next road, follow it left to reach the centre of the holiday park, heading straight on down past the fish & chip shop and entertainment complex to enter Thorness Bay S.S.S.I.*

The routes rejoin at the end of the track, where a rough path continues around the back of **Thorness Bay Beach**, before crossing a bridge and then following a path left along the edge of a field. This starts to climb steadily around the vegetated landslips at the far end of the bay, on the crest of which are the remains of a series of World War II gun emplacements. The narrow path winds pleasantly along the top of the slope round **Gurnard Head** and Stone Point, before dropping down to the road on the edge of Gurnard. Beyond Gurnard Luck creek, turn left on Footpath CS35 to follow a concrete path along the shore of **Gurnard Bay**. The Luck, local dialect for a small stream, was once navigable and a ferry crossed from here to Lepe on the mainland before the development of Cowes.

After 300m along the shore, the path leads back to the road, which heads up the hill into **Gurnard** (originally known as Gurnet and named after a bottom-dwelling fish with a large spiny head). Turn left at the end, then bear left on the bend to follow a rough footpath down through the trees to emerge on the beach by the start of the concrete Shore Path. Beyond Gurnard Sailing Club, this joins the start of **Prince's Esplanade**, which leads round **Egypt Point.** Named after a nearby gypsy camp in the 16th century, this is the northernmost point on the island and has a squat lantern-style lighthouse.

It is an enjoyable walk along the sea wall and beachfront, before rounding the **Royal Yacht Squadron** building at the mouth of Cowes Harbour. Follow Victoria Parade to its end, then turn right along Watchouse Lane and follow **Cowes**' long High Street left all the way through this busy hub. Passenger ferries leave for Southampton from **Town Quay**, while the route continues past the boatyards and marinas. Turn left on Medina Road by the Duke of York to reach the **Floating Bridge** chain ferry service to East Cowes, or turn right to reach the bus stops. The Floating Bridge was established in 1859, replacing a rowing boat ferry between the two halves of Cowes.

Cowes

Though there was a settlement here since 11th-century Viking raiders made use of it, Cowes was only named in the 15th century after a pair of cow-shaped sandbanks at the mouth of the Medina estuary. The towns of East and West Cowes developed around forts built during the reign of Henry VIII, with the larger town simply becoming Cowes in 1895 (even though locals still know it as West Cowes). Boat- and sail-making dominated the local economy, and the founding of the Royal Yacht Squadron in 1815 transformed Cowes into the world's first centre for yachting. An annual regatta that began in 1826, Cowes Week still takes place every August and attracts around 1,000 boats.

SONG OF THE DAY **Hubert Clifford** – *Cowes Roads (No. 1 from Cowes Suite)*
Commissioned by the BBC for its Light Music Festival in 1958, this was Australian-born Clifford's last composition before his death in 1959. He lived in Cowes in the 1950s and the breezy air of this piece is very evocative of a summer holiday with the Solent full of sailing boats.

Section 5.7 – Cowes to East Cowes

Distance: 15.3km (9½ miles)

Height Gained: 100m

Parking: Pay car parks in Cowes and Newport, with free parking on the seafront ½ mile off the route in East Cowes.

Public Transport: The Floating Bridge chain ferry provides a simple link between East Cowes and Cowes, running every ten minutes year round.

Refreshments: There are various options in the centre of Newport at the midpoint of the day's walk.

Accommodation: There are rooms in East Cowes at Annie's B&B (01983 291306), BoSun's Lodge (01983 293425), the Prince of Wales (01983 292843) and Albert Cottage Hotel (01983 299309). Camping is available just ½ mile from the ferry in East Cowes at Waverley Park Holiday Centre (01983 293452).

Overview: A simple day that some will eschew in favour of the shortcut across the Floating Bridge over the River Medina, but a fine little walk along the estuary into Newport and back. Only the last couple of miles are on roads, the rest following cycleways and pleasant paths along the wooded estuary shore. Visiting Newport provides a sense of completeness at seeing the whole of the island, while the route also takes in the church that Queen Victoria had rebuilt for her at Whippingham.

Route Description

The **Floating Bridge** chain ferry regularly crosses the River Medina year round, but is occasionally closed due to maintenance issues or staff shortages. The England Coast Path will provide an alternative route around the estuary that is not part of the existing coastal path but is already accessible in its entirety. The route round the Medina estuary starts in **Cowes** 100m before the Floating Bridge, turning right along Bridge Road, then left on Thetis Road. Just beyond the entrance to the Classic Boat Museum, turn right through a ginnel. Go left on the next road, then first right up South Road and left at the top along Arctic Road. Continue past the United Kingdom Sailing Academy and boatyards, before turning right up a path then immediately left. Head straight across the road and join the Red Squirrel Trail, a cycleway along the former **Cowes and Newport Railway**.

Follow the cycleway for over 2 miles across a series of creeks and past

COWES

EAST COWES

Columbine Shed

ferries

B

B

B

A3020

P

WC

Floating Bridge

A3021

East Cowes Cemetery

Cowes Power Station

WHIPPINGHAM

St Mildred's Church

River Medina

former railway

Folly Inn

P

Island Harbour Marina

0   1 MILE

0   1   2 KM

N
W   E
S

West Medina Mills

paddle steamer

Dodnor Creek

Newport Rowing Club

Seaclose Park

WC

mermaid statue

Bargeman's Rest

P

Newport Harbour

P

NEWPORT

B

A3020

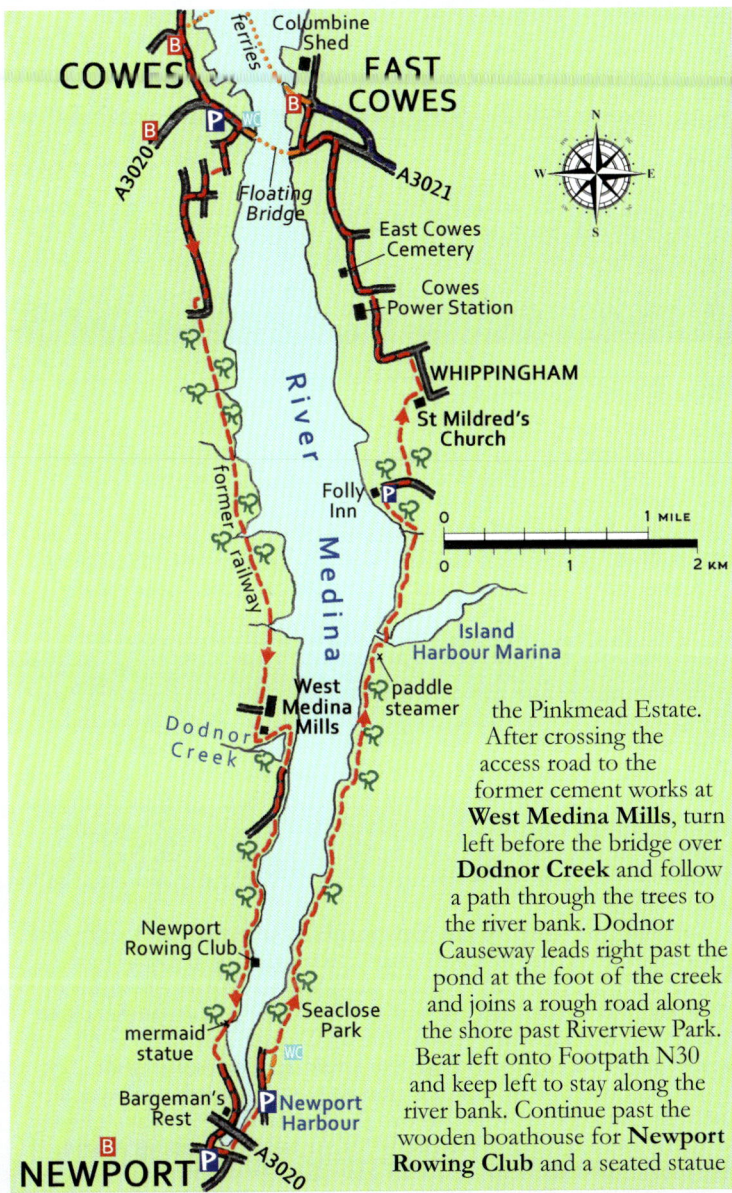

the Pinkmead Estate. After crossing the access road to the former cement works at **West Medina Mills**, turn left before the bridge over **Dodnor Creek** and follow a path through the trees to the river bank. Dodnor Causeway leads right past the pond at the foot of the creek and joins a rough road along the shore past Riverview Park. Bear left onto Footpath N30 and keep left to stay along the river bank. Continue past the wooden boathouse for **Newport Rowing Club** and a seated statue

River Medina

West Medina Cement Works

The River Medina (from an Old English word meaning 'the middle one') is a drowned river valley that once flowed into the River Solent and is navigable as far as Newport. What is now the West Medina Mills complex was one of a pair of tidal mills that stood either side of the estuary. Building started in the 1790s and, from 1841, it was owned by the cement manufacturer Charles Francis & Sons in 1841. It produced Medina Cement, a type of quick-drying Roman cement made with septaria stones dredged from the Medina. Production ended in 1939 and some of the kilns have been preserved alongside Dodnor Creek.

of a mermaid, before rejoining the cycleway at Medina Riverside Park. Keep left to join the road leading through the industrial estates and boatyards into **Newport**. Pass the Bargeman's Rest and duck under the dual carriageway to reach Newport Harbour by the end of the navigable part of the river. Turn left by Quay Arts and, where the route continues round the quay, you can turn right to explore the elegant town centre. Close to the centre of the island but still accessible by sea, Newport became a focal point for trade on the Isle of Wight and is considered its county town.

Rejoining the route around **Newport Harbour**, head back under the dual carriageway and follow Medina Greenway along the quay past Jubilee Stores. Follow the cycleway or walkway that pass either side of the Classic Boat Museum, the routes soon rejoining to enter **Seaclose Park**, now the site of the revived Isle of Wight Festival. At the far end, keep left on the Greenway along the lovely wooded estuary shore. Eventually you emerge from the trees to pass the remains of a paddle steamer that once ran from Ryde to the mainland before being moored here for use as a nightclub in the 1970s. At **Island Harbour Marina** the route continues across the lock gates, though you may need to press the button on the bridge for the lock keeper to close the lock for you. The marina was created in 1966 from the tidal mill pond of East Medina Mill, and the Spice Bus (that featured in the 1997 film *Spin World*) is on display on its south side.

Stay along the grassy shore beyond, then cross a footbridge and skirt along the riverside around the large caravan park. Bend right through the trees and reach the road through the car park of the **Folly Inn** – this pub replaced an illegal drinking den on a former French smuggling barge called *Foliaire*. Follow the road up the hill, before turning left on the bend on Footpath CS24 to wind through the scrub and climb across the fields towards Whippingham. The hamlet is dominated by **St Mildred's Church**, which was rebuilt in the 1860s for Queen Victoria, as she didn't like John Nash's earlier 19th-century edifice. Inside you can view the Queen's comfortable chair and the tomb of her youngest daughter, Princess Beatrice.

The route follows a cycleway left alongside the road, then turns left at the end along Saunders Way. Head back down towards the river to pass the striking outline of **Cowes Power Station**, a gas turbine built in 1982 that looks like a collection of cereal boxes and cardboard tubes. At the end turn left to join Kingston Road and head round past East Cowes Cemetery. Turn left again at the end and follow Clarence Road into **East Cowes** past the boatyards and sheds along the Medina. In the middle of the small town, turn left to return to the other side of the Floating Bridge or reach the vehicle ferry back to Southampton. East Cowes' most striking landmark is the vast **Columbine Shed** of the Wight Shipyard beyond the ferry terminal – it was here that Saunders Roe built the world's largest sea planes and hovercraft from 1935 and painted what is still the largest Union Jack on its doors to celebrate the Queen's Jubilee in 1977.

Newport Rowing Club

SONG OF THE DAY **Level 42** – *The Sun Goes Down (Living It Up)*
Level 42 were formed in 1979, its core members Mark King and the Gould brothers having met on their native Isle of Wight. King, who became famed for his funky slap-bass technique, grew up in Cowes and moved back to the area in 1988. This classic 80s pop-funk single reached number 10 in the charts in 1983.

WORBORROW BAY, PURBECK

Part 6:

The Dorset &
East Devon Coast

The Dorset & East Devon Coast

Start: Mudeford
Finish: Exmouth
Total Distance: 213.5km (132½ miles)
Total Ascent: 5,030m (16,500ft)
Days: 11

The broad steely sea, marked only by faint lines, which had a semblance of being etched thereon to a degree not deep enough to disturb its general evenness, stretched the whole width of his front and round to the right, where, near the town and port of Budmouth, the sun bristled down upon it, and banished all colour, to substitute in its place a clear oily polish. Nothing moved in sky, land, or sea, except a frill of milkwhite foam along the nearer angles of the shore, shreds of which licked the contiguous stones like tongues.

Thomas Hardy, *Far From the Madding Crowd*

Dorset is a hilly county, which reaches the sea in a jumble of ridges and hills, including the highest point on the south coast, at 191m on Golden Cap. It is one of the most varied counties in

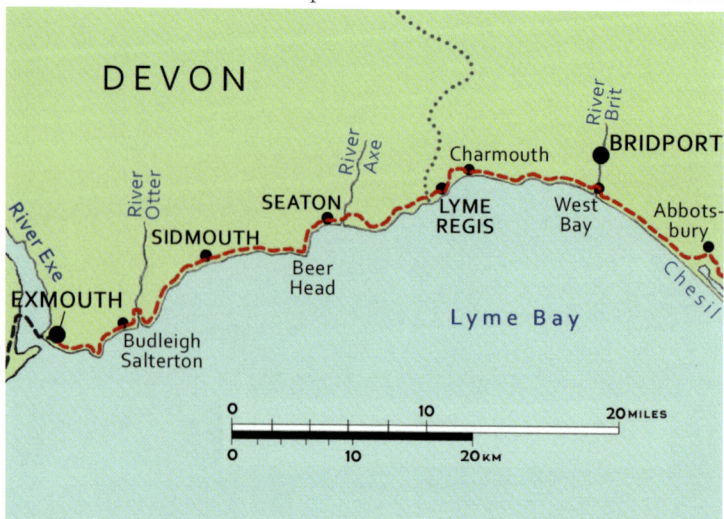

the country, combining the different colours of its soaring chalk, limestone and sandstone cliffs with some of the south coast's finest beaches around Bournemouth, Swanage and Weymouth. The same could be said of east Devon between Lyme Regis and Exmouth, which I have grouped in with Dorset, as the River Exe is a more natural place to end this book and geologically they make sense together. Chesil Beach, the Isle of Portland, Lulworth Cove and the Lyme Regis-Axmouth Undercliffs are among the most distinctive landscapes in the south of England, and the walking is spectacular throughout.

Dorset's name is derived from the town of Dorchester, *sæte* being an Old English word referring to the people of a particular region. The county was first mentioned as part of the kingdom of Wessex in the 9th century, by which time the first Viking raids on Britain had taken place around Portland. It remained a largely agricultural area, its working class still involved in farming rather than industry in the 19th century, when labourers formed the first trade union and became renowned as the Tolpuddle Martyrs. It is this rural landscape that inspired Thomas Hardy, and has made Dorset popular with tourists since George III's frequent visits to Weymouth from 1789 until the end of his reign.

The Dorset and east Devon coast is a geologist's dream, most of it designated by UNESCO as a World Heritage Site. However, the commonly used 'Jurassic Coast' moniker is slightly misleading, as it features a remarkable array of rocks that span the Cretaceous, Jurassic and Triassic periods. These layers dip generally from west to east,

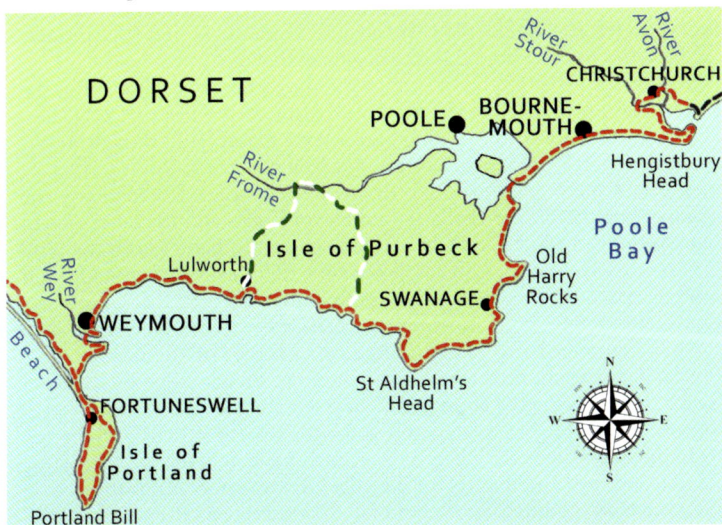

meaning the older Triassic rocks (red sandstones laid down in an arid desert when all the earth's landmass was a single supercontinent called Pangaea) are found in the west. The younger Cretaceous rocks (chalk laid down beneath tropical seas by phytoplankton or algae shedding tiny calcium carbonate shells) are found in the east on the Isle of Purbeck, though some folding has also exposed chalk around Beer. Between Swanage and Seaton though, the bulk of the rocks are truly Jurassic, forming Purbeck Marble, the famous limestone of the Isle of Portland, the pebbles of Chesil Beach, and the loose marl in which are revealed the fossils of Lyme Regis. Giant ammonites can still be seen in several places along the coast of Purbeck, while others of various sizes are found on the rocky tidal platform around Lyme Regis and Charmouth.

The coast path through Dorset begins with a circumnavigation of Christchurch Harbour, before following the sandy arc of Poole Bay past Bournemouth to take the short ferry crossing to the Isle of Purbeck. Here the route joins the existing South West Coast Path, though the England Coast Path provides some newly accessible sections to this long-established trail. Purbeck is dramatic and varied, Studland Bay and heath giving way to the chalk of Old Harry Rocks and the limestone of Durlston Head and St Aldhelm's Head. The path then crosses waves of different rocks – oil-rich shales, limestone, red Wealden clays and chalk – on its spectacular route to Weymouth, with Lulworth Cove and Durdle Door among its most famous features.

After a circuit of the quarried limestone isthmus of the Isle of Portland, the route runs inland of the unique shingle ridge of Chesil Beach, then rejoins the shore at the popular shingle beaches of west Dorset. The route bounds up and down the precarious cliffs all the way to Lyme Regis, beyond which it dives into the lush jungle of the Lyme Regis-Axmouth Undercliffs on the edge of Devon. After Seaton, Devon's cliffs continue to rise and fall dramatically all the way to

Exmouth, where they finally peter out by the Exe estuary. There is barely a dull moment and, with its rich variety of landscapes, it is easy to argue that Dorset's coast provides some of the finest walking in England. Other than on the more remote parts of the Isle of Purbeck, public transport is generally good, particularly in the summer.

Useful Information

Tourist Information – *www.visit-dorset.com*

morebus – 01202 338420 *(www.morebus.co.uk)*

First Wessex, Dorset & South Somerset – 0345 646 0707
   (www.firstbus.co.uk)

Stagecoach South West – 0345 241 8000 *(www.stagecoachbus.com)*

Travel Dorset – *www.dorsetcouncil.gov.uk/travel/travel*

Train Times – *traintimes.org.uk*

Bus Times – *bustimes.org*

Traveline – *www.traveline.info*

Luggage Transfers – 01326 567247 *(www.luggagetransfers.co.uk)*

COUNTY ANTHEM

The Yetties – *Dorset is Beautiful*

This unofficial anthem for the county was written by Bob Gale in the 1960s and first recorded in 1972 by The Yetties, a band hailing from the Dorset village of Yetminster. It is full of smutty West Country humour and includes a reference to the 'wurzel tree', from which the popular band took their name – it is not a tree, however, but local dialect for mangelwurzel, a root vegetable largely used for feeding livestock.

Beer

Section 6.1 – Mudeford to Bournemouth

Distance: 21.5km (13½ miles)

Height Gained: 160m

Parking: Numerous pay car parks in Mudeford, Bournemouth and various places in between. Free parking by the route along Southbourne Coast Road and Southbourne Overcliff Drive.

Public Transport: Buses X1/X2 (morebus, towards Lymington) run regularly from Westover Road in the centre of Bournemouth to Mudeford. More limited service on Sundays.

Refreshments: The Beach House and Hiker Café at Hengistbury Head are probably best placed, but there are also various options in Christchurch and along Bournemouth seafront.

Accommodation: There are various accommodation options in Bournemouth, with a Tourist Information Centre (01202 123800) opposite the pier, but no campsite nearby.

Overview: An amazingly interesting and varied day around the built-up conurbations of Christchurch and Bournemouth. The former is particularly delightful, the route taking its time to wind around Christchurch Harbour and the town's twin rivers, Avon and Stour, to reach Hengistbury Head. Though appearing somewhat convoluted the route gives many different vantage points across the harbour and town, before turning towards Poole Bay and making its way along the long beachfront towards the centre of Bournemouth.

Route Description

Follow the main road left through **Mudeford** to Stanpit, passing the Harbour Hotel and Nelson Tavern, before turning left along Argyle Road after ¾ mile. At the end there are good views across **Christchurch Harbour** as you follow a path right along the shore behind the houses. Rejoin the road briefly to pass the ancient spring of **Tutton's Well**, then turn left at Stanpit Marsh Car Park, following the path to its left out onto the marshes. The main route turns right through a gate before the visitor centre and follows the edge of the recreation ground, *though you can continue round the additional mile loop across* GRIMBURY MARSH *or follow a pleasant path right through the trees just beyond the visitor centre.*

All these routes reconvene to leave the nature reserve, turning left on a tarmac path and left again to continue around the edge of the marsh. Bear left off the surfaced path to join a path through the trees alongside the River Avon by **Little Avon Marina**. Keep left of the council offices at the end to join the road heading left into Christchurch over a pair of bridges across the two forks of the **River Avon**. After the second, turn left along a walkway between the river and the ruins of **Christchurch Castle**, a 12th-century Norman structure that was last used in the Civil War. Historically part of Hampshire, **Christchurch** is an ancient settlement between the mouths of the Avon and Stour rivers and was originally known as Twynham, meaning 'settlement between two rivers'.

Follow Convent Walk alongside the mill stream to round the back of the imposing **Christchurch Priory**. Cross the stream by the medieval Place Mill to reach Town Quay and follow a path right along the bank

Christchurch Harbour and Hengistbury Head from Christchurch Priory

> ### Christchurch Priory
>
> Christchurch Priory was founded in 1094 on the site of an earlier church, though it is said that it was meant to be built on nearby St Catherine's Hill until all the building materials were mysteriously moved to this spot during the night. It was later found that one of the massive beams had been cut too small, only for this to be fitted overnight by a mysterious carpenter thought to have been Jesus – the 'miraculous beam' can still be seen exposed inside the church.

of the **River Stour**, crossing a greensward known as **the Quomps** (a corruption of the Old English word *camp*, for an enclosed piece of ground). Stay along the river until you are forced right to join the road, then turn left along Willow Way, before joining the main road. Keep left at the roundabout to follow the B3059 over the River Stour, then turn immediately left to join the far bank past **Tuckton Gardens**. Keep left along the river bank, passing the historic **Wick Ferry**, which crosses the river from the Quomps between Easter and the end of October, saving around ¾ mile.

As it leaves the riverside, the route joins a gravel path onto **Wick Meadows**. Keep left to cross a bridge and climb slightly onto land formerly used as landfill. Pass a hide looking out across the River Stour, before heading straight across a road to reach **Hengistbury Head Visitor Centre**. A tarmac path leads on along the shore of Christchurch Harbour, but watch out for the land train that also uses this path. The route stays on the tarmac throughout, though it is possible to follow paths through the trees alongside.

Keep left at Hengistbury Head, following a broad track along the shore in front of the beach huts. At the far end of the **Mudeford Sandspit**, looking back across the strait to Mudeford Quay, bend right around the **Black House** and cut through the

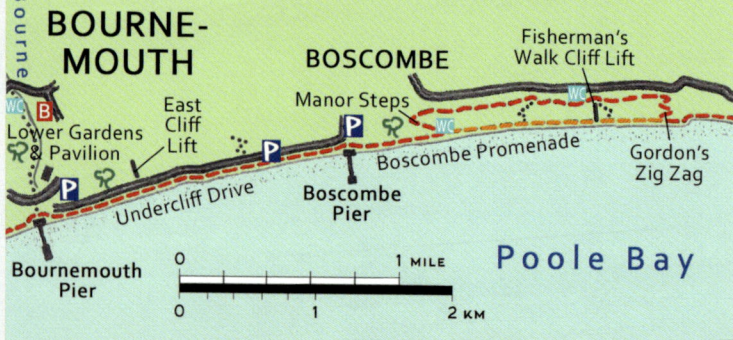

The Black House

The Black House on Mudeford Sandspit was said to have been the refuge of a band of smugglers who were being chased by excise men. According to local folklore, the officers smoked them out, hence the blackening of the walls. Unfortunately the Black House was only built in 1840, by which time smuggling was almost extinguished by lower import duties and the introduction of the coastguard, and the building was painted in oil tar to preserve it against the elements.

dunes to join a path heading back along the other side of the beach huts. This soon turns to sand and it is slow going to reach the steps leading up onto the solid ground of **Hengistbury Head**, formed of clay and iron-rich boulders that have prevented its erosion. This headland once separated the mouths of the Stour and Avon, before they changed their course to form Christchurch Harbour.

A broad track leads on up the crest of Hengistbury Head, past the remains of opencast ironstone quarrying that reduced the size of the

Hengistbury Head looking towards the Isle of Wight

headland in the 19th century. Continue past the coastguard lookout to the summit of **Warren Hill**, a spectacular viewpoint overlooking Christchurch Harbour, Christchurch Bay and Poole Bay. Descending from the headland, keep left along the shore to pass the striking **Double Dykes** that once defended a significant Iron Age port on the headland. A sandy path continues above **Southbourne Beach**, with sections of boardwalk leading to the road on the edge of Southbourne. Now part of greater Bournemouth, Southbourne-on-Sea was created as a rival resort to Bournemouth by Thomas Armetriding Compton in the 1880s and even briefly had its own pier.

You can head down the first set of steps, or take a tarmac path beyond, to join **Boscombe Promenade**, a broad walkway that continues around the seafront of Poole Bay for 7 miles to Sandbanks. Though urbanised throughout, most of Bournemouth is hidden behind the high cliffs and the perfect arc of sand slips appealingly into the bay's turquoise waters. Away from the car parks and access points there is plenty of space to relax on the sand or in the water.

Though it is possible to stay on the promenade throughout, after a mile the coast path is signed up Gordon's Zig-Zag to join a path along the top of **Southbourne** and **Boscombe Cliff**. Staying high for over a mile, this route provides a nice change of scenery and has good views over the beach, before descending Manor Steps Zig-Zag just before Boscombe Cliff Gardens. Rejoin the promenade to pass **Boscombe Pier**, interminable beach huts and East Cliff Lift, which has been out of action since a landslip in 2016. Surprisingly, goats can be seen grazing on the rough slopes as you approach **Bournemouth Pier**, which was built in 1880 to replace an earlier wooden jetty. The onward route continues along the promenade, while **Bournemouth**'s town centre is reached beneath the flyover and through the beautiful Lower Gardens, laid out alongside the tiny River Bourne in 1871.

Bournemouth

No settlement existed at the mouth of the River Bourne until the 1830s, when Sir George Tapps-Gervis began to lay out a new seaside resort on the pine-strewn heathland along this formerly barren stretch of coastline. It was described by Thomas Hardy as 'like a fairy place suddenly created by the stroke of a wand', the town growing rapidly after it featured in *The Spas of England* book. The Pleasure Gardens were once fields, around which the town was laid out, with the Winter Gardens (home to the famous Bournemouth Symphony Orchestra) added in 1875 and the Pavilion Theatre and Ballroom in 1929.

SONG OF THE DAY

The Fall – *Bournemouth Runner*

This song was written by Mark E. Smith in 1986 after an avid fan called Terry Stoate stole the stage backdrop at their gig in Bournemouth in 1985. Stoate only made it 200 yards before being beaten up by the bouncers, but was reportedly so delighted to have a song written about him that he subsequently set up a removals company in the area under the name Bournemouth Runner.

Bournemouth Pier and seafront

Section 6.2 – Bournemouth to Swanage

Distance: 17.6km (11½ miles)

Height Gained: 220m

Parking: Numerous pay car parks in Bournemouth, Swanage and several places along the seafront in between.

Public Transport: The Purbeck Breezer 50 (morebus, towards Bournemouth) runs hourly from Swanage to Bournemouth throughout the year, including a return crossing on the Sandbanks Ferry.

Refreshments: Several cafes in Sandbanks, including the Haven Ferry Cafe just by the Sandbanks Ferry, and various options in Studland.

Accommodation: There are various accommodation options in Swanage, with a Tourist Information Centre (01929 766018) on the beachfront. There are also numerous campsites around Swanage, with the closest to the route being Ulwell Farm Caravan Park (01929 422823), Swanage Bijou Camping (01929 426809, summer holiday only) and Herston Caravan & Camping (01929 422932).

Overview: Very much a day of two halves, bisected by the chain ferry across the mouth of Poole Harbour. Bournemouth's beachfront promenade continues all the way round to Sandbanks, while the Isle of Purbeck's charms are altogether more rugged. After a slog across the sand of Studland Bay, the chalk stacks of Old Harry Rocks dominate the first proper cliffs passed on the mainland since East Sussex and provide a wonderful approach to the resort of Swanage.

Route Description

Rejoin the beachfront promenade by **Bournemouth Pier** and pass the Oceanarium to reach the still-active West Cliff Lift, built along with the East Cliff Lift in 1908. The richly vegetated cliffs are broken only by a series of narrow ravines, known in this part of Dorset as chines; Durley Chine, Middle Chine, Alum Chine (where alum and copperas were mined in the 16th century), Branksome Dene Chine, Branksome Chine, Canford Cliffs Chine and Flaghead Chine. Early in the day, before the crowds descend on the beach, the quiet seafront can be a joy to walk, as Poole Bay slowly bends round towards the distant chalk cliffs of Purbeck. **Canford Cliffs'** sandstone faces tower impressively above the promenade, before diminishing as you near

Shore Road at the start of the Sandbanks isthmus.

The main route is signed straight on along the beach, though it can be hard going until you reach the promenade at **Sandbanks Beach**. Where this ends, continue along the sand for another ¼ mile to the broad Midway Path that leads up to the road. Keep left to reach the **Sandbanks Ferry**, a chain ferry that has been in operation since 1926 – the *Bramble Bush Bay* runs across the narrow strait at the mouth of Poole Harbour every 20 minutes and costs just £1 for pedestrians. *An alternative route avoids the sand by following the old coast path along Shore Road to join the promenade leading left alongside the B3369 and providing great views across* POOLE HARBOUR *towards Brownsea Island.*

Sandbanks is renowned as the most expensive place to live on the British coast, the average house costing more than £1.2 million, and is home to several former footballers and managers.

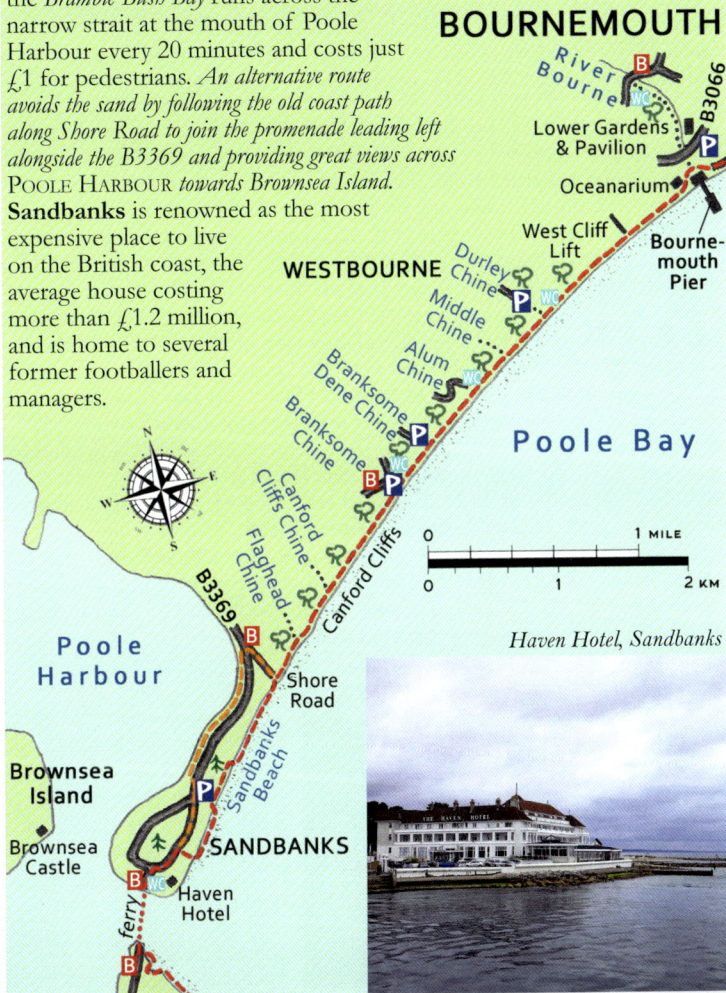

BOURNEMOUTH

River Bourne

Lower Gardens & Pavilion

Oceanarium

West Cliff Lift

Bourne-mouth Pier

WESTBOURNE

Durley Chine

Middle Chine

Alum Chine

Branksome Dene Chine

Branksome Chine

Poole Bay

Canford Cliffs Chine

Flaghead Chine

Canford Cliffs

B3369

Poole Harbour

Shore Road

Sandbanks Beach

Brownsea Island

Brownsea Castle

Haven Hotel

ferry

SANDBANKS

0   1 MILE

0   1   2 KM

Haven Hotel, Sandbanks

> **Poole Harbour**
>
> Poole Harbour is the vast drowned valley of the River Frome and the largest natural harbour in Britain. Poole was established as a port by the Romans and became the country's principal trading port with North America by the 18th century. It has a notably low tidal range as it stands midway between Land's End and the Dover Strait, with the range increasing the further you go in either direction from Poole. Brownsea Island, the largest in the harbour, is famous as the site where Robert Baden-Powell held an experimental week-long camp for boys in 1907, which led to the formation of the Scouting movement.

Disembark the ferry on the **Isle of Purbeck**, a 60-square-mile peninsula that is cut off to the north by Poole Harbour and the soggy heaths along the River Frome that would once have been very difficult to cross. A sculpture marks the beginning (or end) of the South West Coast Path, which runs alongside the England Coast Path for the next 630 miles. Turn left off the road immediately to cross the broad sands of **Shell Bay**, though after heavy rain you may need to head right soon to a footbridge over a shallow inlet. This beach featured in the first episode of *Monty Python's Flying Circus*, in which Michael Palin introduced the show by emerging dishevelled from the sea to exclaim 'It's…'.

Follow the beach round the headland to **Studland Bay**, a shallow expanse of sand that is popular for snorkelling and diving, particularly around the wreck of a 16th-century Iberian merchant ship. The wetland dunes of Studland Heath represent a rare landscape rich in bog plants, including the marsh orchid and Dorset heath flower (a type of heather), though the route sticks doggedly to **Knoll Beach**, part of which is England's most popular naturist beach. Continue past the busiest part of the beach towards Middle Beach, where the coast path is now signed up a sandy path to the car park. Head left to the far end of the car park, and continue straight across the road down to the beach by the thatched **Groom's Cottage** *(though at most states of the tide you can continue along the beach to reach this point).*

The onward path passes **Fort Henry**, built and named by Canadian engineers in 1943, before heading back up to the road through **Studland** village. Follow it left past the Bankes Arms, then turn

Groom's Cottage, Studland

Poole
Harbour

SANDBANKS

B

P

Shell
Bay

Bramble
Bush Bay

Studland
Heath

Little
Sea

Studland
Bay wreck ×

Knoll Beach

Studland
Bay

N

W   E

S

0   1 MILE

0   1   2 KM

P

Middle
Beach

Groom's
Cottage

WC

P

Fort
Henry

STUDLAND
B

P

South
Beach

Handfast
Point

Old Harry
Rocks

Bankes
Arms

WC

Parson's Barn

The Pinnacles

Isle of
Purbeck

Ballard Down

Ballard
Point

Parson's Barn
and the Pinnacles

Ballard
Estate

Shep's
Hollow

WC

Swanage
Bay

B

A351

Banjo
Pier

P T B

WC

Mowlem
Theatre

SWANAGE

> ## Old Harry Rocks
>
> Old Harry Rocks are a collection of chalk stacks standing off Handfast Point which represent a continuation of the line of chalk exposed across the water as the iconic Needles on the Isle of Wight. The hills in between were removed during the last ice age, when the Isle of Wight was created. Old Harry is the last tall thin stack, but Old Harry's Wife stood alongside until it was destroyed by a storm in 1896. It is probably named after the Devil, especially with Parson's Barn (a sea cave formed by a collapsed cliff) standing nearby, although local lore relates it to a pirate called Harry Paye.

second left on the bend (towards Old Harry Rocks, not South Beach). The path through the trees soon opens out into a broad motorway heading across the open ground towards **Handfast Point** (also known as the Foreland). It is understandably popular for the spectacular chalk cliffs that plunge into the sea in a series of precarious headlands, arches and stacks, the most striking being **Old Harry** itself.

The path climbs steadily from the point, passing Parson's Barn and the **Pinnacles** but generally staying well away from the cliff edge. Keep left along the fenceline to round Ballard Point, with Swanage Bay laid out dramatically below, before cutting across the side of **Ballard Down**, then turning left to descend steeply from it. The path winds along the edge of the trees, before dropping down to the bridge at **Shep's Hollow**. *At most states of the tide it is possible to join the beach here and follow it round to Swanage, though you do have to step over some groynes initially.* The main route crosses the bridge and climbs to join the road leading left through the Ballard Estate. Continue to its end, then turn left along the main road leading down the hill to join Swanage seafront. It is a popular and beautiful beach, leading round past the short **Banjo Pier** to the Mowlem Theatre, where you can turn right to reach the town centre and bus/train station. **Swanage** (its name a corruption of 'swainswick' referring to a herdsman) was a traditional fishing and quarrying village before its development as a seaside resort in the 19th century, when the arrival of the railway in 1885 and a new pleasure pier in 1895 made the town far more accessible.

SONG OF THE DAY

Coldplay – *Yellow*

The low-key video for Coldplay's breakthrough single was entirely filmed on the beach at Studland Bay in 2000.

Originally it was intended to feature several extras, but wet weather resulted in them being sent home and this single slow-motion shot was recorded at the last minute, with Chris Martin dressed in an anorak rather than a bright jumper as planned.

Old Harry Rocks

Section 6.3 – Swanage to Kingston or Worth Matravers

Distance: 16.2km (10½ miles), plus 2.5km (1½ miles) into Kingston or Worth Matravers

Height Gained: 500m

Parking: Pay car parks in Swanage, with small free car parks in Kingston (Houns-tout) and Worth Matravers (Renscombe), though the former is far more useful for linking with the bus to Swanage.

Public Transport: The Purbeck Breezer 40 (morebus, towards Swanage) runs hourly from Kingston to Swanage, with a more limited service on Sundays.

Refreshments: There is nothing passed on the route between Durlston Castle and Kimmeridge Bay, though the inimitable Square & Compass pub and the Worth Matravers Tea & Supper Room are only a mile inland.

Accommodation: Rooms are available at the Scott Arms (01929 480270) and Kingston Country Courtyard (01929 481066) in

Kingston, or at Post Office Cottage B&B (01929 439442) and Chiltern Lodge B&B (01929 439337) in Worth Matravers. The closest campsites are back towards Swanage or 4 miles further along the route at Steeple Leaze Farm (01929 480733), a mile inland from Kimmeridge Bay.

Overview: Beyond Swanage, and particularly after Anvil Point, you reach a quieter section of the Purbeck coast, where limestone replaces chalk. It is a dramatic landscape of dry valleys, historic quarries and medieval lynchets, with the wild promontory of St Aldhelm's Head a focal point. As there are no settlements by the coast from Swanage to Lulworth, there are several options to break this long, tough walk into two manageable days; my suggested option is to head into Kingston from Houns-tout.

Route Description

Follow the **Swanage** seafront past the Mowlem Theatre and Swanage Museum, then bear right up to the road before **Swanage Pier**. Fork left soon after on a path that returns to the shore, the main route dropping down some steps to a rough but lovely route right along the shore. It continues past the lifeboat station and turns right up some steps by the Old Watch House, to follow the road left to **Peveril Point**, though you can continue along the shore and take some later steps straight up to the Coastwatch station. *Occasionally the shoreline path may be impassable, so an alternative route is signed up the hill sooner to join the road.* The reef on Peveril Point is formed of **Purbeck Marble**, a type of limestone that could be polished for decorative columns and panels, and was widely used from the 12th century in cathedrals, including those at Canterbury, Salisbury, Ely and Exeter, as well as Westminster Abbey.

Double back at the helipad on a path along the low cliffs around **Durlston Bay**, before bending right to join the road. Follow this left for

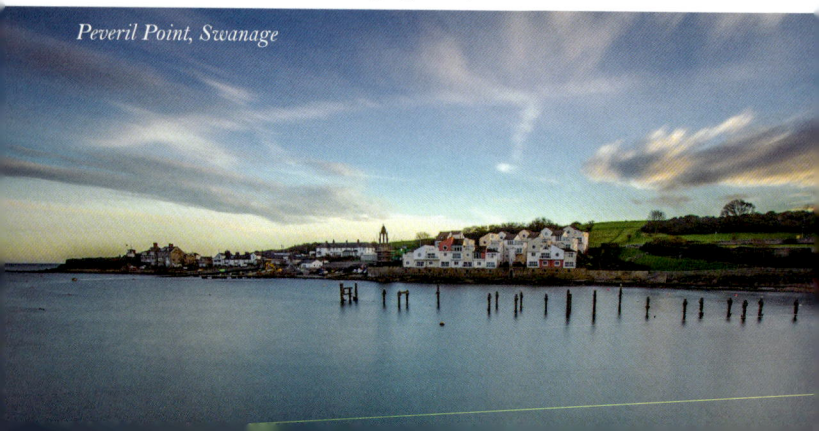

Peveril Point, Swanage

100m and, though a 'Flat Route' is signed along the road, turn left through a gate by the apartments of Purbeck Heights to descend some steps and wind through the woods. Keep left as the Flat Route returns and follow the broad promenade of Isle of Wight Road, with great views across the water to the western tip of the island. At the end, keep left of **Durlston Castle**, descending round Durlston Head (a corruption of Durdlestone, suggesting the existence of an arch here once), before climbing back up the other

The Great Globe at Durlston Head

side to near the **Great Globe**. Said to be the largest stone sphere in the world, this 40-ton globe was created in 1887 by George Burt in Mowlem's stoneyard in Greenwich, before the 15 pieces of Portland stone were transported back to Swanage to be reassembled here.

   Continue along the lovely promenade above the cliffs, passing the closed-off entrance of **Tilly Whim Caves**. Durlston Head is formed of an outcrop of Portland limestone, which was quarried in the 18th century at Tilly Whim (a *whim* being a crane that lowered the stone to waiting ships), the caves later opened as a tourist attraction. Keep left to cross a ravine and climb past the lighthouse on **Anvil Point**, beyond which a smaller grassy path winds along the increasingly remote shoreline. It seems a long time since the coast path has been this quiet and it is a lovely walk as you pass a pair of **mile markers**, which ships could use to measure a nautical mile. The path bounds on past Connors Cove and crosses a dry valley before dropping down to further quarries at **Dancing Ledge**, where it is said the tide dances as it covers the cliffs and a pool was blasted out of the rocks for use by local children. It also

The Halsewell

In January 1786 the *Halsewell*, a merchant ship from London bound for Madras, was dashed against the rocks of East Man in a three-day snow storm. The hull broke up quickly and the sailors tried to escape onto the rocks, some managing to reach a cavern in the cliff and dozens of others clinging to a slanting rock now known as Halsewell Rock. Quarrymen managed to send down ropes to rescue 74 men over the next day and a half, but the rest of the 242 crew and passengers perished in the freezing water. The story provided the inspiration for Charles Dickens' *The Long Journey*.

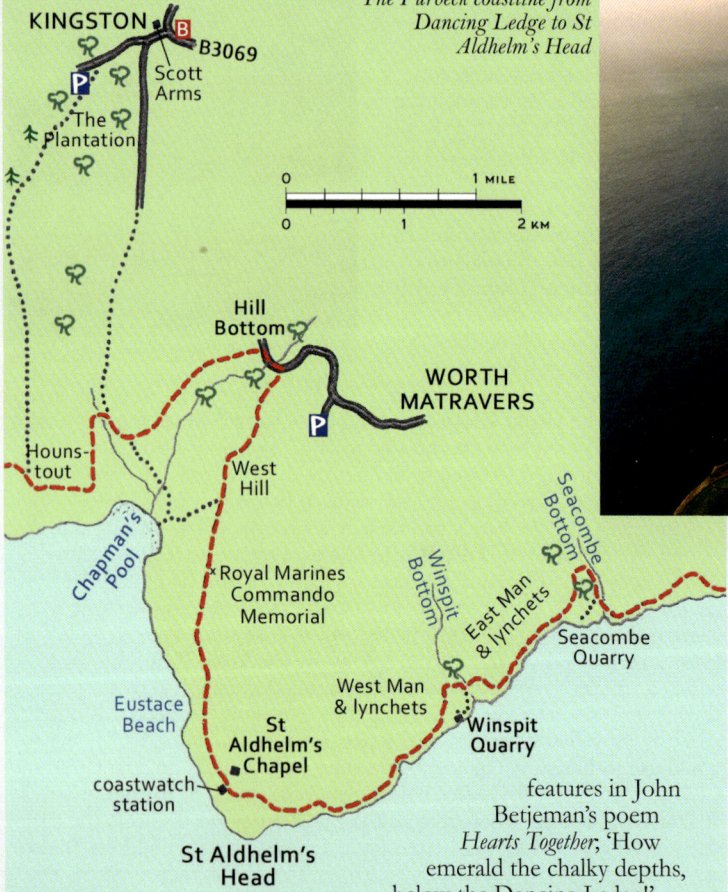

The Purbeck coastline from Dancing Ledge to St Aldhelm's Head

KINGSTON
B
B3069
Scott Arms
The Plantation
Houns-tout
Hill Bottom
WORTH MATRAVERS
West Hill
Chapman's Pool
Royal Marines Commando Memorial
Winspit Bottom
East Man & lynchets
Seacombe Bottom
Seacombe Quarry
West Man & lynchets
Eustace Beach
St Aldhelm's Chapel
Winspit Quarry
coastwatch station
St Aldhelm's Head

features in John Betjeman's poem *Hearts Together*, 'How emerald the chalky depths, below the Dancing Ledge!'

Quarrying dominates the shoreline beyond Dancing Ledge, particularly as you near Seacombe, where the path heads right up the valley for 300m before turning left up some steps. The vast catacombs of **Seacombe Quarry** are fenced off to protect its population of bats, but you get good views over the area from the clifftop beyond. The slopes of **East Man** reveal some of the strip lynchets (or terracing), created by the medieval open field system that was widely practised on Purbeck, but was largely abandoned after the Black Death greatly reduced the local population.

The map shows the coastline with labels: Swanage Bay, Banjo Pier, A351, Mowlem Theatre, SWANAGE, Peveril Point, Pier, lifeboat station, Durlston Bay, DURLSTON, Durlston Castle, Durlston Head, Anvil Point Lighthouse, Great Globe, Tilly Whim Caves, mile marker, Dancing Ledge, Blackers Hole, Connors Cove.

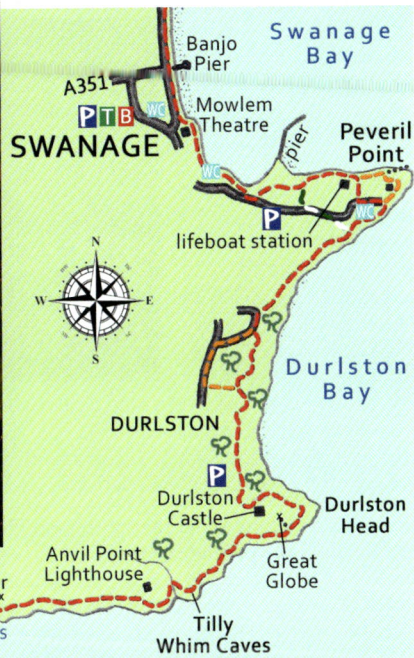

The path soon drops down to **Winspit**, where it is well worth detouring left to have a closer look at the amazing limestone quarries. As at Seacombe, the roof is supported only by pillars of spoil from the fractured Portland stone, an other-worldly scene that has been used for various sci-fi film and TV sets. The route turns right then immediately left at Winspit to climb above the quarry edge and hug the shore around **West Man**. It soon climbs steadily to the Coastwatch station and lonely 13th-century chapel on **St Aldhelm's Head** (also known as St Alban's Head, after the 3rd-century Roman martyr).

Soon after the headland the path plummets down a steep valley above **Eustace Beach** via the first of a series of awkward limestone steps on the Purbeck cliffs, only to climb straight back up onto Emmetts Hill. Limestone parapets here hang dramatically over the undercliffs and huts around **Chapman's Pool**. Continue past the Royal Marines Commando Memorial and go straight on at the next junction to stay along the top of West Hill. *The path that leads down to cross the stream behind Chapman's Pool is very precarious and liable to collapse.*

The path soon drops down to reach a vehicle track in **Hill Bottom**; following this right brings you to Worth Matravers in 1 mile, but the

St Aldhelm's Chapel

St Aldhelm, the Abbot of Malmesbury Abbey and the first Bishop of Sherborne, was responsible for bringing Christianity to Purbeck in the 7th century. Formerly the site of a hermitage, the distinctive square chapel on St Aldhelm's Head was built in the 12th century, reputedly after a Norman knight watched a ship carrying his child wrecked on the headland. The turret was included to house a fire that would warn other ships of the dangers of St Alban's Race. Since 1895 this treacherous headland has also been watched over by a coastguard lookout.

route turns left, then left again beyond Hill Bottom Cottage. The track on through the hamlet is the shortest route into Kingston at just over a mile, but I recommend staying on the route for another mile. Follow the track down the valley then across the foot of the slope, before bearing second left to cross the next valley and head back towards the coast. The path then climbs very steeply up the rough steps onto **Houns-tout** (Houn being a Norman family name and *tout* being a local word for a lookout post). At the top of this eminence ,I recommend bearing right and taking the last route into Kingston past the Houns-tout Car Park – though it is 1½ miles into the village, it is a lovely walk high above the 'Golden Valley' of Encombe and following this route means you won't have to do another big climb in the morning. **Kingston** is a picturesque little village dominated by the 'Cathedral of Purbeck', St James' Church, which was built from local stone in the 1880s, as the old church was not deemed grand enough by the Earl of Eldon.

————————◆◆◆————————

SONG OF THE DAY

Elephant Talk – *Into the Open*

An electronic world folk band from Yorkshire, Elephant Talk's 2000 *Live* album was recorded at the tiny Square & Compass pub in Worth Matravers. Formerly known as the Sloop, the pub became popular with artists and stonemasons in the 1930s and has become one of Purbeck's great attractions, regularly bringing in touring bands. This song captures the move from the urbanity of greater Bournemouth to the open spaces of Purbeck.

Section 6.4 – Kingston or Worth Matravers to West Lulworth

Distance: 17.0km (10½ miles), or 30.4km (19 miles) avoiding military range, plus 2.5km (1½ miles) out of Kingston/Worth Matravers

Height Gained: 550m, or 510m avoiding the range

Parking: Pay car parks at Lulworth Cove and Kimmeridge Bay, with small free car parks at Kingston (Houns-tout) and Worth Matravers (Renscombe), though the former is far more useful for linking with the bus to Swanage.

Public Transport: From May to September the Purbeck Breezer 30 (morebus, towards Swanage) runs every two hours from Lulworth Cove and West Lulworth to Corfe Castle, where you can change for the hourly Purbeck Breezer 40 (morebus, towards Swanage) to Kingston. Out of season Bus X54 (First, towards Poole) runs 3 times a day Mon-Fri from Lulworth Cove/West Lulworth to Wareham station, where you can change for the hourly Bus 40 (morebus, towards Swanage) to Kingston.

Refreshments: Seasonal vans offer food and drink from the car park at Kimmeridge Bay, while Clavell's Restaurant in Kimmeridge is a mile from the main route (though it is passed on the alternative route).

Accommodation: There are several B&Bs, hotels and pubs in West Lulworth and Lulworth Cove, as well as YHA Lulworth Cove (0345 3719331). There is camping nearby at Durdle Door Holiday Park (01929 400200), while Mill Paddock Campsite (07548 879845) at East Stoke is passed on the alternative route. Belhuish Farm B&B (01929 405415) is also passed a couple of miles from the end of the alternative route, handily shortening this option a little.

Overview: A uniquely challenging but spectacular day's walking, one of the finest on the English coast, revealing the full range of Purbeck's Jurassic rock formations. The limestone of Houns-tout and Gad Cliff sandwich Kimmeridge Bay's unique oil-rich shales, before giving way to Worbarrow Bay's red strata and then the chalk ridge that forms the backbone of Purbeck, which is spectacularly exposed around Arish Mell and Lulworth Cove. The coast path rises and falls dramatically over these formations and has interest at every turn, not least because it largely lies within the Ministry of Defence land of Lulworth Ranges. The ranges are open only at weekends, public holidays and throughout August, so I have provided an alternative route around the range should you need to pass it at another time. Though it is a

Route Description

Returning to the clifftop at **Houns-tout**, the coast path immediately plunges steeply down round **Egmont Bight** to cross Encombe, where a waterfall tumbles dramatically over the low cliffs, although it is hard to see from the path above. This remote part of the path is noticeably less trodden. It climbs over a shoulder, further up which stands **Eldon Seat**, erected in 1835 by Lord Eldon of nearby

Clavell Tower

Encombe House, but no longer publicly accessible. Wind on along the dark shale and clay cliffs, with bands of dolomitic limestone (known as basalt because of the colour) stretching out in striking lines off the shore. There are regular collapses along this stretch, meaning the path often has to move inland;. After climbing over **Rope Lake Head**, the path detours around a couple of these collapses, before passing a wartime lookout (on the intriguingly named Cuddle). Ascend Hen Cliff to reach **Clavell Tower**, a folly built

Kimmeridge Oil Shale

The Kimmeridge shale (also known as Blackstone or Kimmeridge Coal) is a 1m-thick band of bituminous Jurassic stone that burns like coal and has occasionally been known to combust spontaneously in the cliffs – indeed at Burning Cliff in Ringstead Bay one fire lasted for many years. It was long used as fuel, mainly by the poor, but Sir William Clavell of nearby Smedmore House began to quarry the shale in the 18th century for its alum content and for use in glass-making and boiling seawater to make salt, though with little financial success. He also discovered oil in the shale, but this was not extracted until the 19th century, when the gas it produced was used in Paris' street lighting despite giving off an unpleasant smell. BP's first oil well began drilling successfully here as recently as the 1950s.

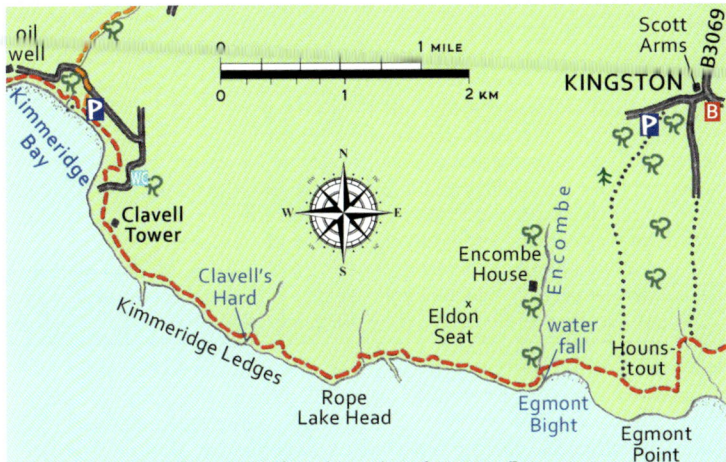

by Sir John Clavell in 1830 for observing the stars. Later used as a coastguard lookout and recently dismantled to move it further back from the crumbling cliff edge, it is now used as a holiday home.

Descend the steps towards the dark arc of **Kimmeridge Bay** and head straight across the road. Cross another stream and keep left past the car park above the beach, which is where the alternative route leaves the coast path. If **Lulworth Ranges** are open for access (at weekends, in August and on occasional other days), you can follow the main coast path, descending steps at the end of the car park to cross a stream behind the beach. Ascend the other side to rejoin the road, then fork

Looking across Kimmeridge Bay towards Gad Cliff

left before the oil well's nodding donkey, in action since 1961 and thought to be the oldest continuously drilled site in the country. Enter the military range and follow the track until it peters out and a path continues along the clifftop fenceline past **Hobarrow Bay**, its shore marked with striking mega-polygon patterns in the volcanic rocks. Climb steadily above Brandy Bay and zigzag across the face of **Tyneham Cap** to join a larger path leading left along the crest of **Gad Cliff**, whose jagged limestone tors plunge precariously into the sea. The remains of **Tyneham**, evacuated in 1943 to make way for the range, can be seen across the valley inland.

   The path descends steadily to Pondfield Cove and the narrow neck of Worbarrow Tout, heading straight on around the back of the beach of **Worbarrow Bay** – its red cliffs are formed of several layers of Wealden sandstones and clays. Ascend to the clifftops and climb steadily towards **Rings Hill**, whose steep flank marks the return of the band of chalk that was exposed back at Old Harry Rocks. The summit is surrounded by a number of ditches and ramparts, which enclosed the large Iron

Arish Mell and Bindon Hill from Rings Hill

Age fort of **Flower's Barrow**, part of which has been lost to the sea. Ghosts of Roman legionnaires are said to march around the ramparts, a myth which once even inspired the local militia in Wareham to take up their posts and barricade the bridge in 1678.

Turn left on the top of Rings Hill and follow the yellow posts down through the bulwarks to join a fenceline descending away from the cliffs to emerge at **Arish Mell**. Once famed for its colourful pebbles, there is no longer access to this beautiful beach due to unexploded ordnance and an effluent pipeline that runs into the sea from the nuclear power station at Winfrith. This is the heart of the well-used Lulworth tank range and the wrecks of burnt out tanks litter the eerie landscape inland. The route climbs very steeply up onto the dramatic chalk ridge ahead, before skirting along its leeward side to ascend steadily onto **Bindon Hill**. Before the summit, turn left with the yellow posts and descend equally steeply to **Mupe Bay**, an idyllic beach backed by a wall of chalk cliffs. Stay along the clifftops past Mupe Rocks and a concrete bunker on the headland to reach the far edge of the range. Just before the gate it is worth descending the steps to the remarkable **Fossil Forest**, exposed on a shelf halfway down the cliffs.

The Fossil Forest

A limestone shelf halfway up the cliffs has been exposed by erosion to reveal the remarkable remains of fossilised trees and the thrombolites that grew around them. The forest was composed of cycads that date from the era of the dinosaurs, 150 million years ago, and were fossilised by the subsequent laying down of calcareous sediment from which the Portland limestone was created. Thrombolites (or algal burrs) are the doughnut-like shapes of fossilised algae and mud that originally formed around the foot of these cycads and now stand out clearly, along with the ripples of the ocean floor.

Continuing out of the range, you quickly emerge on a headland overlooking the breathtaking arc of **Lulworth Cove**, formed by more rapid erosion of the softer chalk behind the limestone headlands at the entrance to the cove. Several informal paths descend roughly to the pebbly beach, which you can follow round to the road at the far end, although the official route turns right shortly before the headland to wind through the dense vegetation behind the cove. Keep right to climb steeply back up onto the chalk ridge, then turn left and follow the fenceline around the top of the cove. The path descends steadily round the edge of the hillside to reach the edge of **West Lulworth** village, following a road left to reach the B3070, with the main car park reached to the left and the bus stop to the right.

ALTERNATIVE ROUTE: *This is not an official alternative route, although there is an expectation that one may at some point be created. Instead this is my preferred route around the military range, aiming to minimise walking on busy roads. As such it is not signed, other than those parts of it that follow the Purbeck Way, and care will be needed with navigation.*

At the KIMMERIDGE BAY car park, follow the road left round the bend, then turn immediately right and follow the edge of the fields. Keep right along the trees (in which there is sometimes a small stream), then turn right at a sign to head up the field to the road in KIMMERIDGE. Follow it left through the thatched village and, where the road bends right, head straight on up a path past ST NICHOLAS' CHURCH and on up the slope. Turn left along the road at the top for 200m, then go right over a stile and descend across

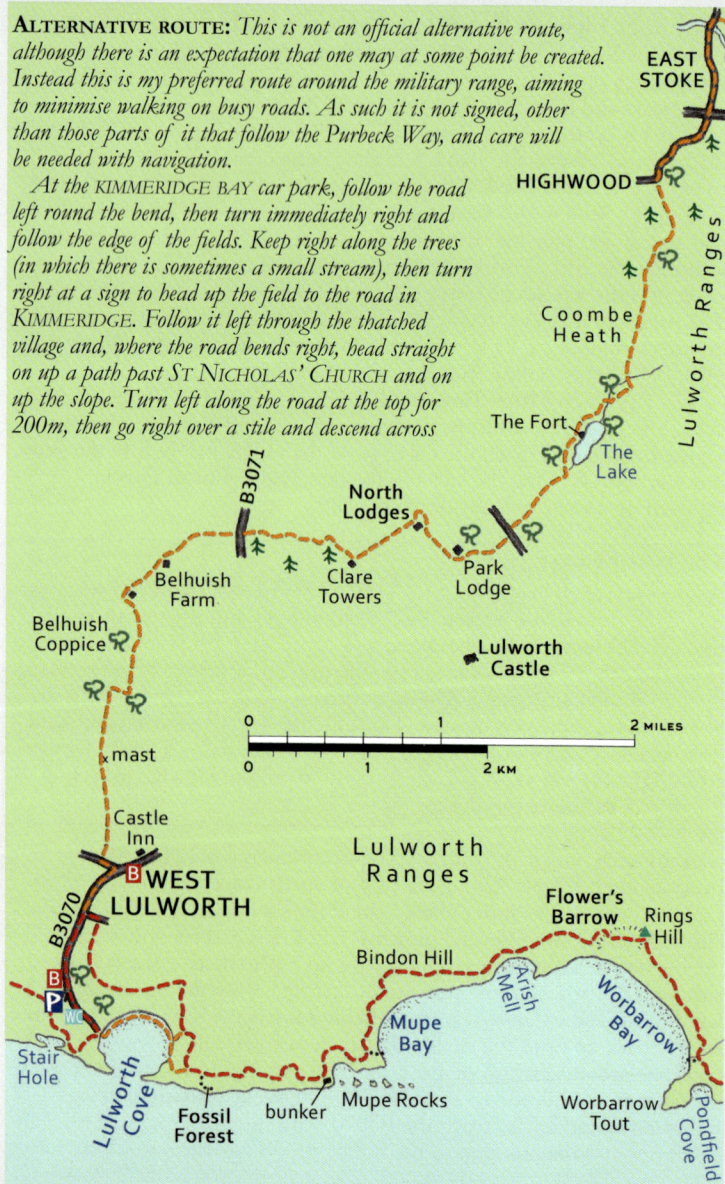

EAST STOKE

HIGHWOOD

Lulworth Ranges

Coombe Heath

The Fort

The Lake

B3071

North Lodges

Belhuish Farm

Clare Towers

Park Lodge

Belhuish Coppice

Lulworth Castle

mast

0   1   2 MILES

0   1   2 KM

Castle Inn

B WEST LULWORTH

B3070

Lulworth Ranges

Flower's Barrow

Rings Hill

Bindon Hill

Arish Mell

Worbarrow Bay

B P WC

Stair Hole

Lulworth Cove

Fossil Forest

bunker

Mupe Bay

Mupe Rocks

Worbarrow Tout

Pondfield Cove

Holme
Bridge

Rushton
Farm

River Frome

Priory
Farm

EAST
HOLME

B3070

East Holme
Rifle
Range

Three Lord's
Barrow

Bridewell
Plantations

**L u l w o r t h
R a n g e s**

Grange Heath

Breach
Pond

Creech
Barrow
▲ Hill

Creech
Grange

Ridgeway Hill

Whiteway
Farm

Corfe
River

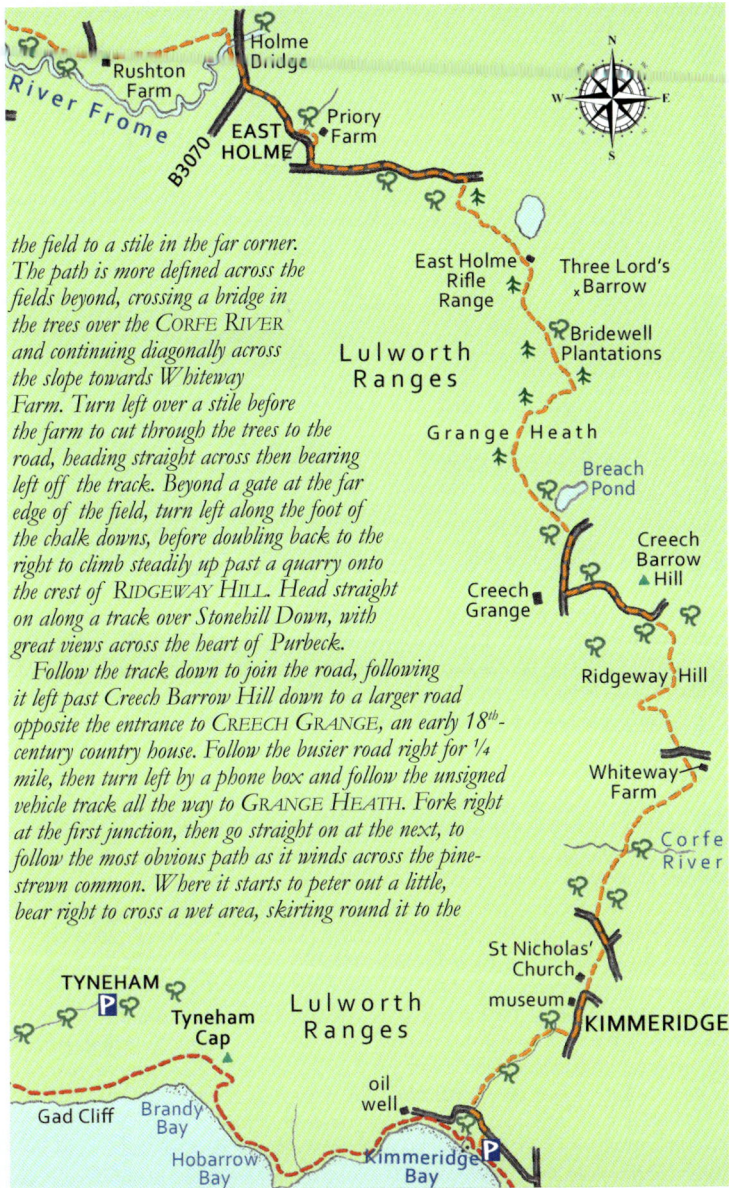

the field to a stile in the far corner.
The path is more defined across the
fields beyond, crossing a bridge in
the trees over the CORFE RIVER
and continuing diagonally across
the slope towards Whiteway
Farm. Turn left over a stile before
the farm to cut through the trees to the
road, heading straight across then bearing
left off the track. Beyond a gate at the far
edge of the field, turn left along the foot of
the chalk downs, before doubling back to the
right to climb steadily up past a quarry onto
the crest of RIDGEWAY HILL. Head straight
on along a track over Stonehill Down, with
great views across the heart of Purbeck.

Follow the track down to join the road, following
it left past Creech Barrow Hill down to a larger road
opposite the entrance to CREECH GRANGE, an early 18th-
century country house. Follow the busier road right for ¼
mile, then turn left by a phone box and follow the unsigned
vehicle track all the way to GRANGE HEATH. Fork right
at the first junction, then go straight on at the next, to
follow the most obvious path as it winds across the pine-
strewn common. Where it starts to peter out a little,
bear right to cross a wet area, skirting round it to the

TYNEHAM
P

Tyneham
Cap ▲

**L u l w o r t h
R a n g e s**

St Nicholas'
Church
museum

KIMMERIDGE

oil
well

Gad Cliff
Brandy
Bay

P

Hobarrow
Bay

Kimmeridge
Bay

Purbeck Heaths

The sandy heaths on the north side of the Isle of Purbeck represent one of the UK's most biodiverse landscapes, with rare butterflies, bats, snakes, dragonflies and orchids found here. It was the sort of landscape that once covered large parts of southern Dorset and inspired the fictional Egdon Heath that features in many of Thomas Hardy's novels. In 2020 it became a vast new National Nature Reserve, stretching from Grange Heath to Studland Bay, and part of a rewilding strategy that will see the reintroduction of osprey and beavers, as well as grazing by free-roaming horses, cattle and pigs.

right if necessary, then picking up a small path through the gorse that emerges at a gateway. Follow the more obvious bridleway left on a fenced path into the dense BRIDEWELL PLANTATIONS *that can sometimes be muddy. Emerging at the far end, follow the vehicle track past a large quarry (which blocks out a view of the Bronze Age burial chamber of Three Lord's Barrow) and* EAST HOLME RIFLE RANGE. *Continue past the buildings at Doreys Farm, then bear left by a gravel lay-by to pick up a path through the scrub alongside to reach Holme Lane.*

Follow the road left for nearly a mile; though it cuts through lovely scenery past Holme Priory, it can be unpleasant as there is no verge and cars tend to race along it. You can continue all the way to East Stoke, though you'll probably want to escape at the first opportunity, turning right on a smaller lane towards EAST HOLME. *By the entrance to Priory Farm, follow a path to the right of the road to avoid having to splash through the ford, then rejoin the road to its end. Briefly turn right along the B3070, before crossing the River Frome by the 17th-century* HOLME BRIDGE, *site of a Civil War skirmish in 1644.*

Here you join part of the Purbeck Way and turn left before the buildings beyond the bridge, following a path across the heart of a long field. A track continues past the buildings of Rushton Farm, where you bear left on the lane and pass in front of Elmley Cottage to pick up a grassy bridleway through the trees. This path can be overgrown and wet in places, before it opens out across a field to reach the road by the railway crossing in EAST STOKE. *Follow the road left over the river and through the hamlet to return to busy Holme Lane, following the dead-end road ahead through the* woods towards Highwood. *After less than ½ mile, turn left off the Purbeck Way on a bridleway towards* Coombe Heath. *The faint path is largely fenced in as it winds through the beautiful mixed woods, though it does open out to cross a wet area* Reaching COOMBE HEATH *soon after, you skirt along the fenceline on the edge of the military range. Bear left towards Shaggs and, beyond the trees and a gate, turn right along the edge of the field. The permissive path provided by* Lulworth Castle Estate *soon cuts right into the next field and is fenced in as it passes round* THE LAKE *and a 19th-century folly, the* Fort.

Emerging through a gate beyond the lake, turn right across a field to pick up a narrow path through the trees. Keep straight on to join a vehicle track and reach the road, bearing

North Lodges, Lulworth Castle

left across it to follow a concrete track that is another permissive route around the LULWORTH CASTLE ESTATE. *Keep straight on past Park Lodge, then bear right onto a grassy path beyond to pull up the slope towards the striking towers of* NORTH LODGES. *This was an ornamental gatehouse built in 1785 as an entrance to Lulworth Castle, a Jacobean hunting lodge built in the style of a castle – it can be made out in the distance looking back across the park.*

Head round to a stile to the right of the gatehouse to reach the far side, then turn left along the track, rejoining the Purbeck Way. At the end turn right by CLARE TOWERS, *another 18th-century gatehouse, and follow the track to the main road. Head straight across the B3071 and follow the lane down to Belhuish Farm, set in a beautiful dry valley within the chalk downs. Continue past the barn, before turning left up the slope and crossing a couple of fields. Turn right in the trees at the top, then go left after 100m to follow a track along the edge of the field. Continue straight on over the top of the hill and cross a lane by the mast to descend steadily down the edge of the fields towards* WEST LULWORTH. *The path emerges in the village down some steps, the road leading left to join the A3070 by the bus stop.*

SONG OF THE DAY

PJ Harvey – *White Chalk*

The title of her 2007 album, this haunting song recalls Polly Jean Harvey's childhood in Dorset. Though Lyme Regis is mentioned, it seems more appropriate for the chalk cliffs around Lulworth. Having been born in Bridport and grown up in the downs inland, she sings 'And I know these chalk hills will rot my bones, Dorset's cliffs meet at the sea where I walked our unborn child in me.'

Section 6.5 – West Lulworth to Weymouth

Distance: 18.6km (11½ miles)

Height Gained: 480m

Parking: Pay car parks at Lulworth Cove and along the front in Weymouth (though the latter is considerably cheaper for day parking).

Public Transport: Buses X52 /X53 (First, towards Monkey World) run every two hours from Weymouth to West Lulworth and Lulworth Cove from Easter to September, as does the open-top Purbeck Breezer 30 (morebus, towards Swanage). Out of season, Bus X54 (First, towards Poole) runs 3 times a day Mon-Fri from Weymouth to Lulworth Cove and West Lulworth.

Refreshments: Ringstead Bay Kiosk and the Smuggler's Inn at Osmington Mills are passed along the route, as well as several places along Weymouth's long seafront.

Accommodation: Various accommodation options are available in Weymouth, with a Tourist Information Shop on St Mary's Street. There are campsites near the route before Weymouth at Eweleaze Farm (01305 833690, during the summer holidays only) and Rosewall Camping (01305 832248), and beyond the town at Martleaves Farm Campsite (07785 565059) in Wyke Regis.

Overview: Another dramatic day that begins with the dizzying chalk undulations around Durdle Door and White Nothe, before gradually working its way round to the gentle sands of Weymouth Bay. There are spectacular chalk and limestone formations and the first of Dorset's undercliffs, as well as many wonderful places to swim.

Lulworth Cove

Route Description

Follow the main road down from West Lulworth to **Lulworth Cove**, where a path doubles back right just before the beach. Climb up to the cliff edge overlooking the dramatic cove of **Stair Hole**, whose contorted limestone is known technically as the Lulworth Crumple and features in Mike Leigh's film *Nuts in May*. Keep right to head back towards the road, then cross the huge Lulworth Cove car park and follow the obvious pitched path up the side of **Hambury Tout**, the first climb of a serious morning. As a section of the path has collapsed into St Oswald's Bay, follow the new fence to a gate below Newlands Farm campsite, then turn left down the main path towards the chalk cirque of **Man O' War Cove**, an idyllic spot for an early dip. The headland and line of rocks offshore are outcrops of hard Portland limestone, through which the iconic arch of **Durdle Door** is carved. Its name comes from an Old English word for a hole and has the same root as the Thurlestone arch in south Devon.

The coast path follows the line of precipitous chalk cliffs over Swyre Head to **Scratchy Bottom**, the first of a series of dry valleys dropping down to the shore. The path continues to roll exhaustingly but dramatically, passing Butter Rock and **Bat's Head**, which is thought to resemble a bat's head, with the tiny arch of Bat's Hole its eye, said to glow red with the setting sun twice a year. From the headland there are stunning views along the inaccessible Lone Beach, dominated by the vertical chalk column of **Fountain Rock**. The ground finally flattens out after passing the navigational obelisk, which once helped to guide ships into Portland Harbour, and stays along the edge of the fields to reach the Victorian coastguard cottages at **White Nothe** ('white nose').

The chalk cliffs shelter a vast area of undercliffs, formed by prehistoric landslips. Though a smugglers' path winds its way down to the beach here, stay along the crest with extensive views across the beaches of Ringstead and Weymouth Bays, before dropping down towards the scattered houses above **Burning Cliff**. This apparently unremarkable, densely vegetated cliff spontaneously set fire in 1826 due to the decomposition of iron pyrites in its bituminous oil shales. It burned continuously until 1838, giving off thick sulphurous fumes and becoming a tourist attraction.

Turn right then left onto a tarmac track, before branching off through the vegetation behind the shattered cliff. Stay along another track into **Ringstead** village, turning left at the road end by the shop as a track continues along the shore. A number of paths lead down to the shingle of **Ringstead Bay**, while the coast path weaves through the dense scrub and eventually climbs up past the observation posts on **Bran Point**. These were part of the World War II radar defences along this

West Ringstead

West Ringstead was mentioned in the *Domesday Book*, although the medieval village was entirely abandoned by the late 15th century. It is said the whole fishing fleet was wiped out in a storm, after which the women fled the village, but it is likely the Black Death and other plagues gradually depopulated the settlement from the mid-14th century. The earthworks of the village and its church remain, as do the strip lynchets on the escarpment above.

stretch of coast, whereas the now-converted Upton Fort just inland was an earlier Victorian battery. On the rocks below is the wreck of the *Minx*, a coal barge that was washed across the bay from its moorings in Portland Harbour one night in 1927.

Descend steadily to **Osmington Mills**, where you emerge by the Smuggler's Inn, originally known as the Crown Inn but renamed in honour of the nefarious activities of its former landlords. Follow the road right for 300m, then turn left up a narrow pathway. Keep left where the Dorset Ridgeway branches off; an alternative inland fork of the South West Coast Path leading all the way to West Bexington, this was the only option until a more coastal route was opened in 2003.

At the top of the hill, the prominent mound of **Goggins Barrow**, a possible ancient burial chamber, has been partially removed

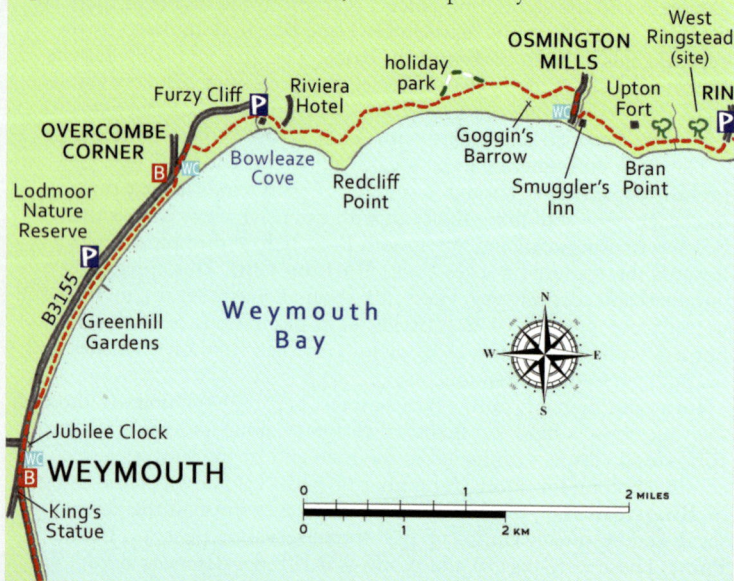

by the cliff's collapse. The route stays inland beneath the willows, then bears left through a campsite to cross the grassy slopes of **Black Head**. *A rather unnecessary alternative route follows the fenced path alongside,* rejoining the main route to skirt around the activity centre above **Osmington Bay**. Follow the edge of the broad fields beyond, tiptoeing around the collapsed edges of Redcliff Point before descending towards **Bowleaze Cove**. On the downs inland you should see the **Osmington White Horse**, a representation of King George III on horseback carved in 1808. The King never saw the figure himself, but it is said the artist committed suicide after realising he had portrayed him leaving the town.

Keep to the left of the 1930s Art Deco magnificence of the **Riviera Hotel**, a former Pontins holiday camp, then cut through the fun park at Bowleaze Cove. Through the car park, head up across the grassy common above Furzy Cliff. At the far end, keep to the right of the Spyglass Inn and join the road heading down to the long esplanade around Weymouth Bay. It is an easy 1½ mile stroll past the beach huts and traditional amusements along the back of the beach into **Weymouth**. The town centre is reached soon after the **Jubilee Clock Tower**, built in 1887 to celebrate Queen Victoria's Golden Jubilee. Buses leave from the roundabout just beyond the clock tower, by the **King's Statue**. This was erected in 1810 to celebrate the Golden Jubilee of George III, whose regular visits had helped popularise Weymouth as one of the first seaside resorts.

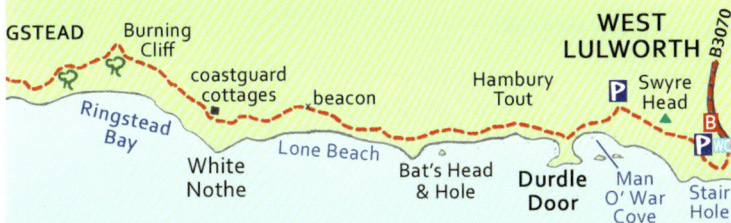

WEST LULWORTH

B3070

GSTEAD
Burning Cliff
coastguard cottages
beacon
Hambury Tout
Swyre Head
Ringstead Bay
Lone Beach
White Nothe
Bat's Head & Hole
Durdle Door
Man O' War Cove
Stair Hole

Durdle Door

George III in Weymouth

George III came to Weymouth in 1789 to convalesce after falling ill with the condition that would keep him confined for the rest of his reign. It was recommended by Dr John Crane that he swim in the sea every day, so he used the sort of bathing machine that was common at the time, a basic shed on a cart that preserved one's dignity and a replica of which can be found on the seafront. Banners lined the streets and a band played as he swam, a scene recorded by the diarist Fanny Burney. The King would return almost every year until 1805, staying at Gloucester Lodge.

SONG OF THE DAY

Tears For Fears – *Shout*

The video for this 1984 single was shot on the chalk cliffs around Durdle Door and cost just £14,000 to make. Despite being nearly six minutes long, this call to protest reached No. 4 in the UK charts annd No. 1 in the US.

Bat's Head, looking towards Durdle Door

Section 6.6 – Weymouth to Chiswell/Fortuneswell

Distance: 23.2km (14½ miles)

Height Gained: 450m

Parking: Pay car parks in Weymouth, with free parking at the Masonic and Hambro Car Parks in Chiswell/Fortuneswell, as well as several places along the east coast of Portland.

Public Transport: Bus 1 (First, towards Weymouth) runs regularly year round from Chiswell/Fortuneswell to King's Statue in Weymouth 7 days a week, with the open top Bus 501 doing the same in summer.

Refreshments: Lobster Pot Restaurant and Pulpit Inn at Portland Bill, and various places at Portland Marina.

Accommodation: Rooms are available at several places in Chiswell/ Fortuneswell, including a hostel at the Bunker (07846 401010). The only campsites on Portland are closer to Portland Bill, including Portland Bill Camping (07810 485351, summer holidays only) and Sweet Hill Farm (07792 689591), so the best option is probably to continue back across the spit to Martleaves Farm Campsite (07785 565059), which is right by the route in Wyke Regis.

Overview: A fine circuit of the Isle of Portland, starting in Weymouth to reach the causeway via Weymouth Harbour, Nothe Fort and Sandsfoot Castle. The island itself is a striking limestone tableland sloping gently from the high ground around the Verne in the north to the southern tip of Portland Bill. The landscape is dominated by the quarrying of Portland stone, as well as a number of huge correctional institutions and fortifications. Despite being rather scruffy in places, it is a unique and fascinating place to explore, with obvious highlights at Rufus Castle and Portland Bill Lighthouse, and wonderful views off the high cliffs on either side of the island.

Route Description

Rejoin the **Weymouth** seafront at the King's Statue to pass various traditional trappings of the English seaside, as well as Sandworld, where sand carvings are displayed using what is said to be finest sculpting sand in the world. At the far end of the beach, turn right before the Pavilion and cut across to join the harbourside, where a rowing boat ferry crosses the **River Wey**, saving you about ½ mile. The main route follows the quay right back into the heart of Weymouth, before heading up steps to cross **Town Bridge**, a swing bridge built in

1930 that you may have to wait for to be lifted. Return along Brewer's Quay the other side of the harbour and continue along Nothe Parade to the other side of the ferry, where the coast path heads up some steps into Nothe Gardens. Turn left at the top and keep left to cross a bridge over the entrance

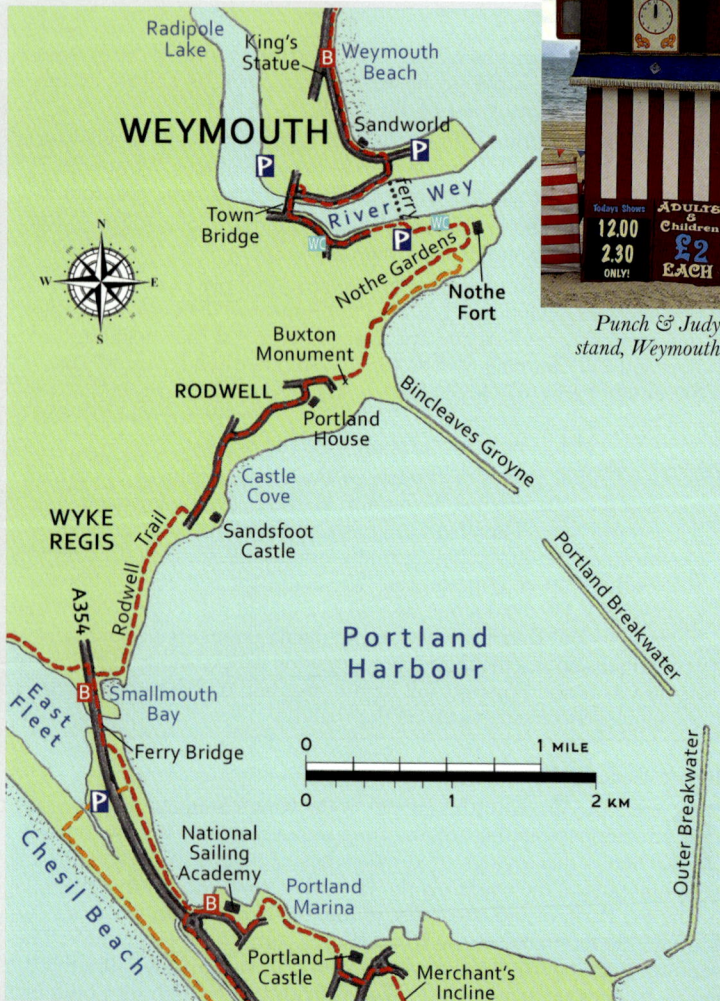

Punch & Judy stand, Weymouth

to **Nothe Fort**, a well preserved D-shaped defence built in the 1860s on Nothe Point.

The route continues round the other side of the headland, staying on the high ground through the trees, *though at most states of the tide you can drop down to the shoreline promenade*. These routes rejoin to cross a bridge over Newton's Road, which gives access to Bincleaves Groyne, part of the breakwater that protects Portland Harbour. Follow the path up through the Bincleaves Green, passing the **Buxton Monument** to Thomas Fowell Buxton, who was responsible for the 1833 Slavery Abolition Act, and join the road. Turn left onto Belle Vue Road by the lodge for Portland House, then left again at its end, continuing past Castle Cove. At Sandsfoot Gardens you can detour left to take a closer look at the ruin of **Sandsfoot Castle**, one of Henry VIII's 16th-century Device Forts, with great views across Portland Harbour.

Just beyond the gardens, turn right and join the **Rodwell Trail** cycleway running parallel to the road. Follow it for ¾ mile to Smallmouth Bay, where you join the A354 to cross **Ferry Bridge** over East Fleet, part of the briny lagoon that runs for 8 miles behind Chesil Beach. Beyond the boat park, bear left onto a path along the sea wall parallel to the road to reach the **Isle of Portland**, once an island but now anchored to the mainland by the massed pebbles of Chesil Beach.

Follow the road left at Osprey Quay, Hamm Beach Road leading past the **National Sailing Academy**, then turn left at the end to reach Portland Marina. Follow a path round to the left of the buildings and along the harbour front to **Portland Castle**, built at the same time as Sandsfoot Castle. Keep left along the roads round the castle, then turn right at the roundabout, before immediately turning right again on the **Merchant's Incline**, which ducks beneath a bridge before climbing steadily past the houses of **Fortuneswell**. This was the line of a horse-drawn railway by which Portland stone was brought down from the quarries to the harbour. Stay on its line as it cuts across the hillside beneath another tunnel, then fork left near the far end of Verne Common to head up towards the ramparts of **the Verne**. Now used as

---

Portland Harbour

Portland Harbour was a natural harbour sheltered by the Isle of Portland and important enough for Henry VIII to build two castles to protect it. When the Royal Navy established a base at Portland in the 1840s, they began to construct a series of mammoth breakwaters to enclose an area of 520 hectares. Upon its completion, it was the largest man-made harbour in the world, said to have been big enough to hold the entire British fleet. It has now dropped to 4th on this list, but along with Weymouth it hosted all of the sailing events during the London Olympics in 2012.

Chesil Beach

Portland Castle

Merchant's Incline

Balaclava Bay

FORTUNES-WELL

🅿 🅱

The Verne

1 MILE

Cove House Inn

A354

🅿 **CHISWELL**

High Angle Battery

0

1 KM

Chesil Cove

🅿

🅿

Grove Prison

West Cliff

Tout Quarry

Clay Ope

Isle of Portland

Little Beach

Bowers Quarries

Nickodemus Knob ✕

Durdle Pier

Blacknor Point & Fort

● gun emplacement

Rufus Castle

WESTON

St Andrew's Church

Church Ope Cove

Mutton Cove

N

Cheyne Weares

🅿

Lost Valley

W ✦ E

S

Freshwater Bay

SOUTHWELL

Rufus Castle

Wallsend Cove

coastwatch station

old lighthouses

crane

crane

Magnetic Range

🆆🅱 🅿

crane

Pulpit Rock

lighthouse

Portland Bill

A crane at Sandholes Quarry, looking towards Portland Bill

Portland Stone

Portland stone is a type of Jurassic limestone that is particularly weather resistant and good for working with. It was long used as building stone in Dorset, but by the 14th century was more widely exported to be used in the Palace of Westminster, the Tower of London and Exeter Cathedral. After initially taking advantage of landslips on the island's east coast, other areas were exploited as it became London's primary building stone, particularly after the Great Fire of 1666. It has since been used in St Paul's Cathedral, the UN Headquarters in New York, the Port of Liverpool Building and parts of Buckingham Palace.

---

a prison, this was built as a huge Victorian citadel on the highest point of the island.

Some steps lead up to the road, which you follow round to the left, then continue through the car park at its end to pass a large quarry. Continue to another small parking area, where you join a broad walkway around the Young Offender Institution at **Grove Prison**, once the borstal to which the most serious offenders in the country were sent. Beyond Grove Farm, double back left by an air shaft that ventilated the prison's sewage system, descending below the limestone ramparts to join a broad path leading right further down the rock-strewn slope. This follows the line of a former passenger railway as it ascends gently past Little Beach and the remains of **Durdle Pier**, where stone was exported from this widely worked landscape. Beyond a deep cutting in the limestone by the stack of Nickodemus Knob, fork left and keep left to descend to **Rufus Castle**, whose ruins perch impressively on a natural limestone turret. Rebuilt in the late 15th century, it replaced an earlier Norman castle named after William II, who was known as William Rufus. A plaque here marks the end of the first section of the England Coast Path to be opened back in 2012.

Descend the steps all the way down to **Church Ope Cove**, passing

Portland Bill and its Lighthouses

Portland Bill is a notoriously dangerous section of the south coast for passing ships due to the Portland Race, where tidal streams collide in a maelstrom of churning water that can stretch for over two miles and shifts with the tide and wind. There is an inshore passage very close to the headland, but underwater ledges make this perilous. Beacons were often lit near the point and the island's windmills used as navigation aids before the first pair of lighthouses was built in 1716, the lower being rebuilt in 1789 and again in 1869. After 15 boats were lost here in 1901, they were replaced by the single Portland Bill Lighthouse in 1906, which is now used as a bird observatory.

some steps that lead up to the 15th-century ruin of **St Andrew's Church**, Portland's first parish church and in use until the Great Southwell Landslip in 1734. Just before the bottom, bear right behind the beach huts and climb a rocky path up on to the low cliffs. The path weaves impressively along the shore through the jumbled rock produced by the landslip (the second largest recorded in Britain) and the spoil of the quarrying industry. Where the old route doubles back to the right, a new route continues straight on through the chasm of the **Lost Valley** to reach Cheyne Weares car park.

Join the road at **Cheyne Weares** and, just beyond the point at which the grassy verge on the left runs out, bear left down to a broad track through the shoreline quarries. This winds on between stacks of spoil and worked stone to pass the first of a series of preserved hoists and cranes at Sandholes Quarry, by which stone was loaded onto waiting ships and fishing boats are still lowered into the water. Head up the bank opposite to follow the fenceline to a bridge and continue along the grassy clifftops past another crane. Keep straight on past the colourful beach huts and wild flowers (the golden samphire being most striking here at the right time of year), as the cliffs slowly descend towards **Portland Bill**, where the headland slides into the broiling sea.

Pass the iconic **Portland Bill Lighthouse** and **Trinity House Obelisk**, built as a daymark on the tip of the headland in the 19th century, and continue round to Pulpit Rock (said to resemble a Bible leaning against a pulpit). Turn right here to skirt around the landward side of the Ministry of Defence's Magnetic Range site, where electronic equipment and systems have been tested since the 1950s. Join a path along the cliffs at the far end of the site and climb up past the Coastwatch station and the higher of the two older lighthouses. Stay along the sheer cliffs past the Atlantic Academy and the estates of Weston to **Blacknor Point**, on which stands an observation post for Blacknor Fort, which was built at the start of the 20th century. Keep left of a modern house built into one of the fort's gun emplacements and round the corner to stunning views across Chesil Beach. The path drops down into the quarries and arcs round the impressive ramparts of **West Cliff**, at one point cutting through an arch in the waste stone – *unfortunately two sections of this path have collapsed and there are diversions through the maze of former workings of* TOUT QUARRY, *much of which has been transformed into a stone sculpture park.*

Keep left at the far end of the quarry workings and descend steeply down steps towards Chiswell and **Chesil Cove**, which marks the south-eastern end of Chesil Beach. Keep straight on down to the seafront, where the route doubles back to join the promenade but Chiswell and Fortuneswell are reached straight ahead. **Chiswell** occupies the flatter ground by the beach and **Fortuneswell** scrambles up the steep hillside towards the Verne, though it is hard to differentiate the two now.

The 'R' Word

Local superstition on the Isle of Portland means it is considered bad luck to say the word 'rabbit' due to accidents in the quarries caused by their burrowing. Instead they are known as 'furry things', 'underground mutton' or just bunnies and, when the film *Wallace & Gromit: The Curse of the Wererabbit* was released, it was promoted locally as *There's Something Bunny Going On.*

SONG OF THE DAY **Mik Parsons** – *The Adventures of Portland Bill*
The original theme from the stop-motion animated 1980s TV series, this was sung by creator John Grace's friend Mik Parsons. Portland Bill is the name of the lighthouse keeper, with other characters named after other lighthouses around the country.

Fortuneswell and Chesil Beach from Tout Quarry

Section 6.7 – Chiswell/Fortuneswell to Abbotsbury

Distance: 20.9km (13 miles)

Height Gained: 200m

Parking: Free parking in Chiswell/Fortuneswell at the Hambro and Masonic Car Parks, with pay car parks in Abbotsbury.

Public Transport: Buses X52 & X53 (First, towards Weymouth & Monkey World) run at alternate hours from Abbotsbury to King's Statue in Weymouth, from where Buses 1/501 (First, towards Portland) run regularly to Chiswell/Fortuneswell. The X52 and 501 are both seasonal, so there is a more limited service in the winter.

Refreshments: The only option passed on the route is Moonfleet Manor Hotel, which offers high-end dining to visitors as well as guests, though Cook's Fish & Chips Weymouth in Littlesea Holiday Park is just off the route near Chickerell.

Accommodation: Bed & breakfast is available at several places in Abbotsbury, with the closest campsites at Jurassic Camp (07593 233465) in Rodden, less than a mile off the alternative route, or Portesham Dairy Farm Campsite (01305 871297), around a mile off the alternative route or a short bus ride from Abbotsbury.

Overview: A unique and often overlooked section of the Dorset coast, the day's route clings largely to the shore of the Fleet, whose brackish water is sheltered from the open sea by the shingle bank of Chesil Beach. Though it might seem more obvious to walk along the shingle bank of Chesil Beach than follow the coast path along the inland shore of the Fleet, be warned that it is closed from April 1st to August 31st to protect nesting birds, and you need to make sure that the rifle range at Tidmoor is not in operation. Though shorter (just 10½ miles from Chiswell to Abbotsbury Beach), the walk along Chesil Beach is rather a monotonous slog and is generally discouraged. The signed route is far more pleasant as it winds around the Fleet's shoreline, before becoming more hilly as it nears beautiful Abbotsbury.

Route Description

Follow the seafront promenade in **Chiswell** to the **Cove House Inn**, beside which the official route joins a pebble track running behind the beach, before following the A354 to head back towards the causeway. *However, you can carry straight on along the top of* CHESIL BEACH's *pebble bank to get a taste of walking on this awkward ground and a better*

EAST FLEET

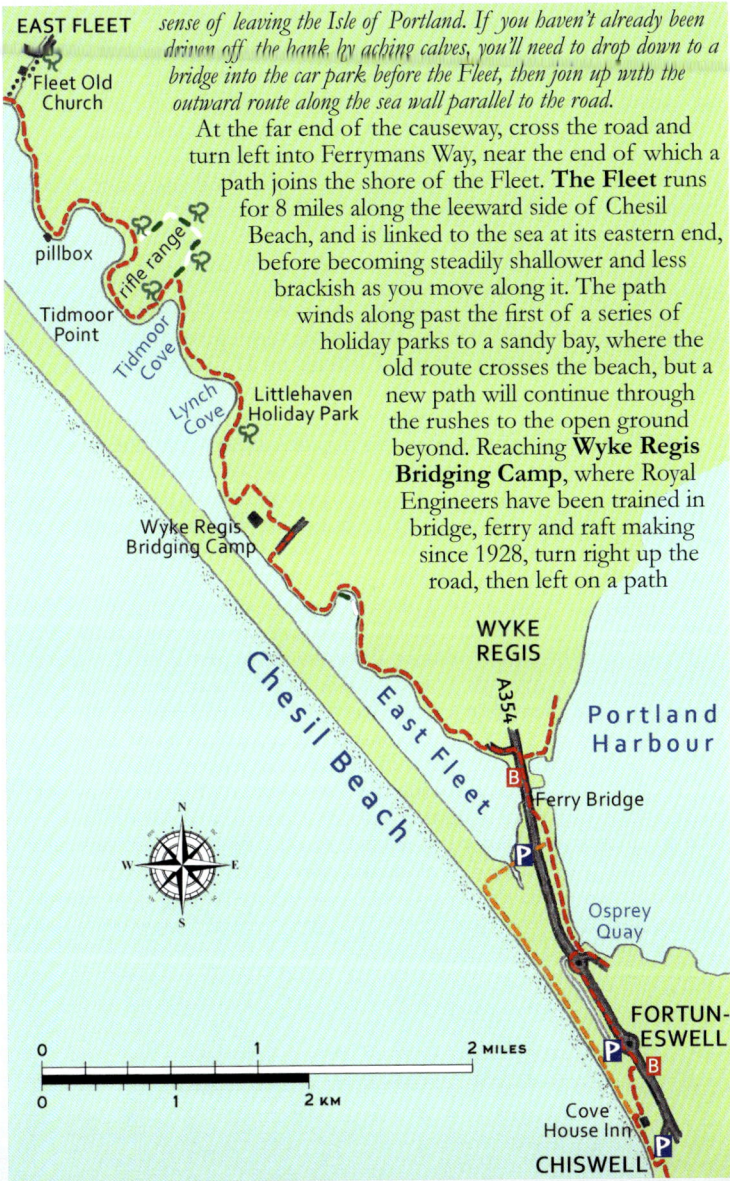

Fleet Old
Church

pillbox

rifle range

Tidmoor
Point

Tidmoor
Cove

Lynch
Cove

Littlehaven
Holiday Park

Wyke Regis
Bridging Camp

Chesil Beach

East Fleet

WYKE
REGIS

A354

Portland
Harbour

B

Ferry Bridge

P

Osprey
Quay

FORTUN-
ESWELL

P

B

Cove
House Inn

P

CHISWELL

sense of leaving the Isle of Portland. If you haven't already been driven off the bank by aching calves, you'll need to drop down to a bridge into the car park before the Fleet, then join up with the outward route along the sea wall parallel to the road.

At the far end of the causeway, cross the road and turn left into Ferrymans Way, near the end of which a path joins the shore of the Fleet. **The Fleet** runs for 8 miles along the leeward side of Chesil Beach, and is linked to the sea at its eastern end, before becoming steadily shallower and less brackish as you move along it. The path winds along past the first of a series of holiday parks to a sandy bay, where the old route crosses the beach, but a new path will continue through the rushes to the open ground beyond. Reaching **Wyke Regis Bridging Camp**, where Royal Engineers have been trained in bridge, ferry and raft making since 1928, turn right up the road, then left on a path

0   1   2 MILES

0   1   2 KM

Chesil Beach

Chesil Beach is an 18-mile long shingle beach, its name derived from an Old English word *ceosel* meaning shingle. Though local legend suggests it was thrown up one night in a great storm, it is now thought to be a barrier beach or natural bar that happens to be connected to the mainland. Unlike a spit, which is caused by the deposition of pebbles by longshore drift, it is not being continually replenished and may therefore eventually be breached. Chesil Beach's pebbles are not uniform along the beach, instead varying in size and colour, with local smugglers said to be able to locate themselves on the bar by the size of pebbles, which are much larger at the Portland end.

around the perimeter fence. Continue along the edge of the fields beyond, before dropping down to **Littlehaven Holiday Park**, where the route keeps left on a path close to the shore of Lynch Cove. Reaching a bridge behind Tidmoor Cove, the main route goes left around **Tidmoor Point**, though this may be closed if the rifle range is in use. *An alternative route heads right, before turning left across the back of the range and skirting round the far side of the range to rejoin the main route.*

Pass the campsite at Seaview Farm and follow the shore round to **Chickerell Hive Point**, where there is a World War II pillbox and a slipway for boats to cross the Fleet to the remote shacks on the back of Chesil Beach. It is also a good place to see the canns at the back of the beach – hollows where water has been pushed through the pebbles by storm surges. The path continues along the shore past East Fleet Farm and crosses the campsite's recreation field to reach a bridge over the stream by **East Fleet**. It is worth diverting 100m right here to **Fleet Old Church** – now serving as a mortuary chapel, the rest of this 15th-century building was swept away in the Great Storm of 1824.

The coast path continues along the open shore of Butterstreet Cove, passing another pair of pillboxes before keeping left of **Moonfleet Manor**, a Georgian manor house made famous by J. Meade Faulkner's *Moonfleet*, a tale of smuggling along this part of the south coast. Continue around the shore of Gore Cove, before turning right across

Herbury Island and West Fleet

ABBOTSBURY

R WC

P B3157

St Peter's Abbey

Tithe Barn

Linton Hill

Swannery

Clayhanger Lodge

Merry Hill

Chesters Hill

Berry Knap

Wyke Wood

West Fleet

Rodden Hive

Chesil Beach

Langton Hive Point

Herbury Island

Gore Cove

Moonfleet Manor

Fleet Old Church

pillboxes

Butterstreet Cove

N
W   E
S

0   1   2 MILES
0   1   2 KM

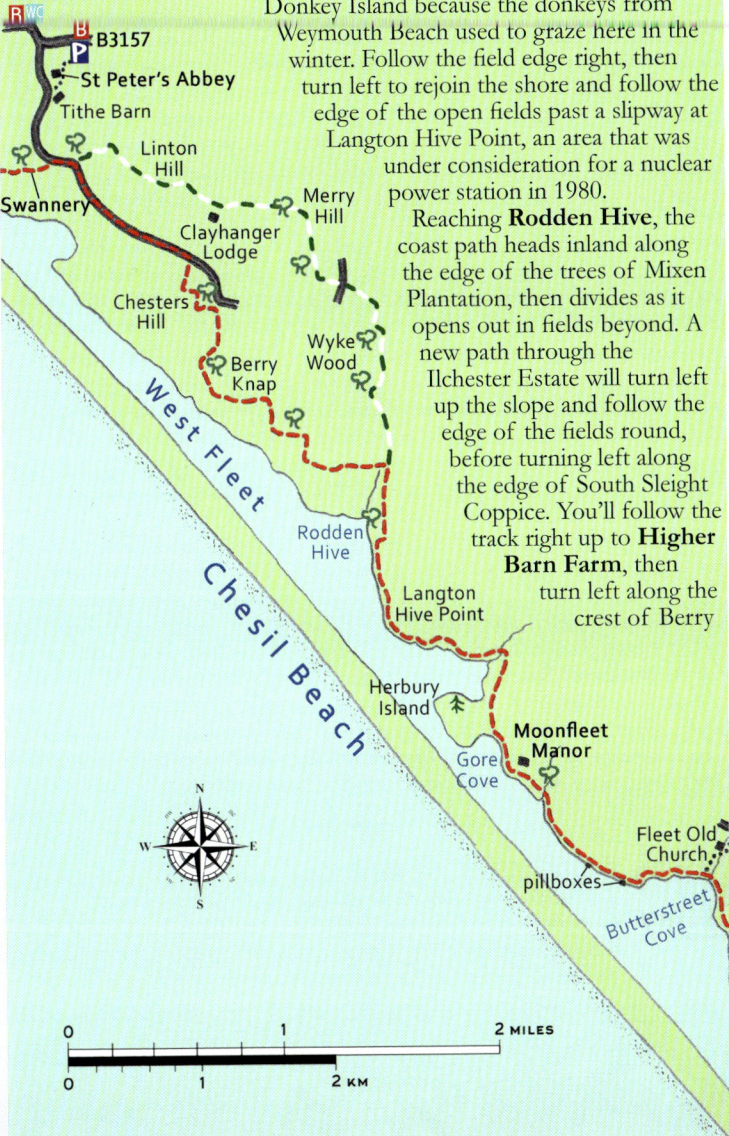

the neck of **Herbury Island**, known locally as Donkey Island because the donkeys from Weymouth Beach used to graze here in the winter. Follow the field edge right, then turn left to rejoin the shore and follow the edge of the open fields past a slipway at Langton Hive Point, an area that was under consideration for a nuclear power station in 1980.

Reaching **Rodden Hive**, the coast path heads inland along the edge of the trees of Mixen Plantation, then divides as it opens out in fields beyond. A new path through the Ilchester Estate will turn left up the slope and follow the edge of the fields round, before turning left along the edge of South Sleight Coppice. You'll follow the track right up to **Higher Barn Farm**, then turn left along the crest of Berry

Knap, with great views across the Fleet. After cutting through Berry Coppice, you'll turn right up the side of Chesters Hill, then head left by the road to skirt around Chesters Coppice. Turn right beyond to return to the road, which you'll follow left for ¾ mile towards **Abbotsbury**.

ALTERNATIVE ROUTE: *Until this section is open, the old route of the coast path can still be followed and is a better walk in some ways, with great views off Linton Hill and less road walking. The path continues across the fields in the bottom of the valley to reach a vehicle track, before immediately turning right to skirt around the outside edge of WYKE WOOD. Turn right then left at the top to follow the field edge down to the road, heading straight across for 300m, before turning right to climb steadily up onto MERRY HILL. Head left through the trees near the top, then follow a path along the high ground above Clayhanger Lodge, before ducking left to join the top of the slope on LINTON HILL, with great views over Abbotsbury Swannery. The path soon winds down the slope at the end of the ridge to rejoin the new route along the road by Horsepool Farm.*

The onward route bears left off the road through the large car park for **Abbotsbury Swannery**, but it is just ½ mile along the road into the picturesque village of **Abbotsbury**. You pass the 14th-century tithe barn and the ruins of the abbot's lodgings, the only remaining part of the great Benedictine monastery of **Abbotsbury Abbey**, which dominated the village until its destruction during the Dissolution.

SONG OF THE DAY

Peter Hammill – *Shingle Song*

A founder member of prog rock band Van der Graaf Generator, this haunting ballad is taken from Hammill's 1975 solo album *Nadir's Big Chance* and is a perfect accompaniment to Chesil Beach's miles of shingle.

Cygnets at Abbotsbury Swannery

Section 6.8 – Abbotsbury to Seatown/Chideock

> **Distance:** 19.2km (12 miles)
>
> **Height Gained:** 290m
>
> **Parking:** Pay car parks in Abbotsbury, Seatown and numerous places along the route in between.
>
> **Public Transport:** Bus X53 (First, towards Bridport/Weymouth) runs every two hours from Chideock to Abbotsbury 7 days a week during the summer, less frequently over the winter.
>
> **Refreshments:** Various options in Burton Bradstock and West Bay.
>
> **Accommodation:** There are rooms in Seatown at the Anchor Inn (01297 489215), and several other options in Chideock, less than a mile away. Camping is available in Seatown at Golden Cap Holiday Park (01308 426947).
>
> **Overview:** A varied day blending the long shingle beaches of Abbotsbury and West Bexington with the dramatic cliffs of West Bay and the wonderful vantage point of Thorncombe Beacon. Some sections early on along the shingle can be tiresome, but these are kept to a minimum and, once the cliffs rear up beyond Hive Beach, it is a fabulous walk with the hills of Bridport as a backdrop inland.

Route Description

Rejoin the route by the entrance to **Abbotsbury Swannery**, where mute swans have been kept for over six centuries, originally as meat for the abbey but now as a nature reserve. Follow the track briefly, then turn left into a field and climb to join a path angling across the side of Chapel Hill. *A couple of paths climb steeply up onto the top of this fine eminence to visit St Catherine's Chapel, a 14th-century place of pilgrimage that was part of Abbotsbury Abbey, but spared destruction for use as a maritime landmark.*

St Catherine's Chapel

As the route descends into the hollow of Coward's Lake, several medieval strip lynchets are clearly seen on the hill opposite. Turn left and follow a path past the marsh at the head of the Fleet to rejoin **Chesil Beach** at the first available opportunity since Chiswell. The path skirts along the foot of the shingle bank, though you might as well walk along the crest as the going is similarly awkward and the views are far better higher up, including the exotic trees of **Abbotsbury Subtropical Gardens**, renowned for its magnolias, camellias and many rare plants.

Beyond the **Abbotsbury Beach** car park, drop down to join the quiet road that runs for a mile behind the beach to the former rocket house by Old Coastguards. It becomes a rougher track beyond, eventually joining the shingle to reach the car park at **West Bexington**. The next section is a bit of a slog as you have no choice but to walk on the shingle beach, which apparently locals get used to but visitors find hard work. Continue for a mile, passing a marker at the site of the **White House**, which stood on the beach in the 17th century as a refuge for shipwrecked sailors. *A 'Summer Route' is signed right at the next bridge, allowing you to follow the edge of the meadow inland – it is accessible all year, but liable to flooding in winter. Stay around the right side of Burton Mere's reedy marsh, before bearing left to rejoin the main route at Cogden Beach.*

The main route ploughs on along the shingle, before a firmer path develops behind Cogden Beach. Keep right of the low cliffs that start to rise up by Old Coastguard Holiday Park, then descend to **Hive Beach** on the edge of the village of **Burton Bradstock**. Head up some steps beyond the Hive Beach Café and cross the car park to a gate, from which a path leads across the fields to the end of Cliff Road. Head

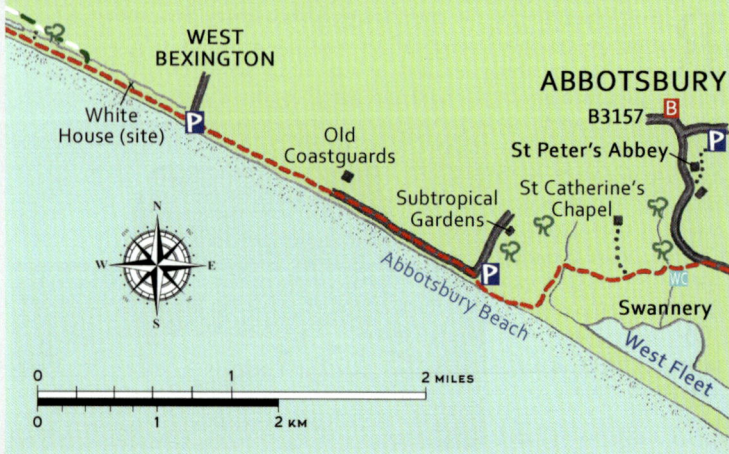

WEST BEXINGTON

ABBOTSBURY

White House (site)

Old Coastguards

B3157

St Peter's Abbey

Subtropical Gardens

St Catherine's Chapel

Abbotsbury Beach

Swannery

West Fleet

0   1   2 MILES

0   1   2 KM

West Bay

Bridport's original harbour lay further up the River Brit, but after this began to silt up, a quay was built at the river mouth in the late 14th century. Despite its distance from the town, it was busy with exports from the local rope-making industry. In the 1740s the river was diverted to create a new harbour to the west and a shipyard developed alongside. There were few buildings around the harbour until the Great Western Railway reached it in 1884, and the small resort of West Bay was born. It may now be most familiar as the location for much of the TV series *Broadchurch*.

straight across, joining the top of the precarious sandstone and limestone of **Burton Cliffs**, before dropping down to the mouth of the **River Bride**. Double back right along the foot of the hill to reach a footbridge, then return along the left edge of the vast campsite at Freshwater Beach.

Cross the back of **Burton Freshwater Beach** to the foot of the dramatic sandstone cliffs beyond. Though it is generally possible to follow the beach to West Bay to get a better view of the dizzying overhang, rockfalls do occur regularly here and so the main route heads steeply up onto the top of **East Cliff**. There is a great swoop down and up in the middle, before you drop equally steeply down to the broad sands of **West Bay**. The route turns right before the Watch House Café

West Bay's East Cliff

to cross the car park and circle round the busy quay of **Bridport Harbour**.

At the far side of the harbour turn right along the Esplanade, then bear right on the path up onto **West Cliff**. Follow the main right fork to skirt around a newly collapsed section of the cliff, then descend steadily to **Eype Mouth**. Cross the stream and follow the steps up to the car park, from where a path climbs steadily up the cliffs beyond. Follow either fork to climb **Thorncombe Beacon**, the main route pulling steeply up its face to be rewarded with one of the finest views in the area, the jumble of shapely hills around Bridport laid out inland, including the distinctive tree-capped peak of Colmer's Hill. The beacon itself was one of a series that were lit along the south coast to warn of the Spanish Armada's approach in 1588, and is also the site of four Bronze Age burial mounds known as the **Devil's Jumps**.

The descent over **Doghouse Hill** and Ridge Cliff is a joyous walk along the grassy crest. Keep left over the higher ground of Ridge Cliff, then bound down the green slopes towards the car park at **Seatown**. The route follows the road briefly

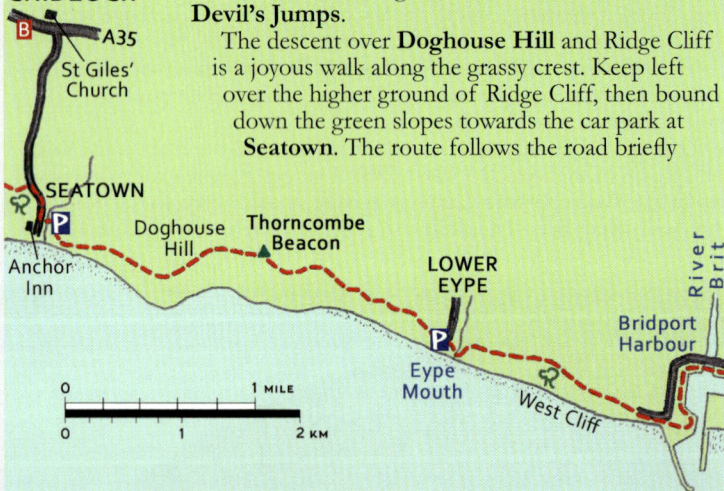

Seatown and Golden Cap from Doghouse Hill

Thorncombe Beacon, looking towards Eype Mouth

right through the pretty hamlet, and it is just over ½ mile further into the larger village of **Chideock**, where buses stop along the main road. Seatown was once a more substantial village, dominated by fishing and smuggling, and was the site where an advance party of the Monmouth Rebellion landed in 1685 in an attempt to depose James II.

SONG OF THE DAY

PJ Harvey – *The Wind*

Though many of Dorset-born Polly Harvey's songs are an evocation of the area's landscape, particularly the album *White Chalk*, this song was written about St Catherine's Chapel at Abbotsbury. Taken from her 1998 album *Is This Desire?* and featuring samples from the theme music from *Planet of the Apes*, it imagines St Catherine listening to the wind blow as she prays on the hilltop for a husband.

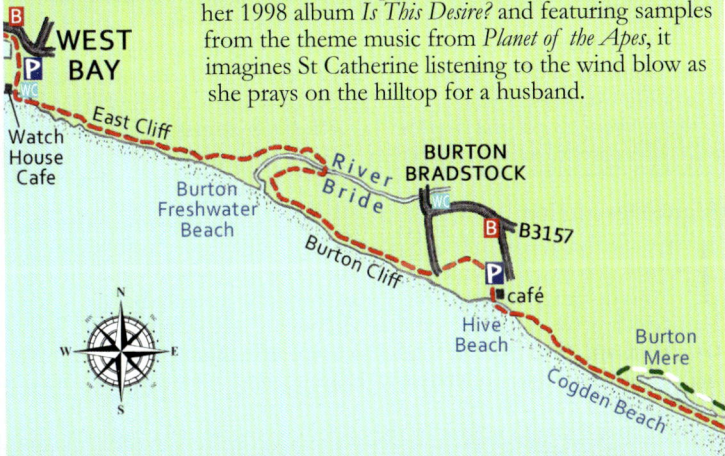

Section 6.9 – Seatown/Chideock to Seaton

Distance: 23.3km (14½ miles)

Height Gained: 930m

Parking: Pay car parks in Seatown, Charmouth, Lyme Regis and Seaton. Free car park just off the route at Stonebarrow Hill above Charmouth.

Public Transport: Bus 9A (Stagecoach South West, towards Lyme Regis) runs hourly from Seaton seafront to Lyme Regis town centre, where you change for the X51 or X53 (First, towards Weymouth), which run to Chideock at alternate hours during the summer and less frequently over the winter. All services run 7 days a week.

Refreshments: Many options in Charmouth and Lyme Regis, the latter perfectly situated at the midpoint of the day's route.

Accommodation: There are various accommodation options in Seaton and a Tourist Information Centre (01297 21388) at the Marshlands Centre. YHA Beer (0345 3719502) is just a couple of miles further along the route, while the nearest campsite is ½ mile from the route at Axmouth Caravan & Camping Site (01297 24707).

Overview: A challenging but very rewarding day's walking, taking in the highest point on the south coast at Golden Cap and the famous undercliffs between Lyme Regis and Axmouth. The crumbling fossil-rich cliffs mean there is always a possibility of diversion or closure of paths due to collapse, which has already necessitated an inland section between Charmouth and Lyme Regis. Yet it is the 7-mile walk through the Axmouth-Lyme Regis Undercliffs that takes centre stage, transporting you into another world of dense foliage and fabulous wildlife like nothing else on the English coast. The fact that you can rarely ever glimpse the sea after Lyme Regis is immaterial – start early and prepare to be blown away!

Route Description

Follow the lane up through **Seatown** for 200m, then turn left on a path across a field and through the trees back towards the clifftop. You don't see much of the sea as you climb steadily, before bearing left across the open ground and pulling steeply up towards **Golden Cap**. Turn left and follow the steps up to the 191m summit, the highest point on the south coast of England; the best views are from the far end of the table-top summit, overlooking Lyme Bay. The bare yellow cap is given its colour by the upper greensand, a Cretaceous sandstone, although this rock used to be more striking before vegetation developed around the summit in recent years.

Steps zigzag down from the far end of Golden Cap to a field, where you fork left unless you want to visit the ruins of **St Gabriel's Church**, part of the village of Stanton St Gabriel, which was abandoned in the early 19th century. The route stays close to the fractured cliff edge, before dropping down to cross the stream near **St Gabriel's Mouth**. Skirt along the edge of the fields above well vegetated Broom Cliff, then descend to cross Ridge Water. Over the next shoulder you drop down again across Westhay Water, before keeping to the left of Westhay Farm to climb steadily up onto **Stonebarrow Hill**. Keep left to skirt along the loose edge on the summit and descend towards Charmouth. A recently collapsed section means you have to keep right and cut into the adjacent field to pass a beautifully carved gate that commemorates the Danes landing at Charmouth in 833. Following a battle here with the locals, a 15,000-strong Danish army plundered the region until forced to retreat.

Continue descending to cross a footbridge over the **River Char** and keep left around the shore to the Charmouth Heritage Coast Centre. *If you want to hunt for fossils, it is possible to stay on the beach all the way to Lyme Regis for 2 hours either side of low tide, but the possibility of landslips can make this difficult.* The loose shale cliffs of **Black Ven** that lie between Charmouth and Lyme Regis are so prone to collapse that the route is now forced to make a significant inland detour. Formed of the blue lias beds that make Lyme Regis renowned for fossil hunting, the cliff's frequent collapse has regularly exposed ammonites, belemnites and more substantial skeletons on the shore.

The formal route heads up some steps beyond the **Charmouth Heritage Coast Centre** and keeps left up the greensward. Follow a path from the end that soon emerges on Higher Sea Lane, then turn right for 300m until a path leads left between the houses to cut up to another road. Bear left off this on a road that climbs steeply to the top

Lyme Regis seafront

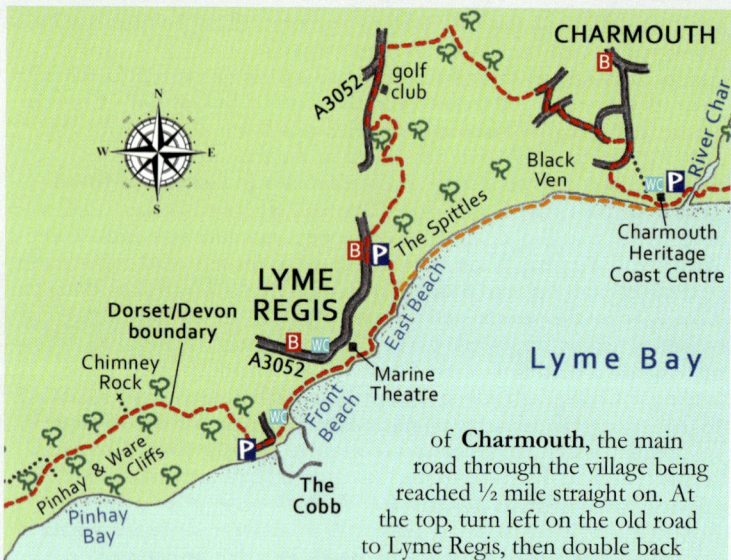

CHARMOUTH

golf club

A3052

B

River Char

Black Ven

WC P

Charmouth Heritage Coast Centre

The Spittles

B P

LYME REGIS

East Beach

Lyme Bay

Dorset/Devon boundary

Chimney Rock

B WC

A3052

Marine Theatre

Front Beach

WC

Pinhay & Ware Cliffs

P

The Cobb

Pinhay Bay

of **Charmouth**, the main road through the village being reached ½ mile straight on. At the top, turn left on the old road to Lyme Regis, then double back right on a narrow lane. Turn left at the end, still climbing as the road becomes a gravel path and soon bends right to wind through the woods across the bottom edge of a golf course. Double back left on a footpath that was the old route of the South West Coast Path and follow the intermittent white stones straight across the middle of the fairways, watching out for golf balls. Turn left on the main road, then bear left on the bend and descend past the golf club. Turn left halfway down on a path around the top of the wood, before dropping down to a gate and crossing the meadows below. Having rejoined the main road, turn left through the car park and follow

Mary Anning

The 'Mother of Palaeontology' was the area's most famous fossil hunter. Selling fossils to tourists from an early age and inspiring the tongue-twister 'she sells seashells on the sea shore', she was just 11 in 1811 when she and her brother discovered the first complete skeleton of an ichthyosaurus, a 50ft-long aquatic dinosaur. She would later find the world's first plesiosaurus and the UK's first pterodactyl, and compel the scientific world to take note of her. She eventually became the first woman to be an honorary member of the Geological Society.

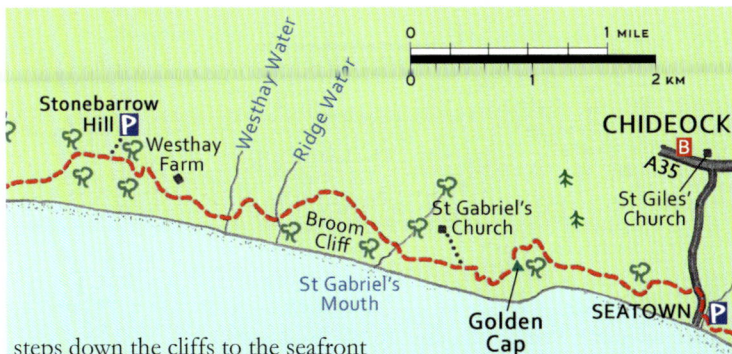

steps down the cliffs to the seafront promenade along **East Beach**. Keep left along the front, passing the Marine Theatre to reach the centre of **Lyme Regis** by the Rock Point Inn. Long before it developed into a prosperous Georgian resort, Lyme was a medieval port that developed around saltworkings at the mouth of the River Lym. It was granted its royal title in 1284 by Edward I after his fleet was granted shelter here. In 1685 the Duke of Monmouth landed at Lyme Regis to seize the crown from James II, only to be defeated at the Battle of Sedgemoor.

The route continues along the Marine Parade behind the beach to reach **the Cobb**, an arcing 13th-century breakwater that forms the backdrop to famous scenes in Jane Austen's *Persuasion* and John Fowles' *The French Lieutenant's Woman*. At the far end of Monmouth Beach, some of the most remarkable ammonites are preserved on the rocky foreshore, although the coast path turns right in the middle of the car park beyond the Cobb to head up some steps through the chalets and into the woods that cloak most of the shoreline between here and the River Axe. Turn left at the top to cross a brief open area and head from

Charton Bay in the Axmouth–Lyme Regis Undercliffs

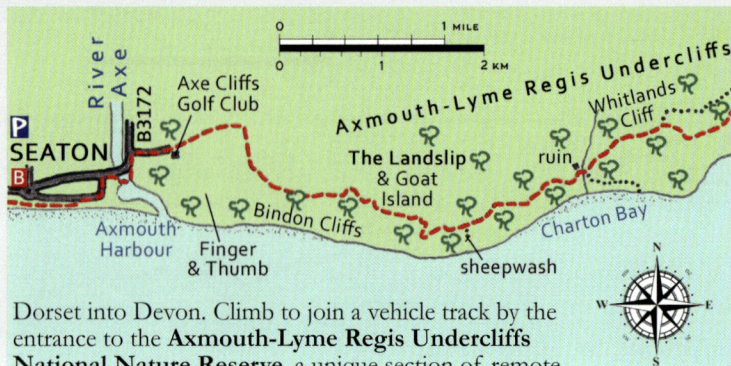

Dorset into Devon. Climb to join a vehicle track by the entrance to the **Axmouth-Lyme Regis Undercliffs National Nature Reserve**, a unique section of remote coast walking with no escape route for the next 7 miles.

The route soon narrows beyond a path leading up to the chert stack of **Chimney Rock**, forking left up some steps as it winds through the dense quasi-tropical foliage. The path can be muddy and slippy in places, picking its way up and down the remnants of ancient landslips in the shade of the ivy-clad ash and maple trees, interspersed with the odd striking evergreen Holm oak. At **Pinhay Cliffs**, towering rock faces loom over the undercliffs and there is a viewpoint offering a glimpse of the sea down in **Pinhay Bay**. The route continues straight on through a glade of beech trees, before climbing steadily above Whitlands Cliff to pass some chalk rock faces. After a steep descent to **Charton Goyle**, you join a larger path, then bear right by the ruins of a building from which freshwater was pumped up to the Peek House estate on the cliffs above. A private path off to the left winds circuitously down to the wonderfully remote sandy beach of **Charton Bay**, of which you get a good view from a bench shortly after.

The main path winds on along Rousdon and Dowlands Cliffs and passes close to a well preserved **sheepwash** from around 1800, much of the undercliffs having been grazed by sheep and cattle until the end

---

The Undercliffs

One of the largest areas of landslip in the country, the Axmouth-Lyme Regis Undercliffs are a mass of contorted ground that began to form centuries ago. Sandstone and chalk have slipped over the underlying limestone and clay for several miles, and the further west you go, the more recent the landslips. In the Great Landslip of 1839, a huge chunk of clifftop collapsed at Bindon Cliffs, with a small woodland and wheatfield surviving intact as Goat Island. The field here was harvested halfway down the cliff while a large crowd watched and the area became a major tourist attraction, with Queen Victoria even paying a visit.

of the 19th century. The landslipped ground under the trees becomes increasingly jumbled as the path picks its way between hunks of ivy-strewn rock, before bending right and climbing steeply up the slope at **Bindon Cliffs**, where the Great Landslip of 1839 occurred. The path soon opens out on the flower-rich meadow of **Goat Island**, the first open ground encountered since the edge of Lyme Regis.

Descend steps across the chasm that formed when this hunk of land fell away from the cliffs, then climb out of the trees to follow a path along the top of the slope beyond. You soon bear right across a field to head away from the cliffs, continuing to a hedged path, where you turn left and descend straight on across the steep golf course on **Axe Cliff**. Follow the lane down to join the B3172 and keep left over the old bridge across the River Axe by **Axmouth Harbour**, which was created in the 19th century but is much smaller than the medieval port that flourished here until the river began silting up. Construction of the first bridge in 1877 indicated that Axmouth's shipbuilding days were over, but the structure now represents Britain's oldest concrete bridge.

Turn first left along Trevelyan Road and join the Esplanade along Seaton's seafront into the heart of the town. **Seaton** developed from a small fishing village to a seaside resort after the arrival of the railway in 1868 (a line now used by Seaton Tramway), with the large Warners Holiday Camp opening in 1935.

SONG OF THE DAY

Show of Hands – *Golden Cap*
Formed in 1986, acoustic roots duo Show of Hands hail from Devon but now call Dorset home. This atmospheric instrumental is taken from their 2013 album *The Path*, a musical journey around the South West Coast Path.

Axmouth Harbour

Section 6.10 – Seaton to Sidmouth

Distance: 15.6km (10 miles)

Height Gained: 770m

Parking: Pay car parks on the front in both Seaton and Sidmouth, as well as at Beer and Branscombe Mouth.

Public Transport: Bus 9A (Stagecoach South West, towards Lyme Regis) runs hourly from Sidmouth Triangle to Seaton 7 days a week.

Refreshments: Beer Head Bistro and the Sea Shanty Café at Branscombe Mouth are both well placed right on the route.

Accommodation: There are various options in Sidmouth, with the closest campsites being less than a mile before the town at Salcombe Regis Camping & Caravan Park (01395 514303), or 2½ miles further along the route at Ladram Bay Holiday Park (01395 568398)

Overview: A beautifully varied day that is deceptively hard due to the severe undulations, especially towards the end. Beyond Branscombe, the striking chalk cliffs of White Cliff and Beer Head give way to the Triassic red mudstone that characterises so much of east Devon. There are some fantastic areas of undercliffs and woodland as the path stays back from the fragile cliff edge in the main.

Route Description

Follow the promenade out of **Seaton** towards the prominent White Cliff, the start of Devon's only chalk coastline. At low tide it is possible to continue along the beach to **Seaton Hole**, where a path leads up onto the cliffs. *If the tide is in, turn right by the former Chine Cafe (now the Hideaway) and join the road above near the striking Check House, built in the 1860s as CALVERLEY LODGE for the geologist Sir Walter Calverley Trevelyan. Stay on the B3172 until it descends into some woods and a path cuts back to the left. Head left along the lower road, then turn right to meet the low tide route from Seaton Hole.* Continue up Beer Hill, then turn left on a clear path along the top of **White Cliff**. Keep left to descend the steep steps to **Beer**'s attractive cove, once a smuggling hotbed with numerous caves in the chalk cliffs (including Tom Tizzard's Hole and Connett's Hole) being ideal for storing contraband goods. Beer's name refers not to the drink, but rather an Old English word *bearu*, referring to a woodland grove.

Turn left up the road in front of the **Anchor Inn** and climb towards the main car park, bearing left along Little Lane just before it. Continue past Beer Head Caravan Park and out onto the open common.

Rounding **Beer Head**, the chalk cliffs drop away, opening up dizzying views along Hooken Beach, which is dominated by the bright white pinnacles of **Sherborne Rocks**. These stacks slid unbroken down the cliff in one of a series of landslips that formed the undercliffs here, the most recent being in 1790.

The path soon forks, the main route descending into the undercliffs, *while an alternative stays along the top of Hooken Cliffs before descending steeply to Branscombe Mouth*. The path through the undercliffs is a delight though, winding through the dense undergrowth while the white cliffs tower above. Look for a rope that hangs tantalisingly from the mouth of a mine entrance high on the cliffs – this was one of the many workings in the distinctive **Beer Stone**, from which Windsor Castle, Westminster Abbey and Winchester Cathedral are all built. It is possible to drop down to the pebble beach, although the coast path persists above to reach a caravan park hugging the cliff. Bear left down the slope beyond, rejoining the alternative route to cross **Branscombe Mouth**, a beautiful spot that was the site of a 19th-century gypsum works.

Beyond the cafe, bear right across the field and skirt around the Lookout, a lavish private residence, before climbing steeply up **West Cliff**. Look out along this stretch of coast for **purple gromwell**, a busy flower that is rare elsewhere in England. Before the top, the path bears off into the ash woods on the leeward side and the coast suddenly feels a world away. After ½ mile, turn left up a track through a landscape shaped by extensive lime quarrying, then fork right at its end, ignoring a lower path that leads to a warren of chalets beneath **Berry Cliffs**. Some

Seaton from White Cliff

The MSC Napoli

On 20th January 2007, the MSC Napoli (a 900-foot 62,000-tonne container ship that sounds like a football team) was unable to reach Portland Harbour in a storm, and so intentionally grounded on the beach at Branscombe Mouth. It was thought this would allow the safe salvage of its hazardous cargo, including 3,800 tonnes of oil, but it soon became a victim of widespread looting. People descended from all over the country to gather the wine, vodka, coffee, perfume, shampoo, motorcycles and dog biscuits that spilled out of the containers, and the salvage operation would ultimately take nearly three years to complete.

of these huts were used for small-scale farming of fruit and vegetables in plats (or small fields) during the late 19th and early 20th centuries. Rejoining the clifftops you soon pass through the low earthworks of **Berry Camp**, an early Iron Age encampment. The open common beyond is also scored with the lines of an associated prehistoric field system and a number of clearance cairns, which have been preserved due to the limited value of the land here. An unlikely path leads down the cliff to the beach at **Littlecombe Shoot**, but the route stays along the fields above, heading inland to cross a dry valley, before returning to the high precipices of Coxe's Cliff and **Weston Cliff**.

The final section of the day's walk is the hardest, the first of two brutish climbs coming after the heady descent into the green swathe of **Weston Combe**. Turn left at the bottom and drop down to cross the stream on the remote beach at Weston Mouth, which has long been used by naturists. Steps lead straight back up the cliff and, from the field above, a short diversion leads left to **Weston Plats**, another area used for small-scale market gardening and complete with a restored linhay (a stone shelter for the donkeys that once worked the ground). The route zigzags up through Dunscombe Coppice to emerge above the greensand pinnacles of **Rempstone Rocks**. Soon after, bear left to cross the dry valley of Lincombe by a gate and continue along the grassy crest of Higher Dunscombe Cliff. At the far end, keep left down

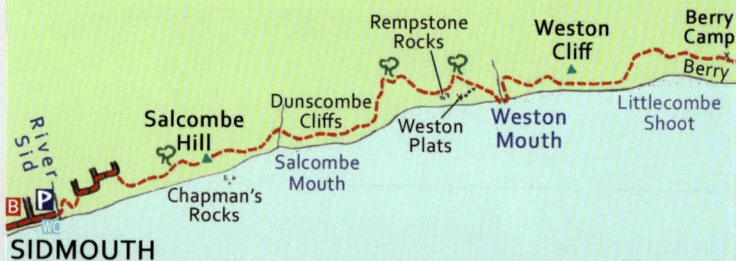

Hooken Cliffs and Sherborne Rocks

the steps towards **Salcombe Mouth**, backed by fragile red cliffs composed of the Triassic mudstones and sandstones that surround Sidmouth. The red colour betrays its origins, laid down when the area was a desert, 200-250 million years ago.

You don't drop down all the way to the shore this time, but cross a bridge over the stream and pull up the long field edges to the top of **Salcombe**

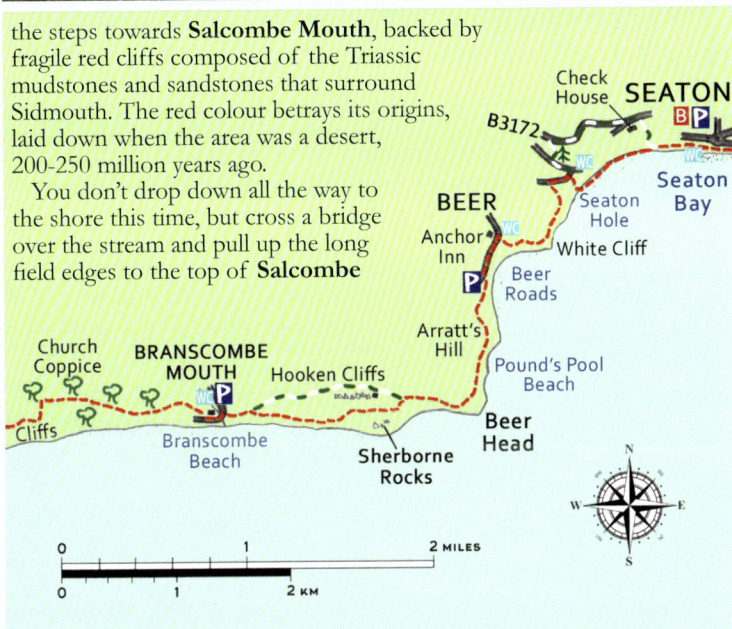

Hill. There is little sign of the cliff edge as the route bears inland beyond the crest, before turning left down through the trees. Keep left to emerge in a long field overlooking Sidmouth. The cliff path has disappeared here, so you have to turn right into a lane at the bottom, then keep left to rejoin a path heading down the cliff to a bridge over the mouth of the **River Sid**. Follow the Esplanade along the beach into the heart of the town. Buses leave from the Triangle, which is reached by turning right at the second mini-roundabout. **Sidmouth**, described by John Betjeman as 'a town caught still in its own timeless charm', developed as a fashionable Georgian resort and has preserved much of its grand architecture.

Sidmouth Folk Festival

A festival has been held in Sidmouth in the first week of August since a folk dance festival was hosted by the English Folk Dance and Song Society in 1955. It grew to become one of the country's premier folk festivals, with the Sidmouth International Festival attracting major artists and up to 65,000 visitors Since 2005, funding cuts mean it has been pared back to a more grassroots folk week, with the town's pubs full of the joyous skirl of fiddles, pipes and hurdy-gurdies.

SONG OF THE DAY **Penelope Swales** – *Sidmouth Song*

Taken from Australian songwriter Swales' 1998 album *Justifying Your Longings to the Doctor*, this is a song about being lost while hunting for her roots in England. She sings 'Another long walk in the sun, the Southern rocks of a Northern land, the jagged coast of my ancestral home, I'd have thought it would mean more to me'.

Sidmouth from Salcombe Hill

Section 6.11 – Sidmouth to Exmouth

Distance: 20.5km (13 miles)

Height Gained: 480m

Parking: Pay car parks on the front in both Sidmouth and Exmouth. There is also a free car park on Peak Hill, a short distance from the coast path near Sidmouth.

Public Transport: Bus 157 (Stagecoach South West, towards Sidmouth) runs hourly from Exmouth town centre to Sidmouth Triangle, with a less frequent service on Sundays.

Refreshments: The Sea View Shack at Ladram Bay and Beachcomber Cafe at Devon Point Holiday Park are right by the route, while various shops and cafes in Budleigh Salterton are only a short distance away.

Accommodation: There is plenty of accommodation in Exmouth, with a Tourist Information Centre (01395 830550) in the town centre, and a couple of options across the estuary in Starcross *(see Book 2)*. The nearest campsites are Prattshayes Campsite (01395 276626) and the vast Devon Cliffs Holiday Park (01395 226226), both a couple of miles before Exmouth, so you may prefer to cross the estuary to Hunters Lodge Caravan & Camping Park (07718 090345), ½ mile from the ferry in Starcross.

Overview: A dramatic day at the end of the Jurassic Coast, featuring its oldest rocks, exposed in a series of rich red sandstone cliffs that continue all the way to the High Land of Orcombe on the edge of Exmouth. Apart from a pleasant excursion up the River Otter and into Budleigh Salterton, this is a great clifftop walk throughout.

Route Description

Follow the seafront Esplanade out of the centre of **Sidmouth**, joining the Millennium Walkway beneath the red cliffs to **Jacob's Ladder Beach**. Climb up either the tarmac pathway or the wooden steps that give the beach its name, joining a path running up the open greensward parallel to the road above. When this runs out, turn left up the old road, before briefly joining Peak Hill Road, then heading left up through the woods onto **Peak Hill**. The view opens out towards the riven face of High Peak, with Big Picket Rock offshore. Follow the path down to **Windgate**, then turn left to climb through the young pines that cloak **High Peak**. The route carries on down through the trees, but a short diversion leads steeply up to the left onto the summit trig, which is set within the earthworks of a Neolithic encampment and

Ladram Bay

offers impressive views over the red cliffs.

The lower cliffs beyond High Peak are carved from the vibrant red Otter sandstone, creating a series of dramatic coves dotted with sea stacks, including Ladram Rock, Hern Point Rock, Hern Rock and George III Rock (once said to resemble the king). At its heart is **Ladram Bay**, surrounded by a large holiday village that the route skirts around. Stick to the clifftops, following the grassy swathe past **Smallstones Point**, then join a lovely path along the edge of the arable fields beyond. Climb up to the observation post on **Brandy Head** (its name a nod to smuggling), which was used by the RAF to test gunsights during World War II.

The path bounds pleasantly past **Danger Point** to the mouth of the **River Otter**, where the route is forced inland for ¾ mile past a narrow band of windswept Scots pines. Turn left at the road, crossing **White Bridge**, then turn immediately left to enter the Otter Estuary Nature Reserve. There are hides along the path from which to spot waders and wildfowl, which are particularly populous during the winter months. Head through the Lime Kiln car park at the far end and join the

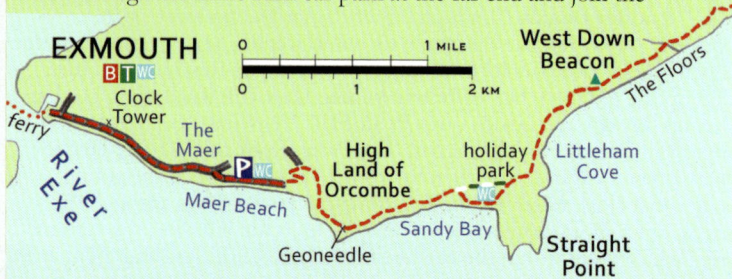